SPIRITUAL HISTORY

For Margarette

SPIRITUAL HISTORY

A Reading of William Blake's
Vala or *The Four Zoas*

ANDREW LINCOLN

CLARENDON PRESS · OXFORD
1995

Oxford University Press, Walton Street, Oxford OX2 6DP
Oxford New York
Athens Auckland Bangkok Bombay
Calcutta Cape Town Dar es Salaam Delhi
Florence Hong Kong Istanbul Karachi
Kuala Lumpur Madras Madrid Melbourne
Mexico City Nairobi Paris Singapore
Taipei Tokyo Toronto
and associated companies in
Berlin Ibadan

Oxford is a trade mark of Oxford University Press

Published in the United States
by Oxford University Press Inc., New York

British Library Cataloguing in Publication Data
Data available

Library of Congress Cataloging in Publication Data
Lincoln, Andrew.
Spiritual history: a reading of William Blake's Vala, or The four
Zoas/Andrew Lincoln.
p. cm.
Includes bibliographical references and index.
1. Blake, William, 1757–1827. Four Zoas. 2. Historical poetry,
English—History and criticism. 3. Prophecies in literature. 4. Philosophy in
literature. I. Title.
PR4144. F683L56 1995 821'. 7—dc20 95-19064
ISBN 0-19-818314-3

1 3 5 7 9 10 8 6 4 2

Typeset by Best-set Typesetter Ltd., Hong Kong
Printed in Great Britain
on acid-free paper by
Biddles Ltd
Guildford & King's Lynn

Preface

This book is intended to serve as a guide to new readers of *The Four Zoas*, although I hope it will also be useful to those who are already familiar with the poem. It presupposes some knowledge of Blake's earlier writings up to 1795, but not of *The Four Zoas* itself, nor of Blake's later works *Milton* and *Jerusalem*. It is concerned with the text of the poem, rather than with the illustrations that appear in the manuscript.

Who reads *The Four Zoas*? Blake specialists, professional students of English literature, a few adventurous undergraduates, some enthusiasts beyond the academic world—the total readership is probably not very extensive. And yet Blake's reputation has been firmly established for decades, and the critical literature on the poem is already considerable. One obvious explanation for the restricted following lies in the unusually heavy demands made upon readers by the long, complex narrative. To this I would add a more contentious explanation: that in responding to the distinctive challenges posed by the work, Blake scholarship has itself created some deterrents for readers.

The difficulties begin with the condition of the text itself. *The Four Zoas* was not printed in Blake's method of illuminated printing, but survived in a manuscript. The work was composed over a period of years—perhaps 10 or more—during which it underwent extensive revision. There are many deletions and erasures in the manuscript; at the beginning Blake erased and replaced whole pages of text. Parts of the poem were transcribed on plain leaves of paper, parts were transcribed on leaves that already contained proof impressions of Blake's illustrations for Edward Young's *Night Thoughts*, while some revisions were even transcribed on leaves made from a print cut in two. Many of the pages have drawings—some vague sketches, others more finished, some touched with water-colour. As a result of these diverse practices the manuscript has a makeshift appearance, and in places looks very untidy, even chaotic.

In his later years Blake gave the manuscript to his friend John

Linnell.[1] It remained for more than 90 years with the Linnell family. When W. B. Yeats and Edwin Ellis examined it in 1889, in preparation for their edition of Blake's works (1893), they found that the leaves were 'unpaged and unsorted'.[2] In attempting to discover the correct sequence they confronted some unusual difficulties: the 'End of The First Night', for example, is announced at two different points; there are two apparently complete versions of 'Night the Seventh'; there are pages on which successive erasures, additions, deletions, and restorations have made the text difficult to decipher. In short, they confronted an editor's nightmare. It is hardly surprising that in sorting the leaves they left some problems unsolved. They outlined the textual difficulties in their edition, an edition which made the poem available to the public for the first time. But they produced a text which gave little sense of these difficulties. In fact they 'improved' the poem by restoring erased passages, conflating the two seventh Nights into one, and making many other editorial emendations.

In 1918 the manuscript was acquired by the British Museum. The museum binding determined the page numbers that would be used in most subsequent editions (which is why pages 19–22 seem to be in the wrong order). The first reliably edited text appeared in Geoffrey Keynes's three-volume Nonesuch edition of 1925.[3] Keynes's editorial practices were unusual: he aimed to record the variants in Blake's texts without resorting to footnotes, arguing that 'The presence of voluminous footnotes on almost every page' would be irksome to the reader and would have 'spoiled the typographical design of the book' (i. p. xiv). The last consideration was perhaps the more important, since the Nonesuch Press was dedicated to producing high-quality editions that were in every way visually pleasing. Instead of using footnotes, Keynes represented corrections and revisions typographically within the main body of the text. Deletions were restored within square brackets and—in the case of *The Four Zoas*—italics were used for lines written in pencil. As a result *The Four Zoas* seemed visually closer to the rough drafts of Blake's notebook poems than to the text of the

---

[1] We do not know precisely when Blake handed over the manuscript. See *BR*, 332–3.
[2] *The Works of William Blake: Poetic, Symbolic, and Critical*, ed. E. J. Ellis and W. B. Yeats, 3 vols. (London, 1893), II: 300.
[3] *The Writings of William Blake*, ed. G. Keynes, 3 vols. (London, 1925).

illuminated poems. The combined effect of brackets and italics gave the text at times a fragmented and even chaotic appearance, reproducing to some extent the effect of the manuscript itself. In the following year Sloss and Wallis published an edition which presented a 'final version' of the text without the typographical devices adopted by Keynes, and with extensive footnotes.[4] In pursuit of a final text they ignored the duplicate Night endings, and they consigned to an appendix one of the two seventh Nights (91–8) on the assumption that it had been superseded. If their editorial practices worked towards coherence and tidiness, their editorial commentary produced a different impression. They described Blake's revisions as quite unsystematic, and as destructive of whatever consistency his narrative may have had, concluding that 'The real interest of *The Four Zoas* appears to us to be in those passages which show the beginnings of doctrines elaborated in the later books [i.e. *Milton* and *Jerusalem*]' (i. 143). Although they avoided making the poem look like a rough draft, in their commentary they made it sound rather like one.

The texts produced by Keynes and by Sloss and Wallis were the standard texts for many years. They were the editions that some of Blake's most influential critics used in their most important works. They helped to establish the widely held assumption that Blake abandoned the poem having reduced it to a chaotic ruin. Northrop Frye's brilliant account of the poem in *Fearful Symmetry* not only gave the impression that much of the narrative had a profound imaginative coherence, but also claimed that we must see 'in its unfinished state a major cultural disaster'.[5] David Erdman, in his indispensable book *Prophet Against Empire*, constructed an account of the poem's development influenced by Sloss and Wallis, and attempted to correlate Blake's revisions with events of contemporary history. In doing so he produced a poem whose design seemed to be determined by external contingencies: 'Each stage in the transformation of Bonaparte from artilleryman of the Republic to lawgiving Emperor seems to have delivered a direct shock to the symbolic consistency and frail narrative frame of Blake's epic.' In Erdman's account the poem was inevitably abandoned, since for

---

[4] *William Blake's Prophetic Writings*, ed. D. J. Sloss and J. P. R. Wallis, 2 vols. (Oxford, 1926).

[5] N. Frye, *Fearful Symmetry: A Study of William Blake* (Princeton, NJ, 1947), 269.

Blake to allow 'his tune to be called by events unfolding as he wrote' was 'as mad as the effort to play croquet in Wonderland with living mallets and balls'.[6] Later studies based on a fresh examination of the manuscript evidence served to deepen the impression of failure and chaos. In 1956 H. M. Margoliouth, convinced that Blake had 'spoilt the poem by incongruous additions', attempted a 'disentanglement' of an earlier, unspoiled version, which he published under the poem's original title, *Vala*.[7] In 1963 Gerald Bentley Jr. gave a much clearer view of the revisions, in the commentary accompanying his photographic reproduction of the manuscript.[8] But by now the established view of the poem seemed hard to question. Bentley concluded, on the basis of little evidence, that the work must have gone through many drafts. He saw the manuscript revisions as a belated attempt to repair a 'fabric . . . so torn and frazzled that the only hope lay in a reweaving of the whole' (166).

The early editions by Sloss, Wallis and Keynes have continued to exert their influence on Blake studies. A one-volume version of Keynes's text appeared in 1957, and an updated version is still widely used.[9] Editions by Alicia Ostriker and Gerald Bentley Jr. both followed Keynes's practice of representing revisions typographically within the main body of the text, ensuring that the poem has an unfinished appearance.[10] The first edition of David Erdman's authoritative text (1965) followed the practice of Sloss and Wallis in consigning one of the seventh Nights to an appendix, a decision followed in turn by the first book-length study of the poem, by Brian Wilkie and Mary Lynn Johnson.[11] Only with the appearance of Erdman's 1982 edition did readers have a version of the poem without regularized punctuation, and without bracketed revisions, that included in the main body of the text

---

[6] D. V. Erdman, *Blake: Prophet Against Empire* (Princeton, NJ, 1954), 269. Erdman acknowleges the limitations of his account in the rev. edn. of 1977, p. 294.

[7] *Vala: Blake's Numbered Text*, ed. H. M. Margoliouth (Oxford, 1956), pp. xxvi, xii.

[8] *William Blake*: Vala, or The Four Zoas, ed. G. E. Bentley Jr. (Oxford, 1963).

[9] *Blake: Complete Writings*, ed. Geoffrey Keynes (Oxford, 1966, rev. 1969, 1971, 1972).

[10] *William Blake: The Complete Poems*, ed. A. Ostriker (Harmondsworth, 1977); *William Blake's Writings*, ed. G. E. Bentley Jr., 2 vols. (Oxford, 1978).

[11] *The Poetry and Prose of William Blake*, ed. D. V. Erdman (New York, 1965); B. Wilkie and M. L. Johnson, *Blake's* The Four Zoas: *The Design of a Dream* (Cambridge, Mass. and London, 1978).

both seventh Nights (here conflated into one Night in an editorial arrangement).

In view of this history it is perhaps not surprising that Blake criticism has often emphasized the disrupted and unfinished nature of the narrative. In recent years it has done this with fewer expressions of regret. Indeed, in the present age, which delights in rupture and disjunctions, the evidence of fragmentation and incompletion has been savoured. Vincent De Luca has argued that editions which iron out the textual difficulties and present the poem in a neat uniform typeface 'deprive the reader of one of the most powerful effects that acquaintance with the manuscript can give, its layered turbulence: the agon of Blake, wrestling with a tale that he cannot get to the bottom or end of, superimposed on the agon of his obstreperous giants in their unsettled chaos'.[12] The *visual* impression of disorder created by the manuscript continues to haunt the reception of the poem like a spectre.

While I can hardly deny the fragmented nature of parts of the narrative, I suspect that scholars have often responded more readily to the impression of disorder than to the question of how the different 'layers' of the text might be related. And that in doing so they have made the poem seem less accessible than it might be. In this study, therefore, I have attempted to take the process of revision into account. My aim is not to provide a comprehensive history of the poem's development, but to allow a staged reading— one that moves, as Blake himself moved, from simpler to more complex forms of writing. After a preliminary discussion of Blake's earlier work, I approach the narrative in four stages. In the first I examine the earliest part of the surviving manuscript, generally known as Blake's copperplate text. In the second I consider the narrative as a whole, but leave out of account the references to Jesus and his role in history (mostly contained in revisions), which are considered separately in the third stage (Part 3). In the fourth stage (Part 4) I examine Blake's unfinished attempt to place the myth within a specifically British framework. I do not assume that the revised narrative does or should constitute a perfect unity—but I do attempt to provide a reading that has more coherence, and may be more accessible, than the disordered appearance of the manuscript might lead us to expect.

[12] V. A. De Luca, *Words of Eternity: Blake and the Poetics of the Sublime* (Princeton, NJ, 1991), 117.

Apart from the textual problems and their critical reception, there is another factor that may have had a significant influence on the reputation of the poem: there has been a tendency to see *The Four Zoas* as a work that opposes the dominant intellectual traditions of its own age, but which otherwise shares little common ground with those traditions. The poem has often been seen as a psychological epic, a view which has focused attention on remarkable analogies between Blake's thought and modern psychoanalytical theory, but which has also tended to move attention away from the contemporary intellectual context of the narrative. Christine Gallant, for example, claims that '*The Four Zoas* is above all a study in man's psychology, and it seems entirely appropriate to use modern depth psychology in an attempt to understand this poem.' She passes lightly over Blake's political and philosophical interests, since she believes that 'it is only through attention to the changing pattern of Jungian archetypes in the poem during its ten-year period of composition that one can see the profound change occurring in Blake's myth as it expanded from a closed, static system to a dynamic, ongoing process'.[13] The critical emphasis on the 'layered turbulence' of the narrative may itself have encouraged a tendency to 'psychologize' the poem. In treating the narrative primarily as a record of inner states and struggles, one can explain the disrupted, fragmentary form of the poem in terms of the disruptive, arbitrary world of the disordered psyche. In their very helpful study *Blake's Four Zoas: The Design of a Dream*, Brian Wilkie and Mary Lynn Johnson approach the poem as 'psychodrama', suggesting that the work 'has some affinity to dream narrative,' and that it 'seems to exist without a context' (2,1). Although they show that the narrative 'often expands to include political, social and religious commentary', such commentary appears to be subsumed by a concern with psychic conflict and reintegration (4). The emphasis on psychology has yielded insights of great value, but it has also, I think, tended to produce a restricted view of Blake's enterprise in *The Four Zoas*.[14]

---

[13] C. Gallant, *Blake and the Assimilation of Chaos* (Princeton, NJ, 1978), 4.

[14] Among other psychological studies, see D. H. George, *Blake and Freud* (Ithaca, NY and London, 1980); B. S. Webster, *Blake's Prophetic Psychology* (Athens, Ga., 1983); H. F. Brooks, 'Blake and Jung: Blake's Myth of the Four Zoas and Jung's Picture of the Psyche', *The Aligarh Critical Miscellany*, 1 (1988), 47–74; P. Youngquist, *Madness and Blake's Myth* (Pennsylvania and London, 1989).

In the most impressive study of *The Four Zoas*, Donald Ault's formidable *Narrative Unbound*, the poem is quite deliberately divorced as much as possible from its historical context, while its disrupted form is seen as the manifestation of a complex intellectual strategy.[15] Blake is described as experimenting with narrative structures that could have a therapeutic effect upon imaginations damaged by Newtonian 'single vision'. Ault explains 'single vision' as consciousness bound by the assumption that there is a single unified world of truth behind appearances, a world against which subjective impressions must be judged. A Newtonian narrative is one that strives to realize a complete world and a preordained 'end', resolving conflict into unity. In contrast, Blake's narrative substitutes a transformational (or 'continuously originary') process: characters and events come into existence the moment they are narrated (they are not presupposed or contained in any fashion, potential or otherwise, until they enter the poem). Past narrative facts can therefore be altered and revised by present ones, so that present events can resist being absorbed into 'a static, dead and unrevisable underlying world' (5). Such a narrative, which represents a radical challenge to the very notion of history, might seem to resist any attempt at analysis. But actually the transformational process 'retroactively resembles a deep structure'—since characters 'behave as if they belonged to an underlying world' (4). In fact Ault finds a conflict in the poem between the desire to renovate readers' perceptions and 'the powerful temptations of Newtonian narrative', a conflict that is 'played out in the radical process of revising that the poem underwent' (4).

I have enormous admiration for Ault's book, which is in several respects quite dazzling. No other study has confronted the difficulties of reading Blake's text as strenuously or in such detail, or proposed such challenging strategies for 'making sense' of it. But some of Ault's assumptions and methods seem questionable. The fact that the poem's characters 'behave as if they belonged to an underlying world' may show just how powerful the temptations of Newtonian narrative are, but may also undermine the very assumption that the poem offers a 'continuously originary' process of the kind Ault describes. If we accept the assumption at face value, we seem committed to losing contact with the historical conditions

[15] D. Ault, *Narrative Unbound: Revisioning William Blake's* The Four Zoas (New York, 1987).

that make that process necessary: Ault attempts to avoid as far as possible any reference to sources and influences (or 'intertextual lures') in his discussion of the narrative. The poem is made to refer almost exclusively to itself—its cultural significance constricted to the anti-Newtonian concern with 'single vision' by Ault's self-imposed 'tunnel vision' (p. xii). Ault is motivated by a wish to provide an account of Blake that is 'fundamentally incommensurable with previous criticism' (p. xvii). This aim seems admirable in many ways, but one might wonder why he should allow his own critical practice to be circumscribed so drastically by previous criticism. Paradoxically, it could be argued that he concedes even more authority to that criticism than is conceded by writers who remain in dialogue with it.

My own study has more in common with those critics who, like Jackie DiSalvo and George Anthony Rosso Jr., emphasize the work's cultural vision and context. Jackie DiSalvo argues that the poem attempts to reconstruct from the Bible and other sources—especially Milton's *Paradise Lost*—'the first consciously historical epic of social and cultural evolution'.[16] Whereas Ault sees the poem as working against the very notion of an underlying world, she suggests that the narrative can be correlated fairly directly with such a world, since in her reading the poem refers to a linear sequence of distinct historical eras—ancient, medieval, modern. The notion of history itself thus seems relatively unproblematic in this account, which focuses on the ideological developments that produce, and occur within, the major eras—notably on 'the implications of love, sex roles and the socialization of children' within bourgeois civilization (14). While DiSalvo takes *Paradise Lost* as the central focus for her study of Blake's poem, George Anthony Rosso Jr. emphasizes the contemporary intellectual context, focusing on two areas for special consideration.[17] He cites eighteenth-century 'Newtonian poems, such as Pope's *An Essay on Man* and Young's *Night Thoughts*' as works of particular importance to the study of Blake's narrative (9), and he sets Blake's work in the context of contemporary views of biblical history and typology. In his account Blake's approach to history resembles that of his

---

[16] J. DiSalvo, *War of Titans: Blake's Critique of Milton and the Politics of Religion* (Pittsburgh, 1983), 11.

[17] G. A. Rosso Jr., *Blake's Prophetic Workshop: A Study of* The Four Zoas (Lewisburg, Va., London, and Toronto, 1993).

German contemporaries (notably Herder) who 'avoid reducing history to the empirical by raising the fact claim of an event into the higher category of understanding' (102). Since the 'fact claim' is transformed rather than abandoned, Rosso argues that an 'emphasis on historical actuality remains crucial to Blake' (105), whose narrative at times closely follows the linear development of biblical history, and proceeds, at one level, through the dark ages to the eighteenth century. Like DiSalvo, then, Rosso sees the poem as representing a linear sequence of historical eras, although in this reading the sequence is continually transformed and disrupted by a prophetic rhetoric that presents 'past events' so as 'to trigger their typical or figural meaning' (97).

Both of these books invite us to see the poem as a work that needs to be contextualized, and as one that engages closely and consistently with cultural issues. My own study shares some of their interests, while differing from both. Like DiSalvo I see the Bible and *Paradise Lost* as particularly important contexts for the study of Blake's poem. And like Rosso, I try to set the work in relation to contemporary intellectual developments. I read the narrative as a field in which two contrasting approaches to experience are made to engage with each other. One approach is derived primarily from the Bible, and views life in the context of fall and judgement. The other is a supposedly demythologizing approach derived from the Enlightenment, which attempts to see life in terms of progress. In emphasizing the relationship between these views, the study focuses less on psychology than on history—not on history as a given sequence of events, but on history as a discourse that shapes and is shaped by consciousness. This reading constructs the text as a 'spiritual history', a history that attempts to delineate the forms which all temporal developments must take, forms that may illuminate eras widely different in chronological time. It is a history that is nearly always in dialogue with other versions of history, and which is often closely engaged with other texts.

I hardly need to point out that my reading makes no claim to exhaust the possibilities of such a complex and encyclopaedic text. Blake, it has often been noted, is at once a systematizer and an attacker of systems.[18] The language of his narratives both invites

---

[18] For a helpful discussion of this problem, see S. Shaviro, ' "Striving with Systems": Blake and the Politics of Difference', in N. Hilton, *Essential Articles for the Study of William Blake, 1970–1984* (Hamden, Conn., 1986), 271–99.

and overwhelms analysis. His idiosyncratic or non-existent punctuation, his frequently uncertain syntax, his use of puns and
wordplay, his dense allusions—all combine to foreground the indeterminacy of language. Nelson Hilton observes that 'each of the
various influential interpretations of Blake shows us that the other
critical contexts are incomplete and that the text that prompted
them all is polysemous'. Hilton shows very clearly, in his own
examination of the multiple contexts evoked by Blake's use of
terms such as 'veil', 'spectre', or 'polypus', what any particular
reading of a Blake narrative will tend to exclude or simplify.[19] But
Hilton's approach does not, of course, escape the condition of
incompleteness, which is not an avoidable constraint but the condition of all interpretation. In this study I concentrate on only one of
the interpretative procedures outlined by Hilton: I am concerned 'to
string the text's words in order along a line of thought', an attempt
conducted at the expense of other lines of thought. The contexts
that I select are certainly used as controlling limits on meaning—
not in order to disqualify other contexts or readings, but in order to
focus attention on possibilities that have sometimes been neglected.
If my attempt encourages more readers to explore the work for
themselves, it will have served its purpose.

   While studying *The Four Zoas* I have incurred many debts of
gratitude. The first is to David W. Lindsay, who introduced me to
the poem and encouraged me to explore its textual problems. The
following scholars have read and commented on early drafts of
parts of this work: David V. Erdman, David Fuller, Morton D.
Paley, Julian Rees. I am grateful for their criticisms and suggestions.
I am also deeply indebted to my wife, Margarette Smith, for her
critical guidance and support. Parts of this book incorporate material revised from three published articles: 'Blake's Lower Paradise:
The Pastoral Passage in *The Four Zoas*, Night the Ninth', *Bulletin
of Research in the Humanities*, 84 (1981), 470–8; 'Blake and the
Natural History of Creation', *Essays and Studies* (1986), 94–103;
'Blake and the Reasoning Historian', *Historicizing Blake*, edited by
Stephen Clark and David Worrall (London, 1994), 73–85. I am
grateful to the editors of these volumes for their permission to
include the material here.

                                                              A. L.

[19] N. Hilton, *Literal Imagination: Blake's Vision of Words* (Berkeley, Los
Angeles, and London, 1983), 11.

Contents

Abbreviations

A Note on Texts

Unless specified, all quotations of Blake are from *The Complete Poetry and Prose of William Blake*, edited by David Erdman, Commentary by Harold Bloom (New York, 1982).

Warning: Readers who use the Newly Revised Edition of this text (New York, 1988) should note that some pages of the text of *The Four Zoas* have been renumbered in order to bring the edition into line with the arrangement in the photographic facsimile published the previous year ('The Four Zoas' by William Blake: A Photographic Facsimile of the Manuscript with Commentary on the Illustrations, edited by Cettina Tramontano Magno and David V. Erdman (Lewisburg, London, and Toronto, 1987)). This renumbering has led to confusion (for example, two pages are numbered 21). In the case of renumbered pages, readers are advised to use the original numbers (which Erdman supplies in square brackets) and to note that [87] should read [85].

In line with Erdman's practice, deletions are represented in italics enclosed in square brackets [*thus*]. Additions are enclosed in angled brackets ⟨thus⟩.

References to *The Four Zoas* are given in the following form—page number: line number(s) (e.g. 23: 1–2).

References to works in Illuminated Printing are given in the form—plate number: line number(s) (e.g. pl. 4: 10–14).

All quotations from Milton are from *The Poems of Milton* edited by John Carey and Alistair Fowler (London, 1968).

References to *Paradise Lost* are given in the following form—book number: line number(s) (e.g. x: 1–5).

All quotations from Edward Young are from *Edward Young, 'Night Thoughts'*, edited by Stephen Cornford (Cambridge, 1989).

References to *Night Thoughts* are given in the following form—Night number: line number(s) (e.g. IX: 765–9).

Introduction

The Four Zoas is a universal history which incorporates, and attempts to harmonize, strikingly different approaches to history. It aligns itself with a Christian tradition that places all human experience within a providential framework; but it is also influenced by an Enlightenment tradition that seeks to liberate history from this framework. Its universalizing perspective suggests the fundamental identity of different cultures; but the poem also responds to the growing contemporary interest in national traditions, and attempts to place world history within a specifically British framework.

Some of these different elements entered the poem through successive revisions. Their presence might suggest that Blake changed his mind about his poem in a quite arbitrary way, but they can be seen as stages in an intelligible process of development, a process of engagement with, and final renunciation of, Enlightenment assumptions. In this chapter I shall consider Blake's relationship with these assumptions in order to identify some of the issues that helped to shape and re-shape *The Four Zoas*.

New Views of History

Blake's imaginative investigation of history placed him in a partial alignment with those writers of the Enlightenment who sought to replace the biblical cosmographic tradition with more reasonable or scientific accounts of human development. He did not seek to elevate scientific explanation over the sublime allegories of scripture. Instead he attempted to reconstruct those allegories in the light of secular discourses, in a way that would expose the errors in both kinds of discourse. Many of the challenges in *The Four Zoas* arise not from the use of obscure sources, but from an extraordinary interplay of contrasting perspectives, in which elements derived from familiar mythical sources—most notably from the Bible and Milton's *Paradise Lost*—appear in an unfamiliar form.

In *Paradise Lost* Milton aligned himself directly with a tradition of prophecy that went back to Moses and was assumed to have a unique authority. Since the publication of Milton's visionary epic, Christian scholars had continued to assert the authenticity of the biblical history, but the status of the Bible as a historical document had been increasingly called into question, either implicitly or directly, by scholars, scientists, Deists, and *philosophes*.

During the second half of the eighteenth century, detailed critical studies of the textual evidence by Jean Astruc, J. G. Eichorn, Johann David Michaelis, Alexander Geddes, and others suggested that Genesis, other areas of the Old Testament, and even parts of the New Testament, were compilations or redactions in which traces of different documentary sources might be identified.[1] Such investigations challenged the assumption that the scriptures were written directly under divine inspiration. It had become possible to see the Bible more clearly as a product of history, a text that was conditioned by the circumstances of its own production.

The authority of the scriptures was also increasingly called into question by evidence drawn from other sources. Historical researches into ancient civilizations in Egypt, Assyria, Chaldea, China, and India revealed alternatives to the Hebraic version of history, some apparently of more ancient origin. Studies in comparative mythology began to challenge the assumption that the scriptures were a unique revelation of God's will. Christian scholars continued to assume that pagan traditions were derived from biblical sources, but Deists such as John Toland and Matthew Tindal argued that God had originally extended his providence to humanity universally, and they implied that the Bible itself was, like pagan mythologies, a corruption of divine truth. Such arguments helped to promote the view that all religions shared fundamental similarities, that (as Andrew Michael Ramsay explained) 'There are traces of the principal doctrines of reveal'd religion . . . to be found in the mythology of all nations'.[2]

---

[1] The tradition that Moses was author of the Pentateuch was attacked in the 17th cent. by Hobbes: *Leviathan* (Cambridge, 1991), 261, 265; and Spinoza, *Tractatus Theologico-politicus* (Leiden, New York, Copenhagen, Cologne, 1991), ch. 8, p. iv. Geddes referred to Jean Astruc's *Conjectures* (Brussels, 1753) and summarized Eichorn's theories concerning Genesis, in his version of *The Holy Bible* (London, 1792), i. p. xix. Michaelis's *Introduction to the New Testament* (London, 1793), argued that the Evangelists had 'made use of written documents' in their Gospels, iii. 94.

[2] A. M. Ramsay, *The Travels of Cyrus in Two Volumes* (London, 1730), ii. 2. See A. J. Kuhn, 'English Deism and the Development of Romantic Mythological Syncretism', *PMLA* 71 (1956), 1094–5.

The physical sciences provided evidence that seemed to conflict with the biblical account of human origins. Developments in the study of geology appeared to show that the earth had undergone immense physical changes during its existence, that mountains had been transformed into plains, plains into mountains, dry land into sea. In the face of such evidence, natural historians and others began to set aside as quite inadequate the Bible's time scale of world history (traditionally a span of about 6,000 years). Evolutionary explanations began to gain ground on the traditional belief in the six days of creation. The French naturalist Georges-Louis Buffon, for example, argued that the earth and the other planets had separated from the sun as torrents of 'liquid fire', and that they had assumed their present form as a result of gravitational forces. Rousseau, in his famous *Discourse on Inequality*, implicitly challenged the biblical view that humanity had come from the hand of God perfectly formed, arguing that it must have taken many ages for human beings to acquire the power of speech and reason. By 1794 Erasmus Darwin was asking his readers to consider the possibility that the earth existed millions of ages before humanity appeared, and that all warm-blooded animals had evolved 'from one living filament.'[3]

As history became liberated from the biblical framework in the eighteenth century, it became increasingly a secular, cultural study. The angle of vision widened, as writers began to look beyond major political events, beyond particular facts and exemplars, to examine general political and social trends. It became possible to write a new kind of universal history, one that could do justice to non-Christian cultures, as Voltaire demonstrated in his *Essai sur les Mœurs et l'Esprit des Nations* (1745–52). And, as Montesquieu showed in his *Esprit des Lois* (1748), it became possible to study religious institutions in relation to political or material circumstances that might influence their development.

The influence of such pioneering works was soon felt in Britain, both in speculative essays such as Hume's 'The Natural History of Religion' (1757), and in monumental studies such as Hume's *History of Great Britain* (1754–62), Robertson's *History of America* (1777), and Gibbon's *Decline and Fall of the Roman Empire*

[3] G.-L. Buffon, *Barr's Buffon: Buffon's Natural History*, 10 vols. (London, 1792), i. 94. E. Darwin, *Zoonomia: Or the Laws of Organic Life*, 2 vols. (London, 1794–6), i. (1794), 505.

(1776–88). These works were committed to revealing in secular terms the causes of cultural, economic, political, or religious development. They were supposedly non-partisan, presenting themselves as 'philosophical' or scientific in spirit.

The philosophical ambition of the new history drew support from the empirical tradition fostered by Newton and Locke, which located the origins of human knowledge in the experience of a natural world governed by fixed and definable laws. The study of history could be thought of as a scientific activity, because human nature was assumed to be a constant. As Hume explains: 'Mankind are so much the same, in all times and places, that history informs us of nothing new or strange in this particular. Its chief use is only to discover the constant and universal principles of human nature.'[4] In view of this assumption, it might seem surprising that progress was an important theme in the new history. But belief in progress could be reconciled with the constancy of human nature simply by assuming that 'man . . . has in himself a principle of progression', as Adam Ferguson explained in his *Essay on the History of Civil Society* (1767). In the light of this view it appeared that the pattern of human development must itself be uniform. Ferguson saw an analogy between the advance of the species 'from rudeness to civilization' and the growth of the individual from 'infancy to manhood', while William Robertson assured his readers that 'In every part of the earth the progress of man hath been nearly the same, and we can trace him in his career from the rude simplicity of savage life, until he attains the industry, the arts, and the elegance of polished society.'[5]

Belief in the uniformity of human development encouraged generalizations about the major phases of history. John Locke's theoretical discussion of the origins of society appeared to associate the initial 'state of nature' with the Golden Age, a condition lost through the rise of ambition and concupiscence which in turn necessitated the establishment of regular government.[6] This

---

[4] D. Hume, *Enquiries Concerning Human Understanding and Concerning the Principles of Morals*, ed. L. A. Selby-Bigge, 3rd edn., rev. P. H. Nidditch (Oxford, 1975), 83.

[5] A. Ferguson, *An Essay on the History of Civil Society (1767)*, ed. D. Forbes (Edinburgh, 1966), 8, 1. William Robertson, *The History of America* (1771), in *The Works of William Robertson*, 11 vols. (Chiswick, 1824), ix. 19–20.

[6] J. Locke, *Two Treatises of Government*, ed. P. Laslett (Cambridge, 1988), 342–3.

three-stage pattern was a common feature of social theory in the eighteenth century (Pope presented a version of it in the *Essay on Man*, III: 147–294); by the 1760s it was being used specifically to explain the course of progress, from a condition of primordial simplicity, through a necessary period of barbarism, to the development of civilization. The pattern appears, for example, in James Macpherson's 'Dissertation Concerning the Poems of Ossian' where the middle state, the period of complete barbarism and ignorance, begins with the establishment of private property.[7] Adam Smith, and a number of other writers who made 'conjectural' reconstructions of the causes and effects of social evolution, defined a four-stage pattern based on methods of subsistence: hunting, pasturage, agriculture, and commerce.[8] This way of visualizing history produced the sense of an inner dynamic or natural potential unfolding in human life, as the major stages were felt to follow each other in a natural progression, each containing within itself the germ of the one that followed.

The idea of progress supported both optimistic and pessimistic views of civilization. Rousseau described the transition from a primeval state of nature into civil order as a disastrous fall into a kind of slavery. In contrast, Condorcet argued that 'no bounds have been fixed to the improvement of the human faculties; that the perfectibility of man is absolutely indefinite'.[9] Generally, historians tended to affirm the advantages that had come with progress, and to warn against the possibilities of regression. Hayden White observes that the sceptical form of Enlightenment rationalism inspired a purely ironical attitude to the past: 'The mode in which all the *great* historical works of the age were cast is that of Irony, with the result that they all tend towards the form of satire.'[10] One might extend this observation: irony is found not only in the attitude to the past, but more fundamentally, in the sense of the historical process itself. In much Enlightenment history the relationship

[7] See M. M. Rubel, *Savage and Barbarian: Historical Attitudes in the Criticism of Homer and Ossian in Britain, 1760–1800* (Amsterdam, Oxford, and New York, 1978), 33–4. J. Macpherson, 'A Dissertation Concerning the Poems of Ossian', in *The Works of Ossian*, 2 vols. (London, 1765).

[8] See R. L. Meek, *Social Science and The Ignoble Savage* (Cambridge, 1976).

[9] A.-N. de Condorcet, *Outlines of an Historical View of the Progress of the Human Mind* (London, 1795), 4.

[10] H. White, *Metahistory: The Historical Imagination in Nineteenth-Century Europe* (Baltimore and London, 1973), 54–5.

between actions and consequences seems paradoxical. Robertson's review of 'The Progress of Society in Europe' (in his *History of the Reign of The Emperor Charles V*, 1769) emphasized both the terrible brutality of the crusades and their beneficial effects on the development of medieval Europe. Hume's *History of England* showed how violent internal dissension might have a liberalizing effect on the state. Ferguson characterized the fortuitous nature of social development in general terms: 'Every step and every movement of the multitude, even in what are termed enlightened ages, are made with equal blindness to the future; and nations stumble upon establishments, which are indeed the result of human action, but not the execution of any human design.' As Ronald Meek notes, Ferguson spelled out here what other historians of the late eighteenth century appeared to take tacitly for granted: history seems governed by 'the law of unintended consequences'.[11]

The paradoxical relationship between causes and effects did not always work to ensure progress. In some cases civilization appeared to be threatened by the very same forces that allowed it to develop. There was a general recognition that increased affluence could undermine the stability or vigour of the social order by stimulating corruption and luxury. More specifically, Adam Smith, Ferguson, and others feared that the division of labour, identified as the mainspring of economic growth, could have a disastrous effect on the well-being of the labourer. Perhaps the best-known exploration of the self-destructive dynamics of a civilization was provided by Gibbon, who not only argued that 'Prosperity ripened the principle of decay' in the Roman Empire, but also provided a highly controversial account of the way in which religion had contributed both to the development and the decline of Roman power.[12]

The Passions

The general movement towards the production of secular or scientific accounts of life also gave rise to new ideas about the place of the passions in civil society. In Milton's vision of fallen existence, restraint of the disordered passions is enforced by visions of

---

[11] Ferguson, *History of Civil Society*, 122; Meek, *Social Science*, 150.

[12] E. Gibbon, *The History of the Decline and Fall of the Roman Empire*, ed. J. B. Bury, 7 vols. (London, 1926–9), iv. 173.

spiritual reward and punishment. But since the Renaissance, writers had been attempting to base ethical systems on a reasonable view of things as they are, rather than on the prospect of possible damnation. As Albert O. Hirschman observes, it became common for social theorists to think of '*harnessing* the passions, instead of simply repressing them'.[13]

The recognition that commerce was founded on competition made it necessary to accommodate self-interest more clearly within the social system. In eighteenth-century theory, self-love could mean not only selfishness but also self-preservation or self-approbation.[14] It could be described as the principle of all action, as Pope showed in his *Essay on Man*, where 'Self-love and Social' are 'the same' (II: 93–4, III: 317–18). Many writers, while taking a generally hospitable view of self-love, also felt the need to describe an unselfish natural principle that worked to unify the individualistic social order by keeping self-love in check. The idea of natural sympathy or benevolence became a commonplace of moral and social theory in the eighteenth century. It had an important bearing on the development of primitivistic thought, as Lois Whitney explains: 'If benevolence can be shown to be "natural" to man, the goodness of primitive man who lives "naturally" is almost axiomatic.'[15] Thus Rousseau, who identified pity as the basis of primitive social life, argued that its unifying function had effectively been usurped by the imposition of formal government: 'Pity is a natural Sentiment which, by moderating in each Individual the Activity of Self-love, contributes to the mutual Preservation of the whole Species . . . it is this pity which, in a State of Nature, stands for Laws, for Manners, for Virtue.'[16] For others, benevolence or sympathy was a characteristic of civilization, dependent on contemplation for its full development. Shaftesbury, Hume, Francis Hutcheson, and Adam Smith were among those who theorized the

[13] A. O. Hirschman, *The Passions and the Interests: Political Arguments for Capitalism before its Triumph* (Princeton, NJ, 1977), 16.

[14] D. H. White, *Pope and the Context of Controversy: The Manipulation of Ideas in An Essay on Man* (Chicago and London, 1970), 174–5. See also R. Ferguson, *The Unbalanced Mind: Pope and the Rule of Passion* (Brighton, 1986), 68–91.

[15] Lois Whitney, *Primitivism and the Idea of Progress In English Popular Literature of the Eighteenth Century* (Baltimore, 1934), 22.

[16] J. J. Rousseau, *A Discourse Upon the Origin and Foundation of the Inequality among Mankind* (London, 1761), 101.

ethics of feeling in this way, placing sympathetic emotion against the civilized individual's more selfish impulses. In spite of differences in terminology and emphasis, their attempts to assert a natural virtue all tend to transform the opposition between good and evil into a dynamic system of countervailing emotions that seems necessary to the operation and continued progress of society. When Milton's Adam is instructed to live by 'love, By name to come called Charity', it is understood that such love will repress his potential for evil and so help to redeem his sinful nature. In contrast, the natural sympathy or benevolence in eighteenth-century theory is a power which tends to retard and balance that 'impulse of passion' on which social activities depend.[17]

The new approaches to social development were not necessarily incompatible with Christian belief. If Christian historians had traditionally interpreted events in the light of providence, and found a divine purpose in both the successful development of civilizations and in their decline, it was possible to find a new role for providence through the operation of 'natural law'—to think of history in general terms as a sequence of causes and effects that had been 'determined and set in motion by God at the creation.'[18] And it was possible to harmonize the idea of continued progress with a millenarian view of the Last Judgement, as Joseph Mede, Henry More, Robert Boyle, and other seventeenth-century writers had demonstrated.[19] Nevertheless the new history tended to promote an understanding of human destiny that contrasted with the traditional, biblical view. If the old vision, on which Milton had based his epic, emphasized that humanity existed in a state of sin from which it was to be redeemed by divine grace, the new vision suggested that humanity might liberate itself from a state of ignorance by the power of reason, that it might progress through the arts and sciences towards greater self-knowledge, greater liberty, perhaps greater happiness.

[17] A. A. Cooper, *Anthony Ashley Cooper, Third Earl of Shaftesbury: Standard Edition*, ed. G. Hemmerich and W. Benda, 6 vols. (Frommann-Holzborg, 1981–9), iv. 183. F. Hutcheson, *An Essay on the Nature and Conduct of the Passions and Affections* (London, 1728), repr. (Menston, Yorks., 1972), 54. D. Hume, *A Treatise on Human Nature* book III, part ii, section 2; book II, part iii, section 3, in *David Hume: The Philosophical Works*, ed. T. H. Green and T. H. Grose, 4 vols. (Aalen, 1964), ii. 271, 194. A. Smith, *The Theory of Moral Sentiments* (Indianapolis, 1976), 163.
[18] E. L. Tuveson, *Millennium and Utopia* (Berkeley and Los Angeles, 1949), 119.
[19] Ibid. 71–112.

History and Myth

We do not know the full extent of Blake's reading among the works of the Enlightenment period. He claims to have read and annotated Locke's *Essay Concerning Human Understanding* and Burke's *Philosophical Enquiry* into the sublime when he was a 'very Young' (*E660*). Voltaire and Rousseau are introduced as portents of revolution in *The French Revolution* (1791) and *The Song of Los* (1795). In *Milton* (1804+), Hume and Gibbon are denounced along with Bolingbroke.[20] This brief list could be extended, but we have no way of knowing for certain how well he knew the works of such writers, when he read them, or how many other authors he read whose names do not appear in his writings. We can say that in a general sense, and sometimes more specifically, Blake's work responds to many of the developments that had transformed the intellectual climate since the age of Milton.

Blake's attitude to these developments was of course hostile. As Michael Ackland says, Blake had 'seen the concept of Enlightenment used to justify the slave trade, rapacious mercantilism, domestic repression, and finally wars of empire'.[21] But his work shows a fascination with the ambitions and anxieties of the Enlightenment. When Blake began work on *The Four Zoas* he shared the philosophical historian's interest in exploring the relationship between economic, social, and religious developments; and he shared the contemporary interest in 'stadial' history, which attempted to reconstruct in general terms the major stages of social development. His vision of history in *The Four Zoas* is deeply ironic: the relationship between causes and consequences is paradoxical and tends to demonstrate, in a highly idiosyncratic way, the law of unintended consequences. The narrative presents fallen civilization as a system founded on countervailing emotions, in which apparently selfish passion is harnessed and restrained under the influence of pity—an ambivalent emotion that emerges through contemplation. And like the works of Deists and sceptics, Blake's poem emphasizes

[20] There is evidence to suggest Blake knew something of Gibbon's history of Rome in the early eighties. G. E. Bentley Jr. notes that in the early fragment 'then She bore Pale desire' the reference to the fall of the Roman Empire 'A sacrifice done by a Priestly hand' apparently echoes similar assertions in Gibbon's *Decline and Fall*, vols. i–iii (1776, 1781): *Blake Books* (Oxford, 1977), 439.

[21] Michael Ackland, 'Blake's Critique of Enlightenment Reason in *The Four Zoas*', *Colby Library Quarterly*, 4 (1983), 174.

that the visions of the past and future on which religions base their authority are limited by the circumstances in which they are produced. It is a narrative that consistently satirizes the biblical view of history.

However, if Blake rejected the authenticity of the Bible as a literal history and, like the most outspoken of the Deists, angrily denounced its 'pretence of divine command', he did not accept that such an exposure made the text an irrelevance to the historian. His attitude is quite unlike that of those who attacked the scriptures from a rationalist perspective. He argued that all religions are derived from the Poetic Genius, and his work draws on a variety of mythical sources in a way that suggests imaginative connections between them. But still the Bible retained a central place in Blake's thought, and he seems always to have considered himself a Christian. He shared the Christian historian's assumption that the function of history is to clarify the relationship between humanity and divinity, that human life is for most a condition of spiritual exile, and that fallen history as we know it will terminate in a universal resurrection. The biblical account of existence, stretching from creation and fall to the Last Judgement, provided the most comprehensive and penetrating vision of human destiny.

As the son of a London hosier he was born into a class that was traditionally dissenting in religious matters and radical in politics. It has often been pointed out that some of his beliefs resemble those of radical Christian sects that flourished during the revolutionary years of the seventeenth century, such as the Ranters and the Muggletonians, whose influence seems to have survived into Blake's own day.[22] We know nothing for certain of his religious education, although it has been suggested that Blake's mother may have come from a Muggletonian family, which would explain the derivation of the antinomian elements in his work.[23] In later life he claimed to have been influenced from an early age by the occult

[22] See A. L. Morton, *The Everlasting Gospel: A Study in the Sources of William Blake* (London, 1958), 98–121; E. P. Thompson, *The Making of the English Working Class* (Harmondsworth, 1968), 55–7; C. Hill, *Milton and the English Revolution* (London, 1977), 467–9; M. H. Abrams, *Natural Supernaturalism: Tradition and Revolution in Romantic Literature* (New York, 1971), 51–5; L. Tannenbaum, *Biblical Tradition in Blake's Early Prophecies: The Great Code of Art* (Princeton, NJ, 1982), 15–17; J. Mee, *Dangerous Enthusiasm: William Blake and the Culture of Radical Enthusiasm in the 1790s* (Oxford, 1992).

[23] E. P. Thompson, *Witness Against the Beast: William Blake and the Moral Law* (Cambridge, 1993), 104.

writers Boehme and Paracelsus (*E*707–8), and he certainly had an enduring (if not always approving) interest in the writings of the Swedish visionary Emmanuel Swedenborg. However his beliefs were formed, it is clear that his approach to the Bible has something in common with Boehme, Swedenborg, and other 'inner light' Protestants, who read the text metaphorically, as representing spiritual states and processes rather than as a literal record of historical events. George Anthony Rosso Jr. has argued that Blake's view of the Bible is close to that of contemporary higher critics, who sought to 'salvage revealed religion' by transforming the 'fact claim' of the Bible.[24] But Blake's reading seems to me more radical than this implies. As he explains in his annotation to Watson's *Apology for the Bible*: 'I cannot conceive the Divinity of the ⟨books in the⟩ Bible to consist either in who they were written by or at what time or in the historical evidence which may be all false in the eyes of one man & true in the eyes of another' (*E*618). The 'fact claim' has become an irrelevance. Exploding the historical authenticity of the text did not diminish its value as history, but allowed it to be read as an imaginative key to historical processes. Reading in this way has nothing to do with literal truth or with specific predictions: a prophet 'never says such a thing will happen let you do what you will'. Instead the prophet says 'If you go on So I the result is So' (*E*617). Prophecy is a matter of seeing the relationship between cause and effect, of seeing the underlying pattern to which historical events are likely to conform. As 'a Poem of probable impossibilities' (*E*616), the Bible became for Blake a guide to the universal patterns of human history.

It is here that the link with Enlightenment history becomes particularly pertinent, since Blake uses the Bible as if the modern pattern of progress is already inscribed in it, contained within the larger framework of creation and judgement. We can see part of this pattern if we consider the outline of Genesis from the era of Abraham, the era in which the history of Israel properly begins. The life of the Patriarchs has a primitive simplicity: their social organization is tribal; their relationship with God precludes dependence on priests. They are nomadic, but their vision becomes governed by the idea of possessing the land in which they live. The entry into Egypt is an entry into the realm of civilization, kingly power, and state

[24] Rosso, *Blake's Prophetic Workshop*, 102–4.

religion (in the last Egyptian chapters of Genesis, God does not speak—except in 46: 2–4, i.e. outside Egypt). Genesis can be read as a parable of progress, a parable that is clarified in Exodus: civilization is experienced as a state of spiritual bondage which reveals the hidden implications of the dream or promise of possession. Read in this way the book offers a counterpart to Rousseau's famous account of progress as a disastrous fall into bondage. Indeed, the entire course of biblical history can be reduced to the same pattern—since the vision of the promised land always leads to the experience of civilization as a state of captivity and/or exile. The Israelites' entry into Canaan leads to the reign of kings, the establishment of the Temple, division, imperial domination, and exile in Babylon. The return to Jerusalem and the rebuilding of the Temple are followed by Roman occupation. The vision of a messianic kingdom provides the foundation for a new religion that will be absorbed by imperial power—Paul's story ends in Rome, just as Joseph's ended in Egypt. We can find an epitome of this pattern contained in the opening chapters of Genesis, where Adam is created from dust (like Abraham called in the desert) and is then given possession of Eden—which is the prelude to the experience of law ('thou shalt not') and spiritual exile. Read in this way the Bible becomes a text in which the Christian and secular views of history are brought into relation and encoded in powerful narrative patterns which overlap, repeat, and contain each other. The first eight Nights of *The Four Zoas* allude to the Bible in a way that emphasizes such patterns: in their account of progress they not only draw on the whole range of biblical history, but can also be read as an elaboration of the first three chapters of Genesis, from creation to fall.

Milton's imaginative exploration of biblical myth in *Paradise Lost* was also a particularly important model for Blake's work, even though Milton's Puritan theology was obnoxious to Blake. In transposing biblical material into an epic form, Milton brought to it something of the rationalizing tendency of his age. He drew the elements of the story into an intricate system of causes and effects, and in doing so he supplied what the Bible excluded: complex analyses of motives; sophisticated parallels between divine and infernal activities; a detailed exploration of the sequence of creation; elaborate descriptions of heaven, hell, and chaos. In expanding and humanizing the myth, he invited close inspection of its hierarchical assumptions, and in that way he destabilized it. The famous claim, in *The Marriage*, that Milton was 'of the Devils party without knowing it', suggests one kind of instability arising from variations in dramatic interest and sympathy. But the method of narration itself also destabilizes the narrative's theology. Since Milton's epic begins *in medias res*, and ends with the exit from Eden, much of the poem's vision of history—whether divine or human—is presented either in retrospect or in prospect, described by the characters rather than by the narrator, mediated through recollections, visions, particular acts of speech, in a narrative which shows that dreams and speech can be deceptive. This procedure foregrounds the rhetorical or ideological function of such accounts—their importance in influencing the behaviour of the listener, whether the case is Sin recalling her own separation from Satan, Raphael recounting creation and the wars in heaven, or Michael unfolding a vision of the future course of history. The relationships between doctrine and point of view, between point of view and historical context, are emphasized, and to that extent values are relativized. Of course the narrative works to contain this effect, since the narrator is consciously on the side of the angels. But the very clarity with which the narrator's doctrine is expounded and dramatized allows its ambivalences to be seen more easily. *The Four Zoas* makes continual reference to Milton's myth, recreating in new forms its visions, dreams, and recollections, in a way that plays on their apparent contradictions.

The narrative of *The Four Zoas*, then, can be seen as an attempt to bring secular and mythical discourses together in a highly unusual way. Like some other eighteenth-century histories, it demythologizes history, by showing that religious and political systems are rooted in particular historical conditions that determine their structure. In this respect the investigation of human origins might be described as naturalistic. But paradoxically Blake's naturalism is visionary, exposing not an objectively fixed and limiting natural world, but a limiting vision of nature that is 'fixed by the Corporeal Vegetative Eye' (*E*563). The mythical form of the narrative consistently locates the mainspring of history in deformations of vision. It emphasizes that the causes of history are spiritual rather than natural, and it retains the possibility of escape from fallen existence through a clarification of vision.

Blake's poem has sometimes been regarded as the product of a retreat into a private world of myth, a withdrawal from the contemporary realities that had occupied him in some of his earlier works. But although his narrative is in many respects highly idiosyncratic, it can be seen as an attempt to engage with the mainstream of contemporary thought, an unprecedented effort to grapple with the divergent traditions he had inherited, and to force them to illuminate each other.

Towards Vala

The Four Zoas acquired its present title at a relatively late stage in its composition. When Blake began work on the poem in the mid 1790s he used the title *Vala*, the name of one of the characters, a goddess of love. Although Vala appeared nowhere in his earlier writings, the new poem did not represent a completely new departure in Blake's thinking: it was an attempt to elaborate and synthesize elements already explored in some of his illuminated books.

The Book of Urizen (1794) introduces the approach to history that Blake was to develop in *The Four Zoas*, and it raises a number of issues that were to receive much more attention in the later poem. It rewrites Genesis in a satirical form that undermines the idea of the sacred text at the same time as it undermines ideas of science and progress.[25] It uses material drawn from both kinds of discourse in order to satirize both kinds of discourse.

It can be read as a stadial history which presents a bizarre counterpart to contemporary ideas about the stages of human development. The common assumption in eighteenth-century history that human nature was essentially the same at all times meant that the capacity for rational order was held to be present, at least as a potentiality, in the darkest, most chaotic ages of history. As we have seen, the historical process was sometimes given a curving pattern, in which a primal state of simplicity gave way to a condition of barbarism (implicitly a temporary suppression of reason), from which humanity escaped into civil order.[26] Blake's narrative in *Urizen* develops its own highly idiosyncratic three-stage pattern, in

---

[25] For a discussion of *Urizen* and the authority of books see P. Mann 'The Book of Urizen and the Horizon of the Book', in *Unnam'd Forms: Blake and Textuality*, ed. N. Hilton and T. A. Vogler (Berkeley and Los Angeles, 1986), 49–68.

[26] See Rubel, *Savage and Barbarian*, 40–2.

which reason is suppressed during a fall into primitive life, and subsequently re-emerges to establish civilization.[27] The central ages, from which the civilized being appears to have escaped, determine fundamentally the pattern that civilization must take.

As a myth of creation the narrative includes references to a prehistory of creation, in which humanity participated in eternal life. We learn that before the creation of earth, 'The will of the Immortal expanded | Or contracted his all flexible senses' (3: 37–8, E71). If sensation is subject to will, no vision of reality can become a fixed mental horizon. The forms of life may change continually according to the desire of the individual. This view of eternal life helps to determine Blake's problematic use of gender relations in his mythology, which seems bound by what Anne K. Mellor terms the 'linguistic prisons of gender-identified metaphors' supplied by the culture in which he lived.[28] Blake's Immortal is male, and as the narrative of *Urizen* unfolds we learn that in eternity there is no separate female form. This implies that each individual identity (whether of a man or of a woman, apparently) is eternally 'male', while the 'female' is the outward form of the individual's vision. It follows that in eternity, where vision changes continually according to the creative will, the female can have no independent existence, and no permanent form. In this respect the communal life of eternity seems not only strenuous, but pitiless. The male who pities the female, and attempts to preserve her form, has already begun to set a limit to his own vision. In *Urizen*, the female only becomes completely distinct from the male in the fallen, finite world. Once the female has emerged into separate form, the relationship between 'male' and 'female' assumes many connotations, which vary according to context. It can suggest the relationship between, for example, spirit and body, or subject and object, or active and passive states of being, as well as between man and woman. But as Susan Fox observes, Blake consistently portrays the female 'as inferior and dependent . . . or as unnaturally and disastrously dominant'. And while his representations can be seen to satirize patriarchal views of women in a way that is sometimes compared to Mary

[27] Robert N. Essick relates the three stages of *Urizen* specifically to the three stages of culture outlined by Thomas Paine in *The Rights of Man*, i.e. priestcraft, conquerors, and reason: 'William Blake, Thomas Paine, and Biblical Revolution', *Studies in Romanticism*, 30 (1991), 200.

[28] A. K. Mellor, 'Blake's Portayal of Women', *Blake: An Illustrated Quarterly*, 63 (1982–3), 154.

Wollstonecraft's critique of limiting sexual roles, the structure of Blake's myth appears to reinforce some of the conventional assumptions it questions.[29]

The three stages of *Urizen* mentioned above are contained within a two-stage pattern, as the process of creation takes place both before and after the fall from eternity. In developing this distinction Blake may have been influenced by the contemporary theory that Genesis is a composite text which includes two contrasting views of creation. These are the so-called Elohist account (ch. 1 to ch. 2: 4a) and the Jahwist account (ch. 2: 4b–23), which Blake could have learned about from the Preface to Alexander Geddes' translation of the Bible.[30] Leslie Tannenbaum suggests that Blake derived from this distinction two separate mythical creators, Urizen and Los.[31] I shall argue that Blake's work reflects the distinction as two separate modes of vision, and that both Urizen and Los come to operate in the second mode.

In Genesis the Elohist creation includes the division of time and space into an unchanging order, and the generation of organic forms. The account expresses confidence in the power of thought and language, rather than in physical activity or love. It celebrates the power of a will superior to and separate from nature, rather than a sense of community with the natural world. If eternal life is a condition in which the 'all flexible senses' expand or contract at will, the Elohist creation can be seen as the product of a state of contraction, a state in which the mind has withdrawn from engagement with the fluidity of immediate experience in order to contemplate it in abstract terms. The first three chapters of *Urizen* show that the attempt to impose such an unchanging order on experience will inevitably make the instability of the elements and the spontaneity of organic life seem a threat to that order. Creation must involve 'conflictions' between the urge for stability and the recalcitrant instability of existence. The being who creates in this embattled mode is Urizen, the reasoning power, whose name may be derived from a Greek word (οὐρίζειν) which, as Geddes explains,

---

[29] S. Fox, 'The Female as Metaphor in William Blake's Poetry,' *Critical Enquiry*, 3 (1977), 507. See also M. Ackland, 'The Embattled Sexes: Blake's Debt to Wollstonecraft in *The Four Zoas*', *Blake: An Illustrated Quarterly*, 63 (1982–3), 172–83.

[30] See J. J. McGann, 'The Idea of an Indeterminate Text: Blake's Bible of Hell and Dr Alexander Geddes', *Studies in Romanticism*, 25 (1986), 305–6.

[31] Tannenbaum, *Biblical Tradition*, 203–8.

means 'to bound or terminate'.[32] Urizen's search for order is motivated by a vision of the individual as set apart from the rest of
existence, as an autonomous centre that is 'self balanc'd'. The
individual conceived in this way has rights that need to be pro-
tected, but such protection can only be secured by regulating the
powers of action and of thought. Urizen is therefore driven to make
'Laws of peace, of love, of unity: Of pity, compassion, forgiveness.'
His quest is that of a reasonable mind, which seeks to establish the
values of innocence on the basis of justice and duty instead of
impulse.

In *Urizen* this quest is placed at the beginning of the narrative, as
if the rational basis of civil order is formulated in a prelapsarian
condition. It determines the subsequent form of existence because it
entails the loss of the eternal sense of interrelatedness, and so forces
humanity to reconstruct life in relation to a world that seems
separate and alien. With the fall of Urizen into intellectual chaos,
the myth of creation begins again, in terms that in some ways
correspond to the Jahwist account of creation in Genesis. The God
of the Jahwist account is not a distant being who creates by giving
commands: he works within the world, becoming involved in
physical processes, making use of limited materials: dust of the
ground, Adam's rib. The Jahwist creation is not the perfect realization of a preconceived order. Instead it emerges from an activity
that seems pragmatic and progressive, since a first attempt may be
subsequently improved ('It is not good that man should be alone').
In comparison with the Elohist creation, this account seems to
reflect a more confined sense of the human condition, an awareness
that the world has to be transformed by labour, even by trial and
error. The reference to planting a garden presupposes an experience
of land as property, as a possession marked off and invested with
toil and expectation. In the Elohist account men and women are
created at the same time, but in the Jahwist account woman is
created almost as an afterthought. The story not only denies the
dependence of the male upon the female (by eliminating natural
childbirth), but also reinforces the idea of monogamous marriage.
It seems to reflect, that is, a fearful, patriarchal consciousness of
sexuality as an area of life that must be carefully regulated.

In Blake's narrative the Jahwist account provides a model of a

[32] See McGann, 'The Idea of an Indeterminate Text', 317.

mode of vision in which humanity sees itself as subject to external nature and must therefore construct its life in naturalistic terms. This is the mode which gives rise to evolutionary theories of creation, speculations about a primitive state of nature, a view of the family as the primary unit of social life, and a progressive vision of history. The creator who first presides within this mode of vision is the embodiment of Urizen's own displaced creative energy: Los, the 'Eternal prophet'.

In the fallen world of *Urizen* Los assumes the familiar role of the prophet only gradually: at first his creativity appears primarily as an instinctual capacity for adaptation and invention. Whereas Urizen was 'self contemplating', and strove to divide time and space by his own power, Los struggles to contain a chaotic external world that seems to evolve and divide itself naturally, as if following its own mysterious purposes. The account of the environment Los contends with recalls Milton's description of the sulphurous landscape of hell (in which the fallen angels become metal workers) and, in the obscure progressive changes that continue 'Ages on ages,' contemporary evolutionary theories of the earth's development.

In the figure of Los, the artisan is not a liberator, as he was in *The French Revolution* (see lines 231-2, E296). In this context he is a repressive power. His labour is reactive and pragmatic: knowledge must flow primarily from experience, in response to the pressure of urgent physical need. As a result the dormant reasoning power of Urizen becomes subject to, and contained by, the natural limits of the body. The naturalistic vision that Los helps to establish determines not only the sense of the mind's relationship with the body, but also the forms in which love can appear in the fallen world. Since love must now become attached to separate, finite objects which the individual seeks to preserve and protect, it takes the form of an inherently possessive 'Pity'. Its attractive power is at once disruptive and stabilizing: it transforms sexuality into a source of anxiety and jealousy (the emergence of pity is seen as the division from Los of his female counterpart, Enitharmon), and it helps to establish the family as the basic unit of social order. From the female aspect of love a male form soon emerges: a 'resistless' child, Orc, whose fiery power recalls the burning eternal life from which Urizen withdrew. At this point the ambivalent nature of pity is revealed more clearly. As the child of pitying parents, Orc is fed and bound, stimulated and repressed. In the power of Los he is not repressed by law or by any rational principle, but by an emotional compulsion. As in Rousseau's vision of the state of nature, the influence of pity takes the place of law.

The binding of Orc corresponds, of course, to the binding of Isaac by Abraham in Genesis, an act which leads to a revelation of the Lord's promise to His chosen people. In *Urizen*, since vision is now bound to a temporal world, the possibility of fulfilment will be conceived not as eternally present, in communion with Eternals, but as lying in the future, in a promised land to be won by gaining control over the unruly passions. In this way Los's world, unforeseen and unplanned, becomes the 'natural' foundation of subsequent experience.

Once Orc has been bound, Urizen, the fallen reasoning power, begins to emerge from his contemplative sleep to become once again the dominant force in human life. The vision of future fulfilment takes on a new significance as we begin to move from a culture in which labour was governed by immediate needs, to one in which it is driven by an ambition to master nature through knowledge. Urizen now seems more like the Jahwist than the Elohist creator, becoming involved in physical processes, learning from experience, even planting a garden. His labour is scientific, depending on measurement and active exploration of his 'dens'. Under his leadership humanity is brought, like the children of Abraham in search of the promised land, into a state of civilization that Blake identifies as Egypt (traditionally associated with science, mathematics, astronomy, and state religion). Since Urizen cannot contemplate the interdependence of life without fear, his religion is another manifestation of Pity, an urge to protect humanity from the moral chaos of its own selfish appetites and passions.

Many aspects of *Urizen* were revised and elaborated in *The Four Zoas*. Some of the most important may be outlined here:

1. The two modes of vision in the narrative can be seen as opposites. The first is teleological and homocentric: initially Urizen formulates abstract laws by contemplating his own nature (he is a 'self-contemplating shadow'). The second is empirical: after the fall Los strives to organize an external world, while Urizen assumes that truth lies outside himself and can be discovered by exploration and accurate measurement. This kind of distinction assumes a

major importance in *The Four Zoas*, where each mode of vision is developed much more elaborately, and a series of intricate parallels is established between them.

2. Although *Urizen* shows the formative role of labour in the historical process, it gives little sense of the importance of economic activity. In *The Four Zoas*, the development of civilization is related to particular modes of subsistence—hunting, pasturage, agriculture, and commerce. The description of the commercial phase of development shows a keen awareness of the economic significance of labour.

3. The narrative of *Urizen* shows that in the fallen world the passions can only be experienced in terms of self-defeating conflict. Orc's desire inspires Urizen's search for mastery of the fallen world, which in turn leads Urizen once more to regulate life by laws that repress desire. As the process leads to a religion founded on 'Pity', we can see that desire stimulates repressive pity, just as pity fosters the desire that it must repress. This understanding of social order—as a system that is generated by conflicting emotions—has its milder counterpart within the secular discourse of eighteenth-century social theory in which, as we have seen, civilization was often shown to be sustained by the balanced opposition of selfish and sympathetic passions. In this opposition, both kinds of passion seem ambivalent: self-love drives the social order, but may disrupt it; the sympathetic passions work to restrain selfishness, and to stabilize a social order that protects self-interest. The complex relationship between pity and desire in *Urizen* presents a dramatic exposure of such ambivalence. But the ambivalence of *Urizen* drives deeper than this. The deliberately reductive distinction made in *The Marriage* between active evil and passive good is here completely exploded, since the terms of the distinction may be reversed: evil may appear in passive forms (the perverse and cruel delight of the female as object of desire), while energy may drive the search to formulate and actively enforce principles of goodness. Indeed, the interrelations between pity and desire suggest that what is held to be good may simultaneously be repressed, and what is condemned as evil may also be sanctioned.

This interest in the complex relationships between desire and pity may help to explain why the original title of *The Four Zoas* was *Vala*, the name of a powerful goddess of love. The myths of *Urizen* and of other illuminated works of the 1790s show that as the historical process develops, the softer aspects and objects of human feeling, which supposedly unify civilization, begin to appear and exert their influence. These are given female forms in Blake's mythology, forms that satirize and reproduce the gendered stereotypes of the patriarchal traditions that the mythology explores. The influence of these female embodiments of mercy, pity, peace, and love is various and often sinister.

In *Ahania*, for example, the repressed Ahania finds expression as a haunting sense of loss. Her song recalls among other biblical contexts the communal and individual laments in the Psalms and the book of Lamentations, which focus on the destruction of Jerusalem, the dispersal of the royal household, the experience of exile. Such laments illustrate the importance of emotions of defeat in the Old Testament, in which the present is repeatedly seen as a condition of spiritual exile from which a dependent (and often self-pitying and reproachful) humanity must look back, as Ahania does, to a lost communion with a divine master. The preoccupation with loss can be seen as another manifestation of emotional ambivalence: the vision of innocent sexuality in Eden, for example, is at once a lost ideal which focuses desire and a tantalizing representation of what must now be repressed. In the New Testament, Mary Magdalene—who weeps at the sepulchre, and fails to recognize the unascended Christ—provides another image of this ambivalence (Luke 8: 2; John 20: 17). Ahania corresponds to the Magdalene; her despairing sorrow at once expresses and inhibits love. She is not only a symptom of repression, but also an insidious instrument of it. Ahania is described as 'The mother of Pestilence' (*E*85).

In *Europe*, Enitharmon embodies an emotional ambivalence that is related more overtly to the Christian vision. She emerges as a power of bliss and joy, who evokes the sensuous beauty of the natural world. But she is also a repressive power, who promotes the conviction that 'woman's love is sin', and who seeks to 'Forbid all Joy'. She inspires 'immortal songs' and 'enormous revelry', but she also presents a vision of Eternal life as an illusory reward for the repression of desire. Enitharmon is an immensely powerful vision of love that takes possession of an entire era of civilization, a tyrannical complex of emotion that exerts its seductive influence over 'horned priest' and 'furious king' alike. The relationship between her rhapsodic song and the turbulent dream it encloses represents that between the dominant Christian ideology of 'Mercy Pity Peace and Love' and the pitiless history of conflict, repression and cruelty it actually produces.

These explorations of love suggest that fallen humanity is imprisoned not only by the prohibitions of law which restrain desire, but also by the powers that stimulate and focus desire. This idea is relevant not only to Blake's representations of creation and fall, but also to his view of revolution. For Blake, as for many other radicals in the 1790s, revolution acquired an apocalyptic significance, as a means by which the errors of tradition might be escaped. Blake's series of continental prophecies 'Africa', *America*, *Europe*, 'Asia' can be read as a sequence that ends optimistically in universal resurrection through revolution. But the events of contemporary history provided little evidence to support any notion of revolution as a triumph over the limited vision of the selfhood. By events I mean not only the political outcomes, but the political ideals that were voiced during the revolutionary era. It seems fair to assume that Blake's response to the revolution was to some extent a response to the debate stimulated in England by Price, Burke, Paine, and others. If hereditary rights were formally challenged in that debate, the challenge did not lead away from the realm of selfhood and law, but if anything, further into it, giving a new significance to the Lockian doctrine of natural rights, and to the analogy between the principles of government and principles of science. To James Mackintosh, author of *Vindiciae Gallicae*, 'The rights and the nature of man are to the Legislator what the general properties of matter are to the mechanic'. In the *Rights of Man* Paine set against the hereditary monarchial system (which 'reverses the wholesome order of nature') the representative system 'which is always parallel with the order and immutable laws of nature, and meets the reason of man in every part'. Richard Price eagerly foresaw 'the dominion of kings changed for the dominion of laws'.[33] The desires of many prominent radicals in the debate seem to be centred firmly on the rights of the selfhood.

The possibility that revolutionary desire might be imprisoned by

[33] J. Mackintosh, *Vindiciae Gallicae* (London, 1791), repr. (Oxford, 1989), 113. T. Paine, *Political Writings*, ed. B. Kuklick (Cambridge, 1989), 163, 172. R. Price, *A Discourse on the Love of our Country* (London, 1789), 50. See also H. T. Dickinson, *British Radicalism and the French Revolution 1789–1815* (Oxford, New York, 1985), 14.

its own objects is dramatized most clearly in *America*. The main part of this prophecy is a narrative of opposition: Orc, the embodiment of revolutionary energy, confronts what he hates—Urizen, a monstrous parody of Jehovah, and the angelic agents of Urizen's religious and political power. Here, restraining error stands clearly revealed before emergent desire and is rejected. But the optimism of this narrative is qualified by the 'Preludium', in which Orc confronts not what he hates, but what he desires. Here, attended by the mysterious Urthona's shadowy daughter (whose helmet and bow suggest the self-protective power of the selfhood), Orc is nourished and stimulated by powers that repress him. The myth implies that it is precisely because Orc is fed and strengthened in his captive state that he can become strong enough to break his chains. The relationship between cause and effect here recalls the paradoxical processes of Enlightenment history; as Gibbon might say, repression ripens the principle of rebellion. And here the conditions of imprisonment seem to determine the nature of the rebellion. In his captive state Orc is seen as an embodiment of what, in *The French Revolution*, Blake's Abbe de Seyes called 'Strength madden'd with slavery, honesty, bound in the dens of superstition'. When Orc breaks free his energy is released as what Seyes might describe as 'savage love' (*E296 228, 230*). His rape of the shadowy daughter recalls the lustful violence of Bromion in *Visions of the Daughters of Albion*.[34] Is desire truly released from bondage, or is it released only as a desire for possession, which implies a subtler form of captivity (hinted at in the female's 'I will not let you go')? The shadowy daughter's partial resistance to the processes of life suggests, at best, the emotional uncertainty that must accompany violent revolutionary change after long experience of deprivation. At worst it implies that the self-protective terrors of the selfhood may be intensified and given voice by revolution.

The female figures that appear in the historical works of the 1790s are patriarchal images reproducing stereotypical views of feminine emotion and behaviour. They may be characterized by a fearful self-pity, or by a terrible resignation to sorrow, or by a seductive beauty that stimulates—and represses—joy. They may be represented as pathetic or alluring, virginal or maternal, submissive

---

[34] As David Fuller notes, the myth is 'redolent of a corrupt male fantasy bred of sexual power structures and aggression which Blake's work aims to combat'. *Blake's Heroic Argument* (London, New York, and Sydney, 1988), 66.

or dominating, threatening or deceptively reassuring—and in each case the image of the female is seen as the counterpart, or product, of limited male vision. Her attractiveness is seen to be an important aspect of her power because in Blake's myth, as in Rousseau's famous *Discourse* on the arts and sciences, civilized humanity is shown to be 'in Love' with its chains.[35] If love in its softer forms is the power that induces self-restraint and submission to law, that craves for peace and for constancy in relationships, that weeps in the face of violence, it can seem necessary to any notion of communal life—even if it simultaneously fosters cruelty, despair, and the very violence over which it cries.

The paradoxical nature of this power may explain much that is most grim in fallen civilization, but also provides some grounds for hope: in the feeding of Orc by the shadowy daughter of Urthona we can recognize another example of the ambivalent force which nourishes and stimulates that which it represses. If it motivates the religion of Urizen, it also fosters the desire which opposes that religion and may be able to liberate humanity from it. In this elusive and protean power Blake had identified a principle that could help to explain both the development and the destruction of fallen civilization. Vala, whose name supplied the title of the long poem that Blake began to transcribe in 1797, was to become the most pervasive and seductive manifestation of this power in the narrative.

Creation and Providence

One aspect of *Urizen* requires separate consideration, because it raises an issue that was to have far-reaching consequences on the development of *The Four Zoas*: the narrative presents a complicated relationship between the fallen powers and the unfallen Eternals. The Eternals' rage and horror in some ways resemble that of Urizen and Los. They do not represent a foreknowing providence: to them, as to the fallen powers, creation unfolds according to the law of unintended consequences. They precipitate Urizen's fall when they spurn his religion. They separate the fallen world from Eternity with a tent called 'Science', in horrified reaction to the birth of Enitharmon and Orc. In short, responsibility for the

---

[35] J. J. Rousseau, *A Discourse to which the Prize was adjudged by the Academy of Dijon in the year 1750*, transl. by R. Wynne (London, 1757), 5.

terrible progress of history seems to lie partly with them. No doubt this can be seen as an ironical reflection on the relationship between divine and human action in Genesis, where humanity is subject to divine wrath, exclusion from Eden, and so on. But such a vision of history makes problematic any idea of communication between fallen humanity and Eternal life (and qualifies the poet's claim to write on the authority of the Eternals, pl. 2: 5–7 E70). In satirizing an unacceptable idea of providential interference, the narrative would seem to leave no room for an alternative view of divine providence.

When Blake began work on *The Four Zoas* he seems to have been untroubled by this problem, since the new narrative also left little room for an alternative view of providence. And yet Blake's vision of the fallen world seems always to have included such an alternative. In an early annotation creation is described as an act of mercy, as 'God descending according to the weakness of man' (E599). This view seems radically different from the view of creation in *Urizen*, although both present humanity as in some way separated from a higher existence, and dwelling in a world whose forms seem predetermined. Blake did not abandon this early view, which finds expression in some of the *Songs of Innocence* and in *The Book of Thel*, and which forms one part of a dialectic in his thinking. In a prose work of 1810 he repeats the view in a different way:

Many suppose that before [*Adam*] ⟨the Creation⟩ All was Solitude & Chaos This is the most pernicious Idea that can enter the Mind as it takes away all sublimity from the Bible & Limits All Existence to Creation & to Chaos To the Time & Space fixed by the Corporeal Vegetative Eye . . . Eternity Exists and All things in Eternity Independent of Creation which was an act of Mercy (E563)

The idea that eternity exists 'Independent of Creation' remains important to Blake, even though he also believes that eternity can be seen 'in an hour' (E490). And the view that creation is an act of mercy remains important, even though it trails in its wake intimations of a divine will that operates independently of our own, and so appears to conflict with the idea that all deities reside in the human breast. Blake seems ultimately to need a separate Eternity, because he needs to retain in some capacity a supervising providence. The necessity is exposed by the very form of the history Blake is developing in *Urizen* and in *The Four Zoas*, a form that reduces all historical developments to a universal pattern which unfolds with a seemingly inevitable momentum. Robert Nisbet has explained this necessity in uncompromising terms:

apart from the use of an omnipresent, omnipotent Providence conceived as author and executor of a design with which all human cultures however widely separated in space and time fit smoothly, there is no possibility whatever of dealing with 'world history' in narrative, unilinear fashion.

Nisbet does qualify this assertion, pointing out that 'secular minds' do in fact dispense with providence, but 'in each instance the obvious and indispensable *modus operandi* is some metaphysical substitute for providence.'[36] As we have seen, the Enlightenment vision of progress through a fixed sequence of stages implies a natural order, an internal dynamic which is the unspoken 'substitute for providence'.

If Blake disliked the idea of a foreseeing providence that could control destiny, there is no reason to suppose that he preferred a blind substitute. In order to avoid handing events over to mere necessity, he would need to reconcile the two terms of the dialectic we have considered: creation must be seen as at once a terrible error and an act of mercy; the vision of a supervising providence must be seen as at once flawed and necessary. It was apparently the need to achieve this kind of reconciliation that led Blake eventually to make a systematic revision of *The Four Zoas*, and to incorporate a specifically Christian vision of providence.

This revision shows the emergence of a new approach to history which is also a new approach to narrative. It ties the myth to a particular historical time-scale: the two thousand years of history since the advent of Christ are superimposed onto an archetypal pattern. It introduces, alongside Blake's invented names, biblical names which align the myth unequivocally with one vision of history. In place of a relativizing perspective which blends different traditions, the revision appears to give universal validity to a single prophetic tradition. The movement may reflect what Molly Anne Rothenberg has called 'Blake's recognition of the dark threat of nondifferentiation lurking in the Enlightenment project of rationalization'.[37]

---

[36] R. Nisbet, *History of the Idea of Progress* (London, 1980), 141.

[37] M. A. Rothenberg, *Rethinking Blake's Textuality* (Columbia, Mo., and London, 1993), 2.

Towards a National Epic

The movement towards a narrative rooted more clearly in particular traditions heralds a movement away from the representation of history as a single, linear sequence of causes and effects. The final step in this direction was the introduction of another, specifically British, framework. This incomplete revision introduced references to Albion, to legends recorded by Geoffrey of Monmouth and by Milton in his *History of England*, and to an ancient Druid culture which is identified with the culture of the biblical Patriarchs.

Although this development in Blake's thinking takes a characteristically idiosyncratic form, it can be seen as a development of its time. As Susan Matthews has pointed out, a number of the long poems published or planned in this period could be seen as attempts to create a national epic, an epic based on a specifically British legend. Such works are evidence of the growing influence of nationalist thinking during the later decades of the eighteenth century, and in particular after the revolution in France, an influence that helped to shape many aspects of contemporary culture, including the writing of history. The revolution has been seen to herald the end of contemporary interest in universal history.[38] But Blake did not abandon his own interest in this subject. By identifying the ancient Druids as the source of biblical history, he could reconcile the British framework with the Christian one, and approach the universal through the national. But as he began to identify the history of humanity with the history of Albion he did begin to lose interest, apparently, in the patterns of progress, in distinctions between the primitive and the civilized, which had been so important to Enlightenment thinking. And it was at this stage that he abandoned the poem which had given so much attention to the rise and fall of civilization—a poem which can be described as the most extraordinary product of the eighteenth-century tradition of philosophical history.

---

[38] G. Barraclough explains: 'From the time of the French Revolution cosmopolitan thinking gave way to national thinking: the nation-state asserted its place as the focus of human endeavour, the natural centre of all activity, and increasingly it was doubted whether there was any wider unity than the sovereign nation.' 'Universal History', in *Approaches to History: A Symposium*, ed. H. P. R. Finsberg (London, 1962), 86.

PART I

The Copperplate Text

The Copperplate Text

The first stage of my reading focuses on the earliest portion of the manuscript, written in Blake's copperplate hand. The first four-and-a-half pages
of this copperplate text were completely erased. The reading therefore
takes as its starting-point the copperplate lines that survive on the lower
half of page 7 (lines 8–13). The text continues, with many additions and
deletions, until it abruptly stops at 42: 18. My reading follows this text,
leaving out of account all of the additions. Readers who want to study the
text in detail will find a useful transcription (with different line numbering)
in the facsimile edition by Gerald E. Bentley Jr. (1963). Here it may be
helpful to identify some of the most extensive additions excluded from my
reading:

1. the conflict between Urizen and Los, 12: 8–31
2. the song sung at the feast of Los and Enitharmon, 14: 6–16: 22
3. the convening of the Council of God, 18: 9–15; 21: 1–22: 41; 19: 1–20:
   15
4. the fall of Albion and Jerusalem, 25: 6–33
5. the description of Urizen's halls and the emergence of Ahania, 30: 15–
   52
6. the description of Urizen's stars, 33: 19–36
7. the dialogue between Los and Enitharmon, and Enitharmon's song, 34:
   16–96

There are many other, less extensive, additions to the text, including, for
example, the passage describing the spaces of Eno (9: 9–19), and a series
of small additions describing the early development of, and conflict between, Los and Enitharmon. The basic copperplate text contains no references to Albion, Jerusalem, the Council of God, Jesus, Eden, Beulah, or
Ulro; and no references to Ahania before Night III.

A History of the Cosmos

The Copperplate Text

Between 1795 and the summer of 1797 Blake was at work on illustrations for an edition of Edward Young's long meditative poem *Night Thoughts*. This was the largest single commission he ever received as an artist and, had the work been a commercial success, it would have greatly enhanced Blake's contemporary reputation. In the event, only 43 of the 537 water-colour designs produced for it were engraved and published. After the first volume appeared the project was abandoned.[1] The hope of public recognition from this venture probably spurred Blake's ambition to compose and illustrate a long poem of his own, and it may have been during these years that the narrative of what was to become *The Four Zoas* first began to take shape. Like Young's poem, Blake's was to be divided into nine 'Nights', the last of which would be a long vision of the Last Judgement.

The first three Nights of Blake's poem were mostly transcribed on paper supplied for the *Night Thoughts* designs. The basic text here is in Blake's copperplate hand, or in a modified version of it, and some of the pages have drawings in a relatively finished state (*see* Appendix 1). The care apparent in this part of the manuscript is unusual, and rather puzzling. David Erdman has argued that Blake began to write only after the *Night Thoughts* project had failed and that—knowing he could never afford to produce the poem in illuminated printing—he began to create a unique illuminated manuscript.[2] More recently it has been suggested that Blake may have received some copper plates from the publisher of *Night Thoughts*, and that he could have intended to make a pro-

---

[1] Blake's illustrations are reproduced in *William Blake's Designs for Edward Young's Night Thoughts*, ed. D. V. Erdman, J. E. Grant, E. J. Rose, and M. Tolley, 2 vols. (Oxford, 1980).

[2] D. V. Erdman, 'The Binding (et cetera) of *Vala*', *The Library*, 5th ser., 19 (1964), 112–29, p. 125.

duction mock-up for the publication of text and designs as intaglio etchings/engravings (the text could be transferred in reverse to copper plates by viewing the mock-up in a mirror).[3] In the absence of firm evidence this question must remain unsettled. What seems beyond doubt, though, is that Blake's original plans were subsequently modified. The copperplate text ends abruptly on page 42, and the rest of the narrative is transcribed in Blake's normal handwriting, mostly on leaves containing proofs of engravings for the *Night Thoughts* edition (which I shall refer to as the 'proof text').

This break in the manuscript coincides almost exactly with a major transition in the narrative. The text up to page 42 contains an account of progress from a primitive condition to civil order, and it ends at the point where this order begins to collapse. The original copperplate text on these pages was revised in places, and some was completely obliterated. But much of it survives, so that we can form some impression of how the narrative looked before revision. The surviving copperplate text forms the subject of this present chapter.

A Universal History

Blake's title page originally read as follows:

VALA | OR | The Death and | Judgement | of the | Eternal Man | a DREAM | of Nine Nights | by William Blake 1797

The poem offers a universal history as the story of one person, an Eternal Man, whose experience contains all the possibilities of development in the fallen world. The framework of this history is ostensibly Christian, since the narrative moves between a fall into error (or Death) and a clarifying resurrection (or Judgement). But as we shall see, the narrative revises orthodox Christian views of history.

Seen in the context of the 1790s this project does not signal a retreat from politically sensitive territory into a neutral or merely private world of myth. Church leaders were denouncing as dangerously subversive any work which challenged or departed from the

---

[3] See P. Mann, 'The Final State of *The Four Zoas*', and R. N. Essick, '*The Four Zoas*: Intention and Production', *Blake: An Illustrated Quarterly*, 18 (1985).

'authentic records' of scripture.[4] Their protests did not prevent the publication of such histories. The radical bookseller Joseph Johnson (who at one stage planned to issue Blake's poem *The French Revolution*) published translations of two sweeping surveys of history by French writers, both of whom traced the primitive origins of religion and foresaw the liberation of humanity from its legacy of superstition. The first, Volney's revolutionary dream vision *The Ruins* (1792), proved enormously influential in radical circles, going through several editions in a few years. The second, Condorcet's *Outlines of an Historical View of the Progress of the Human Mind* (1795), was less popular in its appeal, but no less visionary in its argument (it divided history into 'nine grand epochs', and concluded with speculations about the perfectibility of humanity in a future tenth epoch). In 1796 Richard Payne Knight published *The Progress of Civil Society*, a didactic poem which drew on the naturalistic social history of Lucretius. The poem was parodied as a godless and politically subversive work in the *Anti-Jacobin*.[5] Blake's own treatment of the idea of progress was to be just as challenging to the 'authentic records' of scripture as these works, but it would also subvert rationalist assumptions about the historical process.

In several respects Blake's poem aligns itself with a primitive tradition of prophecy. The name of the goddess Vala may have been derived from Henri Mallet's study of Scandinavian mythology *Northern Antiquities*, in which the prophetess who chants the *Völuspa* of the Elder Edda is identified as Vola.[6] The tone and settings of the poem frequently recall the turbulent world of the Icelandic Eddas and of Ossian. Vincent De Luca has characterized the style of the narrative as 'Bardic', an attempt to reproduce 'The abrupt, artless mode of chronicle practised by the ancient, primitive bards'.[7] Blake rejects the iambic pentameter favoured by English

---

[4] The bishop of St David's, Samuel Horsley, for example, defended the historical authenticity of the scriptures whilst condemning as potentially seditious all speculations concerning natural rights or an original state of nature. *A Sermon, Preached before the Lords Spiritual and Temporal, on Wednesday, January 30, 1793. Being the Anniversary of the Matyrdom of Charles the First* (London, 1793). See also Blake's annotations to Watson (E611–20). For the reactions of other contemporary churchmen see W. T. Laprade, *England and the French Revolution 1789–97* (New York, 1970), 154–7 and notes.

[5] *The Anti-Jacobin—or Weekly Examiner*, Monday 19 Feb. 1798, 119–20; Monday 26 Feb. 1798, 126, Monday 2 Apr. 1798, 166.

[6] Frye, *Fearful Symmetry*, 270.　　　[7] De Luca, *Words of Eternity*, 62.

poets since the Renaissance; the line of the poem, like that of earlier works such as *The French Revolution* and *America*, is a septenary, used with an exuberant irregularity, and often with biblical cadences.[8] The prophetic form of the narrative might have led contemporary readers—had there been any—to associate it with a popular tradition of radical enthusiasm. The revolutionary upheavals of the 1790s gave rise to a flood of popular, millenarian prophecies, some of which, like those of the notorious Richard Brothers, emulated the style of biblical prophecy. The controversy stimulated by Brothers led to many reprints from earlier prophetic texts including, as Jon Mee has pointed out, those of seventeenth-century enthusiasts with whose antinomian views Blake's had much in common.[9] Blake's narrative, then, can be related to quite different kinds of discourse. It is a work in which radical enthusiasm contends with both rationalism and religious orthodoxy.

Night Thoughts

The reference on the title page to 'Death' and 'Judgement', like the organization of the poem as a 'DREAM of Nine Nights', recalls *Night Thoughts*, which was also divided into nine 'Nights', the last of which contained a long vision of the Last Judgement, and whose first Night was headed 'On Life, Death and Immortality'. Although forgotten today, *Night Thoughts* had remained one of the most popular philosophical poems through the second half of the eighteenth century, since its first appearance between 1742 and 1744. In the advertisement to the edition Blake illustrated, Young is referred to as 'the great poet of christianity'. The poem would have been of interest to Blake as an example of Christian apologetics: much of it is devoted to cosmological, teleological and analogical arguments to prove the existence of God and the immortality of the soul. Although Young asserts the superiority of revelation to the evidence of creation, and seeks to emphasize the importance of Christ's redeeming sacrifice, at times his arguments appear to reduce faith to a hypothesis necessary to redeem the intellect from the

---

[8] David Punter notes that Macpherson's prose versions of the poems of Ossian often take the septenary as a model, 'Blake: Social Relations of Poetic Form', *Literature and History*, 8 (1982), 191.
[9] Mee, *Dangerous Enthusiasm*, 33.

prospect of chaos, since all is 'unresolvable, if Earth is All' (VII: 605). When the poet's Hopes and Fears look down over 'life's narrow verge' they confront two alternatives: 'A fathomless abyss! A dread eternity!' (I: 62–5). And although Christ is identified as the key to salvation, the poet's belief still finds its most immediate support in the evidence of creation. Earth's map may be predominantly melancholy, but beyond it arches 'The Mathematic Glories of the Skies; In Number, Weight, and Measure, All ordained' (IX: 1180–1). The canopy of the stars is seen as a defence against the intellectual chaos of unbelief; the heavens seem like the temple of their maker:

> Bright legions swarm unseen, and sing, unheard
> By mortal Ear, the glorious Architect,
> In This His universal Temple, hung
> With Lustres, with innumerable Lights
> That shed Religion in the Soul
>
> (IX: 765–9)

The starry heavens thus function as 'a golden Net of Providence' to capture the soul into belief (IX: 1402).

Young's poem offered no sublime myth to engage with, but it did provide an elaborate example of the function of the creation in a reasonable defence of religion. This aspect of Young's work may have been particularly interesting to Blake, who had already satirized the concept of the designed creation in *Urizen*. In the copperplate text Urizen's creation is seen not as the horrific consequence of an arbitrary assumption of power, but as an unfortunate spiritual necessity, a work of seductive beauty that helps to preserve Man from the chaos of unbelief. Blake's new account, that is, places the teleological activity of reason in a historical context, showing it as an inevitable feature of humanity's spiritual development in the fallen world, during the progress from primitive life to civil order.

Religion and Progress

In the eighteenth century the development of primitive religion was often discussed in terms of the corruption of original truth (either the truth of scripture or, for Deists, the truth of natural religion); or in terms of the transformation of poetic images and tales into religious systems (the terms Blake himself had used in *The Mar-*

riage, pl. 11, *E*38). It was also discussed explicitly in terms of progress. Since the seventeenth century Fontenelle and others, noting similarities between the myths of geographically distinct peoples, had considered the existence of a primitive mentality that determined the form of religion. The Christian scholar Thomas Burnet, for example, accepted the orthodox view that pagan myths derive from scripture, but also argued that religions are the expressions of particular states of mental development: 'In all Learning we must begin from the Rudiments; and like as Men proceed from Childhood to mature Age, they go from Superstition to a chaste and solid Religion.'[10] In this view, polytheism and idolatry become not corruptions of true religion but, as Ernest Tuveson says, 'necessary and normal parts of human belief at certain stages of development.'[11] Hume presented a comparable view, with a quite different intention, in his provocative essay *The Natural History of Religion* (1757). Setting out to examine the origin of religion in human nature (as opposed to its foundation in reason) he argued that polytheistic religions were the most ancient. The earliest theologians did not consider their deities to be the conscious creators of the universe. Primitive peoples (so unlike Milton's Adam, as Hume insists) had little leisure for detached contemplation of the physical world. Instead, casting the world in their own image, they 'seem throughout to have rather embraced the idea of generation than that of creation, or formation; and to have thence accounted for the origin of this universe'. 'Generation' refers to the idea that natural phenomena originally came into being through the sexual activities of the gods, a notion that appears for example in Hesiod's *Theogony*. In Hume's view the primitive mind rises gradually from polytheism to theism 'By abstracting from what is imperfect', according to 'the natural progress of thought'.[12] Adam Smith, in his essay on 'Ancient Metaphysics' (published posthumously in 1795), ascribed the origin of theism in ancient times specifically to the development of science: by producing a unified system of nature, science inevitably suggested 'the unity of that principle, by whose art it was formed; and thus, as ignorance begot superstition, science gave birth to the first theism that arose among those nations, who

[10] T. Burnet, *Archaeologiae Philosophicae*; or, The Ancient Doctrine Concerning the Originals of Things (London, 1736), 160.

[11] Tuveson, *Millennium and Utopia*, 170.

[12] *David Hume: Writings on Religion*, ed. A. Flew (La Salle, Ill., 1992), 125, 110.

were not enlightened by divine revelation'.[13] While such accounts do not deny the influence of divine revelation, they show that the forms of religion may be determined purely by what Hume calls 'the natural progress of thought'. Volney made no concessions to revelation in *The Ruins*, where he offered an elaborate, naturalistic account of the 'genealogical order' in which religious error progresses: from the primitive worship of the elements, to the worship of stars (when the introduction of agriculture made observation of the heavens necessary), to the introduction of dualism, the belief in a future state, and the idea of a designing creator.[14] Seen in this context the Mosaic and Christian religions appear to have purely natural origins (Volney derives Christianity from the allegorical worship of the sun).

Blake's copperplate text presents the development of religion in terms of both natural progress *and* divine revelation. In a way that recalls the arguments of Hume and others, it makes a distinction between the generated world of the primitive mind and the designed cosmos of civilization, and it shows how humanity progresses from one to the other. But the distinction forms the basis of an intricate reconstruction of Milton's myth of creation, and the mythical mode of the narrative at once preserves and transforms the visionary nature of religious experience.[15]

Imagining Creation

In *Paradise Lost* the relationship of creator to creation is defined in two different ways. The creator is first seen as a detached architect, setting limits to the universe with the precision (and one of the instruments) of a mathematician:

> in his hand
> He took the golden Compasses, prepared
> In God's eternal store, to circumscribe
> This universe, and all created things:

[13] *Adam Smith: Essays on Philosophical Subjects*, ed. W. P. D. Wightman and J. C. Bryce (Oxford, 1980), 114.

[14] C. F. de Volney, *The Ruins or a Survey of the Revolutions of Empires* (3rd edn.; London, 1796), 220.

[15] For a different view of Blake's use of *Paradise Lost* here, see DiSalvo, *War of Titans*, 101–38.

> One foot he centred, and the other turned
> Round through the vast profundity obscure,
> And said, Thus far extend, thus far thy bounds,
> This be thy just circumference, O World.
>
> (VII: 224–31)

This image accounts for the principles of order and proportion manifest in the symmetrical form and harmonious revolutions of the spheres, principles that give the heavens the character of a perfectly tuned mechanism turning on its 'great axel'. The second image of the creator as the spirit of God suggests a more intimate relationship between creator and creation:

> on the watery calm
> His brooding wings the spirit of God outspread,
> And vital virtue infused, and vital warmth
> Throughout the fluid mass
>
> (VII: 234–7)

This image accounts for the internal energies manifest in the evolution of the earth and in the generation of organic life. In Milton's poem 'two great sexes animate the world' (VIII: 151). In response to the divine command, life on earth issues from the sexual union of earth and sea: the 'Main ocean' fertilizes the 'embryon' earth in the 'womb . . . Of waters' (VII: 276–84); organic life forms burst vigorously from the womb of the earth in a spontaneous generation. In elaborating the creation myth of Genesis 1, then, Milton accounts at once for the organic vitality of the earth and for the mechanical precision of the heavens by combining ideas of generation and design.

In Blake's poem these two views of creation—as generated organism and as intricately designed cosmos—have their bases in two quite different aspects of consciousness. The distinction appears to reflect a fundamental dissociation of sensible and intelligible qualities. This division in experience is dramatized in the relationship between Tharmas and Urizen, the two agents of creation in this part of the narrative. In the account of their activities the imagery of generation and the imagery of design are separated and express two distinct phases in the development of the fallen mind.

In the Realm of Tharmas

If, as Blake claimed in an early annotation, 'God is in the lowest effects as well as in the highest causes' (E599), then all of the apparently involuntary or unconscious processes we see in nature—from the movement of tides to organic growth—can be seen as the effects of a loving divine will that consciously shapes them and delights in them. In the new myth, Tharmas is the divine power that presides over such process. Daniel Stempel suggests that 'Tharmas . . . almost certainly derives his name from the Anglo-Saxon *thearmas* "bowels".' Blake may have known little about Anglo-Saxon, but he would have had access to Dr Johnson's *Dictionary* which, as Stempel notes, lists 'tharm' and defines it as 'intestines twisted for several uses'.[16] Stempel's suggestion makes a connection that Blake himself emphasized: in *Milton* Tharmas is said to have founded Bowlahoola, 'the Stomach in every individual man' (E121). The digestive process can be seen as a type of the submerged and seemingly involuntary activities on which life and growth depend. In *The Four Zoas* Tharmas is associated with the body ('The Body of Man is given to me' 69: 11, E346), with the instinct for survival, with the ceaseless motion of the sensible world. He is a protective power, a form of pity (the bowels were traditionally regarded as 'the seat of the tender and sympathetic emotions', *Oxford English Dictionary*). Enion is his female counterpart, the material world in which his divine power is manifest, and the expression of his delight in that world.

In Blake's narrative the fall of Tharmas initiates the development of fallen consciousness. There are several reasons why this should be so. As we have seen, pity, the urge to protect, is an ambivalent feeling which lies at the root of the selfhood. In any account of natural development, the processes governed by Tharmas constitute the foundation from which all other powers arise: the growing foetus is enclosed in the realm of Tharmas, as is the new-born child until the first stirrings of self-consciousness appear. The processes that control such growth are perhaps the most difficult to see as governed by a conscious will—even when they are thought of as

---

[16] D. Stempel, 'Blake, Foucault, and the Classical Episteme', *PMLA* 96 (1981), 395.

essentially divine. This last point may help to explain why Blake identifies the collapse of Tharmas with the idea of creation as generation. In Milton's account, quoted above, the generative image not only suggests an intimate relationship between the divine will and the natural world, but also reveals a sense of distance between them. The spirit of God initiates the processes of natural growth as a loving progenitor, but once he has allowed his 'vital virtue' to be absorbed by the 'fluid mass' he is in a sense redundant: the evolution of natural forms proceeds independently and earth becomes effectively self-sustaining, 'self balanced'. In this respect, a myth which describes the origin of the world in terms of generation implies the loss or absence of the originating consciousness as an operative force.

Blake's narrative shows this by presenting an act of divine generation as the fall of the generating power. The final stages of this fall are described in the surviving copperplate text, on page 7. The first four pages of copperplate text, and six lines at the top of the seventh page, have been entirely erased and are largely undecipherable.[17] As far as we can tell the erased text ended with an account of how the unfallen Tharmas appealed to his female counterpart Enion, who had begun to assume an independent existence:

> And said Return O Wanderer when the day of clouds is o'er;
> So saying he . . . ? fell . . . into the restless sea
>
> (E822)

In these lines Tharmas apparently loses his power as a controlling consciousness and is completely submerged in the waters of the material world. Subsequently the fallen Tharmas is always associated with the waters of the 'Sea of Space and Time', and is usually characterized as a powerful and unpredictable sea god. In the copperplate text his fall is followed immediately by his coupling with Enion (lines 8–13, E304), a 'primitive' myth of generation (the

[17] The first 6 lines on p. 7 were apparently transferred in a modified version to p. 5 (ll. 9–14). The lines on p. 5 have a number of verbal echoes of Milton's description of the spirit of God (compare Milton's 'vast profundity obscure', 'his brooding wings outspread', 'surging waves' with Blake's 'vast Deep sublime', 'stretching out his holy hand', 'restless sea'). John B. Pierce suggests that the male and female figures who mate here may not have been identified originally as Tharmas and Enion: 'The Shifting Characterization of Tharmas and Enion in Pages 3–7 of Blake's *Vala* or *The Four Zoas*', *Blake: An Illustrated Quarterly*, 22 (1988/9), 95. That possibility does not, I think, necessarily alter the mythical function of the figures at this point.

names Tharmas and Enion recall Thaumas and Eione from Hesiod's myth of generation in *Theogony*).

Fallen consciousness is engendered in the mating of Tharmas and Enion, as the latter, emerging from the sea in which Tharmas remains, gives birth to twin powers, Los and Enitharmon, who will control the awareness of time and space respectively. The copperplate text originally showed that organic life forms emerge with the birth of these powers, and nature begins to appear luxuriantly fertile. The passage, subsequently deleted, is a miniature counterpart to the magnificent descriptions of spontaneous generation in *Paradise Lost* (v: 310 ff.):

> The barked Oak, the long limbd Beech; the Ches'nut tree; the Pine.
> The Pear tree mild, the frowning Walnut, the sharp Crab,
>   & Apple sweet,
> The rough bark opens; twittering peep forth little beaks & wings
> The Nightingale, the Goldfinch, Robin, Lark, Linnet & Thrush
> The Goat leap'd from the craggy [*Rock*] <cliff>, the Sheep awoke
>   from the mould
> Upon its green stalk rose the Corn, waving innumerable.
>
>   (E824)

Los and Enitharmon become the Adam and Eve of Blake's primitive world. He is the imaginative power in fallen Man, the vessel of the Poetic Genius, 'the true faculty of knowing' (*ARO*, *E1*). He stands at the centre of consciousness and, as we shall see, he determines to a considerable degree the activities of Urizen in the fallen world. As Blake explained in an early work, 'If it were not for the Poetic or Prophetic character. the Philosophic & Experimental would soon be at the ratio of all things & stand still, unable to do other than repeat the same dull round over again' (*NNRb*, *E3*). Los therefore prompts Urizen's activities, and gives him ideas to build on. Enitharmon is at once the embodiment of Los's vision, the medium in which he creates, his perception of the spatial world and, in her independence from him, the limitations that constrain his creative power.

As an account of social progress Blake's copperplate narrative has some parallels with Rousseau's *Discourse on Inequality*. It shows that progress does not mean an increase in happiness, and that civil order brings inequality and repression. As in Rousseau, a state that stands midway between the primitive and civil state seems to be the happiest condition, a state before the introduction of metallurgy and agriculture, before the division of labour, and before the imposition of centralized government.

Los and Enitharmon are initially much closer to Rousseau's savage in the state of nature than to Milton's Adam and Eve in Eden. They do not come into being fully formed, but must pass through all the stages of natural growth. They are governed by the instinctual need for self-preservation, and must strive to achieve mastery of their environment, which means securing autonomy from their mother.

Blake registers the subsequent development of Los and Enitharmon in terms of their means of subsistence, in a condensed account of progress from gathering and hunting towards pasturage:

> Nine Times they livd among the forests, feeding on sweet fruits
> And nine bright Spaces wanderd . . .
> Snaring the wild Goats for their milk they eat the flesh of Lambs
>   (9: 20–2, E305)

The lines allude to Milton's description of the fallen angels, who lie rolling in the fiery gulf 'Nine times the space that measures day and night', before they become fully conscious of their fallen condition (*PL*I: 50). Los and Enitharmon arrive at such consciousness after the emergence of their troubling 'embryon passions', when they have developed the ability to 'controll' their perception of space and time, and Los has begun to assume a prophetic voice. Specifically, they begin to acquire self-consciousness once they have reached the boundaries of their world:

> They wanderd long, till they sat down upon the margind sea
>   (9: 32, E305)

In the *Discourse on Inequality* Rousseau explains that human passions, in the early, animal-like state of existence, do not go beyond physical needs, as the only evils to be feared are pain and hunger—'the Knowledge of Death and of its Terrors, is one of the first Acquisitions made by Man, in consequence of his deviating from the Animal State'.[18] In Blake's narrative the arrival at the 'margind sea' corresponds to the emergence from the animal condition. It is the moment at which Man begins to look beyond his

---

[18] Rousseau, *Inequality*, 41.

immediate physical needs and contemplates his condition in more abstract terms. Here he confronts the 'cold expanse where watry Tharmas mourns' (11: 18, E306), his own mysterious origins in the sea of space and time. It is here that Los first names Enitharmon, just as in Genesis Adam first names Eve after they have both eaten the fruit of the Tree of Knowledge (3: 20); and it is here that Enitharmon sings her 'Song of Death', which is a vision of Man's fall.

Imagining the Fall

The highly condensed narrative at this point gives a fascinating view of how the prophetic powers shape Man's sense of reality. The naming of Enitharmon points to the function of language in defining and controlling experience. In the Song of Enitharmon, and in Los's reply to it, a geography of consciousness is mapped out and a sense of hierarchy is established. Heart and brain are defined as distinct centres of activity, reason (Urizen) and the passions (Luvah and Vala) are identified as separate powers that have been brought into conflict. As soon as they are named these powers can become operative in human consciousness.

The Song and Los's reply were heavily revised, but the surviving portions of the original copperplate text show that Blake was exploring an idea already developed in his earlier work: in the fallen world love can only be experienced in contradictory forms. Enitharmon's vision provides the ethical basis of an emerging ideology, a basis that will justify emotional restraint. In her 'Song of Death' love is seductive in its female or passive form, Vala, and usurping in its male or active form, Luvah:

> Man takes his repose: Urizen sleeps in the porch
> Luvah and Vala woke & flew up from the Human Heart
> Into the Brain; from thence upon the pillow Vala slumber'd.
> And Luvah siez'd the Horses of Light, & rose into the Chariot
>   of Day
>   (10: 10–13, E305; in 10: 11 'woke & flew' originally read
>   'wake & fly')

This myth seems to reflect the tensions that have begun to appear between Los and Enitharmon as their 'embryon passions' develop.

In its characterization of desire as a dangerous power that usurps the role of reason it recalls the assumption that Blake's Devil attributes to all sacred codes in the *Marriage*—that energy is evil and reason is good (pl. 4, *E*34). Specifically it recalls the upward flight that Milton associates with the temptation of the Tree of Knowledge (*PL*v: 86–90).

If Enitharmon's vision of the fall justifies an ethic of restraint, Los's vision of the consequences of the fall apparently provides the spiritual basis of the emergent ideology. Here the passive aspect of love, Vala, is not seen as a seductive temptation, but in terms of an unsatisfied urge to give and receive comfort. As man tries to comfort her,

<blockquote>
she will not be comforted
She rises from his throne and seeks the shadows of her garden
Weeping for Luvah
</blockquote>

(11: 7–9, E306)

In a complementary vision, Luvah has become a transcendent god who descends to earth:

<blockquote>
I see, invisible descend into the Gardens of Vala
Luvah walking on the winds
</blockquote>

(11: 12–13, E306)

This vision recalls the biblical image of God walking in Eden after the fall, and Milton's elaboration of that image in *Paradise Lost*, where the Son descends to Eden in order to judge Adam and Eve and announce the possibility of redemption (Genesis 3: 8; *PL*x: 90 ff.). In Los's vision then, the male form of love is a divine power that may influence human destiny, while the female is a feeling of separation from that divine power. The two forms complement each other, providing the basis of religious faith in the fallen world, the sense of dependence on a transcendent god.

Taken together, the visions of Los and Enitharmon constitute a complex and inherently paradoxical vision of the human condition, in which love is defined as *both* usurping *and* redemptive, as dangerously seductive *and* as sorrowfully dependent. These visions determine fundamentally the subsequent organization of life. If Los's vision encourages an attitude of submission to a higher power, Enitharmon's suggests that the passions should be controlled by reason. These two suggestions are reconciled at the conclusion of the visions, when 'Man bow'd his ... head and Urizen descended.'

The Advent of Reason

The awakening of reason in the primitive mind is described as the advent of a God of dazzling magnificence:

> Ten thousand thousand were his hosts of spirits on the wind:
> Ten thousand thousand glittering Chariots shining in the sky:
> They pour upon the golden shore beside the silent ocean
>
> (12: 32–4, E307)

The unfallen potential of Urizen, referred to in *Ahania*, is clearly acknowledged here. With the arrival of this power the earth becomes a place of beauty and wonder spread out for Man's delight. The golden feast is at once a communion celebrating the sacrificial transubstantiation of reason's infinite power in a finite world, and a nuptial feast, celebrating the union of Los and Enitharmon. Although this union seems fragile, it brings the outer world into harmony with Man's inner life. Humanity enters a mode of existence that corresponds to Rousseau's 'infant Society', a communal life that flourishes before the introduction of centralized government, a condition which Rousseau describes as 'the just Mean between the Indolence of the primitive State and the petulant Activity of Self-love'.[19] In Blake's narrative existence becomes recognizably Edenic. As reason casts its light over the realm of Tharmas, sensation is spiritualized, and each part of Man's world comes alive with 'Elemental Gods' and their harmonious music:

> The Nuptial Song arose from all the thousand thousand spirits
> Over the joyful Earth & Sea, and ascended into the Heavens
> For Elemental Gods their thunderous Organs blew; creating
> Delicious Viands. Demons of Waves their watry Eccho's woke!
> Bright Souls of vegetative life, budding and blossoming
> Stetch their immortal hands to smite the gold & silver Wires
> And with immortal Voice soft warbling fill all Earth & Heaven.
>
> (13: 20–14: 2, E308)

---

[19] Rousseau, *Inequality*, 117.

These lines have a musical resonance that is unusual in *The Four Zoas*. The extraordinary vision of humanized nature recalls the joyful existence of Milton's Eden, which echoes with 'Celestial voices' (*PL*iv: 680 ff.). But unlike Milton's Eden, the paradisal world of Blake's narrative is shown to have a recognizable economic basis, essentially pastoral:

> the clear changing atmosphere display'd green fields among
> The varying clouds, like paradises stretch'd in the expanse
> With towns & villages and temples, tents sheep-folds and pastures
> Where dwell the children of the elemental worlds in harmony.
>
> (13: 12–15, E308)

Blake's use of *Paradise Lost* frequently suggests that Milton's complex interpretation of the Bible provides—in its paradoxes and suppressed contradictions—an unintentional clarification of the Bible's psychological significance. In Genesis 1, for example, light is created on the first day, producing Day and Night, but not until the fourth day is this initial distinction refined, when God creates lights in the firmament of heaven. For Milton, who admits in *Christian Doctrine* that 'we cannot imagine light without some source of light', this distinction poses a problem.[20] His solution actually draws attention to the paradox: in his description of the first day of creation, Etherial light is 'Sphered in a radiant cloud, for yet the sun | Was not; she in a cloudy tabernacle | Sojourned the while' (*PL*vii: 247–9). In Blake's narrative the distinction can be related to two stages in the development of human perception. In the primitive phase the perception of time and space is unmethodized, childlike, and imaginative. Los and Enitharmon experience 'times' and 'spaces' rather than Time and Space. Hence 'purple night' and 'golden day' appear, but 'the bright Sun was not as yet; he filling all the expanse | Slept as a bird in the blue shell that soon shall burst away' (12: 38–9, E307). It is not until Urizen reshapes the perception of nature into an intelligible system, that a new consciousness of time and space begins to emerge, and Man becomes preoccupied with finite sources of light in the heavenly bodies.

---

[20] *The Complete Prose Works of John Milton*, ed. D. M. Wolfe, *et al.*, 8 vols. (New Haven and London, 1973), vi. 312.

Suffering

In Rousseau's account of human origins, infant society is 'the best for Man', and humanity can only have left it as the result of 'some fatal Accident, which should never have happened'. The great revolution in life is produced by the invention of metallurgy and agriculture, on which advanced civilization is founded. As we shall see, Blake also places these inventions at the beginning of civilization. His narrative shows, however, that civilization is not caused by material accidents but by a spiritual development—the recognition of a void at the heart of life. The peace and plenty of the nuptial feast are not manifestations of a genuine innocence. In innocence a joyful awareness of the interrelatedness of life triumphs over suffering and there is no fear of death. But when the mind begins to develop the capacity for abstract thought it tends to recoil in terror from pain and death. Once Urizen has descended, his reasoning power inevitably begins to cast its shadow over experience, and a horror of suffering arises, expressed by Enion. As a pitying earth mother Enion recalls the innocent Matron Clay in *Thel*. But Enion offers no reassuring faith in the universal presence of divine love. She is a profoundly disconcerting figure, blind and age bent, who introduces haunting visions of a godless world. As a result the children of the elemental worlds can know joy only as a temporary evasion of Enion's fear:

> Not long in harmony they dwell, their life is drawn away
> And wintry woes succeed; successive driven into the Void
> Where Enion craves: successive drawn into the golden feast
> (13: 16–18, *E*308)

Enion's terror will stimulate the reasoning power to construct a unified vision of existence, in which each aspect of nature embodies a providential design.

Blake's account of this process seems to have been coloured by his awareness of contemporary optimism. The optimistic theories expounded by Shaftesbury and others attempted to reconcile suffering with divine providence by showing that the apparent imperfections of the world are attributable to our limited perceptions. Pope had provided an elegant expression of the view, shared by many, that all apparent discord in the world is 'Harmony, not understood', and 'All partial Evil, universal good' (*Essay on Man*, I: 291 ff.). For Pope, the inability to see divine purposes is itself a mercy:

> The lamb thy riot dooms to bleed to-day,
> Had he thy Reason, would he skip and play?
> Pleas'd to the last, he crops the flow'ry food,
> And licks the hand just rais'd to shed his blood.
> Oh blindness to the future! kindly giv'n,
> That each may fill the circle mark'd by Heav'n;
> Who sees with equal eye, as God of all,
> A hero perish, or a sparrow fall
>
> (*Essay on Man*, I: 81–8)

One of the effects of Blake's copperplate text is to expose the spiritual poverty of such optimism. Enion's 'happy blindness' seems to offer an ironical commentary on Pope's vision of providence. Her lamentation at the feast is a deeply disturbing response to a life that seems full of purposeless cruelty and pain. Her questions recall those that emerge from Thel's grave plot:

> Why does the Raven cry aloud and no eye pities her?
> Why fall the Sparrow & the Robin in the foodless winter?
> . . . .
> Why is the Sheep given to the knife? the Lamb plays in the Sun
> He starts! he hears the foot of Man! he says, Take thou my wool
> But spare my life, but he knows not that winter cometh fast.
>
> The Spider sits in his labourd Web, eager watching for the Fly
> Presently comes a famishd Bird & takes away the Spider
> His Web is left all desolate, that his little anxious heart
> So careful wove; & spread it out with sighs and weariness.
>
> (17: 2–3, 18: 1–7, E310)

The first line alludes to Job 38: 41, a verse which refers somewhat ambiguously to God's providential care. The second line alludes (as Pope's passage does) to Matthew 10: 29, 'Are not two sparrows sold for a farthing? and one of them shall not fall on the ground without your Father'. Enion's questions seem to refute both the biblical reassurance and the optimism of Pope's lines: unlike Pope's lamb, this one knows enough about predatory human nature to suffer terror at the approach of man, while ignorance of the future merely breeds false hope. The empathy here seems irresistible, and yet Enion's questioning is a symptom of her blindness. It reveals her

inability to see beyond a finite and corrupt world, or
divine comfort.

Enion's world is a challenge to any conception of pr
Blake's narrative such a negative vision gives clear defin
void that makes the concept of a benevolent creator n
the reasoning mind. Los and Enitharmon can survive the haunting
fears of Enion, but when Man confronts Enion's void with his
reason it threatens 'to draw Existence in' (24: 1, E314). Los and
Enitharmon can listen to the 'Sphery song' without being troubled
by the motions of the spheres, but in the light of reason the spheres
'sicken' into mysterious objects that must be brought within the
range of understanding. As a result Urizen must labour to save
Man, by creating a world-view that will transform his environment
into an intelligible system.

Converging Perspectives

In reviewing this account of the prelude to Urizen's first creation we
can see that, while it presents an evolutionary view of human
development, it also follows Milton's myth closely. Milton's Adam,
whose first impulse is to turn to the heavens, learns at the very
dawn of consciousness that God is the author of the world. But a
full explanation of creation is given to him only when Satan has
entered Eden. After Eve tells Adam of her dream, in which she was
tempted to eat the forbidden fruit and subsequently flew up to the
clouds with her tempter, Raphael is commanded to descend to Eden
and advise Adam of 'his happy state'. The placing of Raphael's
account of creation emphasizes the moral significance of the perception of design in the universe, as a reinforcement against the
encroachments of evil. In Blake's narrative, evil does not intrude
into Man's world from without: Man's entire vision of reality is an
error that fosters delusions. He naturally comes to see that he is
fallen and must restrain his passions, and his consequent dependence on reason leads him to see a providential design in the world.
Urizen descends to the golden feast after Los and Enitharmon have
begun to speculate about the fall, just as Raphael descends to the
feast of Adam and Eve after Eve's dream (PLv). Urizen's descent
with ten thousand thousand hosts and glittering chariots recalls not
only Raphael's descent to Eden, but also Milton's description of the

Son coming to the task of creation. There is no distinction between the revelation and the act of creation in Blake's myth: creation is a reorganization of perception.

The narrative here, then, presents a 'natural history' of religion dramatized in imagery derived from one of the best-known accounts of a divine revelation in English poetry. Two types of explanation are evoked simultaneously, each qualifying the other. The natural history reveals the provisional nature of the creation, by showing its origin in man's fallen perceptions. The providential myth suggests the spiritual power and function of creation, which preserves Man from mental chaos.

Creation as Design

Tharmas's creation evolved from his submergence in the sensible world. In order to reshape Man's vision, Urizen separates himself from that world:

> Urizen rose from the bright Feast like a star thro' the evening sky
> (23: 9, E313)

While Los and Enitharmon dwell in an elemental environment that seems bursting with exuberant life, Urizen surveys from a distance a world that seems cold and alien (the word 'beheld' recurs in this part of the narrative, suggesting the contemplative quality of his vision). The detachment of reason produces an environment that is vertiginous and vacuous, a new kind of chaos:

> Pale he beheld futurity; pale he beheld the Abyss
> Where Enion blind & age bent wept in direful hunger craving
> All rav'ning like the hungry worm, & like the silent grave
> Mighty was the draft of Voidness to draw Existence in
>
> Terrific Urizen strode above, in fear & pale dismay
> He saw the indefinite space beneath & his soul shrunk with horror
> His feet upon the verge of Non Existence
> (23: 15–17, 24: 1–4, E313–14)

As the mind withdraws into abstraction, the unknown becomes more important than the known. Whereas Los controls 'times and seasons, & the days & years', Urizen is haunted by 'futurity'. And whereas Enitharmon controls 'spaces, regions, desart, flood & forest', Urizen contemplates 'indefinite space'. While Los and Enitharmon feed on the 'sweet delights' of their mother Enion, Urizen sees Enion's maternal love as a craving to reclaim her children in death.

In emphasizing the chaotic nature of Urizen's vision, Blake calls into question the traditional conception of the self-moved creator. One of the most important models of Urizen's cosmos is the creation described in Plato's *Timaeus*, which Blake probably studied in Thomas Taylor's translation. As Lovejoy has noted, Plato's creator is 'Two-Gods-in-One ... a divine completion which was yet *not* complete in itself'.[21] He is a self-sufficient being who yet creates in response to a chaos that he seeks to reduce into order. Plato sees the production of a stable order from disorder as the triumph of intellect over 'necessity'. In Blake's account, reason is governed by necessity. Responding to his fear of the unknown, Urizen is

> urg'd by necessity to keep
> The evil day afar, & if perchance with iron power
> He might avert his own despair
>
> (25: 42–4, E317)

Urizen is neither self-sufficient nor self-moved, and his role is thus similar to that of the Gnostic *Demiourgos*, an agent of creation whose autonomy is illusory, and who becomes a repressive tyrant as a necessary consequence of his given function.

The description of his activities shows that his compulsion to escape from chaos will not be satisfied unless the sense of beauty and harmony that has already emerged in human experience can be reconciled with a purposeful order. The world he brings into being is an ideal creation, the most perfect construction that fallen reason can place upon the external world it contemplates. The rational ideal is an unchanging order, clear, distinct, and predictable, the embodiment of absolute certainties on which the mind can rest. The world must therefore be conceived as a unified system, designed by a single intelligence and constructed with mathematical precision. In exploring this world-view, Blake emphasizes the intimate relationship between the metaphysical, social, and economic organization of civilization. The naturalistic perspective of his myth shows that a designed and constructed cosmos can only be conceived in a

---

[21] A. O. Lovejoy, *The Great Chain of Being: A Study of the History of an Idea* (Cambridge, Mass. and London, 1936 and 1964), 50.

society that has the capacity to design and construct. His account begins with a technological revolution. Like Rousseau, Blake places the invention of metallurgy and agriculture at the beginning of the process that transforms 'infant Society' into civilization, and he shows that such developments require the division of labour and social inequality. Like Rousseau, he links the division of labour with inherent inequalities (the 'Spirits of strongest wing' and 'the weak' perform different tasks in the creation). At Urizen's command his bands divide 'influence by influence' in order to create a range of instruments which includes the anvil, loom, plow, harness of silver and ivory, golden compasses, rule, balance, furnace, bellows, and mills. Urizen's instruments are not in themselves limiting. Indeed they become essential to the eternal economy: in the Last Judgement the resurrected Urizen is a ploughman, while the resurrected Urthona is a blacksmith and a miller. But here the instruments are used to divert Man's energies from their appropriate functions and so repress them: the tygers of wrath put on the harnesses that belong to the horses of instruction; the plough is used to constrain energy rather than to generate new life. The activities recall Milton's account of the building of Pandæmonium in Hell: like Satan, Urizen is engaged in an attempt to reconstruct a lost order in an abyss. From a natural point of view this technological development may appear to be a major advance, but it also indicates a new division in human experience. Urizen's relationship with his creation is not primarily sexual, as Tharmas's was. Instead he begins to treat his experience objectively, as raw material that can be shaped according to an impersonal will. The energy that drives his cosmos is merely an instrument of his design.

Nature and Energy

In pre-scientific accounts of creation the energy of the natural world is typically described as a spiritual power. In the *Timaeus*, for example, each manifestation of energy in the creation is endowed with soul, from the highest (the heavenly bodies), to the lowest (the vegetables). In the medieval cosmos there is a comparable distribution of spiritual energy (there are three kinds of soul in the natural world: rational, sensitive, and vegetable). Such conceptions may express the conviction that everything that lives is holy, but they subordinate the infinite potential of the spirit to a finite, static hierarchy. The energy that drives Urizen's cosmos is not the spontaneous generative power of Tharmas: from the perspective of reason such a power is indistinguishable from the chaotic flux of the sensible world. Instead the energy is Luvah, a power that is now subject to the constraints of an intelligible order.

The heavenly bodies form the foundation of Urizen's cosmology, perhaps because they offer the most impressive example of predictable motion. Blake emphasizes their importance by reversing the biblical sequence of creation. In Genesis the firmament is given form before the heavenly bodies, which are subsequently installed as lights and as a measure of time. In Blake's narrative Urizen creates the stars first, and then closes the heavens from the chaos beyond. The sequence represents the progressive perfection of a unified system of belief, in which the stars are created 'like a golden chain | To bind the Body of Man to heaven from falling into the Abyss' (33: 16–17, E322). The process by which Luvah is reduced in a furnace, and enclosed in the geometrical forms of the stars, provides a vivid image of the cosmologist's attempt to reconcile divine energy with the fixed appearances of the astral world. It also symbolizes an aesthetic transformation. As the reasoning mind has ceased to perceive the world in human terms, desire must be reconciled to a beauty conceived in terms of mathematical proportion. The myth suggests that only a drastically impoverished form of desire could find satisfaction in such an abstract notion of beauty.

Nevertheless, this creation must have a seductive appeal if it is to sustain a form of belief, and it is quite unlike the horrific world described in *Urizen*. After the stars have been created, the atmospheres are woven. Urizen's 'strong wing'd Eagles' hang 'The universal curtains' on golden hooks, domesticating 'the vast unknown' (like the creator celebrated in Psalm 104, who 'stretchest out the heavens like a curtain'). The resulting vision of the heavens as a work of harmonious beauty provides the basis for a complete transformation of Man's view of earth. All other manifestations of energy in the physical world can now be drawn into a single conceptual framework:

innumerable the nets
Innumerable the gins & traps; & many a soothing flute

> Is form'd & many a corded lyre, outspread over the immense
> In cruel delight they trap the listeners, & in cruel delight
> Bind them, condensing the strong energies into little compass
> Some became seed of every plant that shall be planted; some
> The bulbous roots, thrown up together into barns & garners
>
> (30: 1–7, E319)

This Urizenic harmony stands in direct contrast with the harmony of the golden feast. In both, each aspect of life is spiritualized. But whereas the harmony of the feast is a spontaneous expression of elemental souls, here it becomes the expression of a system which formally attributes a spiritual energy to each of its components.

The Golden World

Having transformed Man's sense of the relationship between energy and nature, Urizen begins to transform more thoroughly the perception of space (his attention moves from the male to the female aspects of his creation). As the 'Architect divine' he begins to build 'a Golden World' to receive the 'eternal wandering stars'(32: 8–9, E321). The 'infinite' becomes finite ('The heavens were closd', 32: 13, E321), and is conceived as the presence chamber of divine power, fashioned with porches and pillared halls. The earth is seen as a realm that has been consciously shaped, like a landscaped garden, by an intelligence sensitive to order and proportion:

> Sorrowing went the Planters forth to plant, the Sowers to sow
> They dug the channels for the rivers & they pourd abroad
> The seas & lakes, they reard the mountains & the rocks & hills
> On broad pavilions, on pillard roofs & porches & high towers
> In beauteous order
>
> (32: 16–33: 3, E321; in 32: 16 'Sorrowing'
> originally read 'Then')

The surprising elevation of mountains on pavilions suggests the heroic futility of Urizen's attempt to transform a world which has lost human form into a masterpiece of architectural harmony.[22] The aesthetic appeal of his world—its purity and stability—is determined and justified by Man's vision of his experience as chaotic.

---

[22] The creation of the rivers and hills here recalls Ovid's descriptions in *Metamorphoses* I.

Thus although the heavens are closed by this Golden World, the abyss remains visible. Unlike Plato's universe, which is 'indigent of nothing external', and unlike the creation in Genesis which is closed off completely from chaos by the firmament, Urizen's Golden World has ornamented windows which look 'out into the World of Tharmas, where in ceaseless torrents | His billows roll where monsters wander in the foamy paths' (33: 6–7, E321).[23] In this, as Alicia Ostriker notes, it resembles Heaven in *Paradise Lost*, beyond whose gates chaos is seen (*PL*vii: 212).[24] This refinement emphasizes that the cosmos is actually sustained by the vision of a chaos that lies beyond it.

Love and Pity

The transition from the world of the golden feast to Urizen's cosmos corresponds to the transition from the predominantly pastoral world of Genesis to the bondage under Egyptian civilization at the beginning of Exodus. In Genesis, before the entry into Egypt, God speaks directly to his chosen people. In Exodus He uses Moses as intermediary, the priesthood is formally established, and the foundations of state religion are put in place. The separation of Luvah and Vala in Urizen's creation recalls this separation between God and his people. Like Jehovah, Luvah sees himself as a protector and deliverer; while Vala, like the children of Israel, has fallen under the power of a taskmaster, and in her anguish does know her Lord.

The biblical context helps to show how the ideology of love is developed within civil society. Enitharmon's primitive vision of the passions justifies repression, but repression is now seen as refinement: the 'Furnaces of affliction' into which Luvah is cast recall God's attempt to refine his people through suffering (Isaiah 48: 10).[25] Los's primitive vision of a transcendent god and dependent creature defines Man's sense of lost innocence and his hope for restoration, and this vision is now elaborated into a complex history by Luvah himself:

[23] *The Cratylus, Phaedo, Parmenides and Timaeus of Plato*, transl. T. Taylor (London, 1793), 462.

[24] Ostriker, ed., *Complete Poems*, 931.

[25] 'iron furnace' is a biblical term for the bondage in Egypt (e.g. Deuteronomy 4: 20).

in times of Everlasting
When I calld forth the Earth-worm from the cold & dark obscure
I nurturd her I fed her with my rains & dews, she grew
A scaled Serpent, yet I fed her tho' she hated me
Day after day she fed upon the mountains in Luvahs sight
I brought her thro' the Wilderness, a dry & thirsty land
And I commanded springs to rise for her in the black desert
Till she became a Dragon winged bright & poisonous
I opend all the floodgates of the heavens to quench her thirst
And I commanded the Great deep to hide her in his hand
Till she became a little weeping Infant a span long
I carried her in my bosom as a man carries a lamb
I loved her I gave her all my soul & my delight
I hid her in soft gardens & in secret bowers of Summer
Weaving mazes of delight along the sunny Paradise
Inextricable labyrinths, She bore me sons & daughters
And they have taken her away & hid her from my sight
They have surrounded me with walls of iron & brass
(26: 6–27: 9, E317–18; in 26: 13 'Till' originally read 'But')

Luvah's account of his relationship with Vala alludes ironically to the Old Testament history of God's attempts to establish a satisfactory relationship with His chosen people. Luvah's history spans two eras, divided by a deluge. His attitude to Vala in each era seems quite different—in the first he calls her forth, in the second he hides her. The first era corresponds to the leading of Israel from obscurity in the wilderness towards the promised land; the second to the creation of Adam, and his life in Eden. Both of these biblical stories are related here to the account of the captivity in Egypt: in the promised land the recalcitrant Israelites experience a new bondage, which corresponds to the fall from Eden. Luvah's history reverses the sequence of biblical history, so that the creation of Paradise seems a reaction to the appearance of evil. In this way the passage shows how a flawed vision of innocence is produced in the consciousness of civilized Man.

The civilized vision of innocence is quite unlike Blake's own vision. Assured of the need for restraint and stability, Man cannot see hate as a necessary aspect of love. Accustomed to hierarchical forms of order, he cannot see the earthworm as essentially human and divine. He can only construct innocence in a form that will reinforce his present assumptions. The myth of Eden can be seen as this kind of construction. It presents innocence as a condition in which humanity is insulated from aspects of life that disturb the civilized mind: from the knowledge of good and evil, from sexual shame and jealousy. Its vision of innocent sexuality suggests a yearning to stabilize an aspect of experience that resists such stabilization. The patriarchal view of woman, and the distinction between humanity and a subordinate animal world, suggest an attempt to reinforce a hierarchical order that can easily be subverted. Above all the myth suggests a conviction that desire must be—and will not be—controlled. Behind its vision of peace lurks the fallen experience of a world of monstrous appetite.

Luvah's speech therefore describes first an emergent sense of evil and then an attempt to evade that evil. As the once helpless creature begins to lose its helplessness, becoming powerful and dangerous, Luvah's reaction suggests a growing fascination and horror. The deluge is a purification that initiates a new era of dependency. In this era the human form represents an escape from bestial passion (in Eden humanity at first lacks the serpent's knowledge), and in this respect it is a repressive form, a form of bondage. Luvah uses Paradise to maintain a possessive relationship with his creature, but the urge to enclose and hide the loved one leads inevitably to loss and self-enclosure. Subject to repression himself, Luvah now seeks 'to deliver all the sons of God | From bondage of the Human form', and subsides into a weak hope that Vala will return. Luvah's speech points to a fundamental dichotomy in the Old Testament conception of God, who seeks to preserve innocence *and* to build his chosen people up. In Blake's narrative this dichotomy is, of course, rooted in the primitive visions of Enitharmon and Los, where the will to power and the desire for innocence are combined. It lies at the heart of the civil order that Urizen develops.

A number of the drawings accompanying the copperplate text from this point on suggest—often in startling terms—a relationship between repression and the fetishizing of sexuality. The transformation of Vala from a helpless creature to a powerful dragon is illustrated on page 26, in four drawings which emphasize the element of sexual fear in Luvah's vision: a human butterfly with breasts and vulva; a batwinged human figure riding a huge erect penis; a winged monster with mermaid tail, female genitals, and curved neck and beak; a winged dragon with female face and breasts.[26] At the foot of page 27 a sketch shows the figure of a skeletal, bearded male with furrowed brow, and a smiling, naked young female. Their bodies appear to converge (he might be emerging from her womb, she might be emerging from one of his ribs). Both seem to be enclosed in a transparent sheet or integument. This image of enclosure can be related to Luvah's dilemma: it presents female sexuality as a tormenting, captivating focus of—or projection of—jealous male desire, self-denial, impotence.

Other, partly obliterated, drawings present sexuality in terms which suggest frenzied compulsion, an urge for domination, or voyeuristic fascination. On page 39, for example, a huge phallus with testicles was sketched in the left margin, set apart as a kind of totem. Several pictures depict phalluses in the power of women. On page 35, for example, three naked women kneel among a crop of phallic vegetables (or vegetating phalluses). One is picking some of the vegetables, while the other two look on attentively. In the left margin another (clothed) woman carries on her head a basket full of the harvested crop. On page 42 a naked woman chases a bat-winged phallus, which flies away but is apparently secured by a string (perhaps held in the woman's hand). Nearby another woman is measuring with her hand the penis of a cupid who stands smiling before her, while a young girl reaches out to touch the cupid's wing. If these images suggest a fear of female desire, a sketch beneath the text on page 40 might suggest a comparable loathing of male desire. Here, a woman lies prone, while a figure who leans over her, as if to penetrate her from behind, has on his back a small cupid with spurs and reins.[27] On pages 28, 35, and 39, children watch the sexual activities of adults (recalling perhaps Los and Enitharmon, who are drawn down by their delight to witness the torments of Urizen's world). The goading, watching, and measuring shown in these sketches are consequences of 'the furnaces of affliction': subjected to patriarchal constraints, sexuality becomes at once a torment and an obsession.

[26] For detailed discussions of these drawings, see J. E. Grant, 'Visions in Vala: A Consideration of Some Pictures in the Manuscript', in *Blake's Sublime Allegory*, ed. Stuart Curran and Joseph Anthony Wittreich Jr. (Madison, Wis., 1973), 192, and 'The Four Zoas' *by William Blake*, ed. C. T. Magno and D. V. Erdman (Lewisburg, Va., London, and Toronto, 1987).

[27] Magno and Erdman note that the reins may extend to the woman's hands, bent back over her head (46).

After Luvah has been weakened in Urizen's furnaces, his love 'Brought him in various forms' before Vala, but she 'knew him not' (31: 19, E321). Man has lost the ability to feel the power of divine love as an immediate and joyous presence in life. Divinity is now perceived as a distant, inscrutable power, an absence. Vala's lamentations (31: 4–16, E320–1) appear to be addressed to Luvah, but are heard by Urizen, who has effectively taken Luvah's place as divine maker. She addresses her Lord as 'thou piteous one,' but her lamentation points to his apparent lack of pity, while in her appeal for forgiveness there is suppressed indignation. In this context pity has become self-pity. It is a moral demand, a reaction to the consciousness of guilt and cruelty, and is coloured by a sense of justice. As a response to oppression it has little force: Vala's sorrowing protest is a form of resignation. The context suggests that, far from undermining an oppressive civil order, such pity has a useful function within it. Vala speaks for an oppressed people. In her a weak sense of fellow feeling survives, a shared feeling of unhappy dependence and shadowy hope, which helps to bind the downtrodden victims of Urizen's world into a docile community. In short, Vala embodies one of the emotional bases of state religion: her ashes are mingled with the mortar that holds Urizen's world together (30: 13, E319).

In contrast to the self-pity of Vala, Enion continues to express pity for others. But her response is no longer simply an instinctual reaction to suffering—it shows a new moral awareness:

It is an easy thing to talk of patience to the afflicted
To speak the laws of prudence to the houseless wanderer
To listen to the hungry ravens cry in wintry season
When the red blood is filld with wine & with the marrow of lambs

It is an easy thing to laugh at wrathful elements
To hear the dog howl at the wintry door, the ox in the slaughter
     house moan
To see a god on every wind & a blessing on every blast
To hear sounds of love in the thunder storm that destroys
     our enemies house
To rejoice in the blight that covers his field, & the sickness
     that cuts off his children
While our olive & vine sing & laugh round our door &
     our children bring fruits & flowers

Then the groan & the dolor are quite forgotten & the slave
  grinding at the mill
And the captive in chains & the poor in the prison, & the soldier
  in the field
When the shatterd bone hath laid him groaning among the
  happier dead

(35: 18–19; 36: 1–11, E325)

Urizen's drive to construct a unified vision of existence, in which
each aspect of nature embodies a providential design, is a manifestation of cosmic optimism. Blake's narrative implies that any attempt to reconcile providence with a fixed order must depend on a
contraction of human sympathy. If the order of nature and society
is essentially good—if all discord is harmony not understood, and
all partial evil is universal good—the individual is implicitly ab-
solved from genuine identification with the sufferings of other
creatures. Such a system will allow the prosperous to regard the
poor with satisfaction. (Among Blake's annotations to Bishop
Watson's *Apology for the Bible* is an angry comment on the title of
Watson's *The Wisdom and Goodness of God, in Having Made
Both Rich and Poor*: 'God made Man happy & Rich but the Subtil
made the innocent poor', *E612*). Such a system will also tend to
sanction cruelty and even murder in the name of the common good.
Blake's narrative seems designed to show that wherever Man thinks
of the external world as a well-ordered system—as the realization
of a premeditated design—he will have to 'justify' apparent evils,
and contemplate them with detachment. Only when the demand
for justice is actively renounced can there be no justification for
cruelty or slavery, and only then can Man's vision of providence be
freed from the moral taint of which Enion complains. In this
respect, Enion's sense of injustice is a manifestation of the error she
struggles to define.

Flexible Senses

Once the cosmic system has been completed, a new phase begins in
the development of civilization: a period of reflection in which there
is a new awareness of tensions that may threaten the *status quo*.
The reasoning mind has sought an order that is permanent and
static, but it now sees in the imagination the possibility of growth

and change, and of a fundamental reordering of experience. As in *Europe*, the interdependence of reason and imagination is potentially a source of conflict.

As we have seen, in the primitive age the visionary activities of Los and Enitharmon tend to promote rational restraint, and in doing so they stimulate the development of the cosmic world-view. But the imaginative powers are stimulated in turn by the advent of reason. Within the cosmic system the original relationship between imagination and reason is in some respects reversed. Urizen once descended to a limited world, bringing harmony to Los and Enitharmon with his divine light. But now it is Urizen who dwells in a limited world, while Los and Enitharmon descend bringing intimations of a fluid, spontaneous consciousness that is no longer available to the reasoning mind. Having descended they enjoy a remarkable liberty:

> Los & Enitharmon walkd forth on the dewy Earth
> Contracting or expanding their all flexible senses
> At will to murmur in the flowers small as the honey bee
> At will to stretch across the heavens & step from star to star
> Or standing on the Earth erect, or on the stormy waves
> Driving the storms before them or delighting in sunny beams
> While round their heads the Elemental Gods kept harmony
> (34: 9–15, E322)

The ability to expand or contract the senses at will is identified in *Urizen* as a characteristic of eternal vision (*see* Introduction). It is an ability which suggests that Los and Enitharmon might be able to liberate Man from his finite world. However, the unbounded freedom of the imagination now seems to contain a danger within it. When the 'all flexible senses' contract they come to rest on a world that is inherently repressive. In *Urizen*, the Eternals cut themselves off from the fallen world, an act which makes the possibility of redemption seem remote, but which also suggests that eternal liberty depends on the clear definition of the limits of error. Without such definition, Los and Enitharmon seem vulnerable to the powerful fascination of Urizen's system. They exhibit the negative capability which Keats saw as a primary characteristic of the chameleon imagination—its ability to enter fully into everything it perceives, to take as much delight in 'conceiving an Iago as an Imogen'.[28] But as

---

[28] Letter to Richard Woodhouse, 27 Oct. 1818. *The Letters of John Keats 1814–21*, ed. H. E. Rollins, 2 vols. (Cambridge, Mass., 1958), i. 387.

yet they are unorganized and therefore uncritical. They take delight in 'all the sorrow of Luvah & the labour of Urizen' (32: 4, E321), but are 'drawn down by their desires' (34: 1, E322) into a realm that may limit imaginative freedom. Such freedom is deeply disturbing to the reasoning power:

> Urizen saw & envied & his imagination was filled
> Repining he contemplated the past in his bright sphere
> Terrified with his heart & spirit at the visions of futurity
> That his dread fancy formd before him in the unformd void
>
> (34: 5–8, E322)

Imagination once again stimulates those aspects of reason that demand and appreciate order, namely memory and the predictive ability that arises from it. In an attempt to assuage his fear of 'futurity', Urizen must turn from metaphysics to the question of human history.

Visions of Futurity

The 'Elemental gods' that keep harmony around Los and Enitharmon seem out of place in the designed world of the cosmos. The vision of a divine power that manifests itself spontaneously in organic processes must seem potentially subversive to a mind that prefers to see the world in terms of hierarchy and centralized control. As long as the imagination retains the ability to see the world in this way, it may liberate the divine power of love from Urizen's control by transforming it into an immanent power.

This possibility is considered at the beginning of Night III. Here the description of Urizen enthroned recalls two parallel scenes in *Paradise Lost*: Satan enthroned at the beginning of Book II, and God enthroned at the beginning of Book III. In the latter scene God the Father, contemplating his newly created world, foresees that Adam and Eve will not remain in their Edenic state. We learn that both Satan and the Son will be drawn to humanity on earth, Satan to corrupt and Christ to redeem. Although the loss of Eden is not fated it is certain, because no bounds can hold Satan, who will soon pervert man (*PL*III: 81–4). Thus the new world will not long sustain its perfection. In Blake's poem, Urizen detects a comparable instability in his own creation. He foresees that Los will not remain in his state of unorganized innocence, but will 'grow up' to assume a dominant role in human consciousness. When this happens, Luvah and Vala, the love which has been repressed in the cosmos, will be reborn:

> Vala shall become a Worm in Enitharmons Womb
> Laying her seed upon the fibres soon to issue forth
> And Luvah in the loins of Los a dark & furious death
> Alas for me! what will become of me at that dread time?
>
> (38: 8–11, E326)

The rebirth is referred to in terms that recall the incarnation of the Son, who in *Paradise Lost* will be 'Made flesh, when time shall be, of Virgin seed' (III: 284). From Urizen's point of view, however, the rebirth must seem as threatening as the appearance of Satan in God's creation, as it suggests a return to a chaotic world in which energy is submerged within and indistinguishable from the flux of the sensible world. In social terms such a transformation would represent the loss of central control, the collapse of hierarchy, the free distribution of power.

Urizen's vision stimulates a complex reply from his female counterpart Ahania, who is usually described as the embodiment of Urizen's own sense of delight. Here, as in *Ahania*, she shows a pained awareness of what has been lost in the process of developing civilization. But her own vision does not inspire eternal delight and liberty—it is an attempt to rationalize Urizen's fear, by incorporating the foreseen rebirth of love within the existing ideological framework. Her refined version of the myth of Luvah and Vala suggests that the naturalization of these powers will not free them, but will inevitably intensify their constraint.

The complex sequence is partly modelled on Milton's description of the dawn of human consciousness in Eden, and Adam's initial encounters with God and Eve, both of whom first appear to him in dreams. In Book VIII of *Paradise Lost*, Adam recalls how, after awakening into consciousness, he fell asleep:

> there gentle sleep
> First found me, and with soft oppression seized
> My drowsed sense, untroubled, though I thought
> I then was passing to my former state
> Insensible, and forthwith to dissolve:
> When suddenly stood at my head a dream
>
> (PLVIII: 287–92)

Within the dream God takes Adam to His 'mansion,' Eden, where Adam wakes and falls 'In adoration' at his maker's feet (315). God reveals first a mild and generous aspect (in the gift of Paradise) and then a 'dreadful' aspect (in the threat of death for transgression). In a second dream Adam has a vision of Eve, who seems to contain 'what seemed fair in all the world' (472). Eventually, of course, Eve also reveals to Adam a dreadful aspect. If both dreams lead to an overwhelming experience of love, first spiritual, then sensuous, with hindsight it appears that there is danger in such love—for Eve will betray Adam and God will punish him. Love leads to emotional restraint and atonement.

Ahania's vision follows a comparable pattern. It begins with Urizen asleep, while 'Man walkd on the steps of fire before his halls | And Vala walkd with him in dreams of soft deluding slumber' (39: 15–16, E327). Here, then, it is the sleep of reason that places Man in the seductive power of emotion and of dreams. Seeing the Prince of Light with splendour faded, Man (like Adam) apparently interprets his loss of consciousness as a sign of his impending degeneration. He ascends 'mourning into the splendors of his palace' (40: 2, E327) where he falls before a vision of his eternal maker. The loving God of his vision is Luvah, who appears (like Milton's God) within a cloud. But when Luvah descends—as if in judgement—Man indignantly turns his back on Vala. In Ahania's vision, offered as reassurance to Urizen, the god of love inspires a renunciation of love. Vala is now seen as merely an earthly power (she is 'inclos'd' in a body), and because Man now struggles to contain his desire he suffers the torments of repression, 'the terrible smitings of Luvah'. When Man finally succeeds in conquering his passions, Luvah—having assumed the form of divine Father—is forced to play the sacrificial role of the Son, his incarnation being ordained to atone for Vala's deceit. Man says to him:

> Go & die the Death of Man for Vala the sweet wanderer
> I will turn the volutions of your Ears outward; & bend your Nostrils
> Downward; & your fluxile Eyes englob'd, roll round in fear
> Your withring Lips & Tongue shrink up into a narrow circle
> Till into narrow forms you creep
>
> (42: 1–5, E328)

We have already seen the dawn of a new awareness of the body as an outer limit to experience, a confinement. When Luvah was subject to rational restraint in the furnaces of affliction, he attempted to dissociate the human form from animal passions and at the same time spoke of liberating humanity from 'the bondage of the human form'. Both tendencies suggest that the body is experienced as a source of torment and constraint—the inevitable consequence of repressing desire. In Ahania's vision, the sense of constraint is intensified, and it leads to the complete separation of Luvah from Vala:

> Vala shrunk in like the dark sea that leaves its slimy banks
> And from her bosom Luvah fell far as the east & west
> And the vast form of Nature like a Serpent roll'd between.
>
> (42: 15–17, E328)

The separation is an image of impotence, the removal of desire from the possibility of fulfilment. If Urizen sees the rebirth of Luvah as a threat to stable order, Ahania's vision tends to neutralize that threat.

The exchange between Urizen and Ahania, then, shows how a prevailing orthodoxy will attempt to assimilate a potentially challenging new development to its existing assumptions. In this context *Paradise Lost* can be seen as a specific example of the process. Milton interprets the advent of Christ in terms of the doctrine of atonement, transforming a potentially liberating vision of love and forgiveness into its opposite, a vision of sin and punishment. In this way an immanent divinity is contained by a conviction that the body is finite and corrupt. Love is made to reinforce rational restraint instead of undermining it.[29]

Ahania's vision is intended to reassure Urizen, but its account of incarnation provides an image of the event which Urizen most fears (the natural world, that he has constructed as a harmonious system, here assumes 'a vast form . . . like a Serpent'). In response, Urizen's 'wrathful throne burst forth the black hail storm' (42: 18, E328). At this point the copperplate text ends. How far it continued beyond its present point is of course a matter of speculation. Gerald E. Bentley Jr. suggests that Blake completed a poem of nine Nights in copperplate hand on plain leaves, and subsequently replaced most of these leaves after progressive revisions had reduced the manuscript to a chaotic state.[30] But the remaining evidence makes this seem unlikely. Blake's method of working over and

---

[29] Blake seems to have been particularly proud of the passage, as he used it again, almost verbatim, in *Jerusalem* (43: 33–80).

[30] Bentley, *Vala, or The Four Zoas*, 162.

adding to his manuscript frequently produced a text that is manifestly composite and fragmented. It seems hard to believe that such a process of revision could have produced a narrative as coherent and homogeneous as the basic text on the proof pages of Nights IV, V, VI, VIIa, and IX seems to be.[31] The surviving manuscript provides abundant evidence of Blake's economical use of paper (at the beginning of the poem he erased and rewrote whole pages on both sides of a leaf). In view of this it seems quite possible that the copperplate text did not continue far beyond page 42. In the final version of the narrative, the disintegration of Urizen's cosmos is described on page 43. The copperplate text thus contains a complete history of a civilization, from the primeval dawn of consciousness to the brink of collapse. Among the distinguishing features of the myth, the following seem particularly significant:

1. The powers that govern this progress are divine: Tharmas, the divine generative principle; Urizen, divine reason; Luvah, divine love. Matter is always animated in some sense by spirit.

2. The primitive era is relatively short, the movement towards civil society is rapid. Progress is the development of divine potential, which flowers quickly, rather than the gradual evolution, through many ages, of a merely natural process.

3. The Golden World is a teleological, homocentric creation, an ideal and static order. Once it is realized, there is no room for further development. Urizen's activity is dominated by a sense of Man's spiritual needs, rather than by a determination to explore the natural world. In this respect, like the first creation in *Urizen*, it is a 'self-contemplating' activity.

In all of these respects, this era of history contrasts with the materialistic era that follows.

The treatment of the idea of creation in the copperplate text is much more complex than that in *Urizen*, not only in structure, but also in tone. The golden feast and the Golden World are described in a language that reveals simultaneously their limitations and their genuinely seductive appeal, while Urizen himself is at times allowed

---

[31] The basic text of these Nights seems to have been transcribed from a draft that Blake considered finished to his satisfaction. J. B. Pierce notes 'the neatness and clarity of the base text of the manuscript', and that 'Most of Blake's errors on pages 43–84 . . . suggest simple slips of the pen typical of copying errors'. 'The Changing Mythic Structure of Blake's *Vala* or *The Four Zoas*', *Philological Quarterly*, 64 (1989), 505 n. 1.

an almost tragic dignity. Here Blake had developed a poetic style that rarely appears elsewhere in his work, one that presents forms of error in terms of dazzling exuberance.

The pages containing the copperplate text were bound together in a separate binding at one stage. We do not know when—or why—the binding took place, but it *may* have followed the transcription of the copperplate text, which could then have been put aside for some time before being revised.[32] As we shall see, Blake's revisions of this text not only complicate it, but also darken it considerably.

[32] The stitch marks in the manuscript were detected by G. E. Bentley Jr. (*Vala, or The Four Zoas*). They tell us little for certain about Blake's practices. Pages 43–84 and 111–12 were once held together in a separate binding. Pages 111–12 are an integral part of Night VIII, the rest of which was never bound. Presumably the leaf containing these pages was bound before the text on them was transcribed—which raises the possibility that this binding predated the transcription of any of the text on pp. 43–84. Perhaps Blake bound unused leaves to protect them from damage. Erdman has argued that the 'copperplate pages range in inception from 1797–1803'. His dating is based on the presence in the text of a 'g' which 'Blake adopted after Nov. 1802'—although he admits that the 'rule of g' may be 'less invariable than I have supposed' (E817). Following Erdman, Joseph Viscomi suggests that *Vala* may have consisted of only the leaves of the copperplate text in 1803, and that Blake may have considered engraving the poem in this form: *Blake and the Idea of the Book* (Princeton, NJ, 1993), 318.

PART II

A Dream of Nine Nights

A Dream of Nine Nights

The second stage of my reading is presented in Chapters 2–8. It considers the poem as a whole, excluding all of the references to Albion, Jerusalem, Jesus, the Council of God, Eden, Beulah, and the Ulro. It includes:

1. Some of the revisions made to the copperplate text—notably material added on 5–7 concerning the Spectre of Tharmas; additions on pages 8–13 concerning the deteriorating relationship of Los and Enitharmon, and Urizen's descent; the song sung at the feast of Los and Enitharmon (14: 6–16: 22); the material added to Night II concerning Urizen's twelve halls and the separation of Ahania (30: 15–50), the geometry of the stars (33: 19–36), and the relationship between Los and Enitharmon (34: 16–96).
2. The basic (i.e. unrevised) text of pages 43–85, written on leaves used for proofs of *Night Thoughts* engravings.
3. Selected passages from Nights VIIb and VIII
4. The basic text of Night IX, including lines added at the top of page 119 (1–23), but excluding lines referring to Christ and Jerusalem (122: 1–3, 16–20; 123: 20–124: 5).

As we shall see, the material in (3) may have been transcribed later than the material in (1), (2), and (4), since the basic text of Night VIIb and VIII includes symbolism of a kind that appears in other Nights only as a result of interpolation. But late transcription does not necessarily mean late composition. The relative times of composition of the elements drawn together in my reading must remain open to question. I am concerned primarily with thematic relationships between them.

2

Breaking the Bounds of Destiny

The first half of Night III, which contains Ahania's vision, is part of the copperplate text. The second half (pages 43–6) is part of the proof text; here Urizen casts out Ahania, an act which leads to the complete destruction of the Golden World and so plunges humanity into a state of chaos. We do not know whether Blake intended to show the destruction of the cosmos at this point when he began to transcribe the copperplate text. His use of *Night Thoughts* proofs from page 43 onwards suggests a radical change of plan; and as Gerald E. Bentley Jr. has argued, he may have begun to use the proofs no earlier than 1802.[1] There are several reasons for thinking that much of the basic proof text was composed while Blake was living under William Hayley's patronage at Felpham on the Sussex coast. H. M. Margoliouth has suggested that some of the passages describing Tharmas, 'especially in Nights III and IV, point to a knowledge of the sea which we have no reason to suppose Blake had before he went to Felpham'.[2] The description of the harvest and vintage in Night IX certainly shows a detailed knowledge of agricultural processes that Blake would have had good opportunities to observe in the countryside around Felpham. Perhaps most significant, at Felpham Blake may have had access to Hayley's library (Hayley showed some interest in Blake's education at Felpham, helping him to learn Latin, Greek, and Hebrew). This library contained an impressively wide range of ancient and modern works, including many volumes by eighteenth-century historians, social theorists, and natural philosophers.[3] The free use of such a facility would have represented a unique opportunity for Blake. As we shall see in later chapters, the proof text shows evidence of engagement with a wider range of ideas than the copperplate text.

[1] On p. 48 of the manuscript Bentley has detected a mirror image from William Hayley's Ballads, which Blake probably engraved in the spring or early summer of 1802 (Vala *or* The Four Zoas, 161). See App. 2.

[2] Margoliouth (ed.), *Vala*, p. xxxiii.

[3] See *Sale Catalogues of Libraries of Eminent Persons*, vol. 2 *Poets and Men of Letters*, ed. A. N. L. Munby (London, 1971).

There may, then, have been a break in the composition of the poem, between 1797 when Blake began to transcribe the copperplate text, and some time after Blake's arrival at Felpham in September 1800. In any event, a number of revisions to the copperplate text seem designed to link it more closely with the basic text on the proof pages (*see* Appendix 2). These revisions are the subject of the present chapter.

In its version of historical development, the surviving copperplate text shows a broad movement through three visions of divinity. After the fall of Tharmas divine power is totally submerged within the sensible world. Then at the golden feast elemental gods are seen to burst spontaneously from that world. Finally the cosmic system is built, in which divine power gives order, energy, and purpose to a realm of matter that would otherwise be chaotic. The development of the cosmos, then, entails a growing awareness of spirit as separable from the physical realm. In the world-view that emerges after the destruction of the cosmos there are no ideal forms in nature. As in the Cartesian account of life, there is a complete severance of matter from spirit, and the latter becomes a purely mental substance. The transition from the cosmos to the post-cosmic world, then, is a transition between two modes of vision—one in which the operative principles that form the world are seen as divine, and one in which they are seen as natural.

As we shall see, this movement corresponds in many respects to the change from the teleological, homocentric world-view that survived until the Renaissance, to the scientific universe that displaced it in the seventeenth century. But although in Blake's myth the transition initiates a completely new era of history, in an important sense it returns us to the point at which the first era began. Urizen's cosmos is destroyed when Man attempts to pursue, in defiance of all spiritual constraints, what Bacon would call 'the pure knowledge of nature and universality'.[4] As all knowledge is subsequently derived from experience, the active powers of the mind become totally dependent on the external world. In consequence, Urizen is completely submerged in the material realm—a fate which parallels that of Tharmas at the beginning of the poem. With the fall of Urizen, then, the course of history has completed a kind of cycle, having moved from one kind of submergence in the

[4] F. Bacon, *The Advancement of Learning*, ed. William Aldis Wright (Oxford, 1900), 5 (book I, section i, paragraph 3).

material world to another. Some of Blake's revisions at the beginning of the copperplate text clarify the cyclical nature of this progress.

Tharmas and his Spectre

If the cosmic era ends with the division of spirit from matter, a new account of the fall of Tharmas includes a similar division. The original description of Tharmas's fall was apparently moved from page 7 to page 5, allowing Blake to insert an elaborate prehistory to the sexual union with Enion. In the new text, the vision of creation as generation is seen as the product of an age that has already become alienated from the natural world and has arrived at a dualistic view of existence. We can approach this revision by reconsidering Blake's model in *Paradise Lost*. Milton's account of creation presupposes a fundamental separation of the spiritual from the material. The energies of nature appear to be derived from the spirit of God in a single, originating act of infusion:

> on the watery calm
> His brooding wings the spirit of God outspread,
> And vital virtue infused, and vital warmth
> Throughout the fluid mass
> (*PL* vii: 234–7)

The relationship between the spirit and the fluid mass of matter here is not a harmonious, loving partnership, as they are complete opposites: one contains the potentiality for form, purpose, and consciousness which the other lacks. In this respect, the source of life seems fundamentally at odds with its medium. Blake's additions show how such a view of origins could emerge.

In the new version, when Tharmas falls from his 'innocent' condition he has no power to achieve a sexual union with Enion. He falls into a state of complete passivity, while she at first becomes a creative power not by giving birth but by weaving:

> Tharmas groand among his Clouds
> Weeping, then bending from his Clouds he stoopd his innocent head
> And stretching out his holy hand in the vast Deep sublime
> Turnd round the circle of Destiny with tears & bitter sighs
> And said. Return O Wanderer when the Day of Clouds is oer

So saying he sunk down into the sea a pale white corse

In torment he sunk down & flowd among her filmy Woof
His Spectre issuing from his feet in flames of fire
In gnawing pain drawn out by her lovd fingers every nerve
She counted. every vein & lacteal threading them among
Her woof of terror. Terrified & drinking tears of woe
Shuddring she wove—nine days & nights Sleepless her food was tears
Wondring she saw her woof begin to animate. & not
As Garments woven subservient to her hands but having a will
Of its own perverse & wayward Enion lovd & wept

Nine days she labourd at her work. & nine dark sleepless nights
But on the tenth trembling morn the Circle of Destiny Complete
Round rolld the Sea Englobing in a watry Globe self balancd

(5: 8–25, E302)

Tharmas's belief that Enion may 'Return' forms a limit to Man's
fall because it allows him to see his fallen condition as provisional:
it gives history a redemptive form, 'the Circle of Destiny'. This
would seem to be Blake's version of the circumscription of chaos,
an act not accomplished by mathematical design (unlike Milton's
creator Tharmas has no compasses) but by an instinctive faith in
the possibility of recovery. As the Circle of Destiny is woven into
Enion's web, faith becomes fatalism, dependent on mysterious
powers manifest in the growth of the earth from primal chaos to
'self balancd' autonomy.

Weaving is often an ambivalent activity in Blake's work.[5] In
Urizen, after the first emergence of 'Pity', the Eternals weave a
covering tent named 'Science' to seal off, and protect themselves
from, Urizen's fallen world (pl. 19, E78). In the *Songs* woven
materials and 'shades' are protective but may also threaten to stifle
individuality. Weaving, then, is associated with that pitying urge
for protection that can give rise to the selfhood. This may help to
explain why it becomes the first art to appear in the fallen world of
The Four Zoas. It provides a model of divine creation, one which
might allow the material world to be seen as a temporary, protective covering for humanity, but which actually makes it seem like a

[5] For a discussion of some of the traditional and contemporary contexts evoked
by Blake's weaving imagery, see Hilton, *Literal Imagination*, 102–26. Kathleen
Raine relates Blake's association of weaving with birth to Thomas Taylor's version
of Porphyry's treatise on *Homer's Cave of the Nymphs: Blake and Tradition*, 2 vols.
(Princeton, NJ, 1968), i. 75–98; 231–3.

form of bondage, the product of a sinister goddess of fate. Enion's 'Woof' is a labour of love, but the reference to counting and threading every nerve, vein, and lacteal suggests an emergent awareness of the body as a complicated web that binds the individual to the natural world, as an object that inspires not delight but mystery and terror.[6]

The growing sense of alienation from the body is personified in the Spectre of Tharmas.[7] In the symbolism of *The Four Zoas* a 'spectre' may be described as a mind that tends to see the natural world as finite and corrupt, and that sees itself as essentially incorporeal—a pure spirit. Such a mind is doomed to live in a state of exile both from the pleasures of the body and from an eternal life that is conceived of in abstract terms. The Spectre of Tharmas is therefore separated completely from the body (he issues from the feet of Tharmas, as the soul was traditionally thought to leave the body).[8] The nine days and nights of Enion's weaving recall the nine days and nights through which the rebel angels fall from Heaven in *Paradise Lost*. In Milton's poem, life begins in Hell when Satan rises up from the burning lake (*PLi*: 221). In Blake's account fallen consciousness becomes active when the Spectre

> Reard up a form of gold & stood upon the glittering rock
> A shadowy human form winged   & in his depths
> The dazzlings as of gems shone clear, rapturous in fury
> Glorying in his own eyes   Exalted in terrific Pride
>
> (6: 5–8, *E*303)

The Spectre seems quite unlike the world from which he springs: he is like a precious artefact in Enion's 'Desart', like a fallen angel in an abyss. He speaks of an inner spiritual world as the source of his being, and sees the material world as a mere 'Diminutive husk & shell' (6: 9, *E*303), a sinful emanation of the mind that can be reabsorbed at will. In him Tharmas's yearning to be reunited with

---

[6] As Peter Otto observes, as this point 'The body is no longer the embodiment of the self but the horizon of the self's constituted world', 'The Multiple Births of Los in *The Four Zoas*', *Studies in English Literature*, 31 (1991), 635.

[7] In the 18th cent. the term 'Spectre' meant a terrifying ghost, an unreal object of thought, a faint shadow or imitation of something. Each of these meanings seems appropriate to Blake's use of the term. Hilton relates Blake's use of the term to the 'impartial spectator' of Adam Smith's *Theory of Moral Sentiments*: *Literal Imagination*, 154.

[8] D. V. Erdman, 'The Suppressed and Altered Passages of *Jerusalem*,' *Studies in Bibliography*, 17 (1964), 24, n. 23.

Enion assumes a grotesque form. His words to her are a horrific counterpart to the words of the serpent in Milton's Eden, who opens to Eve the prospect of a godlike existence:

> This world is Thine in which thou dwellest that within thy soul
> That dark & dismal infinite where Thought roams up & down
> Is Mine & there thou goest when with one Sting of my tongue
> Envenomd thou rollst inwards to the place whence I emergd
>
> (6: 13–16, E303–4)

In historical terms the Spectre represents the first conception of spiritual power in the fallen world—as an infinite power which is defined in opposition to (and in reaction to) an alien, dependent material world. The Spectre's sense of autonomy is of course an illusion, his inner world a formless abstraction, his dazzling brightness merely reflected. In the revised myth it is the Spectre who enters into a sexual union with Enion: threatening to absorb, he is himself absorbed, and Enion becomes a 'bright wonder . . . Half Woman & half Spectre'.

Los and Enitharmon Reconsidered

In the light of this new myth of the Spectre, the birth of Los and Enitharmon acquires a new significance. The absorption of the Spectre's power by Enion dissolves the separation of spirit from matter. Enion is no longer seen as the mere 'husk & shell' of consciousness but as its natural parent, fostering it from a state of complete dependence by 'pity & love':

> The first state weeping they began & helpless as a wave
> Beaten along its sightless way growing enormous in its motion to
> Its utmost goal, till strength from Enion like richest summer shining
> Raisd the bright boy & girl with glories from their heads out
>   beaming
> Drawing forth drooping mothers pity drooping mothers sorrow.
>
> (8: 3–7, E304)

Fallen consciousness still develops by a process of abstraction, as the mind has to deal with a finite world and can only gain independence by withdrawing to contemplate its own ideas. But mental (or 'Spectrous') power is no longer seen to be self-sustaining; it is derived directly from the experience of the natural environment: 'Ingrate they wanderd scorning her drawing her Spectrous Life'

(9: 4, *E*304). Unlike the Spectre, Los and Enitharmon can take delight in the sensuous pleasures of the natural world, while pushing to the margins of consciousness the inhibiting awareness of the natural limits of their existence. In the movement from the reign of the Spectre to the reign of his children, then, fallen humanity loses its primal sense of alienation and learns to reconcile itself to an external world.

The Birth of Anarchy

In the copperplate text the transition from primitive life to civil order was described primarily in terms of an intellectual crisis, the confrontation of reason with Enion's awareness of suffering, and with the void of indefinite space. But as we have seen, in contemporary social theory the transition usually involves a middle stage in which the condition of primal simplicity breaks down into a period of barbaric warfare, a state which motivates the development of a centralized order. Blake had followed Rousseau in showing that civil order depends on metallurgy and agriculture, but Rousseau had shown that these activities emerge before there is a central power to govern society, and that they help to produce the state of anarchy that motivates the establishment of strong government. A series of revisions to Blake's copperplate text brings the myth more closely into line with such thinking.

We have already seen that the arrival of Los and Enitharmon at the sea of space and time is a crucial moment in primitive history: here Man develops a myth of the fall which provides a justification for emotional restraint, and which heralds the descent of Urizen. In revising the text Blake elaborated the historical significance of this development. The arrival at the sea of time and space now marks the awakening of Man's interest in the heavenly bodies and in war. Enitharmon's speech begins with these words:

> We hear the warlike clarions we view the turning spheres
> (10: 7, *E*305)

Enitharmon, who controls the perception of space, is now clearly seen as a power that stimulates the repression of energy both in war and in the construction of abstract cosmologies (in *Paradise Lost* it is Eve who first shows curiosity about the stars, IV: 657). In the revised version of her Song Enitharmon identifies herself, rather than Vala, as the seductive influence that draws Man into the fallen world. Her vision incites Los to violence ('Los smote her upon the Earth', 11: 3, *E*306) and inspires in him visions of war ('I see the swords and spears of futurity', 11: 14, *E*306). After Los has spoken Enitharmon urges Urizen to descend in order to crush the rebellious passions and thus confirm Man's subjection to war:

> Descend O Urizen descend with horse & chariots
> .   .   .   .
> The Human Nature shall no more remain nor Human acts
> Form the rebellious Spirits of Heaven. but War & Princedom
>   & Victory & Blood
> Night darkend as she spoke! a shuddring ran from East to West
> A Groan was heard on high. The warlike clarions ceast. the Spirits
> Of Luvah & Vala shudderd in their Orb: an orb of blood!
>
> (11: 21, 23–4; 12: 1–3, *E*306)

Having been defined in the visions of Los and Enitharmon, Luvah and Vala become operative in the fallen world, and their contradictory influence (as both victims and dominating powers) is immediately felt. Urizen descends to Los and Enitharmon in an act of love and pity that rescues them from self-destruction ('the one must have murderd the other if he had not descended', 12: 6, *E*306). But his descent is simultaneously a denial of love and pity. He now offers love in exchange for obedience to law (like Milton's Raphael, who descends to reinforce Adam's obedience in Eden, where nuptial bliss is 'ordained' by God). He tells Los:

> Thou art the Lord of Luvah into thine hands I give
> The prince of Love the murderer his soul is in thine hands
> Pity not Vala for she pitied not the Eternal Man
> Nor pity thou the cries of Luvah. Lo these starry hosts
> They are thy servants if thou wilt obey my awful Law
>
> (12: 13–17, *E*307)

Although Los attempts to resist Urizen's authority, he is unable to resist the power of love and pity, which reconciles him to Enitharmon:

> Los saw the wound of his blow he saw he pitied he wept
> Los now repented that he had smitten Enitharmon he felt love
> Arise in all his Veins he threw his arms around her loins
> To heal the wound of his smiting
>
> (12: 40–3, *E*307)

Seen as a stage in the progress of fallen humanity this represents a major advance, as love exerts a moderating and healing influence that appears to bring harmony to a disjointed world. But as the myth now makes clear, such protective love does not really bring peace. In this context Los's embrace of Enitharmon's loins epitomizes a possessive urge to control the means of producing life. It is an urge that places sexual and economic activity on a basis of property rights, a desire that will breed rage, violence, and the repression of love and pity. The harmony of the golden feast now seems far from Edenic. The Song sung by 'Demons of the Deep' (added on pages 14–16) dramatizes the eruption of anarchy and warfare as an indignant reaction to the imposition of agriculture:

> Let us refuse the Plow & Spade, the heavy Roller & spiked
> Harrow. burn all these Corn fields. throw down all these fences
>   (14: 8–9, E308)

Luvah and Vala are seen once more as dominant powers (who ride 'Triumphant in the Bloody sky') and as victims (who are actively suppressed by the metallurgy of Los and Enitharmon, rather than by Urizen):

>   Los was born
> And Thou O Enitharmon! Hark I hear the hammers of Los
>
> They melt the bones of Vala, & the bones of Luvah into wedges
> The innumerable sons & daughters of Luvah closd in furnaces
> Melt into furrows. winter blows his bellows: Ice & Snow
> Tend the dire anvils.
>   (15: 19–16: 4, E309)

This alternative myth can be seen as a clarification of the power relations that exist in the fallen world. Reason must build on the foundations supplied by the imaginative powers. It is these which produce both the ideology of repression and the technology that will sustain the cosmos. As the Song implies, this pattern will be repeated later in the narrative (the Demons look forward to the rebirth of Luvah, and his binding by the Spectre of Urthona, events described in Night V).

Body and Spirit

If the descent of Urizen at first reconciles Enitharmon to Los, the creation of the Golden World eventually allows her to triumph over him. The completion of Urizen's labours does not immediately prevent Los and Enitharmon from exercising their 'all flexible senses'. An abstract conception of order that sustains rational conviction will not necessarily assume complete control of the human sense of reality (the conviction that the earth moves round the sun does not prevent us from seeing the sun as rising). Los and Enitharmon can at first still enter imaginatively into each aspect of their environment (34: 9–15, E322). But as we saw in the last chapter, there is a danger inherent in this liberty: they are drawn down by their desires to a world that threatens imaginative freedom. Their vision of Elemental Gods is radically at odds with Urizen's world: it makes no distinction between the material and the spiritual because every aspect of nature is seen to have its own essential divinity. In contrast, Urizen's abstract system reintroduces a distinction between matter and spirit: within it all life and form are derived from a central divinity; spiritual power is distributed to a material world which of itself is dark and chaotic. Blake's revisions show that this distinction inevitably begins to exert its influence on the imaginative powers. After the completion of the Golden World, Enitharmon—the personification of Los's vision of space—is 'dissolved' in Urizen's system. She tells Los

> Secure now from the smitings of thy Power
> Demon of fury If the God enrapturd me infolds
> In clouds of sweet obscurity my beauteous form dissolving
> Howl thou over the body of death tis thine But if among the virgins
> Of summer I have seen thee sleep & turn thy cheek delighted
> Upon the rose or lilly pale. or on a bank where sleep
> The beamy daughters of the light starting they rise they flee
> From thy fierce love for tho I am dissolvd in the bright God
> My spirit still pursues thy false love over rocks & valleys
>
> (34: 23–31, E323)

Los begins to lose his intimate sense of communion with nature as his vision degenerates into an inert material world ('the body of death') which is fleetingly illuminated by an elusive, tantalizing spirit. The elusiveness of Enitharmon's spirit reduces Los to the status of the frustrated, jealous lover whose life depends on the uncertain grace of the female. Enitharmon's hymn celebrates the harmonious beauty of the cosmos in lines that emphasize this new sense of dependence. In the cosmic system, everything that

lives may be holy, but holiness is experienced as a gift from above
that brings relief to a life largely deprived of joy:

> For every thing that lives is holy for the source of life
> Descends to be a weeping babe
> For the Earthworm renews the moisture of the sandy plain
>
> Now my left hand I stretch to earth beneath
> And strike the terrible string
> I wake sweet joy in dens of sorrow & I plant a smile
> In forests of affliction
> And wake the bubbling springs of life in regions of dark death
>
> (34: 80–7, E324)

Before the construction of the cosmos, the awareness of suffering
existed at the margins of consciousness: the lamenting Enion was
excluded from the golden feast. But because the cosmos is a formal
response to 'regions of dark death' it inevitably brings the awareness of suffering closer.

The Separation of Urizen and Ahania

One of the many differences between the myth of *Urizen* and that
of *The Four Zoas* appears in the presentation of Urizen's fall into
chaos. In the earlier work Urizen begins his labours of abstraction
in Eternity, and falls into 'dark desarts' when the other Eternals
indignantly reject his laws. In *The Four Zoas*, he falls into the
'Caverns of the Grave' when he attempts to dissociate himself from
what he sees as the law-giving aspect of his own nature—embodied
in his female counterpart Ahania:

> Shall the feminine indolent bliss. the indulgent self of weariness
> The passive idle sleep the enormous night & darkness of Death
> Set herself up to give her laws to the active masculine virtue
> Thou little diminutive portion that darst be a counterpart
> Thy passivity thy laws of obedience & insincerity
> Are my abhorrence.
>
> (43: 6–11, E328–9)

The immediate cause of Urizen's rejection of Ahania is her vision of
Man's fall in Night III. But Blake made extensive additions to Night
II (which originally contained no mention of Ahania) in order to
clarify Urizen's reaction to this vision. The seeds of conflict are now

shown to lie ultimately in Urizen's constructive activity itself, and in particular in his growing preoccupation with the structure of his world.

The Emergence of Pure Knowledge

According to Thomas Kuhn, only in Western civilization has the explanation of the observed details of nature's behaviour been considered a function of cosmology. Our cosmology has typically assumed a dual purpose:

The requirement that a cosmology supply *both* a psychologically satisfying world-view *and* an explanation of observed phenomena like the daily change in the position of sunrise has vastly increased the power of cosmologic thought. It has channelled the universal compulsion for at-homeness in the universe into an unprecedented drive for the discovery of scientific explanations. Many of the most characteristic achievements depend upon this combination of demands imposed upon cosmologic thought. But the combination has not always been a congenial one. It has forced modern man to delegate the construction of cosmologies to special-ists, primarily to astronomers, who know the multitude of detailed obser-vations that modern cosmologies must satisfy to be believed. And since observation is a two-edged sword which may either confirm or conflict with a cosmology, the consequences of this delegation can be devastating. The astronomer may on occasions destroy, for reasons lying entirely within his speciality, a world-view that had previously made the universe mean-ingful for the members of a whole civilization, specialist and nonspecialist alike.[9]

Urizen's cosmos is designed to meet two kinds of demand: it pro-vides Man with a vision of divine creativity and care, and at the same time it attempts to satisfy his intellectual curiosity about the structure and motions of the physical world. It collapses because these two concerns appeal to two different aspects of fallen reason, embodied in Ahania and Urizen respectively. The desire for comfort and reassurance promotes the vision of a personal deity that is concerned with human welfare, and that may intervene on behalf of the individual. This need for a particular providence is met in the cosmos by Ahania, the 'feminine' aspect of Urizen's power, who

---

[9] T. S. Kuhn, *The Copernican Revolution* (Cambridge, Mass., 1957), 7.

becomes the centre of an organized religion. But the vision of a particular providence is less important to that part of the mind that seeks to understand the structure and motions of nature. The drive for such understanding is typically satisfied by general principles that are immutable, and therefore independent of the whims of a personal deity. A conflict between these interests becomes inevitable.

The history of science since the Renaissance had provided vivid examples of this kind of conflict. The mechanistic world-view established in the seventeenth century could be reconciled with Christian belief, but it did place some strain on the notion of a particular providence. For Robert Boyle, as for many of his contemporaries, the world functioned like a clock in which 'all things proceed according to the Artificer's first design', and which did not require 'the peculiar interposing of the Artificer, or any Intelligent Agent imployed by him'. Boyle argued that such a view of the world was more respectful to providence than the idea that God had appointed an intelligent and powerful Being ('called *Nature*') to be His vice-regent, 'continually watchful for the good of the Universe in general, and of the particular Bodies that compose it'.[10] When Newton wrote of the role of providence in his 'General Scholium', he argued that God 'governs all things, not as the soul of the world, but as Lord over all', a description which seems to imply a general rather than a particular providence. Elsewhere he argued that God might make periodic adjustments to the motions of the planets; but as Leibniz pointed out, this made the creator seem an unskilful designer.[11] Richard Westfall comments, 'Despite all his attempts to retain a meaningful idea of providence, Newton could not free himself from a position to which nearly all of the virtuosi were driven. Indeed there seems to have been no possible alternative. If the mechanical universe is a reality, as Newton firmly believed, providence can only mean God's concurrence in the operation of its laws.'[12] Such a position would itself prove vulnerable to attack. By

[10] R. Boyle, *A Free Enquiry into the Vulgarly Receiv'd Notion of Nature* (London, 1685), 11, 13.

[11] *Newton's Principia*, ed. F. Cajori, 2 vols. (Berkeley and London, 1934, 1962), ii. 544. Samuel Clarke, *A Collection of Papers ... Relating to the Principles of Natural Philosophy and Religion* (London, 1717), 5.

[12] R. Westfall, *Science and Religion in Seventeenth-Century England* (Ann Arbor, 1973), 203.

the mid eighteenth century, Hume was openly questioning the idea that the argument from design could be used to support belief in a personal God.[13]

The difficulty of reconciling a mechanical conception of creation with an active providence can be seen as a correlative of the fundamental shift in natural philosophy from teleological to empirical approaches to nature. From the time of Galileo science had become increasingly concerned with the *how* rather than the *why* of events. The new science involved, as Alexander Koyré observes,

the disappearance—or the violent expulsion—from scientific thought of all considerations based on value, perfection, harmony, meaning and aim, because these concepts, from now on merely subjective, cannot have a place in the new ontology.[14]

This means that while scientists continued to assert the purposeful nature of the world, they did not deduce its structure from a purpose. Final causality itself was not a subject of study. God had, as it were, already been excluded from creation, and could be readmitted only when scientists shifted their attention from the particulars of their work to reflect on its wider significance.

In order to illustrate the emergence of this kind of tension between religion and science, Blake elaborated both the geometrical nature of the stars in Urizen's cosmos, and the nature of the temple-like world that contains them. The 'Globes' of the heavenly bodies became 'cubes' and 'pyramids', or were given more elaborate geometrical shapes, reminiscent of those in Plato's discussion of the structure of regular solids:

> Trapeziums Rhombs Rhomboids
> Paralellograms. triple & quadruple. polygonic
> In their amazing hard subdued course in the vast deep.
>
> (33: 34–36, E322)

The search for a 'pure' knowledge of irreducible clarity and precision is satisfied by the abstract certainties of mathematical form. In its context the specificity of this language seems wildly extravagant: the process of explanation has become an end in itself. On the other hand Blake made Urizen's Golden World more specifically the

---

[13] See Hume, *Enquiries*, 138. The *Enquiries* were first published in 1748 and 1751. Hume made a more elaborated assault on the argument from design in his posthumously published *Dialogues Concerning Natural Religion* (1779).

[14] A. Koyré, *Newtonian Studies* (London, 1965), 7.

archetype of religious temples (in a long addition on page 30, 15–50, E319–20). The concern with destiny is now expressed in its very structure: the temple has twelve halls named after Urizen's sons (evoking astrological and Christian symbolism), and three domes named after his daughters (recalling the Fates and Graces of classical mythology). At the centre of the structure is Urizen's Golden hall, and it is here that Ahania now makes her entrance to the narrative:

> His Shadowy Feminine Semblance here reposd on a White Couch
> Or hoverd oer his Starry head & when he smild she brightend
> Like a bright Cloud in harvest. but when Urizen frownd She wept
> In mists over his carved throne & when he turnd his back
> Upon his Golden hall & sought the Labyrinthine porches
> Of his wide heaven Trembling, cold in paling fears she sat
> A Shadow of Despair therefore toward the West Urizen formd
> A recess in the wall for fires to glow upon the pale
> Females limbs in his absence & her Daughters oft upon
> A Golden Altar burnt perfumes with Art Celestial formd
>
> (30: 23–32, E319–20)

The natural imagery associated with Ahania ('a bright Cloud in Harvest') is played against the ornate grandeur of Urizen's artifice, and Ahania's mists are opposed unexpectedly to the order and clarity that the cosmos is designed to embody. Ahania begins to assume a separate identity as Urizen turns his back upon his Golden hall and seeks 'the Labyrinthine porches | Of his wide heaven' in search of knowledge remote from the spiritual concerns of Man (30: 43–9, E320).

Much of Urizen's activity is now outside the temple, which in his absence becomes the province of ritual and sacrifice, but which remains in contact with the human needs that Urizen descended to serve. If the cosmos represents a harmonious synthesis of two kinds of explanation, this synthesis is shown to be inherently unstable. It tends inevitably to break down into the separate spheres of religion and natural philosophy, which, having different aims, will come into conflict.

In the revised text, the tensions that bring Ahania and Urizen into conflict are analysed with considerable subtlety, and in a way that demonstrates the interdependence of reason and imagination. The initial freedom of the imagination to respond to each part of its world—to the negative as well as the positive aspects of experience—ensures that reason cannot escape the doubts and fears that its order is designed to overcome. As Los and Enitharmon are drawn down to Urizen's world, they begin

> To plant divisions in the Soul of Urizen & Ahania
> To conduct the Voice of Enion to Ahanias midnight pillow
> (34: 3–4 E322)

The voice of Enion generates tension between Urizen and Ahania because it expresses a horror at suffering that can only be soothed by the vision of a caring personal providence, Ahania. As Los's paradisal vision disintegrates into a dead material world and an elusive world of the spirit, he begins to confront faith and doubt as troubling alternatives (he sees Enitharmon 'Now taking on Ahanias form & now the form of Enion' 34: 38, E323). The more Man confronts the possibility that he lives in a blind and purposeless world, the greater the burden thrown upon his faith. Ahania's attempt to persuade Urizen to reassume his fields of light is now seen as her response to Enion's cries (36: 14–19, E325–6).

The Casting-Out of Ahania

Ahania is usually identified as pleasure in Blake criticism, but as we have already seen, her role in *The Four Zoas* can be read in more complex terms. She is the sense of beauty and fulfilment that should inspire Urizen's labours (she is related to the biblical figure of Wisdom, who stands before the Lord inspiring His creativity in Proverbs 8). In the cosmos, she has been compelled to take a religious form, wrapped in mystery and ritual: a source of inspiration has become an established authority which now appears to resist the labours of reason instead of promoting them. In this context, Ahania's vision of Luvah's atonement gains a new significance. Since it implies that the material world is corrupt and limiting (the body a terrible confinement, the 'vast form of Nature like a Serpent') it typifies religious prejudice against the study of nature. Accordingly Urizen's rejection of her 'laws of obedience' typifies the refusal of natural philosophers to allow their work to be constrained by such prejudice, as well as the expulsion of all teleological assumptions from the scientific field of vision.

Blake's description of the casting-out is at once the violent break-ing-up of a carefully ordered world, the beginning of a deluge and, as the cosmos has been presented in terms that recall the captivity in Israel, it is also a kind of exodus. Each of these has its counter-part in seventeenth-century accounts of the transition from the closed, organic, medieval world-view to the infinite, mechanis-tic world of the new science. Joseph Addison, for example, cel-ebrated Descartes as one who 'destroyed the Orbs of glass, which the Whims of Antiquity had fixed above' and who 'scorned to be any longer bounded within the Streights and Christalline Wall of an *Aristotelic* World'. The scientist Henry Power celebrated the 'over-flowing of free Philosophy' as an 'Inundation' that would sweep away the old rubbish of the Aristotelian world. Abraham Cowley celebrated Bacon as the deliverer who has led the new age out of its captivity: 'Bacon, like Moses, led us forth at last.'[15] In Blake's narrative the cosmos is destroyed not by particular scientific discoveries or theories that undermine its intellectual basis, but by a change in desires and values. The cycle that begins with the Spectre's disdain for the 'Diminutive husk & shell' of nature con-cludes with Urizen's disdain for the 'diminutive portion' that in-spires vision. In consequence reason becomes merely passive in relation to its own experience. Urizen falls down into the sea of space and time and is submerged within it, as Tharmas was at the beginning of the sequence. But whereas Tharmas turned round the Circle of Destiny as he fell, Urizen's fall breaks the bounds of destiny: the mind becomes an empirical observer, embracing doubt instead of faith.

In reviewing this sequence as a whole we can see that Blake's revisions consistently darken his portrait of this phase of Man's life. Conflicts between males and females are intensified considerably, so that at every stage there is more emphasis on the torments of love and jealousy. Second, Urizen's creation is seen more clearly to contain the principle of its own destruction: the grasp of order that allows the mind to organize the cosmic vision of life is the very thing that destroys that vision. The cycle as a whole establishes a

---

[15] J. Addison 'An Oration in Defence of the New Philosophy ... July 9 1693', included in *A Week's Conversation on the Plurality of Worlds*, by M. de Fontenelle (London, 1737), 185; H. Power, *Experimental Philosophy; in Three Books* (London, 1664), 192; A. Cowley, 'To The Royal Society', *Poems*, ed. A. R. Waller (Cambridge, 1905), 450.

pattern that will be repeated in the next era of history. Urizen's first system collapses when its order and clarity have been clouded by a religious mystery that he rejects. At the heart of his second creation Urizen encounters a new and more powerful manifestation of mystery, Vala, whom he will eventually embrace.

3

A Vision of Progress

The First Principle of Unbelief

The Artifice of the Epicurean Philosophers is to Call all other Opinions Unsolid & Unsubstantial than those which are Derived from Earth. (*Annotations to the Works of Sir Joshua Reynolds* (E659))

Blake's comment was provoked by Reynolds's view that taste is not of too high origin 'to submit to the authority of an earthly tribunal'. Apparently Blake considered the term 'Epicurean Philosopher' appropriate to any writer who set knowledge derived from experience and experiment against inspiration. Bacon's advocacy of scientific method seemed essentially atheistical: Bacon 'says that Every Thing must be done by Experiment his first princip[le] is Unbelief' (E648). Disregarding Bacon's deferential gestures to Christianity, Blake simply identifies his thought with the supposedly godless materialism of the Greek atomists: 'Bacon is only Epicurus over again' (E645).

This sweeping judgement may seem like a gross caricature, but it points to significant features of the new era heralded by Bacon. By the time Newton's *Principia* first appeared in 1687, most scientists took as their field of study a material world which resembled that of the Greek atomists in important respects. It was a world in which change was produced by the motion, combination, and separation of small particles.[1] The quantitative emphasis of the new science encouraged a widespread acceptance of the doctrine of secondary qualities (making colour, sound, and smell subjective appearances that have no place in the structure of the natural world). John Locke's new model of the mind, which brought epistemology into line with science, derived all ideas ultimately from sense impressions. Each of these developments could be seen as a return to Epicurean philosophy. But in practice they were made to

---

[1] See R. Hooykaas, *Religion and the Rise of Modern Science* (Edinburgh and London, 1972), 13–14.

support a world-view that was quite un-Epicurean. In Locke's account the reasoning mind that reflects upon its ideas finds the knowledge of God its 'most natural discovery'.[2] And whereas Epicurus recognized no design in the material world, the scientists described a mechanical universe that implied a designer, and which could therefore be reconciled with the biblical myth of creation (the Neo-Platonist Ralph Cudworth identified '*Moses* the *Jewish* Lawgiver' as 'the First Author of the *Atomical* Philosophy').[3] The development of natural philosophy in the seventeenth and eighteenth centuries had shown very clearly that the first principle of 'Unbelief' could lend powerful support to religious faith of the kind that true Epicurean philosophers seek to undermine. Bacon actually leads to Newtonian physico-theology.

The narrative of *The Four Zoas* explores a comparable development. In the reading presented here, the movement that begins with Urizen's rejection of religious constraint, and his destruction of the Golden World, culminates in his development of a new world order in which state religion has an even greater capacity to restrain thought. The fallen mind thus moves through a second great cycle of error that closely parallels the first one. The pattern of reconstruction in the myth apparently reflects Blake's sense of the relationship between the scientific world-view of his own age and the cosmic order it replaced. But the narrative is far from a simple allegory of recent history. It explores the ontological and epistemological foundations that must be established before a scientific world-view can develop. Blake's use of biblical symbolism implies that, like Cudworth, he saw the assumptions that underlie modern science inscribed in the Mosaic vision of the Old Testament—just as he saw in Bacon's work 'Epicurus over again'. Such a syncretic reading of history would seem to undermine any attempt to relate the narrative exclusively, or even primarily, to one historical period. His myth delineates the archetypal patterns of error through which the fallen mind must travel, processes that may be re-enacted in quite different periods of fallen time.

[2] J. Locke, *An Essay Concerning Human Understanding*, ed. P. H. Nidditch (Oxford, 1975), 95 (book I, chapter iv, section 17).
[3] R. Cudworth, *A Treatise Concerning Eternal and Immutable Morality* (London, 1731), 57.

The Biblical Pattern

The transition from the first cycle to the second brings into focus some of the broad correspondences between the major episodes of Blake's narrative and events in the Bible. As we have seen, the movement from the golden feast to the cosmos parallels the transition from Genesis to Exodus. Overlapping this parallel is a larger one, which begins in some of the revisions to the copperplate text, and continues through the subsequent narrative.

When Urizen descends to the feast of Los and Enitharmon, he delivers Luvah and Vala into Los's hands, and offers control of the 'starry hosts': 'They are thy servants if thou wilt obey my awful Law' (12: 16–17, E307). Urizen's promise heralds the appearance of the Elemental Gods that keep harmony around the heads of Los and Enitharmon. This attempt to regulate human life corresponds to the attempt made in Eden, where God gives Adam dominion over all living things (Genesis 1: 28). After the expulsion from Eden the God of Genesis reveals an unpredictable appetite for offerings (Genesis 4), the first city is built, and the creation degenerates until it is destroyed. In Blake's poem this is the era of the cosmos, in which Ahania becomes the recipient of sacrifices, and which ends when Urizen sends the ruins of his creation plunging into the sea of space and time. In Genesis, after the flood, God seeks to regulate humanity through a series of covenants. The covenant with Noah heralds the reconstruction of life on a new basis: man now has power over the life of 'every living thing that moveth'. In Blake's poem the flood begins at the point of transition from the copperplate text to the proof text. Tharmas becomes the supreme god of the new world, and his covenants with Los and the Spectre of Urthona utterly transform Man's relationship with his world. In place of Urizen's divine hierarchy, all things now lie on the same ontological level. The Elements are no longer inhabited by gods, because spiritual life has been expelled from the material world. The Elemental music no longer arises spontaneously, but is the reward of labour. Man now struggles to make every living thing subject to a vision of existence that is fundamentally lifeless.

Beyond the Bounds of Destiny

In the first era of human development the Circle of Destiny formed a limit to the fall. But with the destruction of the cosmos this limit is lost:

> The bounds of Destiny were broken
> The bounds of Destiny crashd direful & the swelling Sea
> Burst from its bonds
>
> (43: 27–8, E329)

The bursting of the sea from its bonds, like the biblical flood, is both a continuation of human history and a new beginning: it is a baptism into disillusioned adulthood, and a rebirth into a new vision of human origins. The total submergence of Man's powers in a chaos of smoke and water suggests a descent into the boundless and centreless world of pure materialism, the realm in which 'Epicurean philosophy' appears. Here all of life and consciousness is seen to have evolved from the violent and ceaseless flux of matter, while spirit seems merely corporeal (Lucretius describes the soul as a material substance 'Of smaller parts than water, smoke, or mists').[4] The emergence of Tharmas at this point parallels the rise of the Spectre of Tharmas, who 'reard up' his form after the first collapse into the sea. Unlike the Spectre, Tharmas here is not a spiritual power: neither a winged angel nor a dazzling artefact, he is a power whose substance is identical to the sea from which he has emerged. Seen in mythical terms, materialism is an attempt to derive form and intelligence from a chaotic and unintelligent first mover. Tharmas's struggle to take the voice, features, and limbs of a man, and his horrified awareness that his identity is inextricably bound up with the ocean, dramatize the new vision of origins as a grotesque paradox:

> But from the Dolorous Groan one like a shadow of smoke appeard
> And human bones rattling together in the smoke & stamping
> The nether Abyss & gnasshing in fierce despair. panting in sobs
> Thick short incessant bursting sobbing. deep despairing stamping
> struggling
> Struggling to utter the voice of Man struggling to take the features
> of Man. Struggling

---

[4] *Lucretius Carus of the Nature of Things in Six Books*, transl. T. Creech, 2 vols. (London, 1714), i. 226 (book III, line 408).

To take the limbs of Man at length emerging from the smoke
Of Urizen dashed in pieces from his precipitant fall
Tharmas reard up his hands & stood on the affrighted Ocean
The dead reard up his Voice & stood on the resounding shore

Crying. Fury in my limbs. destruction in my bones & marrow
My skull riven into filaments. my eyes into sea jellies
Floating upon the tide wander bubbling & bubbling
Uttering my lamentations & begetting little monsters
Who sit mocking upon the little pebbles of the tide
In all my rivers & on dried shells that the fish
Have quite forsaken.

(44: 14–45: 1, *E*329–30)

The rhythms and distorted syntax of the passage vividly enact the desperate struggle for life and expression. The verse itself bursts its bounds and re-forms. A momentary sense of triumph in the achieved resurrection is immediately dissipated. Fury dissolves into pathos; body and voice dissolve into marine life which seems at once vigorous and aimless. These lines establish the tidal pattern of Tharmas's passion in the Caverns of the Grave, the repeated swaying between anger and pity, and they herald a new emphasis on the physicality of the human body—on its limbs, hands, feet, eyes, and hair, on its bones, nerves, and veins—to which consciousness seems so mysteriously related.

The ontological change that leads Man to identify a spiritless matter as the basis of his reality, and to see the flux of sensation as the source of his knowledge, robs the external world of its maternal aspect. Nature is no longer a caring if ineffectual mother, but a neutral presence.[5] In Epicurean philosophy the natural world is in itself colourless, silent and without smell, a realm that is continually in motion. To Tharmas, Enion now seems even less than the husk and shell of existence. She becomes merely an 'Image of faint waters' (45: 30, 32, *E*330). 'Substanceless' and 'voiceless', she plunges into the sea from which Tharmas has emerged and 'withers away to Entuthon Benithon' (45: 13, *E*330), a state beyond the range of knowledge (the sound of the name suggests 'entombed beneath'; there may also be a derivation from the Greek, ἐντεῦθεν βένθος literally 'hence depth').[6]

---

[5] See Lucretius on the worship of the Earth Mother, *Of the Nature of Things*, i. 146–7 (book II, lines 612–20).
[6] I am indebted to Nelson Hilton and Mike Edwards for this suggested derivation.

A New Limit

With the breaking of the bounds of Destiny then, Man falls into a vision of the world that seems fundamentally chaotic. But however horrific they may appear, the Caverns of the Grave represent the limit of Man's fall. They are the level of vision at which his error is stabilized, and at which it consolidates into a system. No sooner does Urizen collapse than Tharmas begins to assume human form. Tharmas may claim that 'Love and Hope are ended' (46: 5), but he does not entirely lose either his capacity for love or his hope for Enion's return. Although Los and Enitharmon fall with the rest of Man's powers, they soon emerge in strength and brightness above the deluge. Blake's narrative consistently implies that love and hope, and the mind's creative powers, cannot be finally annihilated, no matter how violently they may be suppressed. This is an article of faith that lies close to the heart of Blake's vision of Christianity. In the comprehensive Christian framework introduced in late revisions to the narrative, the persistence of love and hope is seen to be guaranteed by divine providence. But even before the introduction of this scheme, the basic text of Nights III to VIIa contained hints that Man's fall is limited by a power beyond his own will. Urizen falls 'As when the thunderbolt down falleth on the appointed place' (44: 1). The phrase 'the Caverns of the Grave and Places of Human Seed' suggests both death and the possibility of new life, as if this realm, like the dark earth of Matron Clay in *Thel*, is given 'to enter and return'. Other similes relate the events of this world to the natural cycle in a way that emphasizes the possibility of rebirth after apparent death (*see*, for example, 57: 9–11 and 71: 28–30). And there are also, as we shall see, explicit references to divine intervention which apparently predate, and perhaps anticipate, the providential framework introduced in revisions. The distorted evolutions of fallen history are never shown to be absolutely beyond the range of providence.

Images of Life, Death, and Immortality

At the point where the narrative begins to describe the collapse of the cosmos, Blake began to make use of proofs of his engraved designs for Young's *Night Thoughts*. This decision may have been prompted by the hope of publishing the poem by conventional means. Perhaps, as Paul Mann has argued, Blake was 'influenced by his working association with Hayley during the period 1800–3, and especially by their partnership on an edition of Hayley's *Ballads*', and had hopes of publishing his poem in letterpress form. Mann suggests that Blake 'was either testing the possibility of using the *Night Thoughts* designs directly to frame his own letterpress text, or using those designs as a general model while planning to replace them with new designs'.[7] Certainly, if Blake was thinking in terms of a letterpress edition, it would make little sense to use fresh paper for the fair copy of his text: to reuse the proof leaves would cost nothing. If Blake was guided primarily by economic considerations, that does not necessarily mean that he used the proofs with no heed to their position in the manuscript. John E. Grant, Cettina Magno and David Erdman have argued in detail that many of the proofs can be related in some way to the text they accompany, and that some of the sketches on the versos complement, and help to integrate the designs (*see* Appendix 1).[8]

Blake may have felt that some of the proofs would form generally appropriate illustrations from this point on in the manuscript, since Young's view of 'Life, Death and Immortality' is in many respects typical of the mode of vision dramatized in the Caverns of the Grave. Both are dominated by 'impressions of Despair & Hope'. In both there is a gloomy preoccupation with loss, fallenness, and death, while the faith that eventually emerges in the Caverns is in some respects comparable to Young's—sustained by a scientific vision of the universe, by a belief in a distant eternity 'beyond the bounds of Science' (80: 42, E356).[9] Blake's engraved designs present a world in which hope is defined in stark relation to fear of suffering, transience, sin, and death. Individuals are repeatedly represented as watched, measured, hunted by dominating powers such as Conscience and Time, while Blake emphasizes Young's

---

[7] Mann, 'Final State', 204. See also Essick, 'Intention and Production' and Viscomi, *Idea of the Book*, 316–18.

[8] Grant, 'Visions in *Vala*'; Magno and Erdman (ed.), 'The Four Zoas'.

[9] For detailed discussions of Blake's designs for Young, see *NT*; M. D. Paley, 'Blake's *Night Thoughts*', in *Essays for S. Foster Damon*, ed. A. H. Rosenfeld (Providence, RI, 1969), 131–57; J. E. Grant, 'Jesus and the Powers That Be in Blake's Designs for Young's *Night Thoughts*', in *Blake and His Bibles*, ed. D. V. Erdman, with M. T. Smith (West Cornwall, Conn., 1990), 71–115.

'deification of death'.[10] Blake's narrative explores the ontological and epistemological foundations of the realm of vision in which Young and his contemporaries construct their world, and satirizes attempts to rationalize the anxieties and doubts that haunt the mind in this realm.[11]

Towards a Vision of Progress

Man begins to escape from chaos as soon as the imaginative powers emerge. The arising of Los and Enitharmon is described in terms which suggest the sun rising from the sea. As their light breaks over the dark Abyss, Tharmas feels a paternal affection: 'his bowels yearnd over them' (47: 3, E331). If the love and pity once seen in Luvah and Vala have disappeared with the cosmos, these emotions survive at the level of instinct in the powerful coercive affection of parent for child, providing a motive for order and stability (in the Epicurean system expounded by Lucretius, parental pity emerges at the beginning of social life, and helps to preserve the human race from destruction).

In the sequence that follows, Los and Enitharmon at first resist the power of Tharmas but are soon forced to compromise with it. The confrontation between Tharmas and Los is a confrontation between opposites—between the vision of a spiritless material world and the spiritual, homocentric view of life that has been nurtured in the cosmos. This opposition gives rise to a complete transformation in the sense of being—in the constitution of the self, in the objects and the means of knowledge, in the awareness of time, and in the vision of human destiny. As we shall see, this complex transformation, presented as a series of changes wrought in Los by Tharmas, in some respects parallels the transformation in European thought that produced and followed the scientific revolution.

In the Caverns of the Grave the order of the world is not an ideal, static hierarchy to be contemplated in reverence, but something that has been lost and must be recreated. As knowledge must now

[10] Grant, 'Jesus and the Powers That Be', 84.

[11] Blake used his title page of Young's poem on the verso of the last leaf of *The Four Zoas* manuscript, perhaps to indicate the oppositional relationship between his narrative and Young's poem.

be derived from the chaotic flux of the sensible world, the mind must actively construct what it knows. Knowing becomes a dynamic, progressive activity which is dependent on labour. In Urizen's cosmic hierarchy all labour, from that of 'Spirits of strongest wing' to that of 'female slaves', is governed by 'the great Work master', and fulfils his will. But in the Caverns of the Grave knowledge flows from labour rather than to it, and *homo faber* precedes *homo sapiens*. This development is presented as both an advance and a catastrophe. It gives a new importance to the powers of the individual mind, but at the same time it tends to negate their creativity. If the advancement of learning depends on a heroic effort to bring order out of chaos, the correspondence between what is perceived and what actually exists can only be confirmed by the consistency of experience or (from an eternal point of view) by its deadness.

The sequence begins when Tharmas asserts that the creative roles previously assumed by Enion (weaving) and Urizen (building) must now be taken over by Enitharmon and Los:

> Go forth Rebuild this Universe beneath my indignant power
> A Universe of Death & Decay. Let Enitharmons hands
> Weave soft delusive forms of Man above my watry world
>   (48: 4–6, E332)

This transfer of responsibility gives Los a new sense of his own potential, a new sense of identity, as his reply shows:

> I know I was Urthona keeper of the gates of heaven
> But now I am all powerful Los & Urthona is but my shadow
>   (48: 19–20, E332)

In Blake's narrative Urthona is the unfallen form of Los. He is the liberated imagination that emerges only at the end of the Last Judgement. Los, in identifying himself with Urthona, the 'keeper of the gates of heaven', recognizes for the first time his own potential to lead Man to eternal life. But Los is already falling into the power of Tharmas, whose influence makes the eternal power of Urthona seem shadowy, and the fallen self appear autonomous. Los and Enitharmon resist the prospect of a material world in which all forms are merely transient or 'delusive': they attempt to repel the advances of Tharmas, as they once repelled Enion (Los's words, 'Hitherto shalt thou come. no further. here thy proud waves cease', recall God commanding the sea in Job 38: 11). But Tharmas overwhelms Los by taking possession of Enitharmon.

Under Urizen's power in the cosmos, Los had come to see Enitharmon as twofold: a body of death animated by a beautiful but elusive spirit. Now as 'bright Enitharmon' falls under the power of Tharmas she is separated from Los completely, and the spirit departs from her. When she is returned to him Los sees 'a World Dark dreadful' underneath his feet. The division here seems to correspond to the Cartesian split which transferred 'secondary' qualities from the realm of objects to the perceiving subject, a split that assumed an important place in the new epistemology of the seventeenth century, including the Lockian doctrine that prevailed. As we shall see, the new subject that is defined in relation to the violated Enitharmon is personified as the Spectre of Urthona.

The Spectre as Prophet of Progress

This Spectre in some ways resembles the Spectre of Tharmas. Both are immaterial beings who contemplate a corrupt material world, and both are described in terms of artefacts. The new Spectre is not a dazzling form of gold, nor a winged being like a fallen angel, but

> A Shadow blue obscure & dismal. like a statue of lead
> Bent by its fall from a high tower the dolorous shadow rose
> $$(49: 13-14, E333)$$

The simile suggests an awareness of the fall as a disabling, personal catastrophe. The Spectre corresponds to what Susan Bordo describes as the state of 'epistemological *fallenness*' that seems implicit in the Cartesian division between the knower and the world at large.[12] In this respect he is the symptom of a terrible injury to the integrity of the individual, the death of the primal sense of relatedness to the world (a sense that had survived in attenuated form in the cosmos). But the emergence of the Spectre is also the development of a new power, one that will enable Los to order his world. The activities of the Spectre identify him as a reflective capacity, a faculty that enables the individual to organize the

---

[12] S. Bordo, *The Flight to Objectivity: Essays on Cartesianism and Culture* (New York, 1987), 43.

awareness of time and to learn from experience. Los has previously exhibited a childlike amorality. Now in the Spectre he acquires a haunting self-consciousness that brings a new sense of responsibility and purpose.[13]

The very feeling of epistemological alienation that he personifies can provide the basis of a new vision of destiny. This aspect of Blake's myth can be clarified by examining Bacon's account of human knowledge, in which the fall is reinterpreted in epistemological terms. Bacon suggests that, in falling, humanity lost the power of knowing the creation properly. The study of the material world can be reconciled with the study of God because the ultimate end of learning is to restore 'that same COMMERCE OF THE MIND AND OF THINGS' to its original perfect condition. In his view the order of the world is not a revealed and sustaining presence towering above the human realm, but lies hidden in the depths of nature, waiting to be mastered. His prayer for the great instauration asserts a correspondence between the work of divine creation and the proper work of fallen humanity, and it assimilates the seven days of creation to a vision of progress:

Thou, after thou hadst survayed [sic] the works thy hands had wrought, saw that all was exceeding Good, and hadst rested: but Man survaying the works his hands had wrought, saw that all was vanity and vexation of Spirit, and found no Rest: Wherefore if we labour with diligence, and vigilance in Thy works, thou wilt make us Participants of thy Vision, and of thy Sabbath.

According to Bacon, the scholastic tradition had left science in a state of chaos in which there was 'a perpetual wheeling, Agitation and Circle'.[14] In contrast the Baconian labourer becomes a kind of prophet who works to redeem humanity from the effects of the fall. Manual labour assumes a centrally important place in Bacon's vision of progress, because the advancement of learning must depend on the world of practice and experiment. Bacon's view reflects a more general change in attitudes to labour, a change that found expression in widely different areas of thought, from the speculations of alchemists to the works of the Royal Society, from

[13] As Bordo notes, the consciousness of 'otherness' makes possible the consciousness of self (as Lacan and others have reaffirmed), *Flight to Objectivity*, 45–6.

[14] F. Bacon, *Of the Advancement and Proficience of Learning or the Partitions of Sciences*. Interpreted by Gilbert Wats (Oxford, 1640), 1, 38–9, 2.

the writings of Puritan moralists to the satire of Voltaire's *Candide*.[15]

From Blake's point of view Bacon's exalted vision of labour, like the new epistemology, actually tends to undermine individual creativity. Such labour can only become effective if the powers of vision are suppressed, as Bacon himself explains: 'For God defend that we should publish the ayery dreams of our own Fancy, for the reall Ideas of the World! But rather may he be so graciously propitious unto us, that we may write the Apocalyps, and true vision of the impressions and signets of the Creator, upon the Creature!'[16] The goal is material understanding, to which any intrinsic delight in activity is strictly subordinate. Man is closest to the divine vision when he has surrendered his creativity most completely, and can 'Rest' in contemplation of the 'true vision' he has unearthed.

In Blake's narrative a comparable vision of progress begins to emerge in the confrontation between Tharmas and the Spectre:

> Go Forth said Tharmas works of joy are thine   obey & live
> So shall the spungy marrow issuing from thy splinterd bones
> Bonify. & thou shalt have rest when this thy labour is done
> Go forth bear Enitharmon back to the Eternal Prophet
> Build her a bower in the midst of all my dashing waves
> Make first a resting place for Los & Enitharmon. then
> Thou shalt have rest.
>
> (49: 15–21, E333)

'Bonify' means to make or turn into good, and in particular, to turn evil into good. The Neoplatonist Ralph Cudworth used the term to express the conviction that evils arise 'from the *Necessity* of *Imperfect Beings*' and can be turned to goodness, 'making them like *Discords* in *Musick*, to contribute to the *Harmony* of the *Whole*'.[17] In this context the term implies a new attitude to action. In the cosmos 'regions of dark death' are illuminated and transformed by

---

[15] Voltaire endorses a stoical acceptance of the gospel of work in *Candide*: 'You are in right', said Pangloss; 'for when man was placed in the Garden of Eden, he was put there *ut operaretur eum*, to cultivate it; which proves that mankind was not created to be idle.' 'Let us work' said Martin, 'without disputing, it is the only way to render life supportable.' *Candidus, or All for the Best, translated from the French of M. Voltaire* (Edinburgh, 1773), 129. Milton, of course, emphasized that Adam had to work in Eden.

[16] Bacon, *Advancement and Proficience*, 38.

[17] R. Cudworth, *The True Intellectual System of the Universe* (London, 1678), 876.

divine power. But now the fallen world will no longer be tran-
scended in the contemplation of such power. Instead the effects
of the fall are to be ameliorated by individual effort. Ironically
the chaotic Tharmas is the first to imply that labour can be restora-
tive, the first to refer to Los as the 'Eternal Prophet'. It is he who
suggests that Los should take up 'the hammer of Urthona'. As in
Bacon, the ultimate incentive for labour is not delight in imaginative activity but an escape from perpetual agitation to a state
of 'rest'.

If Tharmas initiates the development of a new vision of destiny,
his vision does not extend beyond the 'dashing waves' of the
material world, in which all forms are ultimately delusive. If he
suggests the ethical basis of the emergent vision, it is the Spectre
who provides the spiritual basis, by connecting labour, and his own
existence, with a higher order of being in a new account of the fall
(49: 27–50: 27). In the first cycle of history Los was a passive
consumer of spiritual delights, but such passivity now occasions
self-reproach ('I slumber here in weak repose'). Whereas Los envisaged a prelapsarian condition in 'Gardens of Vala', the Spectre
envisages a quite different condition in 'Beulah'. Despite is name,
Beulah is not seen here as a garden paradise, but as a place of
labour and responsibility: the Spectre remembers working as a
blacksmith at the forge, a father serving a community.[18] There is a
new sense of organization and culture in this vision (as before, the
fall is conceived in terms of a war in heaven, but the Spectre hears
'symphonies' rather than 'clarions of war'). Remarkably, love is not
a cause of the fall, but a manifestation of it, a feeling born of
separation and loss. Instead of describing a vision of seduction or
usurpation, the Spectre attributes his own loss of creative power to
the retreat of Tharmas. In this view the original 'COMMERCE OF THE
MIND AND OF THINGS' has indeed been lost, as Tharmas has withdrawn into chaos. As a consequence, the Spectre is separated from
Enitharmon (his struggle to free himself from what he sees as the
horrific pipes and caverns of the body merely confirms this separation). He describes himself as issuing from the nostrils of Enion,

---

[18] The name Beulah derives from Isaiah 62, and means 'married'. In Bunyan's
Pilgrim's Progress it lies beyond the valley of the Shadow of Death and out of reach
of the Giant Despair. The pilgrims there 'heard continually the singing of birds and
saw every day the flowers appear in the earth'. *Grace Abounding and The Pilgrim's
Progess*, ed. R. Sharrock (Oxford, 1966), 264.

rather than from the womb, as a spiritual exhalation rather than a corporeal being. But Enitharmon 'strove in vain' against the body. This account is, after all, another version of the rape of Enitharmon: it defines—and rationalizes—the gulf between spirit and body within the new world-view.

The Spectre's account of the fall betrays a growing sense of the body as a labyrinthine prison that threatens to trap human consciousness within it. Although he sees himself as having escaped the body's confines, the division he describes between himself and Enitharmon heralds a new interiorization of the mind. In Blake's narrative, as we shall see, once Man begins to rebuild his world, the body becomes the outward bound of experience, and reason is circumscribed by it as by a terrible prison. Many writers have commented on the sense of mental inwardness that accompanies the Cartesian division between mind and body. As Susan Bordo explains, the body becomes part of the external world, part of what is 'out there', while the construction of experience is thought of as occurring 'deeply *within* and bounded by a self'.[19] The Spectre's horror of the material world offers no way out of the Caverns of the Grave: it can only promote further repression. But the Spectre's protective nature is also emphasized: he sees himself as the preserver of Tharmas, and Tharmas commissions him to protect Los and Enitharmon. His vision of higher possibilities and of the essential dignity of labour helps to reconcile Man to a life that would otherwise be mere decay and death. It is the Spectre who returns Enitharmon to Los, and enables Los to stand on 'solid rocks' in the midst of Tharmas's dashing waves. The distinction between Los and his Spectre points to the doubleness of vision that seems fundamental to the scientific world-view—the tendency both to accept and reject the material world as the horizon of knowledge; to exclude notions of purpose and value from the study of nature, while using them to justify that study. Man now has two conflicting standards of reality, and he cannot escape confusion as long as he seeks to reconcile them.

In reviewing this part of the narrative, one can see that it has many parallels with the events of the first cycle. As before, it is through Enitharmon that Los is drawn into the 'indignant power'

---

[19] Bordo, *Flight to Objectivity*, 49.

of a tyrannical god. A new era begins with a tempestuous sexual union, as Tharmas takes possession of Enitharmon. The reunion of Los and Enitharmon parallels the reconciliation brought about by Urizen in the first cycle, after Enitharmon had suffered violence. There the unity was expressed in the spontaneous harmony of Elemental Gods, but in this new era it is only through work that Man becomes at one with his world. Tharmas promises Los a reward that must be earned:

> All the Elements shall serve thee to their soothing flutes
> Their sweet inspiriting lyres thy labours shall administer
> And they to thee only
>
> (52: 3-5, E335)

The elemental music, no longer the expression of a sense of community, has become a hard-won palliative exclusive to the labouring individual.

Reconstruction

As in the description of Urizen's Golden World, Blake draws on Milton's accounts of divine and satanic creation to describe the reconstruction of Man's world. The relationship between Tharmas and Los parallels that between the Father and the Son in *Paradise Lost*, although the parallel is complicated by allusions which conflate contrasting Miltonic contexts. For example, in Milton, the Son appears 'with radiance crowned' (*PL*vii: 194) as he undertakes the task of creation; the fallen Satan appears with 'eyes | That sparkling blazed' (*PL*i: 193-4) as he contemplates the regrouping of his scattered powers that will lead to the creation of a separate kingdom. In Blake the two contexts are evoked simultaneously with grim irony: Los appears with 'sparks issuing from his hair' as he receives from Tharmas the commission to reconstruct the world. As in the first cycle, the conflation of contexts implies an infernal criticism of Milton. It may remind us that although the Son's creation is presented as a manifestation of divine goodness and wisdom it is—like Satan's—removed from heaven (founded in the abyss) and a place of subjection (where the inhabitants can be 'under long obedience tried' (*PL*vii: 159).

Seen in mythical terms, an account of life that derives all knowledge from the chaotic flux of sensation not only makes chaos the creative principle, but also makes reason itself an unformed chaos initially. The retreat of Tharmas at 52: 7–10 recalls the withdrawal of Chaos that precedes the Son's act of creation in *Paradise Lost* (VII: 295–8). Milton's Chaos exists because, as Fowler puts it, God chooses 'not to extend his form-giving goodness' (see *PL*VII: 166–71).[20] In Blake the chaotic Tharmas chooses not to extend his form-denying power, so that a void space for creation can be found. In this way Tharmas re-enacts the withdrawal described by the Spectre. Subsequently Tharmas is usually seen as fugitive and evanescent in the Caverns of the Grave, as he evades the categories of order that arise in his realm.

Los now assumes the role of creator, and his creative activities are contrasted at every point with those of Urizen in the cosmos (as in *Urizen*, the contrast recalls the two accounts of creation in Genesis, Elohist and Jahwist). Urizen created an ideal system, and functioned at a distance as a guiding influence; his 'Bands of Heaven' formed 'anvils of gold' in order to create the heavenly bodies from the substance of Luvah. Los has no such majestic control over his world. He is placed firmly within it, working with his own hands 'in the wars of Tharmas', attempting to derive order from the ceaseless strife of the material world. One of the most paradoxical aspects of Blake's sequence here is that the imagery of divine creation is used to suggest the negation of divine power. The technique is comparable to Milton's personification of Chaos as an enthroned sovereign who keeps residence upon his frontiers (*PL*II: 959–1009). There are several allusions to Milton's figure in the portrait of Tharmas. Los does not endow phenomena with life, but rather deprives them of it: 'Los formd Anvils of Iron petrific. for his blows | Petrify with incessant beating many a rock. many a planet' (52: 18–19, *E*335). The exclusion of qualitative considerations from reality produces a quantitative world in which all of the components have the same ontological status. In place of Urizen's divine, animated hierarchy, Los creates an inert world that is organized horizontally, as all forms, from planets to rocks, are petrified into equivalent deadness. These material forms become the anvils upon which human reason will now be shaped.

[20] *The Poems of John Milton*, ed. J. Carey and A. Fowler (London and New York, 1968, 1972), 785.

Time and Energy

Blake's account of human development in the first era of history includes successive forms of energy related to Tharmas and Luvah: in the primitive stage, nature is animated by an immanent divine power that is unregulated by a premeditated design, an energy that derives from Tharmas and his Spectre; in the cosmos nature is animated by a divine power that is always subject to the constraints of an intelligible order, an energy that derives from Luvah who is controlled by Urizen. In the Caverns of the Grave there is a comparable movement from the energy of Tharmas to the energy of Luvah.

After the collapse of the cosmos, Luvah is 'hidden in the Elemental forms of Life & Death' (51: 13), and natural energy derives once more from Tharmas. As we have seen, in this chaotic world the energy of Tharmas is neither divine nor regulated by a designing intelligence: it is a merely natural power that finds expression in instinctual drives. This vision of energy becomes operative in Los's world in the rape of Enitharmon which, like the sexual myth of Night I, recalls both the 'brooding wings' of the spirit of God in *Paradise Lost* (PLVII: 235) and the impregnation of the earth by the ocean (PLVII: 279–80). The sequence of Blake's narrative suggests that before the complex mental activities of the human organism can be seen to derive from such an energy, a new understanding of time must appear.

The static, finite world of the cosmos did not exclude a sense of foreboding about the future pattern of history, but it allowed that pattern to be foreseen. Time, like everything else, seemed to be subject to the decree and purposes of the divine creator (*see* 38: 7–10, E326). But in a world-view which formally excludes such purposes from its account of reality, time becomes merely a measurable continuum, its measured units merely links in an ever-lengthening chain. Los, having produced a bedrock of stable form out of the chaos of matter, now works to establish such an awareness of time, forming

> under his heavy hand the hours
> The days & years. in chains of iron round the limbs of Urizen
> Linkd hour to hour & day to night & night to day & year to year
> In periods of pulsative furor.
>
> (52: 29–53: 3, E335)

Los's activity is consolidated by the Spectre, who pours 'molten iron' around the limbs of Enitharmon and the bones of Urizen, like the power of memory that conserves momentary forms of experience as fixed patterns. Los's 'Links of fate' define the future scope of reason. They imply a fatalistic acceptance of the natural limits of knowledge, a confinement within a temporal realm of efficient causes, as Bacon recommends:

Man being the Minister and Interpreter of Nature, acts and understands so far as he has observed of the order; for no Power is able to loose or break the Chain of Causes; nor is Nature to be Conquer'd but by submission.[21]

Under Los's hammer time does not flow from an initiating act of divine creation, but becomes limitless, 'an endless chain' (53: 28). This transformation has some parallels with the emergence of a new awareness of time during the Enlightenment, when scientists and philosophers abandoned the biblical account of natural origins, and began to contemplate an immense time-scale for the creation of the world. The new understanding of time made possible a new vision of human development. In Rousseau's *Discourse on Inequality*, for example, the power of reason is seen as the product of a very long evolutionary process: 'we may judge how many thousand Ages must have been requisite to develop successively the operations, which the Human Mind is capable of'.[22] In Rousseau's account this development is by no means certain or preordained; it is a process that, as Paul Cantor says 'involves many historical accidents and which therefore has an element of arbitrariness in it'.[23] In Blake's myth the new view of time allows human life to be seen as the result of an evolutionary process that proceeds through seven 'ages' (54: 1–55: 9, E336–7). As the Eternal mind is bounded by Los's labours, so its development becomes inextricably linked to the gradual evolution of the body. The evolutionary process is not governed by a foreseeing intelligence but by tormented instinct: anguish, fright, and fear drive the developing organism to writhe, sink, shoot out branches, enclose, and petrify itself, to assume a cavernous form that protects and stifles its identity. Through the irresistible urgency of the impulse for self-protection, the body becomes in every sense

---

[21] *The Philosophical Works of Francis Bacon*, transl. P. Shaw, 3 vols. (London, 1733), ii. 16.
[22] Rousseau, *Inequality*, 48.
[23] P. Cantor, *Creature and Creator: Myth-Making and English Romanticism* (Cambridge, 1984), 6.

the outward bound of consciousness. Its materiality impinges on the mind as never before. Bones, nerves, the circulatory system, the organs of sense—anatomized as the preconditions of conscious-ness—all assume a nightmarish distinctness, while all are bound mysteriously together around the 'dismal woe' of the self. The only signs of hope are associated with the development of the 'Two ears', the doors through which speech can enter.

Blake's imagery of conglobing, upheaving, and sinking in this sequence is derived from Milton's description of the motions that determine the shape of the earth (*PL*vii: 237–42; 276 ff.). In Milton, of course, the motions fulfil a divine intention. Here they result in a form which Los neither plans nor controls. In the first cycle, the imagery of generation and the imagery of construction represented two quite different stages in Man's perception of his world. Here the two kinds of imagery are brought together to suggest the paradoxical nature of the new world-view: in the power of Tharmas and Los, Man labours industriously to bind himself to an evolutionary view of his own life.

The conclusion of Los's labour, the sabbath of rest, is ironically marked by his turning to face the west—to face the prospect of death. In transforming Urizen, Los also transforms his own vision of the world and is inevitably conditioned by his own labour: 'He became what he was doing he was himself transformd' (55: 23, *E*338). In a remarkable passage Los loses his will as he becomes subject to the mechanical reflexes of the body:

> Spasms siezd his muscular fibres writhing to & fro his pallid lips
> Unwilling movd as Urizen howld his loins wavd like the sea
> At Enitharmons shriek his knees each other smote & then he lookd
> With stony Eyes on Urizen & then swift writhd his neck
> Involuntary to the Couch where Enitharmon lay
> The bones of Urizen hurtle on the wind the bones of Los
> Twinge & his iron sinews bend like lead & fold
> Into unusual forms dancing & howling stamping the Abyss
>
> (55: 28–35, *E*338)

The indeterminacy of Blake's syntax makes it impossible to decide where one clause ends and another begins—whether, for example, Los's loins wave in response to Urizen's howl or to Enitharmon's shriek. This sense of different activities merging seems appropriate, as all human activities, from speech to sex, now exist on the same level, and are determined by purely natural drives.

This grotesque view of human life as subject to powerful natural forces beyond the will presents a stark contrast to the hierarchical vision of the cosmos, where reason was divine and subordinated each aspect of experience to its will. Nevertheless Los has given a definite form to error, and has hammered out a new basis upon which life can develop. Like the Circle of Destiny, this new naturalistic view of existence will serve as a limit to Man's fall. It is a limit that will be progressively clarified as Man's subsequent history unfolds.

4

The Progress of Prophecy

Visions of Energy

In the first cycle Man's awareness of the energy that gives life to his world develops through several phases. After the union of Enion with the Spectre, the vital source of life seems completely submerged in the natural world. Once Man has become aware of the passions, reason descends to exert its restraining and harmonizing influence, and each aspect of nature is seen to have its own spiritual life: the world is animated by Elemental Gods. There is no clear distinction between nature and its divine energy until Urizen builds the cosmos, and Luvah is cast into the furnaces of affliction. At this stage Man begins to think of energy as a distinct power that operates within the limits of an orderly system.

In the Caverns of the Grave there is a comparable development in Man's awareness. As before, at first he has no conception of energy as a distinct entity. Luvah is 'hidden in the Elemental forms of Life & Death' (51: 13, E334). Tharmas is the ultimate source of the chaotic motion that animates the material world, and he is now a natural rather than a divine power. His rape of Enitharmon leads to the evolution of Urizen's body, and under his influence all manifestations of human energy are reduced to the level of automatic reflexes. But as soon as reason begins to stir into life it makes its influence felt—Los dances as Urizen howls—and a new consciousness of energy begins to emerge. Blake's sequence parallels the sequence of creation in Milton. In *Paradise Lost* the evolution of the earth is followed by the generation of organic life; in Blake's narrative the evolution of Urizen's body is followed by the eruption of a vigorous new-born energy in the form of Orc. The pattern implies that Orc is the child of Tharmas; conceived in the rape of Enitharmon, and that Los is strictly a foster father, as Joseph was to Jesus. The birth is heralded at the beginning of Night V by Los's dance upon his mountains. This grotesque muscular spasm forms an ironic parallel with the joyful annunciations in the Bible, such as the 'leaping upon the mountain' which announces the coming of a loved one in The Song of Solomon 8: 2, and the appearance of beautiful feet upon the mountain in Isaiah 32: 7, which heralds the coming of peace and salvation. With the birth of Orc energy is once again experienced as a distinct power that must be contained within a fixed order, and nature is animated by spiritual presences.

Fixed Space

Orc is a new manifestation of Luvah, and—as in the first cycle—Luvah appears within the natural world after Man has arrived at a new perception of space. The body is now the outward bound of experience, and vision is limited to a fixed point of view. As Los and Enitharmon shrink into fixed space, so their world begins to assume a more definite topography. A landscape of mountains and valleys appears, in which they journey to and fro between fixed and named locations. Los and Enitharmon no longer have godlike powers, although 'mighty bulk & majesty & beauty remain' (57: 13, E339). They are seen more clearly as figures *in* a landscape, and their activities in this limited environment are sometimes recognizably domestic. In short, the perspective of the myth becomes in several respects more naturalistic.

In the cosmos there was a clear distinction between Urizen's world of ideal forms and the chaotic realm of Tharmas. In Los's new world existence is polarized between the consciousness of the Spectre, who sees himself as an immaterial power (and who appears on 'the iron mountains top'), and the unexpansive world of mere sensory experience (associated with Enitharmon and 'the dark deeps'). Man's power to change his condition seems lost: 'all the furnaces were out & the bellows had ceast to blow' (57: 17, E339). He thus arrives at a new sense of permanence in his life. Los has created a world in which new life will be forced to struggle unsuccessfully against iron limits, a world that is inherently tragic: the fate of Orc recalls not only that of Isaac in Genesis, but also of the tragic heroes Oedipus and Prometheus.[1]

---

[1] The infant Oedipus was abandoned on a mountain by his father, with ankles tied and bound; Prometheus was bound down on a rocky mountain by the divine blacksmith Hephaestus.

The world of fixed space seems more machine-like than the mathematical construct of the cosmos, because its energy seems without purpose, like the blind momentum of a flywheel: 'The wheels of turning darkness | Began in solemn revolutions' (58: 7–8, E339). But although Man can think of natural energy as blindly mechanical, it proves impossible for him to experience it in this way. The qualitative aspects of energy, formally expelled from nature, reassert themselves in the realm of desire. The birth of the fiery child Orc suggests the awakening in Man of an intensely passionate experience of life. In the light of such experience, nature comes to appear neither blind nor mechanical, but organic, purposeful, and holy, a realm of infinite possibilities. Orc therefore becomes an anomaly, a power that is both natural and divine. He is subject to the natural processes of birth and growth, dependent on the material realm that the Spectre regards as corrupt and fallen. But he exceeds the limits of that realm. His sublime energy and the inert world from which it springs are fundamentally at odds, and a reconciliation between them proves exceptionally difficult to achieve. Luvah was quickly (if violently) absorbed into the cosmos, a divine power contained within a divine system. The second cycle of history is much longer than the first because in the Caverns of the Grave the mechanisms of containment are more elaborate and their consequences even more devastating.

Immortal Harps and Horrid Trumpets

With the birth of Orc a pattern of musical imagery that runs through the poem as a whole begins to come into focus. The pattern can be understood in relation to Milton's musical imagery. In *Paradise Lost* and some of the minor poems, Milton associates music with the principle of harmonious order in the universe. But as he is concerned with the disruptive effects of the fall, the musical celebrations in his works are often preludes to discord. In *Paradise Lost* the elevation of the Son as great viceregent is celebrated by a mystical dance to the 'harmony divine' of the spheres, and by 'Melodious hymns', but even as the hymns are performed Satan begins to conspire against the heavenly order (*PL*v: 657ff.). At the creation of the world the angelic hierarchies sing 'Glory . . . to the most high, good will | To future men' (*PL*vii:

182–3), but the poem has already shown that God foresees the fall of man. The creation of Pandæmonium in Hell is accompanied by 'the sound | Of dulcet symphonies and voices sweet' (*PLi*: 711–12), a sweetness that quite belies the Satanic nature of the construction and that gives no hint of its eventual ruin. The existence of evil implies that before the Last Judgement all celebrations of harmonious order are in a sense premature. This is acknowledged most clearly in the hymn 'On the Morning of Christ's Nativity', where Milton develops an imaginative opposition between angelic harmony and the disruptive sound of the trumpet. The hymn celebrates the birth of Jesus in the dead of winter when nature is 'confounded' at her own deformities. The incarnation brings an interlude of peace in which 'The trumpet spake not to the armed throng'. Under the influence of the 'angelic symphony', Nature

> Now was almost won
> To think her part was done,
> And that her reign had here its last fulfilling;
> She knew such harmony alone
> Could hold all heaven and earth in happier union.
> ('On the Morning of Christ's Nativity', 104–8)

This unifying harmony may stir thoughts of an imminent return to the golden age, but such hopes are fanciful. Before the promise of universal peace can be realized

> The wakeful trump of doom must thunder through the deep
>
> With such a horrid clang
> As on Mount Sinai rang
> While the red fire, and smould'ring clouds out brake
>   (156–9)

The contrast between serene harmony and warlike trumpet no longer expresses the triumph of angelic peace over earthly strife, but two aspects of divinity. The God who comes in peace will return in wrath. The trumpet is destined to rouse the earth from sleep, and to shatter temporal order completely.

In *The Four Zoas* Blake develops a similar contrast between musical harmony and clarions of war. As harmony depends on selection and exclusion it becomes associated with the delusive urge for a stable vision of life.[2] Any attempt to create a fixed order is shown to involve the repression of energy, and there are many indications that repressed energy will eventually reassert itself with apocalyptic violence. The Clarions of War that echo through the poem herald this inevitable reaction. The distinction between the two kinds of music sharpens as the narrative unfolds. In the revised copperplate text, the clarions are heard as Man turns his attention to the spheres, those traditional symbols of harmonious order: Enitharmon says 'We hear the warlike clarions we view the turning spheres' (10: 7, E305). When Urizen is about to descend 'The warlike clarions ceast' (12: 2, E306), and a spontaneous harmony subsequently prevails at the feast of Los and Enitharmon (13: 20–14: 5, E308). Fairchild describes the Nuptial Song as 'literally a Grand Chorus', its 'doubling' and 'Responsing' voices suggesting a choral orchestration.[3] The song blends in harmony the voices of Gods and Demons, but this marriage of heaven and hell is delusive. The 'Spirits of Flaming fire on high' may govern the song, but the Demons of the Deep provide an infernal commentary on the action, revealing the destructive implications of Urizen's descent. The Song of the Demons celebrates the perversion of human energies in universal warfare, and asserts that while the warlike passions can be melted, Luvah cannot be permanently repressed—a prophecy that portends the eventual collapse of Urizen's orderly creation: the Clarions of War provide the final notes of the music.

The order and harmony of the cosmos are thus shown from the outset to be provisional, doomed to collapse. In constructing his system Urizen exerts his power absolutely over Luvah, and the turbulent clarions are silenced:

> many a soothing flute
> Is form'd & many a corded lyre, outspread over the immense
> In cruel delight they trap the listeners, & in cruel delight
> Bind them, condensing the strong energies into little compass
> (30: 2–5, E319)

---

[2] Blake's use of musical references is coloured by his association of harmony with rationalism and law, as B. H. Fairchild notes (although it is not limited by this association): *Such Holy Song: Music as Idea, Form and Image in the Poetry of William Blake* (Kent, Oh., 1980), 5.

[3] Ibid. 68.

Harmony has become a powerfully seductive force which threatens to draw all aspects of human life into Urizen's system. Los and Enitharmon succumb to its beauty (34: 1–2, E322), and Enitharmon's song is a triumphant celebration of its power to repress through enchantment (34: 58–92, E323–4). But the music is not able to silence the voice of Enion or soothe the fears of Ahania, and the cosmos inevitably collapses with a 'horrible din' (44: 9, E329).

In the Caverns of the Grave the urge towards order is again expressed in musical terms. As we saw in the last chapter, when Tharmas makes his covenant with Los music is seen as a reward for labour (52: 1–5, E335). The world that Los builds in the midst of Tharmas's waves is not a beautifully proportioned system, but a petrified mass enclosing stifled energy. The harmony that appears in it is not a seductive force that draws in and condenses energy, but a sedative that strives to prevent 'Enraged & stifled' energy finding expression (55: 6, E337). Its delusive nature is revealed in Night V where sweet music swells in a futile attempt to soothe the birth pangs of Enitharmon:

Her pale hands cling around her husband & over her weak head
Shadows of Eternal death sit in the leaden air

But the soft pipe the flute the viol organ harp & cymbal
And the sweet sound of silver voices calm the weary couch
Of Enitharmon but her groans drown the immortal harps
Loud & more loud the living music floats upon the air
Faint & more faint the daylight wanes.

(58: 1–6, E339)

The passage offers an ironic contrast to the peaceful nativity celebrated in Milton's hymn. The Clarions of War, stilled by Urizen's cosmos, erupt violently into the Caverns of the Grave when Orc is born, threatening the new order:

Soon as his burning Eyes were opend on the Abyss
The horrid trumpets of the deep bellowd with bitter blasts
The Enormous Demons woke & howld around the new born king

(58: 19–21, E339)

The Song of the Demons of the Deep gives voice to Man's repressed fears and unacknowledged desires. It is a sequel to the 'Nuptial Song', and it associates the fall and division of Urthona with the seductive influence of Vala. In the larger context of the poem it can be seen as a self-fulfilling prophecy, since the characterization of Vala as a powerful war goddess reasserts the conviction that the passions are dangerous, a conviction which motivates the repression that creates war. When Vala is reborn later in the poem, the intimations of war that have echoed through the earlier Nights will erupt into the foreground of the narrative, as a prelude to the Trumpet of the Last Judgement.

The Birth of Desire

The bleak world into which Orc is born is a state of nature quite unlike the primitive world in which Los and Enitharmon once wandered as children. It is not a state of unorganized innocence, but a state of experience. Although it precedes the redevelopment of organized society, it has the experience of civilization behind it and within it, like the new world of Noah, or the state through which the children of Israel pass on their exodus from Egypt. In this it seems analogous to those visions of human origins which, according to Rousseau, 'have transferred to the State of Nature Ideas picked up in the bosom of Society'.[4] The centre of interest in this world is not the natural man who lives for himself, but natural man as parent: the family emerges as the primary model of communal living. In this state the child does not develop through a random exploration of the environment, or move beyond the range of parental control as Los and Enitharmon once did. The centre of appetite in the narrative shifts from Los to Orc, who is never free to wander or to feed himself. Appetite is now conditioned by the immediate presence of those who feed it, and while Orc is in the care of his parents, his desire inevitably becomes 'Concenterd into Love of Parent Storgous Appetite Craving' (61: 10, E341; *Storge* is the Greek word for parental affection).[5]

As in *Urizen*, the binding of Orc shows the consolidation of the emotional bases on which a moral order will subsequently be built. In this new context the myth is significantly revised. Whereas *Urizen* showed the emergence of pity before the birth of Orc, in the new account pity begins to emerge as a dominant force after Orc

---

[4] Rousseau, *Inequality*, 9.
[5] See S. F. Damon, *A Blake Dictionary* (London, 1973), 388. Damon notes that Blake could have found the word in Swedenborg's *Conjugal Love*.

has been bound. In this respect the sequence can be read as an account of the natural progress of feeling which, like many other accounts, from Lucretius to Rousseau, emphasizes the softening effect of parental relationships.[6] Here the process is developed in terms which offer a complex reinterpretation of the Bible.

In relation to the fixed and unexpansive world that Los has created, the emergence of desire is a 'wonder' as fascinating and as dangerous as a volcanic eruption: Orc springs forth 'In thunder smoke & sullen flames & howlings and fury & blood' (58: 18, E339). For Los this development is terrifying since it challenges the established limits of his world, beyond which he can see nothing: he fears 'Eternal Death & uttermost Extinction' (60: 2, E340). In trying to protect both Orc and Enitharmon, to foster desire and to preserve the *status quo*, he is driven to make a series of compromises that quickly exhausts his ability to act.

As a natural power the raging energy of desire is dependent, passive, totally absorbed in the blind satisfaction of its immediate needs: Los at first takes Orc 'down into the deeps' where the child is nursed and fed by Enitharmon in darkness. As desire grows, so it seems more threatening, and Los is moved to guard Enitharmon:

> Los around her builded pillars of iron
> And brass & silver & gold fourfold in dark prophetic fear
> For now he feard Eternal Death & uttermost Extinction
> He builded Golgonooza on the Lake of Udan Adan
> Upon the Limit of Translucence then he builded Luban
> Tharmas laid the Foundations & Los finishd it in howling woe
> (59: 28–60: 5, E340)

This is probably the earliest surviving occurrence of the name Golgonooza in Blake's work. In later references Golgonooza becomes an extremely complex symbol whose function is elaborated in considerable detail. Here its significance is suggested only by the dramatic context and by the allusive quality of the name. The

---

[6] In Lucretius's account of natural development humanity first began to mellow when male and female learnt to live together in a stable union and to watch over their joint progeny, *Lucretius Carus of the Nature of Things* i. 550–1 (book V: lines 1075–88). Hume asserts that 'Tenderness to . . . offspring . . . is commonly able alone to counterbalance the stongest motives of self-love', *Enquiries*, 300. Rousseau argues that 'The first Developments of the Heart were the Effect of a new Situation, which united Husbands and Wives, Parents and Children, under one Roof; the Sweetest Sentiments the human Species is acquainted with, conjugal and paternal Love', *Inequality*, 108.

dominant suggestion appears to be the discovery of hope in the face of extinction. The name recalls Golgotha, the site of Christ's crucifixion, although Nelson Hilton has suggested that the word is an anagram of the Greek *logon zooa[s]*, the 'living word' (Philippians 2: 16).[7] The lake of Udan Adan, as Frye suggests, is possibly an allusion to the pool of Bethesda, where sick men wait in hope of a cure, and where Jesus healed one who had faith. Raine has pointed out that the name Luban is identified in Bryant's *Mythology* as one of the names of 'the Arkite moon', a symbol of Noah's ark and therefore of humanity's escape from total destruction in the flood. Blake's contemporary, Alexander Geddes, argued that before the Hebrews had written documents their history was transmitted either orally or by 'monumental indexes' such as pillars, which served as links to hand tradition down to posterity.[8] The fourfold structure recalls the traditional division of fallen history into four ages, and perhaps more specifically the dream of Daniel (2: 31–45), a vision in which four periods of subjection are followed by the appearance of the kingdom of God. These hints suggest that in building Golgonooza Los founds a prophetic tradition: responding to the fires of Orc he gives history a shape that implies the eventual fulfilment of desire (which means that desire becomes subject to time). The reference to 'the Limit of Translucence' suggests that Golgonooza is built at the lowest possible level of inspiration. Los does not contemplate an immediate transformation of his world. On the contrary, he builds his pillars 'around' Enitharmon, presumably in order to preserve her from transformation. His vision is grounded firmly in the fallen world.

The compromise of Golgonooza soon proves inadequate. As Orc reaches maturity he threatens to transform Los's world completely: 'Los beheld the ruddy boy | Embracing his bright mother'(60: 7–8, E340). This development is presented exclusively from Los's point of view, but there could be no 'objective' account here. In the youth Los sees his own unacted desire (as he contemplates the 'ruddy boy' his own brows are 'ruddy'). The state of nature begins to resemble a state of war as Los becomes convinced that Orc plots his death, and reacts in 'jealousy'. Orc is not restrained in the name of

[7] Hilton, *Literal Imagination*, 236.

[8] Frye, *Fearful Symmetry*, 380; Raine, *Blake and Tradition*, i. 232; Jacob Bryant, *A New System, or, an Analysis of Ancient Mythology* (3 vols.; London, 1774–6); Geddes, *Bible*, p. xix.

moral law, but in response to the natural urge for self-preservation.
In taking Orc from 'the dark deeps' and binding him on 'the
iron mountains top', Los renders desire subject to the Spectre's consciousness. This does not stifle desire, which continues to rage 'Louder & Louder'. But it allows Los to protect
Enitharmon:

> Los folded Enitharmon in a cold white cloud in fear
> Then led her down into the deeps & into his labyrinth
> Giving the Spectre sternest charge over the howling fiend.
>   (61: 7-9, E341)

The 'labyrinth' is presumably Golgonooza, now insulated from
Orc's fierce hunger.

As we have seen, the Spectre is that aspect of Los's consciousness
which harbours a crippling awareness of its own fallen condition,
and a conviction that the corrupt material world is dependent on
the protective influence of the immaterial spirit. Orc is thus guarded
by a power that denies his promise of fulfilment. In the Spectre's
power Orc remains essentially passive, while the pleasures of sense
are conveyed by spiritual powers:

> Concenterd into Love of Parent Storgous Appetite Craving
> His limbs bound down mock at his chains for over them a flame
> Of circling fire unceasing plays to feed them with life & bring
> The virtues of the Eternal worlds ten thousand thousand spirits
> Of life lament around the Demon going forth & returning
> At his enormous call they flee into the heavens of heavens
> And back return with wine & food. Or dive into the deeps
> To bring the thrilling joys of sense to quell his ceaseless rage
> His eyes the lights of his large soul contract or else expand
> Contracted they behold the secrets of the infinite mountains
> The veins of gold & silver & the hidden things of Vala
> Whatever grows from its pure bud or breathes a fragrant soul
> Expanded they behold the terrors of the Sun & Moon
> The Elemental Planets & the orbs of eccentric fire
> His nostrils breathe a fiery flame. his locks are like the forests
> Of wild beasts there the lion glares the tyger & wolf howl there
> And there the Eagle hides her young in cliffs & precipices
> His bosom is like starry heaven expanded all the stars
> Sing round. there waves the harvest & the vintage rejoices. the
>   Springs
> Flow into rivers of delight. there the spontaneous flowers
> Drink laugh & sing. the grasshopper the Emmet & the Fly

The golden Moth builds there a house & spreads her silken bed
His loins inwove with silken fires are like a furnace fierce
As the strong Bull in summer time when bees sing round the heath
Where the herds low after the shadow & after the water spring
The numrous flocks cover the mountain & shine along the valley
His knees are rocks of adamant & rubie & emerald
Spirits of strength in Palaces rejoice in golden armour
Armed with spear & shield they drink & rejoice over the slain
Such is the Demon such his terror in the nether deep

(61: 10–62: 8, E341–2)

This magnificent passage creates a disturbingly ambivalent impression of natural appetite. Man has reached a stage equivalent to the feast of Los and Enitharmon, gaining a new awareness of the abundance of his world as spirits bring Orc 'wine & food' and the 'thrilling joys of sense'.[9] But there are obvious contrasts with the earlier condition. The spirits who bring the 'virtues of the Eternal worlds', unlike the Elemental Gods who animated the world of Los and Enitharmon, are not exuberant and musical, but lamenting servants who 'flee' and 'back return' in response to the 'enormous call' of Orc's appetite. Their presence makes the ceaseless rage of desire seem not only glorious but tyrannical, and recalls the oppression of Urizen's cosmos, where 'spirits mournd their bondage night and day' (32: 13, E321). In his bound condition Orc is necessarily dependent, a devourer feeding on a prolific world. He may 'mock' at his chains, but his vision is defined by them. Los and Enitharmon could once expand and contract 'their all flexible senses', but Orc can apparently expand or contract only his sight. As Donald Ault points out, Orc's expansion and contraction is quite different from Los's and Enitharmon's.[10] While they had the ability to move through each part of their world, to 'murmur in the flowers small as the honey bee | At will to stretch across the heavens & step from star to star' (34: 11–12, E322), the immobilized Orc's vision explores a world that seems threatening and subject to mysterious constraints (expanded, his eyes see the 'terrors' of the heavenly bodies; contracted, they behold 'secrets' and the 'hidden things of Vala'). There are intimations of both innocence and experience in the description of Orc's body, but the images of abundance and of

---

[9] One source of this passage is Milton's account of creation (PLVII: 309–504): as in Milton the lion is the first named animal, and the eagle is given prominence as the sovereign of birds.

[10] Ault, Narrative Unbound, 200.

fierce, predatory energies are not contraries. Natural appetite is gratified by acquisition and conquest, as well as by the communal rejoicing of the harvest and vintage. Indeed, while desire is bound to a finite material world, peace and prosperity must be won and defended by cruelty and violence. In short, this is the desire that will inspire the exploration and exploitation of nature, the desire that will eventually fuel the construction of empire.

All the Sorrow Parents Feel

As soon as the male aspects of desire have been contained, the female aspects begin to make their influence felt. Free from the immediate pressure of desire, Los feels repentance:

> he thought to give to Enitharmon
> Her son in tenfold joy & to compensate for her tears
> Even if his own death resulted so much pity him paind
> (62: 18–20, E342)

In contrast to the instinctual pity of Tharmas, pity begins to emerge here as a contemplative emotion. It is a manifestation of the triumph of thought over spontaneous feeling, of the Spectre's rule over Orc. It promotes a rudimentary sense of justice, which transforms joy into a compensation for grief, and transforms the urge for self-preservation into an uncertain readiness for self-sacrifice. Such pity is a negation of the fiery desire it seeks to liberate. Los therefore finds that he cannot remove the chain of jealousy:

> for it had taken root
> Into the iron rock & grew a chain beneath the Earth
> Even to the Center wrapping round the Center & the limbs
> Of Orc entering with fibres. became one with him a living Chain
> Sustained by the Demons life
> (62: 32–63: 4, E342)

It becomes apparent that in taking Orc from the deeps up to the mountain top, Los has transformed him from a threat into an unrealizable ideal. In the Spectre's charge, Orc inspires and terrifies but cannot take complete possession of Man's consciousness. The divine inspiration that portends the consummation of the material world is jealously guarded and apparently neutralized. Having consigned Orc to the power of the Spectre, Los himself falls under the Spectre's protection. The reference to the 'herbs of the pit' which revive Los and Enitharmon shows how Orc's desire begins to stimulate research into 'hidden things'. The Spectre's primitive medicine foreshadows the development of more elaborate sciences which preserve and intensify the fallen condition they are intended to ameliorate (or 'Bonify').[11]

The emergence of a self-sacrificial pity heralds the reappearance of Vala prophesied by the Demons of the Deep:

> Enitharmon on the road of Dranthon felt the inmost gate
> Of her bright heart burst open & again close with a deadly pain
> Within her heart Vala began to reanimate in bursting sobs
> And when the Gate was open she beheld that dreary Deep
> Where bright Ahania wept. She also saw the infernal roots
> Of the chain of Jealousy & felt the rendings of fierce howling Orc
>
> (63: 11–16, E343)

History is beginning to fulfil Urizen's decree (38: 7–10, E326) and the demonic claim that 'the times return'. Los's new world had its origins in the rejection of Ahania's pity. With the binding of Orc, Vala begins to emerge as a more powerful form of pity, one that thrives on despair and loss, and that will eventually become a dominant power in human life.

The Natural History of Desire

Los's changing attitude to Orc defines an archetypal pattern that can be traced in both religious and secular discourses. Since the Renaissance, for example, speculative theories about the state of nature had shown a comparable development that could be read as a process of liberalization. In the Hobbesian state of nature individuals, governed by rampant appetites, are in a condition of war that can only be controlled by the rigid imposition of patriarchal power. In Locke the superiority of fathers is temporary—necessary only until the child has acquired sufficient reason to look after itself. In Rousseau individuals in the state of nature are swayed by

---

[11] In his enormously popular study of primitive medicine, John Wesley relates physical illness to original sin, and describes the progressive development of medicine from a traditional body of knowledge wholly founded on experiment to 'an abstruse science quite out of the reach of ordinary men': *Primitive Physick. Or an Easy and Natural Method of Curing most Deseases* (Bristol, 1770), pp. vii, ix.

pity rather than by violent passions; attention has shifted to the negative effects of the constraints imposed by social conditioning, and to the possibility of allowing the child to follow its own wishes.[12]

In religious terms the sequence defines a history of prophecy, which shows how prophets betray the image of divinity that inspires them. In the Bible the pattern can be traced as a broad (and by no means complete) transition from an urge to impose limits on disruptive desire, to an urge to release individuals from the constraints of a life of suffering and unfulfilment. The Old Testament vision of a promised land whose realization depends on sacrifice and strict regulation modulates into an eschatological vision of fulfilment that depends on repentance. In the world-view of Exodus God may appear within the natural world, but the sight of Him is normally fatal. The prophet must therefore act as a privileged intermediary. Orc's initial earth-shattering appearance recalls the terrifying theophany on Sinai, where Moses 'Set bounds upon the mount' in order to prevent the people from breaking through to the Lord (Exodus 19: 18, 24).[13] Los's three attempts to guard Enitharmon with pillars, cloud, and labyrinth, and his decision to leave Orc in the care of the Spectre, form a grim parallel with Moses' attempts to act as mediator between God and the Israelites in Exodus 24–8. In the biblical sequence the building of pillars is followed by a mountain-top encounter with the 'devouring fire' of God in the midst of a cloud (24: 17). The prophet then becomes absorbed in a system of labyrinthine complexity (receiving details of the design of the ark and the tabernacle), while the task of mediation devolves upon the priesthood (28: 1 ff.). For Moses the promised land remains an unrealized possibility; the vision of the later prophets becomes dominated by the loss of God's kingdom and the idea of restoring it. The demand for repentance, for a turning back to the Lord, displaces the demand for sacrifice (Isaiah 1: 11–17; Jeremiah 6: 20 and 7: 21–3; Amos 5: 21–4). Once Los's power of action has been spent in 'Despair & Terror & Woe & Rage' (63: 4, E342), he falls into a state of lamentation. Presumably

[12] See Hobbes, *Leviathan*, chs. 13 and 17; Locke, *A Second Treatise of Government*, ii. 61; Rousseau, *Inequality* and *Émile*.

[13] The description of the feeding of Orc by ten thousand thousand spirits, is modelled, as Morton D. Paley notes, after Daniel's vision of the Ancient of Days (7: 10). See *Energy and Imagination: A Study in the Development of Blake's Thought* (Oxford, 1970), 105.

Blake saw the preoccupation of Old Testament prophets with defeat and exile, and with the distress of the times, as records of this phase in Man's spiritual history. The myth implies that the promise of fulfilment is frustrated from the outset by the limited vision that shapes it, so that it becomes an ideal whose realization is indefinitely deferred.

Blake's sequence also contains many allusions to the New Testament. As we have seen, the birth of Orc corresponds to the nativity. The binding girdle of jealousy recalls the girdle of Acts 21: 11 which prefigures the binding of Paul (Acts 28: 17) and is a type of the binding of Jesus (Mark 15: 1), while the nailing of Orc corresponds to the crucifixion itself. Los and Enitharmon returning in haste from Golgonooza 'to their much beloved care' recall Joseph and Mary returning to Jerusalem to find the young Jesus who has remained in the temple (Luke 2: 41–50). Enitharmon's experience on the road of Dranthon, after the failure to release Orc, suggests Christ's appearance to his disciples on the road to Emmaus (Luke 24: 13–53), and Paul's conversion on the road to Damascus in Acts 9.[14] As an infernal reading of the New Testament, Blake's sequence identifies the birth of Jesus with a messianic hope that is transformed by the prophetic tradition that fosters it. The crucifixion, like the child's introduction to the temple, represents the triumph of orthodoxy over a revolutionary power. It changes a promise of immediate fulfilment into a preoccupation with self-sacrifice and loss.

The sequence establishes the emotional basis on which all further developments in the fallen world must be built. The natural progress from an apparently selfish appetite towards an apparently selfless pity will dominate the subsequent history of civilization. Unlike *Urizen*, the new myth will show that the central concern of fallen civilization—the concern around which its confusion intensifies—is not simply how to repress desire, but how to unbind it, how to liberate its potential for good.

[14] Ostriker (ed.), *Complete Poems*, 938.

5

The Progress of Reason

The Gates of Hell

Once Los's capacity to act has been exhausted, the focus of attention shifts to Urizen, who now has to develop in the conditions shaped by Los. He is 'shut up in the deep dens of Urthona' (63: 23, E343), subject to the limitations of the caverned body, and stirred into thought by the vibrations of natural appetite. His soliloquy at the end of Night V recalls Satan's in Book IV of *Paradise Lost* (32 ff.), in which the fallen archangel considers the prospect of Eden, and struggles to come to terms with the loss of heaven. Urizen's view of his unfallen existence creates a powerful contrast with his present condition, and suggests a partial recognition of error, but his vision is—like Satan's—limited and distorted. He is convinced that he can 'well remember', but has in fact been bound in 'Forgetfulness' (54: 4, E336). He regrets the loss of eternal wisdom but makes no mention of the expulsion of Ahania. He dwells not on the creative activity of eternal life, but on its sensuous pleasures:

> Once how I walked from my palace in gardens of delight
> The sons of wisdom stood around the harpers followd with harps
> Nine virgins clothd in light composd the song to their immortal
>   voices
> And at my banquets of new wine my head was crownd with joy
>
> Then in my ivory pavilions I slumberd in the noon
> And walked in the silent night among sweet smelling flowers
> Till on my silver bed I slept & sweet dreams round me hoverd
> But now my land is darkend & my wise men are departed
> (64: 1–8, E343)

Urizen's attempt to recall an original error appears to be leading him to a new acceptance of love and pleasure as holy, a positive response to the power of Orc. But this is merely the first stage in a process of recollection that proves to be circular. In retrospect his fall seems the result of both wilful action and a refusal to act:

> He gave to me a silver scepter & crownd me with a golden crown
> & said Go forth & guide my Son who wanders on the ocean
>
> I went not forth. I hid myself in black clouds of my wrath
> I calld the stars around my feet in the night of councils dark
> The stars threw down their spears & fled naked away
> We fell.
>
> (64: 23–8, E344)

This confused recollection might refer to Man's command in Night II (23: 5, E313), in which case Urizen has forgotten his own constructive labours. The conclusions drawn from this account seem more significant than the details. The process of recollection leads from the delights of rest to regret at inaction; the refusal to act becomes associated in turn with the indulgence of appetite and with loss of self-control. In this way Urizen moves from ideas of forgiveness ('chariots of mercies') to thoughts of punishment. He sees that Orc is Luvah, and concludes that Luvah has been bound 'even to the gates of hell' as result of a transgression:

> Because thou gavest Urizen the wine of the Almighty
> For steeds of Light that they might run in thy golden chariot of pride
> I gave to thee the Steeds   I pourd the stolen wine
> And drunken with the immortal draught fell from my throne sublime
>
> (65: 5–8, E344)

This account recalls Enitharmon's Song of Death (10: 10–13, E305), and Ahania's vision of the fall (39: 1–11, E326–7). The surrender of horses to Luvah, and Urizen's drunkenness, both imply a dangerous surrender to passion and pleasure. As his thoughts move from the communal joy of 'banquets of new wine' to the guilty pleasure of 'stolen wine', Urizen arrives once more at that fear of passivity, sensuous delight, and love which led him to reject Ahania. He thus finds justification for a new era of repressive activity.

As Urizen's confused recollection shows, his fear of Luvah coexists with a sense of Luvah's purity and life-giving power. Urizen remembers the unfallen Luvah and Urthona (the imaginative power) as guardians of eternal life, keepers of 'the living gates of heaven'. To Los such a vision might seem an image of the reality he has just created. Orc appears to be bound at the summit of the natural world, creating a vision of infinite fulfilment that inspires terror, despair, self-sacrificing love, and distant hope. Urthona, or rather his Spectre, is still a keeper of eternal life, watching over Orc as a prophet guards the vision of God. But to Urizen it appears that Orc is bound with Urthona in an infernal underworld: the gates of heaven have become the gates of hell because they appear to lead into a dark world of wilful error. To Urizen the 'deep pulsation' of Orc can only seem a source of endless and unnecessary torment. His final hope that 'love shall shew its root in deepest Hell' reveals a suspicion that even love's heavenly purity will prove to have been an infernal delusion.

A Journey Through Chaos

In the Caverns of the Grave, where knowledge is derived from experience, reason must begin its activities in a state of doubt. As Bacon explains, 'if a man will begin with certainties, he shall end in doubts; but if he will be content to begin with doubts, he shall end in certainties'.[1] Urizen, like Los, must therefore create a world out of chaos. The account of his difficult progress reflects some of the intellectual preoccupations and problems that appear with the rise of science in the seventeenth and eighteenth centuries, a period that provides many examples of the chaos from which the reasoning mind sees its own activities emerging. When Bacon looked at the legacy of scholastic philosophy he found a dizzying maelstrom of apparently groundless theorizing. When scientists examined the material world they found a realm of spiritless particles in continual motion, a realm that in some ways resembled that described by the Epicureans. Unlike the Greek atomists they found evidence of design in the world, but as Richard Westfall observes, 'their endlessly repeated confutation of materialistic atheism takes on the appearance of a quest for personal certainty'.[2] The evidence of design was itself called into question, most fundamentally in Hume's *Dialogues Concerning Natural Religion*. When Hume's Philo reflected on the natural environment he saw no mechanism that implied a benevolent creator, but a blind world full of 'maimed and abortive creatures' odiously hostile and destructive to each other.[3] Contem-

---

[1] Bacon, *Advancement of Learning*, 41 (book I, section v, paragraph 8).
[2] Westfall, *Science and Religion*, 108.
[3] Hume, *Writings on Religion*, 274.

porary social theory described civil order as the product of a state of barbarism which motivated the establishment of a strong central government. When Enlightenment sociologists and historians examined communities that existed without civil order they frequently saw inhumanity and ignorance: Gibbon recoiled from the barbarity of the ancient Germanic tribes; Robertson described a horrifying state of universal anarchy that had prevailed in every European country following the collapse of the Roman Empire.[4] In Night VI, Blake presents a journey through comparable visions of chaos towards what appears to be a redeeming stability and purpose. If Los is forced to betray his inspiration, Urizen is forced to compromise his doubt. As the reasoning power he moves inevitably towards civil order, a community based not on the model of the family (although it includes that model), but on the impersonal principle of law. And just as inevitably, he comes to develop a religion based not on inspiration (although it subsumes revealed religion) but on apparently reasonable evidences—that is, natural religion.

As we shall see, Urizen moves towards the world of Urthona in search of Orc, in a sequence that parallels Satan's journey through Chaos to Eden in *Paradise Lost*. The topographical explanation at 74: 14ff., *E*351 implies that he begins his journey in the West. He travels through the South and East before approaching Urthona's kingdom in the North, having traced a circle. He can only enter the realm of desire by passing through what he sees as the gates of hell, because he must pass beyond the limits of the finite material world. The narrative shows how he succeeds without abandoning his commitment to that world. On his journey he discovers once more a design in nature, and thus a designing providence. He finds, that is, his own vision of the infinite, a vision that does not threaten to consume the finite natural world, but is actually dependent on it. At the end of his journey Urizen can thus confront Orc with a rational alternative to self-torturing desire.

Urizen as Explorer

In the cosmos each aspect of life expresses a single creative intelligence. Urizen's sons and daughters obey his will, and their names

[4] See Gibbon, *Decline and Fall*, i. 230–55 (ch. 9); W. Robertson, *The Progress of Society in Europe*, ed. F. Gilbert (Chicago and London, 1972), 18.

are given to the halls and domes of his Golden World. In this creation everything that lives is holy, all creatures are instruments of divine power. Among those who perform the work of creation are 'the Lions of Urizen', 'leopards', the 'tygers of wrath', 'the Spider & Worm', 'the strong wing'd Eagles'. The system may be cruelly repressive, but within it nothing seems alien to the mind except the dark chaos of Tharmas.

The collapse of the cosmos reverses the relationship between Tharmas and Urizen. Tharmas is the true God of the Caverns of the Grave, because all knowledge is now derived ultimately from the sensible world (at 74: 21 we learn that he rolls his billows 'All thro the caverns', $E351$). Mind becomes secondary, and reasoning therefore involves, in Locke's words, 'search, and casting about, and requires Pains and Application'.[5] At every step of his journey Urizen finds the given data of experience resisting or opposing his efforts. All manifestations of life seem alien to each other (animal powers are now quite remote from human intelligence). There is no common purpose, no divine sanction for authority, no principle of cohesion apart from a coercive parental affection. As we have seen, in the Caverns of the Grave parents rule their children by force: Tharmas gains control over Los by an act of violence; Los chains Orc. All stability, order, and knowledge now appear to depend on such conquests. Night VI begins with a confrontation between Urizen and his daughters, and ends with a confrontation between Urizen and his sons.

At the beginning of a new era of activity Urizen appears not as a powerful god of a civilized community, but as a primitive hero armed with helmet and spear. The armour associates him with the armed 'Spirits of strength' who rejoice in the power of Orc (62: 6–7, $E342$). But Urizen's first action immediately makes clear that reason cannot be satisfied with the pleasures of natural appetite:

> taking off his silver helmet he filled it & drank
> But when unsatiated his thirst he assayd to gather more
> Lo three terrific women at the verge of the bright flood
> Who would not suffer him to approach
>
> (67: 3–6, $E345$)

These lines may allude to a similar incident in the sixth book of Richard Glover's *Leonidas*, where the Greek warrior Diomedon

---

[5] Locke, *Human Understanding*, 52 (book I, chapter ii, section 10).

receives the waters of a stream into his 'concave helm'. In Glover
the stream leads to the temple of the Muses, and a train of 'nine
bright virgins round their priestess ranged'.[6] In contrast, Urizen
finds no inspiration in nature, but a baffling sense of alienation. He
fails to recognize his daughters, just as Milton's Satan fails to
recognize his daughter Sin at the gates of Hell. Like Sin, the three
women seem both fair and terrible. In Blake the ambiguity suggests
a life-giving potential that is denied. The daughters seem generous:
the urn is poured forth abroad, the fountain is a symbol of life, the
four rivers recall the rivers of Eden (Genesis 2: 10; *PL*iv: 233).[7] But
they are also joyless and threatening: we may remember that there
are 'four infernal rivers' in Milton's hell (*PL*ii: 575), while the
daughter who 'stretchd her arms' recalls contemporary representations of Milton's Sin.[8] Urizen recalls how his daughters once reflected his own activity ('I pourd the beauties of my light... I
gave... I taught them... I invented... They pourd their radiance
above all', 68: 7–14, *E*345). Now he gives nothing. Like Orc he is
a devourer contemplating a prolific world, but in his case appetite
stimulates a search for knowledge. He no longer teaches, but asks
questions. The conviction that knowledge comes from without
transforms each aspect of experience from a source of inspiration
into an object of enquiry. The daughters thus assume an independent power. The name written on the forehead of the eldest associates her with the figure of Mystery in Revelation. The second is, like
the Virgin Mary, 'clad in blue', while her attractive power associates her with the moon (and hence with the Greek Fates, who
constitute a threefold Moon Goddess). The third is clad in green, a
colour associated with Venus, natural fertility, and envy. Their
appearance reflects the conviction that nature is governed by mysterious forces which, like the 'attractive power' of the moon, exert
their influence inexorably over human life. Together they have
begun to assume the sinister threefold appearance of the Fates in
Greek and Teutonic mythology.

Although there is a moment of recognition between parent and
children as 'Urizen raisd his spear' (68: 1–2, *E*345), the daughters

---

[6] R. Glover, *Leonidas*, 5th edn. (London, 1770), 204.

[7] For an erudite discussion of possible sources for this passage, see Raine, *Blake
and Tradition*, ii. 93–4.

[8] Cf. James Gillray's *Sin, Death, and the Devil*, which influenced Blake's own
Satan, Sin, and Death (*c.* 1808).

hide themselves from his eyes, and the waters that were poured 'forth abroad' dry up. Their retreat reflects his own withdrawal from creative involvement with the world. His curse entails an acceptance of the supremacy of Tharmas, Los, and Orc. He curses his children

> That they may curse Tharmas their God & Los his adopted son
> That they may curse & worship the obscure Demon of destruction
> That they may worship terrors & obey the violent
>
> (68: 24–6, E345–6)

Having acknowledged the supremacy of Tharmas, reason must now enter chaos and confront the full horror of a godless materialism, as Los did in Night IV. But there is a difference between these two confrontations. Los and Enitharmon inspired love and pity in Tharmas, who urged his son to 'choose life' (52: 2, E335). Los's creation is thus founded on the slender triumph of love over despair. Urizen on the other hand has renounced love, and attempts to view his world as coldly as possible: in his presence the waves of Tharmas 'froze to solid' (68: 30, E346). Having put himself beyond all positive influences he must confront a world in which there seems no shadow of hope. The swarming life of the sensible world is seen as an inexplicable futility, endlessly repeating itself to no purpose, a nightmare that makes universal death seem like a desirable release. The opening words of Tharmas's speech to Urizen echo the words of Satan's speech to Death in *Paradise Lost*.[9] But unlike Satan, Tharmas longs for a death that seems ever beyond his reach:

> The Body of Man is given to me I seek in vain to destroy
> For still it surges forth in fish & monsters of the deeps
> And in these monstrous forms I Live in an Eternal woe
>
> (69: 11–13, E346)

Tharmas of course reflects Urizen's own approach to experience. This is emphasized when Tharmas urges Urizen to choose death:

> Withhold thy light from me for ever & I will withold
> From thee thy food so shall we cease to be
>
> (69: 15–16, E346)

---

[9] Compare 'Whence and what art thou' (*PL*ii: 681) with 'What & who art thou' (69: 6).

It is because Urizen has already withheld his light that he confronts a realm of ever-shifting impressions that seems always to elude final definition. What Tharmas thinks of as death has become for Urizen the basis of life.

This confrontation with Tharmas, then, dramatizes the challenge that reason must meet in a material world that seems to offer no basis for hope or incentive for constructive action. At the beginning of his journey Urizen has no power to shape an alternative to the vision of life offered by Tharmas, no weapon with which to overcome despair (as soon as Tharmas arrives Urizen's spear darkens). Just as Milton's Satan 'stayed not to reply' to the speech of Chaos (*PL*ii: 1010), so Urizen 'replied not' to Tharmas but passes on his way (69: 23, *E*346). But throughout this Night he is preparing for conflict, and at the end he will be ready to confront Tharmas with apparently irresistible weapons.

The Ruined World

When Tharmas departed from Los in Night IV, Los became aware of Urizen 'In brooding contemplation'. Now the situation is reversed. After his encounter with Tharmas, Urizen continues on his journey to 'the dark world of Urthona' and becomes aware of Los:

> The howlings gnashings groanings shriekings shudderings sobbings
>   burstings
> Mingle together to create a world for Los. In cruel delight
> Los brooded on the darkness. nor saw Urizen with a Globe of fire
> Lighting his dismal journey thro the pathless world of death
> Writing in bitter tears & groans in books of iron & brass
> The enormous wonders of the Abysses once his brightest joy
> (69: 32–70: 4, *E*346–7)

As Donald Ault points out, the gerunds in the first line also appear in the descriptions of Los's binding of Urizen, Enitharmon, and Orc in Nights IV and V.[10] The prophet is now preoccupied with the terrible constraints that he himself has imposed; his 'cruel delight' is perhaps a reflection of the relish with which distress and desolation are sometimes threatened and recorded in biblical prophecy

[10] Ault, *Narrative Unbound*, 212–13.

(e.g. Isaiah 24: 1–12, Jeremiah 10: 19–25). These lines confirm that responsibility for shaping Man's future has passed from Los to Urizen, who is the only power that remains free to act. Urizen is no longer a warrior, but an observer. His globe of fire symbolizes an attitude to nature like that recommended by Bacon, for whom *'The spirit of man is as the lamp of God, wherewith he searcheth the inwardness of all secrets'*.[11]

Armed with his books Urizen enters the South, the eternal realm of reason and hence of civilization, now in ruins. It is now the site of the Cave of Orc, but Urizen can only approach Orc through the realm of Urthona in the North. At this point his vision resembles that of the Enlightenment sociologist who contemplates with horror the anarchy of a world without the benefit of arts and science and secure central government. Until he confronts Orc directly he can have no experience of the infinite visions of desire, but sees only the disastrous external consequences of raging natural appetite. What he observes remains essentially unknown, and can only be judged through its external appearances, the 'shapes & sights of torment' that appal the selfhood:

> Beyond the bounds of their own self their senses cannot penetrate
> As the tree knows not what is outside of its leaves & bark
> And yet it drinks the summer joy & fears the winter sorrow
> So in the regions of the grave none knows his dark compeer
> Tho he partakes of his dire woes & mutual returns the pang
> The throb the dolor the convulsion in soul sickening woes
>
> The horrid shapes & sights of torment in burning dungeons & in
> Fetters of red hot iron some with crowns of serpents & some
> With monsters girding round their bosoms. Some lying on beds of
>   sulphur
> On racks & wheels he beheld women marching oer burning wastes
> Of Sand in bands of hundreds & of fifties & of thousands strucken
>   with
> Lightnings which blazed after them upon their shoulders in
>   their march
> In successive vollies
> .   .   .   .
> Then he came among fiery cities & castles built of burning steel
> Then he beheld the forms of tygers & of Lions dishumanizd men
>
> (70: 12–24; 30–1, *E*347)

---

[11] Bacon, *Advancement of Learning*, 7 (book I, paragraph 3).

The violence here looks back to the armed spirits of Orc's vision, who 'rejoice over the slain' (62: 6–7, E342). The sights of torment and the 'vollies' of lightning recall the divine vengeance of *Paradise Lost* (I: 60–74; VI: 848ff.), which leaves the outcast angels 'far removed from God and light of heaven' (I: 73). The observation of these 'dishumanizd' animal forms, which now seem beyond the power of reason, leads Urizen to a condition of ineffective repentance equivalent to that reached by Los in Night V. Urizen, who began with cursing, begins to find within himself a kind of pity:

> Here he had time enough to repent of his rashly threatend curse
> He saw them cursd beyond his Curse his soul melted with fear
>
> (70: 46–7, E348)

This repentance is inspired by fear rather than by love, and has no power to overcome the constraints of the self: 'He could not take their fetters off for they grew from the soul' (71: 11, E348). But it is still a ghostly manifestation of pity. It brings Urizen to a new recognition of the dreadful vacuum at the heart of life, a new awareness of the absence of love. Thus he arrives at 'the Eastern vacuity the empty world of Luvah' (71: 24, E348).

In the Dark Vacuity

Whereas the cosmos was built in order to save man from falling into the abyss of meaninglessness, Urizen must now explore the abyss in an attempt to derive meaning from it. The attempt is seen to be inherently absurd, a search in the realm of objects for that which has already been confined to the realm of the subject. The dilemma posed by Urizen's fall in this 'bottomless' vacuity would seem to be insoluble, but at this point Blake introduces a device that seems to have no clear precedent in earlier parts of the poem:

> The ever pitying one who seeth all things saw his fall
> And in the dark vacuity created a bosom of clay
> When wearied dead he fell him limbs reposd in the bosom of slime
> As the seed falls from the sowers hand so Urizen fell & death
> Shut up his powers in oblivion. then as the seed shoots forth
> In pain & sorrow. So the slimy bed his limbs renewd
>
> (71: 25–30, E348)

This providential intervention appears in the basic text of Night VI, while no other explicit references to such a merciful saviour survive in the basic text of any of the previous Nights of the poem. The incident has a parallel in *Paradise Lost*, where Satan encounters 'A vast vacuity' in Chaos, and is saved from an endless fall by 'ill chance' (*PL*II: 935). In Milton's narrative human destiny seems paradoxically to depend on this ill chance. In contrast Blake's lines indicate that Man is never beyond the influence of divine mercy, even in the lowest depths of error. But this influence allows no arbitrary escape from his plight. Urizen is guided by a power 'not bent from his own will' (74: 31, *E*351). His ineffective repentance is a dim recognition of humanity's need for love and pity; his determination to explore the empty world of Luvah is an attempt to find a rational answer to this need. The 'Divine Hand' can therefore be seen as an expression of his will, not an agency that actively opposes it. The introduction of an apparently external agency seems to have become necessary in order to show that Urizen's selfish pity has two aspects. Its immediate consequences are devastating, but ultimately it leads to the resurrection of humanity. Providence doesn't lead Urizen out of the Caverns of the Grave. On the contrary, Urizen subsequently assumes control over the Caverns, and gratifies his repressive will by restraining desire in the name of pity. The 'ever pitying one' seems paradoxically to further the progress of tyranny. As we shall see in Chapter 9, this paradox becomes centrally important to Blake's conception of providence. Divine pity has to work in this way, it seems, because error must be fully defined before Man can begin to cast it off. As the reference to 'the sowers hand' implies, Urizen's experience in the dark vacuity serves a purpose that is quite beyond his own immediate understanding.

In the empty world of Luvah, the emergence of life from the slime of blind matter must remain an inexplicable mystery. But it may still make nature seem obscurely purposive. The most sceptical eye may find a shadow of providence in the organic cycle of life and death: there is a kind of mercy in the death that brings 'oblivion', and in the renewal of life and strength to contend with 'pain & sorrow'. The organic renewal of life also sustains Urizen in a quite different sense. The conviction that knowledge must be derived from experience makes wisdom dependent on the continuity of life through successive generations, for as Bacon says 'the experience of

one man's life [cannot] furnish examples and precedents for the
events of one man's life'.[12] If knowledge is progressive, it must be
continually built up, and handed down, from one age to the next:

> But still his books he bore in his strong hands & his iron pen
> For when he died they lay beside his grave & when he rose
> He siezd them with a gloomy smile . . .
>
>   .   .   .   .
>
>   the books remaind still unconsumd
> Still to be written & interleavd with brass & iron & gold
> Time after time for such a journey none but iron pens
> Can write And Adamantine leaves recieve nor can the man who goes
> The journey obstinate refuse to write time after time
>
>   (71: 35–37, 39–72:1, E348–9)

In Urizen's 'Adamantine leaves' knowledge begins to take on a
separate existence, more durable than the writer's. Writing becomes a necessity, upon which the continuation of life seems to
depend.[13]

In the cosmos all forms express and are sustained by an absolute
divine will. Spiritually and spatially it is a world of clear directions,
with 'heaven' above and the 'Abyss' below (33: 16–17, E322). Each
heavenly body has a preordained 'center', and a fixed station. The
architectural symbolism keeps in mind the measured stability of the
cosmic order, an order that can be known with certainty. In contrast, the empty world of Luvah confronts reason with a realm in
which such order seems at first to be inherently impossible. It is a
world which is in every sense directionless and centreless, like the
infinite void of Epicurean philosophers. Within it the stars are not
artefacts following orderly preordained courses, but seem to be
mere rocky masses 'revolving erratic' (72: 4, E349), while 'up' and
'down' exist only in relation to particular fields of force.

In its search for a comprehensive and objective understanding of
this world, reason is hampered by the fact that it is always subject
to the conditions it observes, like a swimmer trying to map an
infinite ocean. There is no fixed external vantage point, no absolute
certainty on which to base a rational interpretation. Blake uses the
idea of the vortex to dramatize this dilemma: Urizen begins to order
his world by 'Creating many a Vortex fixing many a Science in the

---

[12] Bacon, *Advancement of Learning*, 14 (book II, paragraph 3).
[13] David Fuller notes the resemblance between Urizen's dens here and 'the world
of Samuel Beckett', *Heroic Argument*, 119.

deep' (72: 13, E349). In this context the term 'Vortex' probably alludes to Cartesian physics, in which the heavenly bodies are moved by huge vortices.[14] A vortex is a system that accounts for the motions of a particular group of astral phenomena, and is thus analogous to a particular scientific system or theory. There have been several attempts to relate Blake's symbolism closely to its Cartesian model,[15] but one of the most striking aspects of the vortex here is the overriding impression of confusion it creates, as Urizen's sense of direction becomes dependent on limited systems of order:

> For when he came to where a Vortex ceasd to operate
> Nor down nor up remaind then if he turnd & lookd back
> From whence he came twas upward all. & if he turnd and viewd
> The unpassd void upward was still his mighty wandring
> The midst between an Equilibrium grey of air serene
> Where he might live in peace & where his life might meet repose
>   (72: 16–21, E349)

Ironically, Urizen finds relief, a breathing space, only when he gets beyond the immediate influence of his own abstract systems. But reason can never place itself entirely beyond its own structures. In emphasizing this Blake seems to anticipate modern theorists like Thomas Kuhn and Paul Feyerabend, who insist that there is no absolute distinction between scientific theory and data. Kuhn argues that scientific activity is governed by dominant models or 'paradigms', which 'provide all phenomena except anomalies with a theory-determined place in the scientist's field of vision'.[16] There can be no escape from the theoretical structures that condition

---

[14] For a discussion of other contexts suggested by the term 'vortex', see Hilton, *Literal Imagination*, 205–37.

[15] Donald Ault attempts to relate Blake's symbolism closely to both Newton and Descartes. Ault comments 'as soon as he [Urizen] creates a vortex, he finds himself in a Cartesian plenitude in which he cannot obtain a total perspective on the system he has created; and, once outside the vortex he has created, he is in a void': *Blake's Visionary Physics* (Chicago and London, 1974), 149. (Ault seems to have reversed Blake's distribution of matter and void.) Martin Nurmi explains in psychological terms Urizen's view that his journey is 'upward all': 'Negative Sources in Blake', in *William Blake: Essays for Samuel Foster Damon*, ed. A. H. Rosenfeld (Providence, RI, 1969), 309–10.

[16] T. S. Kuhn, *The Structure of Scientific Revolutions*, 2nd edn. (Chicago and London, 1970), 97; See also P. K. Feyerabend 'Explanation, Reduction, and Empiricism' in *Scientific Explanation, Space, and Time* (Minnesota Studies in the Philosophy of Science, 3; Minneapolis, 1962), 95.

observation, no access to a realm of pure fact or absolute certainty. Urizen's wish for an external point of reference, for a void on high 'Where self sustaining I may view all things beneath my feet', or for a route 'beneath' that would allow him to travel 'round the outside' of his dark confusion, is doomed to be frustrated, and contrasts strikingly with his absolute authority in the cosmos, where he 'strode above' the indefinite. Urizen's realization that each movement leads him back in the direction from which he has come is comparable to Bacon's assessment of the science of his predecessors and contemporaries as 'a perpetuall wheeling, Agitation and Circle'.[17]

Urizen's solution to his dilemma is to give up the vain search for an external vantage point, and to choose instead a fixed point within the abyss itself: 'Here will I fix my foot & here rebuild' (73: 14, $E350$). Historically, this is the point at which natural philosophy becomes methodical and programmatic, where it had previously been fragmented and based on inadequate observation—the point at which Bacon locates his own work: 'This one way remaineth that the business be wholly reatempted [sic] with better preparations; & that there be throughout AN INSTAURATION OF THE SCIENCES AND ARTS, and of all Human Learning rais'd from solid foundations.'[18] The foundations of Urizen's world are supplied in part by improved techniques of observation. As in the cosmos, the construction of a new order depends on a technological revolution: once again, instruments of measurement have a central importance. But the ultimate foundation of this scientific programme is not external. The image of Urizen fixing his foot in the abyss suggests an attempt by reason to put itself at the centre of its world once more. The scientific revolution which begins in the subjection of reason's power to an external world, comes to fruition in a determination to subject all of life and nature to the authority of rational judgement. Blake's symbolism implies that the ultimate foundation of Urizen's science is an act of faith (just as Bacon's programme was underpinned by the conviction that there is a divine plan in nature that can be understood by restoring the appropriate 'COMMERCE OF THE MIND AND OF THINGS'). Urizen thus assumes a shadowy semblance of his cosmic authority, and begins to take control of the Caverns of the Grave from Tharmas:

---

[17] Bacon, *Advancement and Proficience*, 2.   [18] Ibid.

So he began to dig form[ing] of gold silver & iron
And brass vast instruments to measure out the immense & fix
The whole into another world better suited to obey
His will where none should dare oppose his will himself being King
Of All & all futurity be bound in his vast chain

And the Sciences were fixd & the Vortexes began to operate
On all the sons of men & every human soul terrified
At the turning wheels of heaven shrunk away inward withring away
Gaining a New Dominion over all his sons & Daughters
& over the Sons & daughters of Luvah in the horrible Abyss
For Urizen lamented over them in a selfish lamentation
Till a white woof coverd his cold limbs from head to feet

                              (73: 16–27, E350)

For Bacon the spider's web was an appropriate image of schoolmen's thinking, in which the mind works upon itself. Here the web is associated with the faith that motivates—and is engendered by—empirical science. It is a religious system which flows from the urge to redeem humanity from chaos, while its form is determined by the field of vision (science explores a world in which all elements lie on the same ontological level and are united not by an immanent structure but by general laws; unlike the ideal construction of the cosmos, the web accumulates gradually and continuously as reason explores its domain). The explanatory power of science gives it an authority that seems irresistible. Urizen once more becomes a source of wisdom ('Clothed in aged venerableness', 73: 30, E350). His web enmeshes all who encounter it, although Blake insists that its coercive power is merely an illusion which, like gossamer, can be broken at will:

The eyelids expansive as morning & the Ears
As a golden ascent winding round to the heavens of heavens
Within the dark horrors of the Abysses lion or tyger or scorpion

For every one opend within into Eternity at will
But they refusd because their outward forms were in the Abyss

                              (73: 37–74: 2, E350)

These lines point to a central difficulty in Blake's conception of the relationship between truth and error, one that he will return to in his revisions of The Four Zoas. Refusal presupposes choice, but much of the narrative has shown that Man's vision is limited by the horizons of fixed space, and that his will is fettered by its conditioning. Until the limited horizons are destroyed it is hard to see how Man can escape the chains that grow to his soul. If, as the voice of Blake's Devil claims, 'Truth can never be told so as to be understood, and not be believ'd' (*MHH* pl. 10), then Man remains in error only because truth has not appeared to him in a comprehensible form. In this respect, his will is not free, and he is destined to endure the full consequences of his initial lapse.

An Apocalyptic Confrontation

The final incident in the Night reinforces the grimmer view of Man's destiny. As a created universe requires a divine creator who exists beyond the closed world of the senses, Urizen begins to move towards a conception of eternal life, and thus to trespass on the province of Urthona. As he approaches the 'Abhorred world of dark Urthona' he reaches the limit of the finite material world, and finds that death which has been all round him on his journey now stands in front of him, as an intellectual challenge that must be overcome. Blake's imagery here evokes at once the gates of Eden and the gates of Hell in Milton's myth. The eastern gate of Eden 'was a rock | Of alabaster' guarded by Gabriel (*PL* iv: 543–4); the Vale of Urthona is overlooked by a 'Peaked rock of Urthona' and is guarded by enormous iron walls built by the Spectre (75: 4, *E*351). The gate of Hell is guarded by the monstrous figure of Death with his mortal dart; Urthona's world is guarded by the Spectre, who appears grotesque to Urizen, and whose club is 'Desart among the stars them withering'. As we have seen, the Spectre assumes that the body is dependent on the spirit, and he disdains the material world which is now the object of Urizen's science. As he restrains and protects the fiery Orc, he embodies the hostility of a faith based on revelation to a faith derived from a rational interpretation of the external world. By his side stands Tharmas, whose chaotic materialism is a negation of the design and divinity that Urizen now finds in nature.

The prophetic tradition established by Los in Golgonooza divides history into four descending ages of gold, silver, brass, and iron, and looks beyond these to the eventual consummation of the world of fixed space. This tradition is recalled by the appearance of the

Spectre's armies, led by Urizen's four sons.[19] The 'Four winged heralds' recall the 'four cherubic shapes' that move the chariot of the Son into battle against Satan (*PL*vi: 753). The science of Urizen requires an alternative, ascending vision of time, in which knowledge is progressively perfected, and Man gradually conquers the world of fixed space. The confrontation between these opposite visions is potentially apocalyptic, as it threatens to lead to the complete destruction of one or both world-views. But this possibility is suggested only to be thwarted: the easy triumph of Urizen over his opponents is a remarkable anticlimax. As Ostriker points out, this anticlimax has its precedent in Milton.[20] In Book IV of *Paradise Lost* (877–1015), a confrontation appears imminent between Satan and the angelic guard (who have been set to protect Adam and Eve from his encroachments). The conflict is interrupted by God, who indicates that the parting of these adversaries will have greater consequences in human history than the fight and defeat of Satan. The parting leads of course to the fall, and humanity's ultimate redemption through Christ. Blake's poem recreates the pattern of interruption, with similar implications. The triumph of Urizen will lead to laws of good and evil, and a catastrophic intensification of error. But it also prepares the way for Man's resurrection, as the full potential of error must be realized before Man can escape it.

The Comets and Globes that prove irresistible weapons suggest the triumphant use of the new science to argue for providential design (for Newton it seemed beyond dispute that 'blind Fate could never make all the Planets move one and the same way in Orbs concentrick . . . Such a wonderful Uniformity in the Planetary System must be allowed the Effect of Choice).[21] But Urizen's triumph depends on his retreat. Up to the point of confrontation he secreted his web behind him. Now he moves back into it and begins to use it as an armament. This movement heralds his further dependence on religion to achieve control of experience. If the predictive power of science, its ability to 'command' the Comets and massy Globes, gives reason authority over the realm of prophecy, in doing so it

[19] David Erdman relates this passage to the American War of Independence: 'The raising of fifty-two armies from his [Urizen's] fifty-two counties for the American war is re-enacted in language drawn from *America*': *Prophet Against Empire*, 374.
[20] Ostriker (ed.), *Complete Poems*, 941.
[21] I. Newton, *Opticks* (New York, 1952, 1979), 402.

leads reason inexorably back into the power of mystery. If the prophet Los is doomed to compromise his vision of the infinite by subordinating it to the world of fixed space, Urizen is doomed to compromise his vision of reasonable order by depending on an authority that transcends reason. Together the two compromises will lead to the emergence of an uncontrollable mystery, as the next Night shows.

6

The Human Abstract

As we have seen, in Blake's account of life in the Caverns of the Grave control of events shifts from Tharmas to Los to Urizen. In the natural development of consciousness, reason becomes active only in maturity, after the transactions of sense, instinct, and the imaginative powers have consolidated a fixed schema of the world. The reasoning of the scientist may appear to reveal an unshakeably factual order of reality, but the instruments of science merely alter the 'ratio' of the closed senses, allowing new relationships to be seen within a predetermined field of vision. From his own point of view Urizen appears to be a pioneer, blazing a trail through an uncharted chaos towards a secure understanding of the universe. But the repetitions in Blake's myth show that Urizen is condemned to follow a path that has been set by Los. His struggle to establish a stable order parallels the struggle of Los in Nights IV and V; he seeks an intellectual understanding of the space that has already been 'fixed'. He only begins to seek an understanding of desire once it has been repressed, and he will approach this task having experienced an emotional development—from cursing to repentance and selfish lamentation—that follows the development of Los. As we might expect, his response to Orc closely parallels that of Los.

Urizen's triumph over Tharmas and the Spectre of Urthona represents that moment in the history of a people when reason, having gained prestige from the rise of science, becomes in Locke's words, 'our last Judge and Guide in every Thing'.[1] We can approach Blake's presentation of the consequences of this triumph by considering some aspects of the relationship between science, religion, and social theory in the seventeenth and eighteenth centuries. As the works of Locke, Boyle, Newton, and countless other writers amply demonstrate, the rise of science does not signal the immediate demise of revealed religion. Instead it stimulates efforts to show

---

[1] Locke, *Human Understanding*, 704 (book IV, chapter xix, section 14).

how science may demonstrate and elaborate the essential truths of revelation. The response to Newton's work provides a centrally important example of this process. Newton himself asserted both the theological significance of his system and the general continuity between natural science and moral philosophy.[2] The ideological implications of his physics were expounded by many writers, and perhaps most influentially in the series of lectures endowed by Robert Boyle, especially in those by Bentley, Clarke, and Derham.[3] Samuel Clarke, for example, considering the evidences of natural religion, was able to deduce from the operation of the physical world that 'There is such a thing as *Fitness* and *Unfitness*, eternally, necessarily, and unchangeably, in the Nature and Reason of Things', and that good and evil are absolute values: 'For if there be no difference between Good and Evil, antecedent to all Laws; there could be no Reason given why any Laws should be made at all.' He also deduced that goodness required strict control of the passions, and that 'there must necessarily be a *Future State of Rewards and Punishments after this Life*, wherein all the present difficulties of Providence shall be cleared up, by an exact and impartial Administration of Justice'. As the operation of physical laws seemed to require the subordination of each part of the universal system to a Supreme Cause, the natural order appeared to provide a justification for a hierarchical social order. Clarke argued that each individual must 'attend to the duties of that particular station or condition of life . . . wherein providence has at present placed him', and that everyone is 'obliged to obey and submit to his superiors in all just and right things, for the preservation of society'. Just as the harmonious working of the creation revealed the benevolence of the creator, so everyone was 'bound by the law of his nature' to practise universal love and benevolence.[4]

---

[2] 'And if natural Philosophy in all its Parts, by pursuing this Method, shall at length be perfected, the Bounds of Moral Philosophy will be also enlarged. For so far as we can know by natural Philosophy what is the first Cause, what Power he has over us, and what Benefits we receive from him, so far our Duty towards him, as well as that towards one another, will appear to us by the Light of Nature'. Newton, *Opticks*, 405 (book III, part 1).

[3] Robert Boyle founded the series of lectures with the intention of proving the Christian Religion against 'Atheists, Theists, Pagans, Jews, and Mohametans'. Margaret Jacob points out that by 1711 the reading of the Boyle lectures formed a part of an educated man's knowledge: *The Newtonians and the English Revolution 1689–1720* (Hassocks, Sussex, 1976), 162.

[4] Samuel Clarke, *A Discourse Concerning the Being and Attributes of God*

Such arguments, which had wide currency in the eighteenth century, allowed poverty to be seen as part of the regulating mechanism by which providence worked to maintain order in the world.[5] Indeed, in the light of such reasoning even the most terrible disasters could be contemplated with a certain detachment, as manifestations of a providential order. Long before the appearance of Malthus's first essay on population, Derham argued that plagues, diseases, floods, and war could be seen 'not only as a just Punishment for the Sins of Men, but also a wise Means to keep the Balance of Mankind even'.[6] The Newtonian idea of a stable, balanced social order did not of course preclude economic expansion, just as the emphasis on the sinful nature of the passions did not prevent a recognition of the importance of self-love and the pursuit of self-interest. As Margaret Jacob observes, for Clarke and others 'the necessities of the marketplace presented no contradictions to the dictates of natural religion'.[7] Self-aggrandizement was necessary and justified as long as it did not work to disrupt (or transform) the social order. Derham was able to find a providential design in the development of empire, since 'the great Improvements . . . in Arts and Sciences, in Navigation and Commerce, may be a means to transport Our Religion, as well as our Name, through all the Nations of the Earth'.[8]

In expounding the religious and social implications of their universal order, the Newtonians undoubtedly helped to give a new prestige to natural religion but, unlike the Deists (who sought a substitute for the scriptures) they argued, as Locke and some earlier scientists had done, that natural religion was complementary to revelation. Both forms of religion were essentially 'reasonable', although revelation was felt to make a deeper impression on the general mass of humanity. Clarke insisted, for example, that revelation remained necessary in spite of other evidences of God's will, since 'men are apt to be more easily worked upon, and more

(London, 1712), 115, 125, 258–9. *A Discourse Concerning the Unalterable Obligations of Natural Religion and The Truth and Certainty of the Christian Religion*, in *A Collection of Theological Tracts*, ed. R. Watson, 4 vols. (London, 1785), iv. 148, 122, 145.

[5] See Blake's angry reaction to the title of a book by Richard Watson, Bishop of Landaff: *The Wisdom of God, in having made both* RICH *and* POOR (E612).

[6] William Derham, *Physico Theology, or, a Demonstration of the Being and Attributes of God from his Works of Creation*, 4th edn. (London, 1716), 177.

[7] Jacob, *Newtonians*, 177.   [8] Derham, *Physico Theology*, 280.

strongly affected, by good testimony, than by the strictest abstract argument'. In a comparable way orthodox churchmen adapted and inverted the Deist view that the Gospel was an obscure 'republication' of natural religion: thus Joseph Butler saw Christianity as a republication of 'natural or essential Religion, adapted to the present circumstances of mankind', while William Warburton argued that the Mosaic revelation was a republication of the natural religion of the Egyptians (who were traditionally regarded as the first to develop the sciences).[9]

From Blake's mythical version of the accommodation between reason and prophecy one might conclude that the Bible is a combination of natural religion and prophecy, and that its moral doctrines are the result of a rationalization and harnessing of the prophetic tradition.[10] The myth shows that reason assimilates and remains dependent on prophecy because, as in *Europe*, the prophet is able to shape the affections, to inspire and stimulate where the reasoner can only restrain. The prophet thus becomes instrumental in furnishing reason with the most powerful of the 'soft mild arts' on which commercial civilization is founded, the vision of love which—like the universal benevolence of the eighteenth century— can be reconciled with restraint of the passions, punishment for sins, economic competition, social deprivation, and the development of empire.

Love and Justice

One of the discoveries that Urizen makes in the Caverns of the Grave is that social order depends not only on reason but also on love and pity. This is shown in his repentance, which gives rise to a guilty and fearful determination to redeem humanity from the tyranny of natural appetite and desire. The melting of Urizen's soul,

[9] Clarke, *Unalterable Obligations*, 204; Joseph Butler, *The Analogy of Religion*, 5th edn. (London, 1754), 174; William Warburton, *The Divine Legation of Moses Demonstrated*, 10th rev. edn., 3 vols. (London, 1864) ii. 65. For a discussion of Warburton's views, see Tannenbaum, *Biblical Tradition*, 56–7, 187–8.

[10] Thomas Sprat had already claimed that the Bible contained natural religion— in Genesis, Job, the Psalms, and parts of other books: *History of the Royal Society*, ed. J. I. Cope and H. W. Jones (London, 1959), 350. For a discussion of the relationship between natural and revealed religion in 17th- and 18th-cent. thought, see John Dillenberger, *Protestant Thought and Natural Science* (London, 1961).

the apparent softening of temper inherent in the civilizing process, motivates an attempt to ease repression. Of course, desire is not in any real sense liberated by his efforts—his science is founded in the 'empty world of Luvah' and depends on the repression of subjectivity. In the social order he constructs, repression will actually be intensified by the proscriptions of law, while love will promote cohesion by validating restraint.

When he was in the abyss, looking outward, Urizen saw only the external effects of desire, the 'horrid shapes & sights of torment'. Having invaded the world of Urthona in search of the inner source of desire, Urizen re-enters the world of Orc and encounters once more the 'southern terrors'—the animal forms of his children. Now he becomes aware that their fire and fury give rise not only to cruelty, but to an impulsive mercy:

> But Urizen silent descended to the Caves of Orc & saw
> A Cavernd Universe of flaming fire the horses of Urizen
> Here bound to fiery mangers furious dash their golden hoofs
> Striking fierce sparkles from their brazen fetters. fierce his lions
> Howl in the burning dens his tygers roam in the redounding smoke
> In forests of affliction. the adamantine scales of justice
> Consuming in the raging lamps of mercy pourd in rivers
> The holy oil rages thro all the cavernd rocks
>
> (77: 5–12, E352–3)

It was Urizen's confrontation with such howling animal forms that first prompted his repentance (70: 46, E348) and his attempt to 'take their fetters off' (71: 11, E348). Now Urizen's pity is implicitly contrasted with the 'consuming' mercy he finds among them. To fallen reason such mercy can only appear threatening and irresponsible because it overwhelms the sense of detachment on which justice depends. In the interests of a stable social order reason must reconcile mercy with justice, and safeguard liberty with law. He must therefore develop an alternative vision of 'Mercy Pity Peace and Love': the love that can bind individuals into a law-abiding community must triumph over arbitrary impulses.

It proves impossible for Urizen to move close to Orc: he must remain aloof from the urgent pressures of desire, and can only contemplate the 'Demon' from a distance, taking his seat upon the rock of law, and 'brooding Envious'. He has thus reached an impasse comparable to that which has transfixed Los since the binding of Orc (see 70: 1, E346). As the laws of science are essentially descriptive, Urizen will have nothing to say to Orc unless he can find a secure basis for prescriptive moral laws.

The narrative suggests that the transition from natural philosophy to natural religion and moral law involves a radical change in the perceived relationship between the human and natural worlds. This transformation gives new expression to the dichotomy between submission and conquest that characterizes most aspects of vision in the Caverns of the Grave. Science allows Man an element of control over his environment, and in this respect makes nature appear submissive to human will. Conversely, the vision of an unchangeable universal order subordinates individual will to inexorable limits.

The dawning conviction that desire must be sacrificed to the natural order is imaged in the growth of the tree of Mystery. The conviction begins to take shape initially in Los, who feels Urizen's envy in his limbs 'like to a blighted tree' (77: 27, E353). Then as Urizen contemplates Orc, 'fixd in Envy', tracing the dreadful letters of his knowledge, the root of Mystery appears from beneath his heel. It is at first a sinister growth that threatens to engulf both Urizen and 'the heavens of Los' completely. But subsequently it seems to Urizen 'wondrous'. The tree has many precedents in mythology and religion: the oak groves of the Druids, for example, or the great ash tree Yggdrasil of Nordic mythology, the banyan grove in which Milton's Adam and Eve attempt to hide their nakedness after the fall, the biblical tree of knowledge, the tree of Calvary, perhaps also the upas tree.[11] Its most obvious precedents in Blake's work are the tree in *Ahania* (on which Urizen sacrifices his own son) and that in 'The Human Abstract' in *Songs of Experience* (which is associated with 'holy fears', selfish love, deceit, and humility). As the natural philosopher derives the vision of an unchanging order from the study of nature at its most predictable and mechanical level, the conviction that this order governs human behaviour can be seen as a grotesque inversion of human values which allows the head to be ruled by the inert matter beneath the feet. Several images in this Night suggest this kind of inversion: the root of Mystery springs from the rock beneath Urizen's heel, but soon he is 'high roofd over' with branches; Los's

---

[11] See Desmond King-Hele, *Erasmus Darwin and the Romantic Poets* (London, 1986), 52–3.

broodings rush down to his feet; sorrow shoots though Los 'from his feet . . . to his head'.

Urizen's tree is a natural counterpart to the pillared structure of Golgonooza that Los builds to protect Enitharmon. Both are labyrinthine (*see* 61: 8, *E*341), both symbolize faith that develops in reaction to Orc. Golgonooza is built on the limit of Translucence: it preserves the vision of an infinite fulfilment within the natural world, a sense of divine power that arises directly from human appetites and desires, the hope that a messianic kingdom can be established on earth in the fullness of time. Unlike Golgonooza, the tree of Mystery develops independent of the human will. It springs from the rock of law, from the conviction that divine power is expressed in fixed principles of order and justice. As the concept of a just creator has to be reconciled with the existence of injustice in the world, the tree promotes the vision of a future state beyond the realm of nature, in which the rewards and punishments earned in this life will eventually be distributed. In the shadow of the tree, therefore, the messianic vision of an earthly kingdom must be transformed into the vision of a heavenly kingdom.

Once Urizen has encountered the tree, his vision of nature has two different but complementary aspects—one scientific and inviting conquest, one mysterious and demanding submission. His book of iron, which remains in the shade of the tree, corresponds to Genesis, in which humanity becomes subject to the knowledge of good and evil. Having acquired a natural authority for moral law, Urizen can now address Orc directly, and reveal himself 'in a form of wisdom' (78: 31, *E*354).

Dividing the Spirit

Although the meeting of Urizen and Orc is apparently a confrontation of opposites, the sense of opposition is soon exposed as a delusion. Like all of Man's powers, these two are interdependent. It is Orc's 'deep pulsation' that stirs Urizen into his investigation of the material world, and that drives his urge for control of experience. It is the approach of Urizen that allows Orc to become articulate and to rationalize his fury. When the two powers come face to face, the parallels between them are emphasized as much as the differences. Orc's fiery contempt for meddling reason parallels

Urizen's cold detachment from desire. Urizen's troubled speculation on Orc's 'visions of sweet bliss' is matched by Orc's reference
to Urizen's preoccupation with 'the wonders of Futurity'. They
itemize each other's 'Tortures' with the same incomprehension.
Neither will allow the development of a vital relationship between
thought and feeling.

Like Los, Urizen will attempt to reconcile Orc to his own sense of
unchanging order. To Los it appears that Orc is bound on the iron
mountain's top, constrained only by limits that seem necessary for
self-preservation. To Urizen such constraints are quite inadequate:
to him it appears that the demon is still in an illusory 'deep'
suffering unnecessary self-torment, and has yet to be elevated into
the true realm of order, the realm of law. The process of elevation
can only be achieved by moral education.

The eighteenth-century debate about the education of the poor
shows with particular clarity how the idea of the social order as a
hierarchy ordained by providence influenced the understanding of
social love. Charity schools were opposed by those who, like
Mandeville, shared the mercantilist assumption that a vigorous,
profitable trade depended on cheap labour, and by others who
feared that by funding such education they would be damaging the
prospects of their own children.[12] On the other side it was argued
that the schools worked to maintain the *status quo* by reconciling
the poor to their poverty through religious instruction while
enhancing their social and economic usefulness. Thus Steele, sup-
porting the schools in *The Spectator*, condemns those who use
wealth only to support 'Pomp and Luxury', and advocates
charity on the grounds of its benefits for the governing classes, its
tendency to create 'endearing Dependencies' and dutiful servants.
He ends his paper with an extract from a sermon in which this
charitable education is seen as part of the compensation arranged
for the poor by 'wise Providence': 'their Poverty is, in reality, their
Preferment.'[13]

---

[12] See 'An Essay on Charity Schools', in Bernard Mandeville, *The Fable of the
Bees, or Private Vices, Publick Benefits* (1723), ed. F. B. Kay, 2 vols. (Oxford, 1924).
Isaac Watts listed and argued against common objections to charity schools in *An
Essay Towards the Encouragement of Charity Schools* (London, 1728). He advo-
cates a 'slender education' that would not allow the poor to rise above their ordained
station (47, 14–15). For a general discussion of the debate see V. E. Neuberg,
Popular Education in Eighteenth-Century England (London, 1971), 1–15.

[13] 'What would not a Man do, in common Prudence, to lay out on Purchase of

In Blake's narrative, the education of Orc is presented in terms which emphasize its function as a preparation for subservience. Orc has previously been fed on the thrilling joys of sense by spirits of life. He is now to be fed on the bread of knowledge—or sorrow—by Urizen's daughters:

> The heavens bow with terror underneath their iron hands
> Singing at their dire work the words of Urizens book of iron
> While the enormous scrolls rolld dreadful in the heavens above
>
> (79: 33-5, E355)

Urizen's daughters are once more associated with destiny, but as destiny is now linked to moral duty, their primary function is to inhibit spontaneity and individuality. The book of iron instils a grim vision of humanity's sinful nature, and is thus a preparation for the book of brass (or moral law). In the cosmos order was imposed by brute force (Luvah was cast into the furnace of affliction). In this new regime order is enforced by the more insidious methods of indoctrination and psychological manipulation, by what Hume refers to as 'the artifice of politicians'.[14] As before, Blake exposes the tyranny of a system that justifies manifest injustices (see the lamentation of Enion in Night II). But in Urizen's 'soft mild arts' he caricatures the hypocrisy that has to be endorsed or tolerated within apparently liberal societies:

> Compell the poor to live upon a Crust of bread by soft mild arts
> Smile when they frown frown when they smile & when a man
>   looks pale
> With labour & abstinence say he looks healthy & happy
> And when his children sicken let them die there are enough
> Born even too many & our Earth will be overrun
> Without these arts If you would make the poor live with temper
> With pomp give every crust of bread you give with gracious
>   cunning
> Magnify small gifts reduce the man to want a gift & then give
>   with pomp
>
> (80: 9-16, E355)

one about him, who would add to all his Orders he gave the Weight of the Commandments to inforce an Obedience to them?' Paper no. 294, *The Spectator*, iii. 49–50.

[14] Hume argued that all morality depends on our sentiments, and that while the progress of sentiments in favour of justice is natural, it is strengthened by education and '*the artifice of politicians*': *Philosophical Works*, ii. 245, 270–1 (*Treatise*, book III, part i, section 1 and book III, part ii, section 2).

Indoctrination and flattery gradually transform an energy that seems impossible to reconcile with a rational world-view, into an ideal that will help to sustain it. Once Orc is subject to his power, Urizen is able to recognize him as a manifestation of Luvah, the divine power of love which in itself seems dangerously intoxicating. Urizen neutralizes this threatening potential by dividing Orc's spirit:

> Then Orc cried Curse thy Cold hypocrisy. already round thy Tree
> In scales that shine with gold & rubies thou beginnest to weaken
> My divided Spirit Like a worm I rise in peace unbound
> From wrath Now When I rage my fetters bind me more
> O torment O torment
>
> (80: 27–31, E356)

The divided Orc now has two forms, human and subhuman. As we have seen, the human form is 'concenterd' on the natural world embodied in Enitharmon. When Orc's desire was constrained by the finite horizons imposed by Los he mocked at his chains, finding infinite delight within the finite realm of nature. But the constraints of moral law cannot be mocked in this way: they make desire seem evil, and passive obedience seem the essence of goodness. Orc's obedient subhuman form, shining with gold and rubies, has the appearance of an artefact, an appearance that Blake consistently associates with abstract visions of spiritual life (as in the Spectre of Tharmas and, in a different form, in the Spectre of Urthona). This form is centred on the tree of Mystery, which promotes a vision of eternal life remote from the realm of nature and the senses, a 'Godlike State | That lies beyond the bounds of Science in the Grey obscure' (80: 41–2, E356). Such a vision places the individual utterly at the mercy of divine judgement: Orc now feels his own tormenting rage as a punishment, and preys for 'mildness'. But he cannot love Urizen as his God and King. The myth implies that the demand for obedience necessarily entails resentment, deceit, and self-contempt. Although Orc may feel that his own conformity makes him a pusillanimous worm rising 'in peace unbound from wrath', he actually becomes a serpent growing ever more monstrous under the pressure of his own repressed energy, a communicant who scorns the grace of the creator he worships:

> And Orc began to Organize a Serpent body
> Despising Urizens light & turning it into flaming fire
> Recieving as a poisond Cup Recieves the heavenly wine
> And turning affection into fury & thought into abstraction
> A Self consuming dark devourer rising into the heavens
>
> (80: 44–8, E356)

It becomes difficult to tell who is in control of Orc's transformation as the process continues. His obedience seems an act of defiance that Urizen both compels and suffers. Orc himself becomes Urizenic, not only 'turning affection into fury' but also turning 'thought into abstraction'. The two opposed wills apparently converge, suggesting an unconscious conspiracy between them. This suggestion is reinforced by allusion. The elevated serpent recalls the brass serpent set up by Moses in the wilderness—an antidote for the fatal bite of the fiery serpents which God sent to plague the disobedient people of Israel (Numbers 21: 6–9). This incident, in which the serpent is at once the instrument of divine punishment and of redemption, imposing and removing the threat of death, can be seen as an epitome of divine justice in the Bible. The image of Orc on the tree emphasizes the relationship between punishment and redemption as it recalls both the temptation in Eden and the crucifixion (in John 3: 14 the brass serpent is seen as a type of Christ).[15] Like the crucifixion, it symbolizes self-denial raised to the status of a divine ideal. As such it has a seductive power which, like the serpent in Eden, draws humanity into the bondage of moral law. The implicit identification of Satan and Christ here suggests that both are instruments of a repressive legalistic orthodoxy they seek to oppose. It is the sacrifice of the saviour, rather than his acts of rebellion, which forms the basis of state religion, and makes the rebel an instrument of the orthodoxy he defied, as Urizen realizes:

> He knew that weakness stretches out in breadth & length he knew
> That wisdom reaches high & deep & therefore he made Orc
> In Serpent form compelld stretch out & up the mysterious tree
> He sufferd him to Climb that he might draw all human forms
> Into submission to his will
>
> (81: 2–6, E356)

---

[15] Wilkie and Johnson note: 'Christian typology has always recognized the connection between the serpent of Eden and the crucified Christ, a clear example of the way its mythical understanding runs deeper than doctrinal purpose', Blake's Four Zoas, 151.

The breadth and height of Orc, like the crossed members of the crucifix, become the symbol of a faith in which wisdom is associated with submission.

Prophecy in the Age of Reason

As we have said, in Blake's myth, prophecy retains an important place in the rational world-view after the rise of science because it has a persuasive influence that the abstract principles of reason lack. The tree of Mystery provides a justification for the subordination of desire to law. But law, as an instrument of social control, is essentially negative. Prophecy not only helps to justify the ways of God to Man by providing an appropriate vision of human origins and destiny, it can also promote the love that must bind civilization into a stable community.

From a rational point of view the prophetic impulse that longs to release the full potential of human energy in an earthly paradise is the worst kind of visionary enthusiasm. It seems 'reasonable' to conclude that any attempt to build a social order on the basis of unrestrained natural appetite will collapse into anarchy under the pressure of rampant individualism. Enitharmon, the vision of nature that fosters and stimulates Orc's libidinous rage, and Los the prophet who sought to unbind the fiery demon, must both seem subversive to Urizen:

> Lo how the heart & brain are formed in the breeding womb
> Of Enitharmon how it buds with life & forms the bones
> The little heart the liver & the red blood in its labyrinths
> By gratified desire by strong devouring appetite she fills
> Los with ambitious fury that his race shall all devour
> (80: 22–6, E356)

It is inevitably the more reasonable aspect of prophecy, the Spectre, that proves useful to Urizen. Although the Spectre initially opposes Urizen's advance, he soon contributes to it. The rock beneath which he takes refuge (77: 2, E352) is presumably the rock of law on which Urizen builds his society. And the Spectre's belief that spirit and body are separate lends support to Urizen's view of the universe as a world of dead matter given life and form by a divine creator. The Spectre's grim vision of material life has so far been qualified by the eruption of Orc's fiery desires and by the construction of Golgonooza. Now the emergence of reason provides an ethos in which the Spectre's vision can find new expression. As man's perception of nature changes, a new form of Enitharmon begins to emerge. Urizen tells his daughters:

> let Moral Duty tune your tongue
> But be your hearts harder than the nether millstone
> To bring the shadow of Enitharmon beneath our wondrous tree
> That Los may Evaporate like smoke & be no more
> Draw down Enitharmon to the Spectre of Urthona
> And let him have dominion over Los the terrible shade
>
> (80: 3–8, E355)

The emergence of Enitharmon's 'shadow' in the scientific universe parallels her division in the cosmos. When Urizen completed his Golden World—a system of ideal forms remote from the dark chaos of Tharmas—Los began to lose his sense of intimate communion with nature. He experienced it instead as an essentially dead world redeemed by a transcendent holiness: Enitharmon became a lifeless corpse animated by a tantalizing and unpossessable spirit. The scientific universe exerts a comparable influence on Los. He no longer lives in a world that has been shaped by his own efforts, but in one that is subject to a divine creator. Enitharmon becomes once more a lifeless body animated by an elusive spirit. The divine animating power is not a living spiritual presence as it was in the cosmos, because the supernatural in this sense finds no place in the scientific vision. Rather, as Locke says, the idea of God is 'naturally deducible from every part of our Knowledge'—experience supplies evidence of divinity that is appreciated by the reflective mind.[16] The spirit is now a mere abstraction, a shadow which responds only to the Spectre, while Los feels excluded once more from a paradisal beauty enjoyed by 'All things beside the woeful Los':

> Enitharmon lay on his knees. Urizen tracd his Verses
> In the dark deep the dark tree grew. her shadow was drawn down
> Down to the roots it wept over Orc. the Shadow of Enitharmon
> Los saw her stretchd the image of death upon his witherd valleys
> Her Shadow went forth & returnd Now she was pale as Snow

---

[16] Locke, *Human Understanding*, 89 (book I, chapter iv, section 9).

When the mountains & hills are coverd over & the paths of Men
    shut up
But when her spirit returnd as ruddy as a morning when
The ripe fruit blushes into joy in heavens eternal halls
Sorrow shot thro him from his feet it shot up to his head
Like a cold night that nips the roots & shatters off the leaves

(81: 10–19, E356–7)

The psychological implications of this transformation are dramatized with care. Los is now subject to the power of reason, and in
particular to reason's detachment, which resists the flow of feeling,
and transforms the loved one into an object of contemplation. The
resultant possessiveness is a deterrent to love: his sorrow blights
Enitharmon when her spirit returns. Like Urizen on his journey
through the abyss, Los transforms his world by withdrawing from
it, and finds himself at war with 'secret monsters' of anxiety and
doubt.

The Shadow of Enitharmon, then, personifies the conviction that
the divine essence of nature lies beyond the reach of natural appetite, and can only be apprehended rationally. She is a transcendent
beauty who is immune to the fiery desire of Orc's human form, and
who offers a dim spiritual comfort to his serpent form as she
descends to weep over it like the Virgin weeping over the crucified
Jesus.

Beneath the Tree of Mystery

We have already seen that in Blake's narrative each major period of
constructive activity is preceded by a vision of human origins which
provides a justification for the limits that are to govern human
action. Urizen descends to create his Golden World in response to
the visions of Enitharmon and Los, which show Man overwhelmed
by his passions. In the Caverns of the Grave the reasoning or
spectrous power of prophecy supplies the vision of origins: in Night
IV the Spectre's revaluation of labour underpins Los's efforts to
consolidate the world of fixed space. Now the Spectre, with the
Shadow of Enitharmon, provides an account of history that will
justify a new social order. As the reasoning power of the prophet
moves to embrace the abstract vision of nature, the tree of Mystery
begins to bear fruit.

Two passages from *Paradise Lost* have a special importance here: the description of the temptation in Book IX, and the confrontation of Satan with Sin in Book II. The shadow of Enitharmon is brought beneath the tree of Mystery, as Eve is brought beneath the tree of knowledge, to draw humanity into the knowledge of good and evil. The Spectre of Urthona recalls Satan tempting Eve. To him, the Shadow appears 'Shivering', a condition that recalls the first symptoms of the fall in Eden. The Shadow also resembles Sin, who unlocks the gate of Hell in order to allow Satan passage into Chaos, and who recounts her own memories of the fall from Heaven. Both Miltonic contexts refer to the triumph of Sin and Death over humanity. They are evoked at this point in order to herald the rebirth of Vala.

The Poison of Sweet Love

Taken together, the two versions of the fall offered here constitute the fallen mind's most elaborate and sophisticated attempt so far to define the cause of the human predicament. For the first time the prophet develops his vision while reason is in the ascendant. As a result there is an attempt to show more clearly the role of reason in the fall, while the fall is seen as a historical process that continues through several eras. Perhaps the most significant development is a new recognition of the nature of love, as a power that can not only enslave, but can also liberate. This recognition allows a more hopeful view of man's plight to emerge. As in the first dialogue between Enitharmon and Los, the female emphasizes the moral implications of the fall, while the male emphasizes its spiritual implications. Here, though, her account seems dominated by fear, while his includes a new sense of hope.

The dramatic context foregrounds the ambiguous nature of love. The dialogue is presented as a scene of seduction: the Spectre woos the Shadow with 'the poison of sweet love', and she responds with an alluring disdain. Her speech is ostensibly a revelation of secret feeling (taking the bar from Enitharmon's breast), but its emotional significance is revealed only gradually. As in the first cycle, love is seen as the major cause of Man's fall. The first part of the vision (83: 7–18) corresponds to the loss of Eden: Man's melting in high noon recalls Adam sinking to dream of Eve soon after his creation in *Paradise Lost* (VIII: 286 ff.). If the fall is shown to begin when Man succumbs to the sensuous power of love, Man does not realize he is fallen until he acquires the power of reason. With the birth of Urizen he discovers 'a wonder': love which appears blissful in Vala also has an aggressive masculine aspect, Luvah. Man's recoil is apparently a rational reaction to his loss of self-possession in the power of love. Those in heaven similarly recoil from the surrender to feeling ('Wonder seizd | All heaven they saw him dark. they built a golden wall | Round Beulah'). Thus although this account ostensibly shows love as the cause of the fall, its subtext implies that reason is the cause. The rational urge for order makes restraint a necessity, and thus creates desire (Luvah) as an anarchic and apparently sinful power.

This account shows a new sense of the relationship between fallen and unfallen existence. When the Spectre described his fall in Night IV, Beulah seemed the highest condition known to humanity: he spoke of the 'hills of Beulah', and of his labour there. Beulah is now seen as a lower condition, a place of flowers, plains, and unstrenuous joy, clearly distinguished from Eternity or heaven, which is a place of constructive activity ('they built a golden wall'). In this respect the Shadow's view seems more elaborate than earlier accounts, but in another respect it seems more restricted: neither Urizen nor Luvah is seen to have an eternal existence. Urizen is the 'First born of Generation' and 'grew up in the plains of Beulah', while of Luvah the Shadow says: 'Nought he knew | Of sweet Eternity' (83: 19, 24–5, E358–9). In this more naturalistic account, the distance between heaven and the powers that dominate the fallen world seems to have increased. The fall is traced through several distinct epochs: from the intense pleasures of the garden, to patriarchal prosperity in pastures, to slavery.

The latter part of the vision (83: 19–34, E358–9) corresponds to the vision of history shown by Michael to Adam after the fall in *Paradise Lost* (XII: 13–62), describing the transition from the patriarchal prosperity of the descendants of Noah who 'dwell | Long time in peace by families and tribes | Under paternal rule' (22–4) to the usurpation of Nimrod the tyrant, and the confusion of Babel. In Milton the vision is used to support the view that liberty 'always with right reason dwells' (84). Similarly, in the Shadow's account reason is the power that ameliorates the effects of the fall by recreating the conditions of happiness in pastures rather than in gardens. Ostensibly it is desire, Luvah, that enslaves Man as soon as reason succumbs to its power. But the account also shows that reason makes Man forget Eternity and thus delivers him into the tyrannical power of desire (Luvah conferring in 'darksom night' recalls the conspiracy of Satan in Heaven, *PLv*: 667 ff.). The contradictions and parallels in the Shadow's vision indicate that she is subject to the conditions she describes. The avenging, enslaving spirit of Luvah is manifest in her desire to subject Vala to the rage of Orc. In this way the myth exposes the emotional drive hidden beneath justifications of divine vengeance: in *Paradise Lost*, for example, Michael explains that since man permits unworthy powers within himself to reign over free reason, 'God in judgement just | Subjects him from without to violent lords' (XII: 92–3). Blake would no doubt see this justification as an example of the conferring between Urizen and Luvah which the Shadow describes. It is a characteristic manifestation of the fearful view expressed by the Shadow, that fallen humanity is 'enslavd to vegetative forms', imprisoned in the body, and that the surrender of reason to the power of love must be punished. It provides a justification not only for the conventional notion of hell, but also for the state of war that will become a permanent feature of Urizen's civilization.

The Spectre's reply places emphasis on redemption rather than punishment. In this it provides a more positive—and more seductive—rationale for the repression of desire. His words recall his earlier vision in Night IV 50: 1–27, *E*333–4, but this new vision is significantly different. The fall begins when 'the gentle passions' issue through the nostrils to stand 'before the Eyes of Man' in a female form. Man apparently falls into the delusion that his own feelings of pity, mercy, and love express spiritual ideals by which he must regulate his life. The account suggests that Man can only aspire to such ideals at the expense of the masculine aspects of desire. With the emergence of the female Man's creative work is arrested, and his passivity leads him to see himself as subject to the biological necessity of the body.

In the Spectre's earlier vision he saw himself as issuing from the nostrils of Enion. Now he sees himself issuing from her brain, as an intellectual rather than a spiritual power. But like the Shadow, he is subject to the conditions he describes; that is, he is in the power of the gentle passions. Although his vision of Eternal life has become more elaborate, and includes not only active labour but an interdependent brotherhood (or 'Universal Manhood'), it is nevertheless a gentle vision of Eternity, remote from the rage of natural appetite: he remembers 'mild fields of happy Eternity', 'Tharmas mild & Luvah sweet melodious' (84: 4, 8, E359). Whereas he once reproached himself for slumbering in weak repose, he now speaks grudgingly of his labour for Los. And although he wishes to regain a blissful state of 'imbodiment' with Enitharmon, he characteristically expresses disdain for the body and wants to destroy it. Ironically, he sees the path to redemption through the gentle passions: re-enacting the fall he has just described, he adopts the 'soft Vala' as an ideal that can restrain the masculine aspects of desire and thus release humanity from the imperious appetites of the body.

In the conferring of the Shadow and the Spectre beneath the tree of Mystery, Man begins unconsciously to expose with unprecedented clarity the paradoxical nature of his view of love, a view divided between fear and hope. On the one hand the fierce appetites that drive the tyrannical will can be traced back to love: love of pleasure, love of self, love of power. From the point of view of fallen reason, love seems dangerously seductive, not only in its overtly sexual sense, but whenever it takes possession of human judgement. It must therefore be subject to rational restraints and the sanctions of law. But the sense of moral outrage that cries out for the punishment of sin is itself an expression of a fierce repressed passion: thus Vala becomes subject to the rage of Orc. On the other hand love is the source of mercy, forgiveness, and self-sacrifice upon which brotherhood appears to depend. It therefore becomes an ideal by which natural passion can be restrained: in this sense Vala is given to Orc so that he might lose his rage. Blake apparently saw this contradiction at the heart of all attempts to reconcile love with justice, impulse with law, inspiration with natural religion. Its place in orthodox Christianity is vividly defined by Milton's theodicy, where Adam falls through his love for Eve, and is subsequently instructed by Michael to seek happiness through 'love | By name to come called Charity, the soul | Of all the rest' (PLxii: 583–5). The contradiction is traditionally resolved, of course, by distinguishing between earthly and spiritual, or selfish and social love. But in Blake's view such distinctions are founded on the false separation of soul from body, of individuality from the universal community.

The prophetic conference beneath the tree of Mystery, then, finds a place within Urizen's system for love and pity, in a form that will reinforce his moral vision by justifying both the repression of natural appetite, and the violence that results from that repression. As the Demons of the Deep prophesied, the times have returned: Vala is to be reborn. In the Caverns of the Grave she will become one of the most powerful and seductive forms of error that Man has to encounter in the fallen world.

7

The Progress of Empire

The narrative that follows on from the birth of Vala shows evidence of a very full and complicated revision. Blake added new material on paper that had not been used for *Night Thoughts* proofs (pages 87–90), to form what is now known as Night VIIa (pages 77–90). As we shall see in Chapter 9, the added material seems to reflect a radical change in Blake's thinking about his poem. There is a second version of Night VII (on pages 91–8) now generally referred to as VIIb, the basic text of which—like that of Night VIII—also contains material that seems to reflect this change. Gerald E. Bentley Jr. has suggested that VIIb may have come into being as a result of the revision of VIII (the latter may simply have grown under the pressure of new material until it was divided into two parts).[1] In the present chapter I shall be concerned with those parts of VIIb and VIII that seem most closely related to the narrative I have already discussed. I shall be concerned, therefore, with thematic relationships rather than with the existing narrative sequence in these Nights, Nights which contain Blake's most elaborate treatment of the growth and decline of a commercial empire.

In dramatizing the systematic extension of Urizen's power into a Universal Empire, Blake was working in a field that had occupied some of the major historians of the Enlightenment. There were many attempts to reveal the hidden dynamics of growth and decay in the development of particular societies, including Montesquieu's *Considérations sur les causes de la grandeur des Romains et de leur Décadence* (1734), Lévesque de Burigny's *Revolutions of the Empire of Constantinople* (1749), and the most ambitious and scholarly of such works, Gibbon's history of the Roman Empire (1776–88). More generally eighteenth-century history had been preoccupied in defining in general terms the causes of progress and the factors which may threaten its continuation. It is not surprising, therefore, that Blake's study of Empire seems to incorporate a

---

[1] Bentley, Vala, *or* The Four Zoas, 162–3.

number of contemporary assumptions concerning the growth and decline of civilizations.

War and Civil Society

The widely held view that civil government originates in a state of barbarism and war, and that it allows an escape from this state, naturally coexisted with a recognition that war is a continuing feature of civilized life. This paradox is emphasized dramatically in Rousseau's pessimistic view of civilization. In the *Discourse on Inequality*, the social contract that was intended to protect individuals from oppression is seen to lead inevitably to a disastrous intensification of war, because governments remain in a state of nature in their relations with each other, and the conflicts between them are necessarily more violent than those between individuals in the original state of nature:

Political bodies, thus remaining in a State of Nature among themselves, soon experienced the Inconveniences which had obliged Individuals to quit it; and this State became much more fatal to those great Bodies, than it had been before to the Individuals which now composed them. Hence those national Wars, those Battles, those Murders, those Reprisals which make Nature shudder and shock Reason; hence all those horrible Prejudices, which make it a Virtue and an Honour to shed human blood.[2]

Writers who took a less pessimistic view of economic and cultural progress had to take a more accepting view of war, even if their conclusions in some ways paralleled Rousseau's. Adam Smith's account 'Of the Expense of Defence' in *The Wealth of Nations* offers a detailed analysis of how social development influences the conduct of war, and it soberly demonstrates the high military cost of economic growth. As society advances, the progress of manufactures and improvements in the art of war demand the professionalization and, increasingly, the mechanization of warfare. Smith argues that it is only by means of a standing army—often seen as an instrument of government tyranny—'that the

---

[2] Rousseau, *Inequality*, 139. The idea that nations remain in a state of nature in their relations with each other is explained by John Locke in *The Second Treatise of Government* (ii. 14).

civilization of any country can be perpetuated; or even preserved for any considerable time'. He accepts this prospect with equanimity, maintaining that war is 'certainly the noblest of the arts', even if with 'the progress of improvement it necessarily becomes one of the most complicated among them'.[3] The contemporary awareness of the close relationship between war and progress seems to have been reinforced by the tradition of civic humanism mediated by Machiavelli and his successors which continued to influence political theory throughout the eighteenth century.[4] In this tradition, the health or virtue of the state is seen to depend on the military commitment of the citizen, and the soldier is often seen as a type of the virtuous citizen in his acceptance of discipline and self-sacrifice for the universal good. The influence of this tradition can be seen in Gibbon's history of Rome, in which the fortunes of the state are related to the personal willingness of citizens to bear arms. In this account there is an essential difference between the motives of the barbarian and of the civilized soldier, seen for example in Gibbon's comments on the ancient British tribes, who 'possessed valour without conduct, and the love of freedom without the spirit of union'.[5] If the civil state brings to war a new sense of purpose, war itself could be seen to give a sense of purpose to the state. In Adam Ferguson's *History of Civil Society*, war is an essential stimulus to progress as it gives cohesion and direction: 'Without the rivalship of nations, and the practice of war, civil society itself could scarcely have found an object, or a form.'[6] In Enlightenment histories the progress from primitive to civil society is repeatedly shown to entail a new commitment to warfare, a commitment that is often moralized.

Internal Conflict

If progress gives a new significance to war, it is sometimes also seen to generate internal conflict. This idea assumes an important place

---

[3] *An Inquiry into the Nature and Causes of the Wealth of Nations*, ed. R. H. Campbell, A. S. Skinner, and W. B. Todd, 2 vols. (Oxford, 1976), ii. 706; ii. 697.

[4] See J. G. A. Pocock, *The Machiavellian Moment* (Princeton, NJ, 1975), chs. 10–14.

[5] Gibbon, *Decline and Fall*, i. 4 (ch. 1).

[6] Ferguson, *History of Civil Society*, 24.

in Hume's *History of England*, for example, in which the seventeenth-century struggle between king and commons is seen as an inevitable consequence of the progress of commerce and of the arts, which allowed the love of liberty to acquire new force, and therefore produced a new attitude to government.[7] English history provided a particular example of what was taken to be a general principle. The Scottish historian John Millar, for example, in his essay *On the Origin of Ranks*, argues in general terms that commercial expansion will always tend to produce an opposition between the sovereign and the people, because it furnishes the means of tyranny and oppression, notably the much-feared standing army, at the same time as it inspires the people with ideas of independence.[8] The necessity for internal conflict is a subject that Hume returns to in several of his essays. In 'Of the Origin of Government' he asserts that 'In all governments, there is a perpetual intestine struggle, open or secret, between AUTHORITY and LIBERTY; and neither of them can ever absolutely prevail in the contest.' In 'Of Superstition and Enthusiasm' the religious dimension of the conflict is singled out, and the balance of power seems to tilt more decisively against liberty. Hume associates superstition with priestly power and with antagonism to civil liberty, while enthusiasm is a friend to liberty. Of course, Hume is not an advocate of enthusiasm, which he sees as responsible for 'the most cruel disorders in human society'. But 'its fury is like that of thunder and tempest, which exhaust themselves in a little time, and leave the air more calm and pure than before', while superstition 'steals in gradually and insensibly ... Till at last the priest, having firmly established his authority, becomes the tyrant and disturber of human society, by his endless contentions, persecutions, and religious wars.'[9]

---

[7] Hume explains that the rise of commerce and the arts had the effect of redistributing wealth from the barons to the gentry. As a consequence 'the spirit of liberty was universally diffused'. D. Hume, *The History of Great Britain*, 2 vols. (Edinburgh, 1754), ii. 124, 161–2.

[8] 'So widely different are the effects of opulence and refinement, which, at the same time that they furnish the king with a standing army, the great engine of tyranny and oppression, have also a tendency to inspire the people with notions of liberty and independence. It may thence be expected that a conflict will arise between these two opposite parties', John Millar, *The Origin of the Distinction of Ranks* (London, 1779), 289.

[9] Hume, *The Philosophical Works*, iii. 116; iii. 149.

Growth and Decline

The acceptance of war and contentions as ineradicable aspects of civil society does not necessarily imply a pessimistic view of progress. Indeed, Hume's *History of England* demonstrated that conflict could have a liberalizing effect on the state. But the connections that are being made here, between economic development and the increased potential for violence, are typical of the contemporary awareness that civilization can generate powerful destructive forces that must be contained if progress is to continue. And in some writers we can see a paradoxical view of progress, in which the forces that promote social development are the same as those that undermine it.[10]

This paradox appears very clearly in some discussions of the consequences of economic development for the ordinary worker. Adam Smith, for example, who is usually regarded as an economic optimist, warned his readers candidly of the negative effects that could arise from progress. In *The Wealth of Nations* he notes that in barbarous societies of hunters, shepherds, and even of husbandmen, before the improvement of manufactures and the extension of foreign commerce, 'Invention is kept alive' by the variety of occupations, and by the demands they make on the individuals involved. In contrast, the division and specialization of labour, which is the driving force of economic development, can result in 'mental mutilation', as the labourer is given 'no occasion to exert his understanding, or to exercise his invention'. When this happens, Smith says, the labourer 'generally becomes as stupid and ignorant as it is possible for a human creature to become'. Far from enlightening and enlivening the members of society, economic development could, it seems, undermine the 'intellectual, social, and martial virtues' of the vast majority, unless preventative measures could be devised.[11] Smith's views on this subject were reformulated by his pupils Ferguson and Millar. Ferguson's comment that 'manufacturers prosper most where the workshop may . . . be con-

---

[10] Pocock suggests that this paradoxical view of the history of civilization is 'Machiavelli's unintended legacy to Western thought'. 'Between Machiavelli and Hume: Gibbon as a Civic Humanist and Philosophical Historian', in *Edward Gibbon and the Decline and Fall of the Roman Empire*, ed. G. W. Bowerstock, J. Clive, and S. R. Graubaud (Cambridge Mass., and London, 1977), 105.

[11] Smith, *Wealth of Nations*, ii. 783, 782.

sidered as an engine, the parts of which are men' was later quoted approvingly by Marx.[12]

The most elaborate examination of the paradoxical relationship between growth and decay was probably that offered by Gibbon. In his 'General Observations on the Fall of the Empire in the West', Gibbon saw the decline of Rome as

the natural and inevitable effect of immoderate greatness. Prosperity ripened the principle of decay; the causes of destruction multiplied with the extent of conquest; and, as soon as time or accident had removed the artificial supports, the stupendous fabric yielded to the pressure of its own weight.

In practice, of course, his account showed that the principle of decay was rather difficult to identify. But his notorious presentation of the role of religion in the decline of the Empire provides a vivid example of how an activity that initially promotes social development can eventually undermine it. In Gibbon's account the pagan religions served the interests of the state by fostering civil obedience and tolerance:

The various modes of worship which prevailed in the Roman world were all considered by the people as equally true; by the philosopher as equally false; and by the magistrate as equally useful. And thus toleration produced not only mutual indulgence, but even religious concord.

But eventually Christianity rose from among these religions, and with its other-worldly vision of destiny, its preoccupation with sinfulness, and with its fanatical and dogmatic followers, it helped to turn attention away from the former interests of Rome, and to sap the strength of the Empire: 'The clergy successfully preached the doctrines of patience and pusillanimity; the active virtues were discouraged; and the last remains of the military spirit were buried in the cloister.'[13]

Gibbon explains that 'the conquests of Rome prepared and facilitated those of Christianity'. The drive for unification in the Empire provided the conditions in which the new religion could flourish. His account even creates an implicit parallel between Rome's extension of privileges to all within its jurisdiction, and Christianity's promise of divine favour which is, as Gibbon has it, 'universally

---

[12] Ferguson, *History of Civil Society*, 182–3; K. Marx, *The Poverty of Philosophy* (London, 1956), 145.

[13] Gibbon, *Decline and Fall*, iv. 173 (ch. 38); i. 31 (ch. 2); iv. 175 (ch. 38).

proposed'.[14] Ironically, in Christianity the spirit of union appears in a form that could undermine the citizen's commitment to the political interests of the state.

Vala

Blake's own account of the growth and collapse of commercial civilization appears to incorporate a number of the ideas that have been outlined here, although in his presentation of the interaction between feeling and material developments the role of feeling is primary. Vala as the Shadowy Female becomes a central power in his paradoxical vision of materialistic civilization. She is the emotional force that allows fallen reason to develop commerce and industry, to control religion, to channel energy and skills into the arts of war; and she is the power that eventually undermines these activities. In this role she becomes one of Blake's most complex symbols.

As we have seen, the Shadowy Female embodies two contrary views of love, one optimistic, one fearful:

1. *As an expression of the Spectre's hope*, she promotes his vision of a Universal Manhood that can be realized through self-restraint. This vision has its origin in a religious context, but it is clear that the Spectre of prophecy quite underestimates the power of his own vision. The 'soft Vala' he imagines turns out to be an uncontrollable terror whose influence spreads unpredictably. His universalism consequently appears in two quite unexpected forms: in the dream of Universal Empire; and in radical reactions to the divisive power structures of state control. The hopeful visions of unity inspired by Vala are 'Sweet delusions' because love which depends on restraint is a sad and self-regarding shadow of emotion that will thwart the development of genuine brotherhood. Here Blake begins to clarify the historical role of the false prophet, an issue that emerged in his early treatments of revolution: his myth shows that prophets of revolution whose vision is bound by a finite material world can only intensify the repression against which they strive. The Shadowy Female is a grotesque deformation of human sympathy, which finds expression in possessive affection, com-

---

[14] Gibbon, *Decline and Fall*, ii. 60, 7 (ch. 15).

placent pity, calculating mercy, peace based on mutual fear. She is the feeling that inspires and is inspired by reasonable ideals of social benevolence. The spontaneous passion that she represses character-istically finds release in war—the only arena in which the libidinous fury of natural energy can be formally sanctioned by civilized society.

2. *As an expression of the Shadow of Enitharmon's fear*, Vala assumes the appearance of a harlot who conceals her sinful nature under a show of innocence. She is the seductive power which drew Man out of Paradise, the emotional softness or indulgence which leads insidiously to disruptive passion and which must be resisted and punished if reasonable social order is to be maintained. As such she provides a moral justification for the retributive violence that underpins law, and for the martial spirit that must shape and defend civilization. War is thus an inevitable—indeed, complemen-tary—reaction to Vala's gentle passions.

As the Shadowy Female, then, Vala is a manifestation of the profound emotional confusion that Blake sees at the heart of fallen civilization. The consequences of this confusion are complex and various (which is why the narrative that follows on from the description of Vala's birth is the most heavily revised area of the poem).

The Seduction of Orc

As we have seen, in the Caverns of the Grave love and pity are first experienced in the instinctual drives of Tharmas. The narrative sequence emphasizes that Man's subsequent development is deter-mined to a considerable extent by this initial experience. Tharmas lays the foundations of Golgonooza, and thus sets the conditions in which Orc's natural appetite can be expressed: to Tharmas love and rage seem 'the same passion' (47: 18, $E331$); in Orc's burning natural appetite love and rage are united. The emotional confusion found in Vala arises from an attempt to rationalize and moralize experience that is rooted in natural instinct, an attempt to separate love and rage into distinct and opposite categories (sensuous temp-tation/moral indignation; spiritualized love/merely natural desire). The Spectre's vision of a return to an Edenic state of innocence in which the female is the garden of delight, the male the spirit in the garden, derives from the instinctual urge for unfettered sensuous enjoyment, for the free and unselfconscious expression of love. But of course a rational theology does not seek to promote such freedom in what it sees as the corrupt material world. Its paradise is a tantalizing image of what it actually represses. The Shadowy Female thus both stimulates and frustrates the natural urge for sensuous enjoyment, the longing for paradisal innocence.

She has come into being as a result of Los's and the Spectre's reactions to Orc, and is in this respect an expression of Orc's power—even though she appears to control his power. Her relationship with the fiery demon is thus as ambiguous as Urizen's. She takes over from Urizen's daughters the task of feeding Orc, endowing the impersonal demands of moral duty with the appearance of personal sympathy, as mercy is reluctantly reconciled with justice. The feeding is described in Night VIII:

> Still Orc devourd the food
> In raging hunger Still the pestilential food in gems & gold
> Exuded round his awful limbs Stretching to serpent length
> His human bulk While the dark shadowy female brooding over
> Measurd his food morning & evening in cups & baskets of iron
>
> With tears of sorrow incessant she labourd the food of Orc
> Compelld by the iron hearted sisters Daughters of Urizen
> Gathering the fruit of that mysterious tree circling its root
> She spread herself through all the branches in the power of Orc
> (101: 17–25, E373)

The relationship between the fiery Orc and the cloudy Shadowy Female here parallels that in the 'Preludium' of *America*. In the earlier text, the feeding leads to the moment when Orc breaks from his chains to embrace the female, an act which symbolizes the eruption of repressed energy in revolution. As we saw in the Introduction, the myth of the Preludium is highly ambiguous, and registers troubling doubts about the prospects of revolution. In Blake's new version of the myth the ambiguity is developed and clarified, and given a quite new significance. Here the rising of Orc both serves *and* challenges the progress of empire. It is the female rather than Orc who makes the first move, embracing his fire 'that he might lose his rage | And with it lose himself in meekness' (91: 4–5, E363). Orc does not see the female as a virgin, but as the harlot of those powers that have sought to restrain him—Los and Urizen and 'the Kings of Earth' (91: 15, *E*363). Nevertheless he finds her embrace irresistible, and as he responds to her his soul is 'gnawn in sunder' (91: 16, *E*363). As we shall see, the sundering of Orc is a typical manifestation of the Shadowy Female's power to intensify the conflict between opposing tendencies within Urizen's regime. This seduction and its immediate consequences are described in Night VIIb.

Orc responds to the Female in two quite different ways: as a human form, and as 'Serpent round the tree of Mystery'. His human form at last breaks his chains in a jealous attempt to reclaim her. This revolutionary gesture is doomed to fail: Orc's human passion, which transforms the natural world into a source of delight, is negated by an opposing, abstract view of passion—Vala's belief in the transcendent purity of Luvah. The Demons of the Deep identify Luvah with the crucified Christ, and refer to Vala as a 'Melancholy Magdalen', challenging her to 'descend into the Sepulchre'. These taunts help to clarify Vala's emotional significance as the Shadowy Female, because they place her symbolically at the empty tomb, contemplating the loss of her saviour who is in fact, in the form of Orc, a living presence that she fails to recognize.[15]

Orc's human form therefore cannot find a true counterpart in the Shadowy Female, and is soon entirely consumed in his own fires. But his remaining serpent form also rises to her embrace, 'rending the form of life', actively committing himself to an abstract conception of the universal good. The Female's embrace thus heralds a new era in the history of civilization. The search for a unified social order is no longer primarily a matter of restraining individual energies; it becomes a dynamic process, an energetic striving to realize abstract social ideals. Diverted from the fiery joys of appetite, Orc's energy can now be channelled into empire-building— into the industrial and military expansion on which progress is seen to depend.

There is a potent irony in the fact that the Female is able to release Orc from his chains where Los and Enitharmon failed. For whereas Enitharmon 'concentred' Orc's desires, the Female draws him into a realm where desire cannot realize its own object. Like

---

[15] In the Preludium of *America*, the shadowy daughter recognizes Orc as the fallen 'image of God'. Here, although Vala embraces Orc, she cannot accept him as a manifestation of Luvah.

the abstract goals she inspires, she can be embraced but never possessed. A vortex that absorbs human energy without rewarding it, she fosters hope that breeds disillusionment. She creates a distinctive emotional rhythm that will appear in all aspects of life in the empire of Urizen: a rush of hope which collapses into despair, only to be fanned into hope again. This rhythm is apparent in the immediate result of Orc's rising, the state of universal warfare, the condition anticipated in the earlier songs of the Demons of the Deep, and now triumphantly celebrated by them. War has always been a feature of fallen experience, but now it is no longer simply an expression of barbarous appetite (*see*, for example, 62: 6–8, E342; 70: 30–6, E347). As in contemporary histories, it is moralized, governed by ideology, and becomes an essential instrument by which the illusory goal of universal social order is to be achieved and defended. Subsequently its destructive power is enhanced by increasing mechanization (100: 28–31; 102: 14–22, E373–5). The Shadowy Female typically sends warriors out to war 'with Strong Shouts & loud Clarions' only to make them return 'with lamentations mourning & weeping' (93: 30–1, E365).

Universal Empire

In some respects, the seduction of Orc by the Shadowy Female can be seen as another stage in Urizen's triumph over Los. Since the collapse of the cosmos, Los has been responsible for the labour that shapes the human world. As he is in the power of Tharmas, he does not work to a preconceived design but merely responds to the immediate needs of survival. The descriptions of his labour in Nights IV and V are relentlessly grim because he is the slave of physical necessity and must struggle with recalcitrant materials. But the very constraints of his situation constitute a limit to his fall. The close relationship between labour and need subordinates humanity to the fixed bounds of time and space but also ensures that Man is never finally alienated from the world he makes for himself. Under the influence of Los, the artisan stands at the centre of human development, supplying the basic technology of life in the same way as the ploughman and shepherd provide the basic materials of food and clothing. This elementary labour certainly does not liberate the full potential of human creativity, but it allows Man to see that his life is shaped by his own efforts and skills, and it keeps him closely in touch with the inspirational pleasures of the natural environment. Blake's narrative suggests that as long as Man remains responsive to the concrete demands of sense and instinct, he will be able to create a world in which a sustaining hope can emerge, in which the infinite can be seen in the finite, and desire can mock its chains. Thus Los builds Golgonooza 'Upon the limit of Translucence', after 'Tharmas laid the Foundations'.

As reason gains the ascendancy in human consciousness, labour becomes subordinate once more to its ambitious purposes, as in the cosmos. But whereas in the cosmos the eternal will of the creator could be realized in the workmanship of the artisan, in the scientific universe a more abstract conception of universal order is accompanied by a more sophisticated technology which begins to displace traditional craftsmanship:

> And all the arts of life they changd into the arts of death
> The hour glass contemnd because its simple workmanship
> Was as the workmanship of the plowman & the water wheel
> That raises water into Cisterns broken & burnd in fire
> Because its workmanship was like the workmanship of the Shepherd
> And in their stead intricate wheels invented Wheel without wheel
> To perplex youth in their outgoings & to bind to labours
> Of day & night the myriads of Eternity. that they might file
> And polish brass & iron hour after hour laborious workmanship
> Kept ignorant of the use that they might spend the days of wisdom
> In sorrowful drudgery
>
> (92: 21–31, E364)

The development of oppressive and dehumanizing forms of manufacture here is comparable to the process discussed by Smith and others, which transforms the labourer into a mere component of the industrial mechanism. But here the transformation is not simply the result of material developments. The seduction of Orc by the Shadowy Female provides the reorientation of desire that makes such a development possible.

The birth of Vala as the Shadowy Female, then, is initially seen as a triumph for Urizen, as it provides the emotional basis for material expansion. As the Universal Empire of reason unfolds, so its economic structure works to consolidate the suppression of individual creativity:

First Trades & Commerce ships & armed vessels he builded
    laborious
To swim the deep & on the Land children are sold to trades
Of dire necessity still laboring day & night till all
Their life extinct they took the spectre form in dark despair
And slaves in myriads in ship loads burden the hoarse
    sounding deep
Rattling with clanking chains the Universal Empire groans

                          (95: 25–30, E360–1)

As we have seen, 'the spectre form' appears when consciousness is
alienated from the life of the body. It is a shadowy death-in-life, the
inevitable consequence of systematic repression. Blake's symbolism
repeatedly emphasizes that this repression is enforced in the name
of love. The Spectre of Urthona wooed the Shadow of Enitharmon
with the vision of Universal Manhood; Urizen gives the confused
ideology of love its appropriate institutional form, a temple in the
image of the heart:

And he commanded his Sons found a Center in the Deep
And Urizen laid the first Stone & all his myriads
Builded a temple in the image of the human heart
And in the inner part of the Temple wondrous workmanship
They formd the Secret place reversing all the order of delight
That whosoever enterd into the temple might not behold
The hidden wonders allegoric of the Generations
Of secret lust when hid in chambers dark the nightly harlot
Plays in Disguise

                          (95: 31—96: 6, E361)

This is the counterpart of the cosmic temple. But whereas the earlier
temple embodied the principles of order and harmony that appear
in each aspect of the Golden World, the new temple is a violation
of the natural order in which it appears. Its centre is founded in the
centreless vacuum of the scientific world-view; its structure is designed to conceal the absence of love. The harlot becomes the
symbol of an organized religion that offers a substitute for love, a
furtive ritual in which loving gestures are merely simulated. If the
divine image appears in love which is spontaneous and freely expressed, organized religion reverses the order of delight by transforming divinity into a hidden wonder veiled in allegory. The
appropriation of the sun 'that glowd oer Los' suggests a similar

transformation. Los's reduction of the natural world to finite form does not prevent desire from finding a vision of the infinite within it, but a dogmatic religion places nature within a single, fixed interpretative framework, subordinating its visionary potential to a centrally controlled orthodoxy.

The seduction of Tharmas

As we have seen, one of the consequences of material expansion discussed by Hume and others is internal conflict. And here, once the foundations of commercial civilization are laid, such conflict flares into life. As the rending of Orc's soul shows, the embrace of the Shadowy Female works to intensify the oppositions inherent in Urizen's regime. The resistance of the instinctual and imaginative powers to the constraints of rational control is intensified within each individual, and in the world at large it leads to open warfare between state authority and anarchic libertarianism, between priestly superstition and prophetic enthusiasm. The Shadowy Female stimulates both sides of this conflict, giving new impetus to the opposition to Urizen by her seduction of Tharmas.

As the fluid life of sense and instinct, Tharmas eludes the abstract categories of reason: as Urizen advances, Tharmas retreats, remaining forever beyond his control. But if Tharmas cannot be controlled by reason, he is susceptible to the emotional power of the Female. Like Orc, he finds his instinctive urge for unfettered gratification at once stimulated and frustrated by her. She awakens his sense of lost innocence, but if she inspires hope that Enion may return and that love may be brought 'into the light', at the same time she dashes such hope. To her such innocence seems impossible because the purity of love cannot be expressed in a bodily form; the female powers who govern the outward forms of life seem to have conspired to hide the pure spirit of Luvah in the lustful body of Orc:

> Lo him whom I love
> Is hidden from me & I never in all Eternity
> Shall see him   Enitharmon & Ahania combind with Enion
> Hid him in that Outrageous form of Orc which torments me for Sin
> For all my Secret faults which he brings forth upon the light

Of day in jealousy & blood my Children are led to Urizens war
Before my eyes & for every one of these I am condemnd
To Eternal torment in these flames for tho I have the power
To rise on high Yet love here binds me down & never never
Will I arise till him I love is loosd from this dark chain
                              (94: 14–23, E366)

Her speech reveals the terrible consequences of rationalizing love
and rage: a vicious circle of guilt and recrimination that perpetuates
conflict and repression. Her acknowledgement of sin and her implicit appeal for forgiveness are combined with a sense of moral
outrage and a readiness to find sin in others. Guilt and anger
produce a combination of fatalism ('I am condemnd') and wilful
determination ('never Will I arise') that prevents any resolution of
a potentially paralysing conflict.

This self-destructive emotion pervades and taints everything in
Urizen's world. Tharmas may appear to resist Vala in her guise as
the Shadowy Female, but actually he succumbs to her power,
absorbing her paradoxical consciousness of sin:

Tharmas replied Vala thy Sins have lost us heaven & bliss
Thou art our Curse and till I can bring love into the light
I never will depart from my great wrath
                              (94: 24–6, E366)

The confusion that Tharmas feels in the Female's presence ('Art
thou bright Enion') suggests his awareness that she is at once the
embodiment and the negation of his hope. She stimulates and fails
to acknowledge the infinite powers of appetite. In a passage that
looks back to the feast of Los and Enitharmon, and to the description of Orc's desire in Night V, the Female is served by 'those fair
perfections which men know only by name', and with the 'living
souls' of the Elements, 'But in vain delights were poured forth
on the howling melancholy' (94: 37–53, E367). In her presence,
glimpses of paradisal peace and pleasure mingle with intimations of
the disruptive energy of nature and furious discontent. In seducing
Tharmas, she works to bring him under the control of Urizen, so
that reason can achieve an uneasy truce with its own instinctual life:
'To stay him in his flight that Urizen might live tho in pain' (93: 37,
E366). But at the same time she intensifies Tharmas's opposition to
rational constraint, and brings him into violent conflict with the
progress of empire.

Universal Conflict

Under the influence of Vala as the Shadowy Female, the resistance to rational authority begins to assume the moral characteristics of its enemy. As in Night II, Los and Enitharmon are drawn to participate in the cruelty unleashed by the repressive regime of Urizen. Los at last rises from his broodings and becomes for the first time in this poem a prophet of revolution, who eagerly foresees the overthrow of Kings and Princes in an apocalyptic bloodbath (his speech at 96: 24-7 echoes Revelation 19: 17-18, the words of the angel standing in the sun, whose appearance heralds the destruction of the beast and of the false prophet). But like Tharmas, he participates in the error he opposes: in threatening to punish 'lust & murder' he seems lustful and murderous, rapt in the 'cruel delight' that has possessed him since his failure to release the bound Orc (see 69: 33, E346).

Blake's description of the conflict that develops between Urizen on the one hand, and Tharmas and Los on the other ('the War of Urizen & Tharmas'), recalls at several points Milton's descriptions of the war in heaven. Tharmas is the true god of the Caverns of the Grave, the first mover from whom all knowledge is ultimately derived, while Los is his agent of creation. Urizen's relation to Tharmas and Los parallels the relation of Satan to the Father and the Son in *Paradise Lost*—he is an opposing principle who creates an empire out of what he steals from the abyss of Los's material world. In his attempt to 'undermine the World of Los & tear bright Enitharmon | To the four winds' Urizen develops an elaborate technology of warfare which recalls that of Milton's Satan during the war with the hosts of Heaven (see 100: 26-34; 101: 30, E373-4, and *PL*vi: 470 ff.). The Tharmas who laughingly promises Los victory over his enemies (Night VIIb 85: 28 ff., E367) recalls Milton's God, who appoints his Son as leader of the heavenly hosts (*PL*v: 600 ff.), and who is described as laughing as he contemplates the rebellion of Satan (v: 737). In *Paradise Lost* divine providence works to redeem fallen humanity from the power of Satan in order to restore obedience to the divine will; Tharmas seeks to 'rend the Nations all asunder' in order to roll back the tide of material progress and restore his children to the power of Los (96: 29-97: 17, E361-2). The conviction that love can come from revenge, that freedom can be regained and protected by coercive force, makes the revolutionary impulse seem as tyrannical as the power it seeks to overthrow. As Tharmas declares his opposition to Urizen, his resemblance to his enemy becomes particularly close (*compare* 95: 18–24, E360 and 96: 29–97: 3, E361–2).

The Shadowy Female's embrace of Orc signals the failure of Urizen's attempt to liberate humanity from violent passions. War is now moralized, and becomes an instrument of social good. The libidinous fury of Orc's passion—once so abhorrent to the reasoning mind, and remote from its conception of order—can now be seen as essential to the fulfilment of natural, human, and divine purposes. This implies a fundamental transformation of Man's vision of the world. Nature, no longer a realm whose value and purpose are apprehended only by the reasoning power, is now seen to be animated by fierce 'immortal energies', and all creatures seem driven by the same 'warlike desperation' to live (as in Milton's vision of a postlapsarian nature driven by 'fierce antipathy', *PLx*: 709).

If the vision of nature as a battleground undermines the original basis of the rational world order ('Urizens Web vibrated torment on torment'), it also serves the purposes of state power. This last point is crudely emphasized by the introduction of the Prester Serpent, whose name associates him both with the serpent form of Orc and with the legendary Christian priest and king, Prester John. He is a symbol of state religion, which encourages Man to dissipate his energies in self-destructive warfare (he is sketched on page 98 as a hooded cobra with a human face). The opposition between the forces of reaction and rebellion is thus presented in terms that recall in several respects Hume's conception: the priest as the tyrant and disturber of human society by his endless contentions and religious wars (*see* 98: 22–9, E363), the enthusiast as one whose anarchic fury is like that of the thunder and tempest (*see* 96: 19 ff., E361).

The Seduction of Urizen

A dominant idea in Blake's presentation of the unfolding social order is that all activities within it, whether they are directed towards the expansion of commerce and state control, or against it, are at once influenced by and tend to propagate the influence of

Vala as the Shadowy Female. If she allows war to be moralized and motivated by social ideals, military conflict in turn strengthens her influence, which thrives on the hopes and fears aroused by war. If she promotes religious indoctrination, that indoctrination in turn draws 'the myriads of perturbed spirits thro the universe' into her irresistible vortex. Eventually the Shadowy Female's pervasive influence begins inevitably to impede the development of empire, because it tends to expose the widening conflict between the ideals and the practices of the state. Ostensibly, mercy is a guiding principle of civil and divine power. It was Urizen's 'pity' for the furious Orc that moved him to formulate the restraints of law, and which justified their severity. But the desire to establish absolute rational control increasingly resembles the furious rage it seeks to subdue. As his struggle to impose order becomes more desperate, Urizen finds the Shadowy Female's pitying urge for restraint directed against his own activities. In the progress of the Female Blake describes a process that parallels the progress of religion in Gibbon's account of Rome. What is at first a convenient instrument of state power eventually assumes a form that challenges and triumphs over that power. Ironically, it is while Urizen reads the words of his sacred books in his temple that the Female begins to challenge him:

> O might my eyes behold
> My Luvah then could I deliver all the sons of God
> From Bondage of these terrors & with influences sweet
> As once in those eternal fields in brotherhood & Love
> United we should live in bliss as those who sinned not
> The Eternal Man is seald by thee never to be deliverd
> We are all servants to thy will O King of Light relent
> Thy furious power be our father & our loved King
> But if my Luvah is no more If thou hast smitten him
> And laid him in the Sepulcher Or if thou wilt revenge
> His murder on another Silent I bow with dread
> But happiness can never [come] to thee O King nor me
> For he was source of every joy that this mysterious tree
> Unfolds in Allegoric fruit. When shall the dead revive
> Can that which has existed cease or can love & life Expire
> (103: 6–20, E375)

Here the ideal of Universal Manhood, which initially provided a justification for the pursuit of Universal Empire, appears in a form that reveals the gulf between the ideology and the practices of the state. The Shadowy Female represents a more formidable challenge to Urizen's power than Orc did, because her reproach reflects some of his own deepest beliefs. Urizen's distrust of desire made Orc's visions of bliss seem tormenting delusions. But the Shadowy Female speaks of a blissful other-worldly state remote from the 'terrors' of desire. It is one of the great ironies of Blake's poem that the ideals of 'brotherhood and love' should be advocated by this seductive and delusory Female. Typically, there is self-pity and recrimination in her words, instead of the fearless love and forgiveness that create genuine brotherhood. The emotional commitment to a lost saviour promotes fatalistic resignation, brooding sorrow, the death wish of one 'in love with tears'. It is a resignation that reconciles humanity to repression, that accepts the vindictive official murder as a dreadful necessity, and thus endorses the sacrifice of love even while bemoaning the sacrifice. However, the same resignation may also work to soften the constraints of law. Orc's scornful defiance seemed to make rigorous control an absolute necessity, but Vala's submissiveness allows for compromise—the compromise that reconciles the ideal of brotherhood with the need for paternal authority ('our father & our loved King'), that seeks to liberalize state power even while acknowledging that the true sources of happiness lie beyond such power. It is a compromise that may appear whenever there is an attempt to transform religion from a mere instrument of government into the official conscience of the state. Her challenge at once denies and confirms state power, and thus offers a rationale for state religion.

For Blake the most important product of this compromise is of course orthodox Christianity. In the poem as we now have it, the confrontation between Urizen and the Shadowy Female is followed by a complex and much revised sequence describing the descent, judgement, and crucifixion of Jesus (103: 32–106: 17, E376–81). The sequence shows how institutional Christianity emerged from an attempt to neutralize completely the opposition between mercy and justice. As this sequence forms an integral part of the providential framework introduced in revisions to the narrative, I shall reserve discussion of it until Chapter 9. Here it will be sufficient to note that the elevation of Christianity into a state religion is seen as a particular manifestation of an archetypal process, in which Urizen is finally seduced by Vala and begins to judge his own activities by her values.

When Urizen embraces the Shadowy Female, civilization has reached the point at which it attempts to bridge the gulf between its professed ideals and its practices. The result is not simply a new spirit of leniency. Urizen embraces a vision of destiny that negates the very basis of his imperial ambitions. In the light of Vala's vision of other-worldly happiness and brotherhood, all of the activities upon which empire is founded—slavery, warfare, material expansion—must seem essentially evil. The will that drives civilization, the ambition to reduce all aspects of life to rational control, is finally recognized as a manifestation of the same natural appetite it seeks to suppress. At this point Urizen suffers the fate previously endured by Orc, and is divided between an impotent, human form (that embodies the ideals by which he is unable to live) and a fierce, subhuman form (that embodies his own ruthless desire for absolute control of life, and which seems essentially evil). This is the ultimate triumph of false pity: if Urizen's pity for the furious Orc moved him to formulate the restraints of law, his pity for the submissive Female who speaks of redemption through love makes him forgetful of his own laws. His division is the final climax of Night VIII:

> Urizen sitting in his web of dece[i]tful Religion
> felt the female death a dull & numming stupor such as neer
> Before assaulted the bright human form he felt his pores
> Drink in the deadly dull delusion horrors of Eternal death
> Shot thro him Urizen sat Stonied upon his rock
> Forgetful of his own Laws pitying he began to Embrace
> The Shadowy Female since life cannot be quenchd Life exuded
> His eyes shot outwards then his breathing nostrils drawn forth
> Scales coverd over a cold forehead & a neck outstretchd
> Into the deep to sieze the shadow scales his neck & bosom
> Coverd & scales his hands & feet upon his belly falling
> Outstretchd thro the immense . . .
>
> .   .   .   .
>
> A form of Senseless Stone remaind in terrors on the rock
> Abominable to the eyes of mortals who explore his books
> His wisdom still remaind & all his memory stord with woe
>
> And still his stony form remaind in the Abyss immense
>
> (106: 18–29, 32–5, E381–2)

Urizen finally recognizes that his own wisdom serves 'but to augment the indefinite lust' of Orc (107: 20, E382). The course of human destiny is thus no longer seen to depend on the development of reasonable methods of social control. Instead it is felt to be determined by the struggle of the defective individual will for repentance. This transformation seems potentially liberating: the fury of Urizen's struggle with himself gives his subhuman form a majesty and inspirational power that his human form has never achieved in the Caverns of the Grave:

> No longer now Erect the King of Light outstretchd in fury
> Lashes his tail in the wild deep his Eyelids like the Sun
> Arising in his pride enlighten all the Grizly deeps
> His scales transparent give forth light like windows of the morning
> His neck flames with wrath & majesty he lashes the Abyss
> Beating the Desarts & the rocks the desarts feel his power
> They shake their slumbers off
>
> (106: 41-7, E382)

But although there are signs of hope in this struggle, Urizen's repentance offers no way out of the abyss of materialism. Instead it leaves him—and all of humanity—in the power of the Shadowy Female, reduced to a state of 'living Death'. This state corresponds to, and redefines, the condition of sleep described in *Europe*, where humanity is bound in the power of Enitharmon for 'Eighteen hundred years' after the birth of Christ. During this period, the possibility of more effective action remains only in Los, who retains the power to alter the perception of time and space, and thus to find the way out of the fallen world:

> And Tharmas gave his Power to Los Urthona gave his strength
> Into the youthful prophet for the Love of Enitharmon
> And of the nameless Shadowy female in the nether deep
> And for the dread of the dark terrors of Orc & Urizen
>
> (107: 31-4, E383)

The reference to Urthona here (rather than to his Spectre) suggests perhaps the stirrings of the dormant creative potential of the imaginative power.

New Hope

One consequence of Urizen's struggle to repent is that Ahania, the suppressed voice of his own conscience, begins to be heard once more. She once spoke to Urizen of the 'sweet fields of bliss | Where liberty was justice & eternal science was mercy', but now her vision is dominated by 'the dark body of corruptible death'.[16] Her assumption that death triumphs over all creative effort, that the grave mocks 'the plowd field', seems to spring from a horror at the interdependence of life. The particularity of her vision (108: 9–109: 11, E383–4) betrays a deep fascination with the violence she contemplates. Her horror reflects Urizen's own conviction that nature is in the power of the serpent Orc ('King & Priest' appear as manifestations of a fierce predatory appetite). Repentance has apparently brought Urizen round full circle. The nightmare vision in which Man's 'corrupting members | Vomit out the scaly monsters of the restless deep' was once the vision of Tharmas that Urizen confronted at the beginning of his travels through the Caverns of the Grave (69: 11–13, E346). All of Urizen's subsequent activities have been motivated by the urge to redeem humanity from this vision. Now he must confront it again, but this time the relationship between him and Tharmas is reversed. It is Urizen who, forgetting his wisdom, repines in a dark world of death, while Tharmas flies from this haunting vision, pursuing instead an abstract paradise—a 'Vain Shadow of Hope' (108: 2, E383).

In committing himself to 'abstract false Expanses', Tharmas becomes once more a Spectre, 'fleeing from identity', moving further away from Enion even while he thinks he pursues her. The result is the apparent death of Enion. In Night II Enion was reduced to 'a voice eternal wailing in the Elements', but she resisted death: 'do not thou destroy me quite' (45: 17, E330). Now as the Shadowy Female draws the Spectre away from her, Enion is brought to see death as the gateway to new life.[17]

> For I am now surrounded by a shadowy vortex drawing
> The Spectre quite away from Enion that I die a death
> Of bitter hope
>
> (109: 25–7, E384)

Enion's explanation of her enlightenment is reminiscent of the experience of Thel. Like the young shepherdess, she initially finds

---

[16] Ahania cries to the Caverns of the Grave, from beyond them (presumably from the margin of Non Entity).

[17] As Donald Ault points out, when Los and Enitharmon draw away the spectrous life from Enion in Night I, she rehumanizes (*Narrative Unbound*, 345).

little hope in the devouring Earthworm, because she does not see that divine love descends to the lowest forms of existence. But unlike Thel, Enion finds reassurance in the grave:

> A voice came in the night a midnight cry upon the mountains
> Awake the bridegroom cometh I awoke to sleep no more
>
> (109: 20–1, E384)

The reference to the bridegroom is an allusion to the parable of the ten virgins (Matthew 25: 6), which describes the coming of the Kingdom of God. Enion believes there is no such thing as death, and that the mortal body 'disappears in improved knowledge'. But her newfound conviction still seems limited by her experience of a fallen world. She foresees a soothing release from the turbulence of mortal existence as the individual 'gently fades away'. This recalls Thel's dissatisfaction with her life, her wish to 'fade away' from her 'mortal day'. For Enion, the body seems to offer little hope of fulfilment, and is closed off from Eternity. She assumes that the Mortal who fades away will become invisible to those who still remain.

Her description of life in the Caverns of the Grave develops her sense of its limitations. Life is seen to be dominated by anxiety, the anxiety of the seed that knows its natural potential may be thwarted by hungry winds with their 'invisible army' (110: 5, E385). From this perspective nature is a condition of warfare, and the struggle for existence fraught with pain and sorrow. Like the seed, Man begins in a dark state of chaos and must draw all of his substance from the external environment. Nature thus appears to provide the ground of his existence and identity:

> So Man looks out in tree & herb & fish & bird & beast
> Collecting up the scatterd portions of his immortal body
> Into the Elemental forms of everything that grows
>
> (110: 6–8, E385)

Before it can become a home the world requires dogged exploration, a fact which limits Man's imaginative relationship with it. There are no Elemental Gods in his vision of nature, and little imaginative pleasure. If he rides on the angry furrows of the sullen north wind, this is because he 'tries' it. He works continually to gain mastery of an environment that actually controls him. He is therefore condemned to 'Labour & sorrow & learn & forget &

return | To the dark valley whence he came to begin his labours anew'. In her account of this existence Enion shows a greater awareness of the interrelatedness of life than the time-bound Man she describes: she sees everything in the natural world as an expression of human life, and she feels that everything participates in human sorrow. Enion's 'death' is a stage in a process of growth. What has died is the anxious pity she once felt for the victims of the ceaseless conflict in nature, the pity that now haunts Ahania. In its place a new pity arises in Enion, sustained by her faith in eventual resurrection. Where Ahania sees only conflict, Enion sees beyond it to a sorrowful unity. Here the influence of Vala as Shadowy Female begins to assume a new significance, as it has begun to produce a new understanding of universal brotherhood. There is no sense here that the 'Elemental forms' which govern man's life can be a gateway to 'his ancient bliss', and no indication of how Man can escape his timebound existence. But the mood of acceptance and expectancy at least provide grounds for renewed hope.

The Circular Journey

Reviewing the narrative of Blake's poem as a whole we can see that the development of the materialist universe parallels at every stage that of the cosmos. The cosmos, designed to explain both the purpose and structure of nature, contains within it the seeds of a conflict between religion and science. The inevitable collapse begins with the emergence of Ahania as a power distinct from Urizen, an anxious, piteous, and submissive deity, whose concern with spiritual purpose and origins calls into question the ontological basis of the Golden World and threatens to constrain the progress of rational enquiry. In a comparable way, the materialist universe in which Urizen builds his empire contains the seeds of its own collapse. As the Shadowy Female, Vala's inspirational and challenging influence parallels that of Ahania in the cosmos. Both express a yearning for the lost love and delight of eternity. But whereas Ahania urges a return to creative activity, the Shadowy Female inspires hope that leads eventually to inaction and despair. To the Female eternal life seems remote from the life of the body and therefore all human activity seems ultimately futile. The parallel between Ahania and the Female is deeply ironic: whereas Ahania was rejected by Urizen as an intolerable restraint on his activities, the Female proves irresistibly attractive to him. Blake's presentation of Vala's triumph as the Shadowy Female constitutes one of his most powerful and disturbing indictments of the values on which Western civilization is built.

8

The Last Judgement

An Agrarian Vision

The transition from the chaotic world of the Universal Empire to 'The Last Judgment' is one from a civilization dominated by trades and industry to one dominated by agriculture. Blake's presentation of the harvest and the vintage in this Night is of course rooted in the language of the Bible, and especially of Revelation. The Last Day was a popular subject in eighteenth-century poetry, and naturally earlier writers had adapted the biblical symbolism of the harvest to their own purposes. Blake would have known Cowper's description of the Last Judgement in the sixth book of *The Task*, in which 'The fruitful field | Laughs with abundance' and the land 'Exults to see its thistly curse repealed' (VI: 765–6, 768). And he had illustrated Edward Young's account in *Night Thoughts*, where agricultural symbolism is used to describe a complete transformation in human life (as in the figure of 'final Ruin' who 'fiercely drives Her Plough-share o'er Creation!', and 'The Great Proprietor' whose 'all-bounteous Hand . . . sows these fiery Fields With Seeds of Reason' (IX: 167–8; 921–4; NT427, NT511). But such precedents offer nothing like Blake's extended description of the human harvest. This account was almost certainly influenced by his experience of living in the Sussex countryside at Felpham, and observing closely the activities that make up the agricultural year. Ploughing, harrowing, sowing, waiting for the crop to germinate and ripen, harvesting, threshing, and milling—each of these activities is given a precise symbolic place in the narrative. His use of such symbolism reflects more than an artisan's fascination with productive labour, or an interest in developing correspondences between physical and spiritual processes. As David Worrall has pointed out, the Blakes left Lambeth for Felpham during a spate of bread riots, the most serious of their kind for twenty years.[1] The economic significance of

---

[1] D. Worrall, *Radical Culture: Discourse, Resistance and Surveillance, 1790–1820* (Hemel Hempstead, 1992), 46. Worrall finds striking parallels between Blake's

agriculture was an issue of unusually urgent concern. Blake's description of the harvest presents a vision of social development that has its counterpart in contemporary social and economic theory.

Adam Smith is sometimes regarded as the apostle of modern industrial capitalism, but he was critical of the balance in contemporary European states between agriculture on the one hand, and mercantile and manufacturing activities on the other. While he recognized the interdependence of these interests, in his account of the 'Natural Progress of Opulence' he emphasized that 'The cultivation and improvement of the country . . . which affords subsistence, must, necessarily be prior to the increase of the town, which furnishes only the means of conveniency and luxury.' In Smith's view this natural order of things was underpinned by an inherent preference for agriculture: 'as to cultivate the ground was the original destination of man, so in every stage of his existence he seems to retain a predilection for this primitive employment.' Compared to the mechanic who lives in a town, a common ploughman had a superior understanding, having a greater variety of objects to consider (agriculture being more resistant to the division of labour than urban occupations). Moreover the rural labourer was a member of a community, whereas the urban labourer was liable to be sunk in 'obscurity and darkness'. In the modern states of Europe an 'unnatural and retrograde order' prevailed. 'According to the natural course of things . . . the greater part of the capital of every growing society is, first, directed to agriculture, afterwards to manufactures, and last of all to foreign commerce.'[2]

Some of Smith's views were mirrored in a quite different form by those who questioned the prevailing order of society more radically. In *An Essay on the Right of Property in Land* (1781), for example, the Scottish academic William Ogilvie argued that each individual has a natural right to possess and cultivate an equal share of land, and that 'the freedom and independence of cultivation' should be given first priority over all other plans for increasing happiness, especially those for manufactures and commerce.[3] The

harvest imagery and the language of a contemporary seditious handbill urging the men of England to fight for 'a Land of Bread and Vineyards'.

[2] Smith, *Wealth of Nations*, i. 370; i. 378; ii. 795; i. 380.

[3] W. Ogilvie, *An Essay on the Right of Property in Land With Respect to its Foundation in the Law of Nature* (London, 1781), 11, 32.

outbreak of the French Revolution gave a new impetus to such thinking. William Godwin, in his influential *Enquiry Concerning Political Justice* (1793), argued for a radical simplification of economic life. In his parish-based society the burden of labour would be considerably reduced as 'superfluity' was to be banished and agriculture would become a universal male responsibility: 'Justice directs that each man . . . should contribute to the cultivation of the common harvest, of which each man consumes a share.'[4] Coleridge embraced for a while a spiritualized agrarian communism, and celebrated the ideal of common ownership and production in millennialist terms:

> each heart
> Self-governed, the vast family of Love
> Raised from the common earth by common toil
> Enjoy the equal produce.
> 'Religious Musings' (340–3)[5]

One of the most ardent exponents of agrarian communism was Thomas Spence, publisher of the radical weekly *One Pennyworth of Pig's Meat* and author of a succession of political pamphlets designed to spread his agrarian gospel. Like Godwin, but with different aims, he envisaged a simplified economy, in which the parish would 'do all the business of a Landlord'. Unlike Godwin he insisted that, if necessary, force should be used to effect the dissolution of private property. For Spence the common ownership of land was the basis of liberty since 'there is no living but on land and its productions, consequently what we cannot live without, we have the same property in, as in our lives'.[6] Like Coleridge, he sometimes presented his ideal in millennialist terms. Malcolm Chase observes that the agrarian ideal of a return to the land might seem naïve, as intellect and manual dexterity were arguably at a lower premium in rural occupations than basic physical strength.

---

[4] W. Godwin, *Enquiry Concerning Political Justice*, 2 vols. (London, 1793), i. 806; ii. 791.

[5] Coleridge's agrarian theory is developed in his 'Lectures on Revealed Religion'. See the 2nd and 6th lecture, *The Collected Works of Samuel Taylor Coleridge, Volume 1: Lectures 1795 on Politics and Religion*, ed. L. Patton and P. Mann (London, and Princeton, NJ, 1971). See also N. Leask, *The Politics of Imagination in Coleridge's Critical Thought* (Basingstoke, 1988).

[6] *The Political Works of Thomas Spence*, ed. H. T. Dickinson (Newcastle-upon-Tyne, 1982), 31 (*Description of Spensonia*, London, 1795); 1 ('The Real Rights of Man', *Pig's Meat* iii, London, 1795).

But the agrarianism of Spence and his followers 'was centrally concerned with skill, security, independence and status. These were perhaps the greatest constituent of working-class grievances and trade disputes.'[7] One should add that education also had an important place in agrarian theory (Smith and Spence, for example, shared the view that every parish should have its own school maintained at public expense).[8]

In both the agrarian capitalism promoted by Smith and the radical agrarianism that emerged at the end of the century, we find the conviction that independence and creativity can be fostered by the restoration of a natural relationship with the land, which often means giving agriculture priority over other kinds of economic activity. Blake's agrarian 'Last Judgment' presents a comparable view. Urizen, in constructing the Universal Empire, had inverted what Smith saw as the order of nature: 'First Trades and Commerce ships and armed vessels he builded laborious.' In consequence Urizen's sons leave the plough and harrow and are drawn into the deadening workmanship of mechanized industry. In the ninth Night, the restoration of agriculture involves the destruction of empire and its 'sorrowful drudgery'; only after this restoration has been completed is there a celebration of industry, epitomized by 'Golden Looms' rather than by more complex forms of manufacture. Blake's agrarian vision is of course fundamentally unlike that of more reasonable radicals or that of Smith. It is not based on an appeal to justice or natural rights. It begins with a complete rejection of the world-view on which such ideas are based. That is, it seeks to liberate agrarianism from the limited vision of the selfhood.

The Night presents a vision of progress, a development that begins in a decisive moment of illumination but which also involves a gradual clarification of vision. The Enlightenment belief in the power of reason to liberate humanity from the crippling errors of the past is here transformed and reconciled with a belief in the liberating power of revolutionary energy. Those who argue that the poem represents an abandonment of Blake's earlier con-

---

[7] M. Chase, *The People's Farm: English Radical Agrarianism 1775–1840* (Oxford, 1988), 8.

[8] Spence, *Political Works*, 13; Smith, *Wealth of Nations*, ii. 785 (Smith insisted that not all of the funding should come from public funds, otherwise the teachers would soon learn to neglect their duties).

cern with revolution have to discount much of the substance of
the narrative, as the Night contains some of the most disturbing
scenes of violence in Blake's work. David Aers complains that
some critics have accepted unquestioningly the Night's 'reproduction of coercive hierarchy and violence', and he argues
that 'Only the unexamined prejudices of those thriving in such a
fundamentally violent culture as ours could explain how apparently sane people assume that the violence figured in Blake's
poem . . . could have anything to do with "rebirth"'.[9] I would
argue that it is precisely Blake's attempt to challenge the
unexamined prejudices of apparently sane readers that makes this
Night so difficult to come to terms with. The account of the Last
Judgement is in many respects the most horrific thing Blake ever
wrote, and it strikes continually at our normal understanding of
humane values.

Rejecting Error

As we have seen, in my reading of *The Four Zoas* human history
develops through two major eras or cycles, which parallel each
other at every stage. There are two, because the powers that animate the fallen world can be seen either as divine or as natural. The
first era gives rise to an 'ideal' cosmic harmony, the second to a
materialistic and scientific order, and both orders collapse under
the pressure of their inherent contradictions. The failure of the
second leads to a state of almost universal paralysis, in which only
one power seems to retain some potential for action—Los, the
power that can change fundamentally Man's perception of time
and space.

Blake's presentation of the Last Judgement suggests that although Man has been imprisoned in a finite vision of the natural
world, the prison is locked from the inside. Los initiates the process
of regeneration simply by directing his efforts against the 'creation'

---

[9] D. Aers, 'Representations of Revolution From *The French Revolution* to *The
Four Zoas*', in *Critical Paths: Blake and the Argument of Method*, ed. D. Miller, M.
Bracher, and D. Ault (Durham, NC and London, 1987), 264–5. Northrop Frye
described what he called an 'Orc cycle' in Blake's myth, a cycle which implied the
inevitable failure of revolutionary energy. He therefore seemed puzzled to find 'the
old revolutionary doctrine' in Night IX, and thought it might have been 'added as an
effort of will, almost of conscience': *Fearful Symmetry*, 308.

that he has helped to build.[10] Los's action appears in a passage added to the new beginning to the ninth Night, but it was evidently an integral part of Blake's conception of the Last Judgement before it was included here, because it is referred to in the main body of the narrative (121: 24–5).[11] In pulling down the sun and moon Los apparently enacts the kind of transformation described by Blake in the additional notes for his 1810 Catalogue of Pictures. There Blake insists that 'whenever any Individual Rejects Error & Embraces Truth a Last Judgment passes upon that Individual' (E562). 'Error' is synonymous with 'Creation':

Error or Creation . . . is Burnt up the Moment Men cease to behold it I assert for My self that I do not behold the Outward Creation & that to me it is hindrance & not Action it is as the Dirt upon my feet No part of Me. (E565)

If this suggests an absolute rejection of the 'Outward' world, the suggestion is qualified: as soon as Blake asserts that he does not behold creation, it reappears like the dirt on his feet. He has to contend with its 'hindrance', apparently, even after the 'Last Judgment' has passed upon him. The world of nature that gives rise to the idea of 'Creation' is the world in which he must live and work as an engraver and painter while he is in the mortal body. Elsewhere in these notes Blake asserts that Judgement involves 'throwing off the Temporal' (E555), which might suggest that history can be escaped completely. But this suggestion is also qualified: error cannot be rejected once and for all, but must be thrown off 'continually' (E562). The Last Judgement presented in *The Four Zoas* would seem to confirm A. L. Morton's view that for Blake 'history can never come to a conclusion'.[12] A universal Last Judgement that liberated the imaginative potential of humanity would not free mortals from the need to return from the mental exertions of eternal life to a finite natural world. Blake's presentation of the Last Judgement in *The Four Zoas* suggests that the vision of a finite

[10] The description of Los pulling down the heavens recalls a passage at the end of *Night Thoughts*, where 'Time, like Him of Gaza in his Wrath, | Plucking the Pillars that support the World, | In Nature's ample Ruins lies entomb'd' (IX: 2464–6).

[11] Erdman notes that a passage of about 11 ink lines was erased on p. 117 to make room for the new opening. He has partially deciphered the endings of 2 erased lines (2 '?curst the heavens'; 11 'was Ended') which conceivably referred to Los's destruction of the heavens (E843).

[12] Morton, *Everlasting Gospel*, 27.

world will only imprison Man if he accepts it as the horizon of his vision. It can become instead a temporary and inspirational resting place, in which humanity can live in the state of innocence that Blake names Beulah. Much of the ninth Night is concerned with Man's attempt to organize the innocence of Beulah. Only at the conclusion of the Night, when the process of renovation is largely complete, does Urthona rise to form the golden armour of science 'For intellectual war'. We are left to imagine for ourselves what the strenuous life of eternity might be like.

When Los tears down the heavens, then, he is rejecting the fixed view of creation that he has helped to shape, and thus allowing a new view of nature to appear. Although the rejection can be initiated in a 'Moment', it cannot be accomplished without a long and painful struggle. The ninth Night of *The Four Zoas* is remarkable not only for its sustained exuberance, but also for its detailed account of the pain, effort, false expectations, errors, and disappointments that have to be negotiated in the process of recovery. It emphasizes the need to overthrow not only the conceptual frameworks that govern our lives (these are among the first to change in Blake's myth) but also the deeply ingrained habits of feeling that cannot be escaped in a moment of enlightenment. Change here proves to be a slow and at times exceptionally difficult process.

The contrast between the redemptive potential of the regenerative process and its immediate consequences is emphasized throughout the Night. Two levels of action are distinguished more consistently here than in other parts of the poem: on one level the four powers of humanity learn to perform their appropriate functions; on another level the effects of this learning process are felt. In this way the myth develops a disturbing paradox: the despair, torture, and violent conflict involved in the process of renovation are expressed in the imagery of peaceful labour. The hope and pleasure of Urizen or Luvah can be felt as pain and desolation by the individuals in their power. There is an obvious risk in this procedure: the idea that pain is a necessary instrument of redemption can provide a justification for tyranny, and can find expression in the shallowest kind of optimism. Blake's vision in some respects resembles the errors it seeks to expose. But the process he describes undermines the notion of justice on which most explanations of suffering usually depend. The elaborate agricultural myth continually shows that there can be no productive activity without some kind of violence and destruction.

Awakening

The immediate result of Los's destruction of the heavens is a state of Universal Confusion. The description of this state was added to the original beginning of the Night, and it foreshadows some of the major events. The three lines 117: 19–21, E387, for example, anticipate three separate phases of regeneration described at 123: 5–32, E392–3, 125: 6–11, E394, and 134: 18–31, E402–3. At the end of the description we learn that 'Mysterys tyrants are cut off & not one left on Earth', but much of the following narrative is concerned with the elimination of tyranny. The passage can be seen as a kind of overture or 'Preludium' which summarizes some of the central issues of the Night as a whole.

In pulling down the external world, Los destroys the bases on which his own temporal personality has developed. He and Enitharmon are both 'buried in the ruins of the Universe' and will be resurrected, as Urthona and his 'wife', only when the human body has been renovated. Ironically, the destruction of the outer world can be seen as the ultimate triumph of the Spectre, that aspect of Los that has always disdained the body. His desire for union with the abstract purity of Enitharmon's shadow now has its final satisfaction. But 'fierce desire' divorced from the body can only achieve 'a faint embrace . . . as when | Two shadows mingle on a wall' (118: 2–3, E387). The union is revealed as a sterile intellectual fantasy that heralds the disintegration of the exhausted Urizenic ideology.

Once Los has renounced the material bases of his vision, desire begins to throw off the Serpent form of its conditioning (118: 8–13, E387). The appearance of Orc's flames as 'pillars of fire' resembles the pillar of fire that guided the Israelites through the wilderness towards the promised land, and recalls the liberating role Orc played at the end of Blake's prophetic sequence *The Song of Los* (*see* pl. 7: 26–30). Here it introduces a new upsurge of revolutionary violence which is seen not only as physically horrific, but also as potentially humanizing.

The negative and positive aspects of revolution are symbolized as contrasting manifestations of divine wrath: flood and fire. The 'Bloody Deluge' which overwhelms 'Cities Villages | High spires & Castles' destroys both the weak and the powerful alike, but is seen as a terrible necessity that cleanses the world of tyrants. The flames of mental fire that accompany the violence consume the deluge, liberating individuals from the limited horizons that enslave their passions. Under the pressure of a common distress the divisions between individual families begin to break down: women and children 'throughout every nation under heaven', flock like doves and cling around the men 'in bands of twenties & of fifties pale'.[13] On the other hand the dread unleashed by limitless violence also begins to undermine the predatory passions, which take flight (they retreat to the North, the realm of imagination that is to be renewed). For the first time in Blake's poem, energy begins to break out of the closed circle of self-perpetuating violence. Eternal life, which has usually seemed remote from temporal existence, suddenly comes within reach, as 'all the Sons of Eternity Descended into Beulah' (118: 40, E388) to observe the cataclysm.

As trembling millions start forth into flames of mental fire, the creative potential of reason, surrendered when Urizen forsook his realm in the South, is glimpsed once more, and Man at last begins to stir on his deathbed. There is a parallel here with the beginning of the poem, where fear of confusion prompted his resignation to Urizen (120: 11 echoes 23: 4). Now he attempts to regain control:

> Come forth from slumbers of thy cold abstraction come forth
> Arise to Eternal births shake off thy cold repose
> Schoolmaster of souls great opposer of change arise
> That the Eternal worlds may see thy face in peace & joy
> That thou dread form of Certainty maist sit in town & village
> While little children play around thy feet in gentle awe
> Fearing thy frown loving thy smile O Urizen Prince of light
>
> (120: 19–25, E389)

This vision of reason transformed into a loving guardian has an appealing simplicity that contrasts vividly with the complexity of the crisis that inspires it. It recalls the world of *Songs of Innocence*,

---

[13] Wilkie and Johnson note here 'the regenerative effects on society of the enlargement of the family' (*Blake's Four Zoas*, 214). The dove-like women and children recall Hecuba and her children at the sack of Troy in *The Iliad*, Book II.

and the response of many English radicals to the revolution in France: an appeal for educational reform as an alternative to violent revolution. The assumption that redemption involves little more than a sympathetic mode of instruction, one that inspires 'gentle awe' rather than 'dread' is immediately seen to be misplaced. Man's 'awful voice' fails to transform Urizen. Change requires a different response: 'Then wrath burst round the Eternal Man was wrath' (120: 27, E389). Repeatedly the narrative moves from comforting visions of peace and joy to disturbing manifestations of the anger that must break down resistance to change. As Man now sees, peace is not to be achieved by curbing anger:

> Let Luvah rage in the dark deep even to Consummation
> For if thou feedest not his rage it will subside in peace
>   (120: 32–3, E389)

The restraint of Luvah formally began with the descent of Urizen and the feast of Los and Enitharmon (p. 12), where the nervous wine and fleshly bread of mortality were consumed. Urizen now repents of this error on which his fallen civilizations have been founded:

> O that I had never drank the wine nor eat the bread
> Of dark mortality nor cast my view into futurity nor turnd
> My back darkning the present clouding with a cloud
> And building arches high & cities turrets & towers & domes
> Whose smoke destroyd the pleasant gardens & whose
>   running Kennels
> Chokd the bright rivers burdning with my Ships the angry deep
>   (121: 3–8, E390)

This is recognizably an agrarian reaction against the diversion of resources into polluted cities and overseas trade. The wish to return to the pastoral simplicity of the 'pleasant garden' is characteristic of the ambivalent state of Beulah, in which the inspirational qualities of nature are rediscovered. It is a wish that must be gratified and then outgrown in the process of regeneration. The instruments of war and of construction that in Urizen's hands reinforce the natural ties and 'Order the nations separating family by family' (121: 16, E390) must eventually be transferred to the power of Urthona, and civilization must be constructed on a new basis. Before this can happen, a radical reorganization of human consciousness must be achieved.

A Seasonal Pattern

Throughout the poem, Urizen has worked on assumptions that have been shaped by Los. Now Los's renunciation of the external world makes possible Urizen's renunciation of his own limited vision of time. Urizen does not escape time, but begins to experience it differently. The anxious preoccupation with the future is cast off in the realization that 'futurity is in this moment' (121: 22, E390). This recognition immediately liberates reason from its 'aged mantles', its assumption that wisdom comes from experience, and allows it to rediscover the sense of delight in the inspiration of the moment—Ahania reappears 'in joy'. But at this point we are reminded of the fugitive nature of inspiration. Ahania does indeed live in the 'moment', and dies as soon as she arises. This incident presents in startling form one of the central problems of Blake's poem: the life of the mind is not fixed, but is subject to variations, disappointments, departures of vision. Man's anxious reaction to this instability is sometimes seen as a major cause of his fall, as in the various accounts of the primeval darkening of Vala. In this sense the death of Ahania is a re-enactment of a crisis that haunts the fallen mind. It brings Man to the point at which he must confront a potentially baffling sense of loss. As Ahania dies, the Eternal Man 'Darkend with sorrow'.

He now concludes that such loss must be accepted as part of the seasonal rhythm of life:

> The times revolve the time is coming when all these delights
> Shall be renewd & all these Elements that now consume
> Shall reflourish. Then bright Ahania shall awake from death
> A glorious Vision to thine Eyes a Self renewing Vision
> The spring. the summer to be thine then sleep the wintry days
> In silken garments spun by her own hands against her funeral
> The winter thou shalt plow & lay thy stores into thy barns
> Expecting to recieve Ahania in the spring with joy
> Immortal thou. Regenerate She & all the lovely Sex
> From her shall learn obedience & prepare for a wintry grave
> That Spring may see them rise in tenfold joy & sweet delight
> Thus shall the male & female live the life of Eternity
>
> (122: 4-15, E391)

The death of the female suggests the inevitable fading of inspiration, which leaves Man to contemplate an external world that seems static and finite. The 'male' is immortal, because identity can never be destroyed. The 'female' is regenerate because the forms that inspire and express imaginative life have to be renewed continually. The garment here is apparently a symbol of the beauty and hope that sustains innocence when creative power dwindles. It prevents the male's vision from degenerating into the dead world of 'mere nature', and gives promise of renewed life, as the cocoon gives promise of the butterfly. It allows the fixed outer form of the world to be seen as a delightful and merciful protective covering that can be cast away. Man concludes that the sense of loss felt at the death of the female must be accepted as part of the inevitable rhythm of the mind's activity. Instead of reacting in horror and frustration, or developing conceptual structures that are not subject to such a rhythmical variation, reason must prepare itself for a renewal of creative activity when inspiration revives.

The gender roles described here seem oppressively patriarchal, reducing the female to an inescapably subordinate position. The structure of Blake's symbolism seems to endorse this subordination, although the notion that the female should 'learn obedience' harks back to Man's earlier assumptions about order which he is still in the process of outgrowing. The agricultural symbolism certainly reinforces and naturalizes the notion that the male must wait for the renewal of the female.

If the Last Judgement describes humanity's release from its imprisonment in nature, it also offers Blake's most elaborate celebration of the productive relationship between farmer and nature. If it celebrates an escape from a limited vision of time, it describes a process in which the pace and sequence of events are not determined by individual will, but by the natural rhythms of the seasons. The symbolism points consistently to the fact that in agriculture we triumph over nature and direct it to our own use not by working against its rhythms, but by submitting to them. The most crucial part of the harvest sequence—the germination of the buried seed—lies quite beyond the control of the sower, who can only wait in an act of faith. Urizen is reunited with Ahania only after he has committed himself to the process of the harvest: ploughing, sowing—and waiting.

The description of Urizen's daughters rising to guard Ahania's death couch was added to the main body of the text, but it symbolizes this act of faith in a way that is quite consistent with the symbolism of the basic text of Nights IV to VIIa, where they are (sometimes oppressive) guardians of inspiration. However, Man's vision of the seasonal pattern of eternal life is framed by a quite different kind of symbolism, which includes references to the Lamb of God and his bride Jerusalem. These allusions, and the reference to the Cloud of the Son of Man at 123: 21–124: 5, E392–3, are part of the basic text of the Night, but as they are closely related to the elaborate providential framework that usually appears in revisions, I shall consider them when I discuss this framework in Chapter 9.

The Noise of Rural Work

The recognition of the seasonal pattern of life brings reassurance, and allows the reasoning mind to abandon its attempt to reduce the infinite to finite order:

> Urizen Said. I have Erred & my Error remains with me
> What Chain encompasses in what Lock is the river of light confind
> That issues forth in the morning by measure & the evening by
>   carefulness
> Where shall we take our stand to view the infinite & unbounded
> Or where are human feet for Lo our eyes are in the heavens
> $\hspace{6cm}$ (122: 21–5, E391)

This relaxation of reason explodes the normal view of experience. In the fallen world nature is an aggregate of separate objects, each of which is bound by the continuum of space and time. Now a new vision begins to emerge in which all things will be seen as unified in an eternal present. The imagery of resurrection and birth, the rattling bones which join, the breathing clay (122: 26–30, E392), indicates the redemptive potential of this transformation (*see* Ezekiel 37: 7). But the birth pangs of this vision are horrific. The sudden loosening of reason's iron grip allows the fury and terror that have been repressed to erupt with overwhelming force (122: 39–123: 12, E392). There is a recognition here that liberty cannot be achieved without violent revolution, and that before a spirit of brotherhood can emerge there must be a full resurrection of the bestial passions that have been buried deep within the psyche. As the terror in France had amply demonstrated, revolution tends to inflame bitter memories of injustice which can transform the oppressed into pitiless avengers (the 'Cold babe' who 'Stands in the furious air' at 123: 6–7, E392 is apparently an ironic allusion to Shakespeare's image of pity 'like a naked newborn babe striding the blast'). The price of allowing the reptilian Orc to 'consume' and the deluded Tharmas to 'rage' is a chaotic bloodletting in which the spirit of forgiveness is utterly denied.

If reason cannot remain passive in the face of such violence, it no longer strives to resist. Instead it is stimulated into a new kind of creative labour, one that is no longer governed by the vision of a social order unified by law and defended by force. The Sons of Urizen now relinquish the instruments of warfare and, working for the first time in alliance with Urthona's sons, they adopt the tools of peaceful cultivation, 124: 6–22, E393. (The transformation of 'iron engines of destruction' into spade, mattock, axe, and roller recalls the prophecy of Isaiah 2: 4, 9) The development of agriculture becomes the first priority in the creation of regenerated community: the symbolic identification of agricultural and mental growth implies a recognition that deprivation must be eliminated by abundance before individuals can be freed from the anxiety, greed, and envy that frustrate creativity. The image of Urizen himself as ploughman suggests the new orientation of intellectual activity. Reason no longer strives to establish norms and conventions by which to regulate individual behaviour. Just as the plough makes new growth possible by breaking up the hardened surface of the earth, so reason now creates the conditions for unrestrained mental development by working against the stifling mental habits it once fostered, undermining its own principles of order, destroying its fixed vision of creation, driving 'the Plow of ages'

> over Cities
> And all their Villages over Mountains & all their Vallies
> Over the graves & caverns of the dead   Over the Planets
> And over the void Spaces over Sun & moon & star & constellation
>   (124: 26–9, E394)

In this way the ploughing initiates a new learning process. The sowing of souls that follows is a mental rebirth: the souls are committed to earth as to infancy ('howling & wailing'), and must grow into a new maturity, stimulated by the fierce rage of unsatisfied desire and instinct (the fires of Orc, and the trump of Tharmas).

The image of Urizen as the sower of souls (125: 3–16, E394) recalls the image of the sower in Isaiah 28: 25 and Matthew 13: 3–8. The fate of the warriors, Kings, and Princes, driven by winds 'on the unproducing sands & on the hardend rocks', seems quite unlike the bloody vengeance described on page 123. It suggests that the forms and agents of hierarchical power are not favoured by, and will not flourish in, conditions that promote free intellectual development.

The learning process is not joyful, but begins in 'silent fear' towards the South, the rightful domain of Urizen (125: 20–1, E394). In contrast to this fear, throughout the passage there is a growing sense of Urizen's pleasure in his own activity. His limbs 'shone with ardour'; his daughters, as daughters of inspiration, follow the work with refreshments. The ravishing melody of 'flutes & harps & softest voice', previously associated with repressive construction, now accompanies the turbulence of the harrow. As the work of sowing is completed, and Urizen gives time 'to sweet repose', Ahania returns 'like the harvest Moon'. The simile reinforces the view that the life of the delightful, inspiring female is not constant, but has its own rhythm of decline and renewal.

The union of Urizen and Ahania completes the first stage of Man's remaking of his world. He is still not able to rise out of Beulah, because although he has experienced an intellectual revolution, he has not yet recovered the pleasure of the senses, but thinks of regeneration as a release from the body:

> The Eternal Man also sat down upon the Couches of Beulah
> Sorrowful that he could not put off his new risen body
> In mental flames the flames refusd they drove him back to Beulah
> His body was redeemd to be permanent thro Mercy Divine
>
> (125: 36–9, E395)

The renovation of his powers will involve far more than this new beginning: Luvah, Tharmas, and Urthona have yet to be restored.

Organizing Innocence

Orc is eventually consumed by 'Expending all his energy against the fuel of fire' (by stimulating both the terrible violence of retribution and the strenuous activity of ploughing and sowing, 126: 2, E395).

This leads to a period of exhaustion and rest in which Luvah must renew his power. Throughout fallen history Man's fears have represented love either as a usurper or as a seducer, and in either case Man is drawn into repression. As Urizen once more takes control of Luvah and Vala, this pattern is repeated in a new form. Although the commitment to restraint has ostensibly been abandoned, Urizen ('the Immortal') concludes that since Man fell because the Gods overwhelmed him, love must be reduced to obedience: 'Luvah & Vala henceforth you are Servants obey & live' (126: 6, E395). The demand for obedience recalls God's attempt to confine Adam and Eve to paradise, while Man's conviction that love can be excluded from the realm of the brain or heart recalls his earlier deluded assumption that reason can dissociate itself from the energy that drives it. If Urizen's words demonstrate the persistence of habitual assumptions, they also reflect the exhaustion of love, and show the need for its renewal.

The Place of Seed

The phrase 'the place of seed' suggests at once the unseen subterranean world in which the seed germinates, the realm of infancy, and the realm of sexual love. Here the pleasures of sensation, the joys of childhood and parenthood, the mutual trust and intimacy of loving personal relationships, can be seen as direct expressions of a divine love that urges the soul into consciousness. Here Man will begin to discover a sense of delight in his world that has eluded him through fallen history. The inwardness of this condition is carefully emphasized. In Eternity the gates of Urthona are the gates of heaven, as Urthona inspires imaginative activity. In Beulah they correspond to the gates of sleep, and give entrance to a dreamy state in which consciousness is both liberated and limited. When Luvah and Vala enter this world they are insulated from the 'terrible confusion' of the harvest, 'For in their orbed senses within closd up they wanderd at will' (126: 25).[14]

The pastoral interlude that follows has a fluency and a disarming lyrical beauty of a kind that rarely appears in Blake's work. Its

[14] The pastoral interlude forms what Donald Ault refers to as an 'embedded structure'. He argues that Night IX is 'completely organizable around' such 'nested structures or shells of enclosure', although he admits that the narrative includes 'contrary clues' which may interfere with our perception of such an organization, *Narrative Unbound*, 257–358.

thematic and stylistic similarities with *Thel* have often been noted, while Kathleen Raine has considered the episode in relation to sources in Apuleius and The Song of Solomon.[15] The simplicity of its diction and the apparent evenness of its tone seem reassuring, and may seem to invite a relaxed reading, especially in the context of the exuberant Last Judgement described in the rest of the Night. The context suggests an onward movement towards reintegration and regeneration, and thus creates a temptation to overlook or minimize the significance of features which disturb the sense of progress. The passage describes a 'lower Paradise,' and as in other literary presentations of paradise the scale of action is very small. This is another source of difficulty. Whereas Milton rarely allows his readers to forget that in Eden the eating of a single fruit may have profound consequences, Blake is inclined to leave his readers unattended, and so it is never safe for them to relax their vigilance.

One of the most important models for Blake's episode is Milton's account of Eden in *Paradise Lost*. Milton gives a detailed description of the earliest recollections of Adam and Eve, recollections which form a sequence dislocated by the complex narrative scheme (so that Eve's occur first, in Book IV, while Adam's appear in Book VIII). The sequence begins at the dawn of human consciousness, when Adam finds himself lying 'as new waked' in the sun (*PL* VIII: 253). Adam subsequently has two dreams: in the first he ascends into Paradise where, at the sight of fruit trees, he feels the stir of 'sudden appetite'; in the second, Eve is taken from his side and assumes an independent will (the moment from which Eve's recollections proceed). Whereas Adam first remembers lying in the sun, Eve wakes 'Under a shade of flowers' (*PL* IV: 451); and whereas Adam's attention is immediately taken by the sky, and his first words are addressed to the sun, Eve's first inclination is to lie down by the side of a lake, to look into its waters 'that to me seemed another sky'. In the first moments of human consciousness as Milton describes them, there is a progressive movement from the heavenward impulses of Adam to the earthward impulses of Eve, a movement which clearly foreshadows the loss of Paradise. Blake's pastoral passage contains an equivalent sequence of events, embodied in the experience of a single character, Vala.

[15] See S. F. Damon, *William Blake: His Philosophy and Symbols* (Boston, 1924), 393; Margoliouth, *Vala*, 134; Raine, *Blake and Tradition*, i. 182–203.

It is clear that the pastoral world in Night IX will not be insulated entirely from the conflicts, tensions, and delusions that usually occur in Blake's descriptions of fallen experience. Indeed it is a land

> Where the impressions of Despair & Hope for ever vegetate
> In flowers in fruits in fishes birds & beasts & clouds & waters
> The land of doubts & shadows sweet delusions unformd hopes
>   (126: 20-2, E395)

The pastoral narrative as a whole presents a series of contrasts, comparable to those noted in Milton—sun and shade, hill and valley, song and silence, sleeping and waking, rising motions and sinking motions. The significance of Vala's actions in this delicate pastoral setting is suggested by these contrasts.

The interlude properly begins when Luvah, 'Invisible . . . in bright clouds,' calls on Vala to 'Rise from the dews of death' (126: 32, E395). Vala rises, looking 'toward the Eastern clearness':

> Where dost thou dwell for it is thee I seek & but for thee
> I must have slept Eternally nor have felt the dew of thy morning
> Look how the opening dawn advances with vocal harmony
> Look how the beams foreshew the rising of some glorious power
> The sun is thine when he goeth forth in his majestic brightness
> O thou creating voice that callest & who shall answer thee
>   (127: 1-6, E396)

It seems clear that Vala's search for Luvah will not be fully re-warded in this world, for once she has taken possession of her pastoral home Luvah appears and speaks to her only within the gates of sleep (although he does manifest himself to her indirectly, as we shall see). Having made her answer she is then asked, perhaps by Luvah, 'Where dost thou flee O fair one,' and when she replies 'To yonder brightness,' an unidentified voice tells her:

> Eternally thou must have slept nor have felt the morning dew
> But for yon nourishing sun tis that by which thou art arisen
> The birds adore the sun the beasts rise up & play in his beams
> And every flower & every leaf rejoices in his light
> Then O thou fair one sit thee down for thou art as the grass
> Thou risest in the dew of morning & at night art folded up
>   (127: 10-15, E396)

Vala, naturally discouraged by these words, sits down beneath the apple trees, to weep and 'sigh for immortality.' The tone of this unidentified voice seems very similar to Luvah's tone, but the voice does not seek to enlighten Vala. On the contrary, it denies her immortality, and interferes with Luvah's attempt to rouse her. Vala is exposed to two distinct and conflicting voices ('whence came that sweet and comforting voice | And whence that voice of sorrow', 127: 28–9, E396), as might be expected in a land where 'impressions of Despair & Hope for ever vegetate'. The uncertainty that arises from this rather odd intrusion of an unidentified voice once again recalls Milton's Eden, where it was so easy for Eve to mistake the voice of Satan for the voice of Adam (see Paradise Lost Book V, ll. 38–47, 'Why sleeps't thou Eve?'). When Vala is first exposed to the persuasive voice of error, like Eve she receives immediate reassurance and instruction from her true consort—but her confusion is portentous.

After Vala has learned to distinguish herself from the material world, she learns more about the role she is to play in it, arriving at a sense of responsibility by observing the nature of lambs (which are subject to her will), and the contrasting nature of birds (which are not):

> come hither tender flocks
> Can you converse with a pure Soul that seeketh for her maker
> You answer not then am I set your mistress in this garden
> Ill watch you & attend your footsteps you are not like the birds
> That sing & fly in the bright air . . .
> (127: 33–128: 1, E396)

In this world such minor contrasts assume an unusual importance. The events that follow are presented with a subtle ambivalence that arises from the cumulative effect of contrasting impressions.

As Vala takes charge of her flocks she sings 'a new song' to her lord:

> I will cause my voice to be heard on the clouds that glitter in
>   the sun
> I will call & who shall answer me   I will sing   who shall reply
> For from my pleasant hills behold the living living springs
> Running among my green pastures delighting among my trees
> I am not here alone my flocks you are my brethren
> And you birds that sing & adorn the sky you are my sisters
> I sing & you reply to my Song   I rejoice & you are glad
> (128: 9–15, E397)

The song gently expresses a growing feeling of confidence (in the repetition of 'I will') and a sense of solitude that finds comfort, unlike Milton's Adam, in the company of the other creatures, her brothers and sisters. As Vala takes charge of her flocks and leads them into the valley, her thoughts are turned to her own protection: 'Here will I build myself a house' (128: 23, E397). When she falls asleep, her will is fulfilled by the vision of Luvah, who creates a bodily house for her. As this incarnation is seen through the eyes of innocence, the house is quite different from the deadly 'hollow pit' of experience that confronts Thel. The description seems to invite a simple, approving response to this 'pleasant' dwelling-place with its 'pleasant garden'. And yet the approval must be qualified. The first part of the interlude (up to 128: 16, E397) has concentrated on Vala's awakening. The sun rises, the birds sing and fly, Vala is inspired to rejoice. The emphasis on rising, on light, and on song is appropriate, for Vala seeks communion with her divine lover. In contrast, the descent into the valley is a descent into silence (the birds disappear) and shade. The contrast is significant, as it emphasizes that the valley is, after all, a place of limitation. At the beginning of the interlude, Vala responded to Luvah's voice; but here Luvah creates the house in response to Vala's expressed will. His compliant response is an example of the pity and love that renders form permanent. The point is made indirectly, because Vala's bodily house is not a prison, as Thel's threatened to be. To adapt words from another context, she may 'pass out what time she please' to the heights where she was inspired to sing (see Europe III: 5, E60). The cycle of sleeping and waking, descending and returning, that seems to be interrupted in the Lyca poems, and 'Earth's Answer' can here be completed. But the dangers inherent in Vala's descent soon become apparent.

When she wakes, there is no creative voice to rouse her. She assumes that she is to tend her flocks in her 'pleasant garden', but finds that her flocks 'were gone up from beneath the trees into the hills.' She concludes that the will of her unseen Lord manifests itself indirectly by such means: 'I see the hand that leadeth me doth also lead my flocks' (129: 7, E397). When she goes up into the hills to join them, and to explore her domain for a second time, the material delights of the pastoral world are seen not as objects of praise, but as objects of appetite. There are hints that a tension may

exist between the influence of Luvah, and the influence of sensuous
pleasure, as Vala leads her flocks back down again into the shade
and silence of the valley:

> She went up to her flocks & turned oft to see her shining house
> She stopd to drink of the clear spring & eat the grapes & apples
> She bore the fruits in her lap she gatherd flowers for her bosom
> She called to her flocks saying follow me O my flocks
>
> They followd her to the silent vall[e]y beneath the spreading trees
> And on the rivers margin she ungirded her golden girdle
> She stood in the river & viewd herself within the watry glass
> And her bright hair was wet with the waters . . .
>
> (129: 8–15, E397–8)

This last incident—Vala viewing herself within the 'watry glass'—
recalls a similar incident in Milton's Eden, where Eve viewed herself
in a lake (*PL*IV: 457–75). Eve found Adam less fair than herself,
and the incident portends the subsequent tensions in their relationship, and Eve's fatal weakness. In Blake, Vala's eyes are 'opend to
the world of waters,' and she has a vision of the degenerate
Tharmas and Enion. The vision, another 'impression of despair,'
seems to act as a warning, perhaps a timely reminder of the dangers
of wilful self-absorption, for Vala suddenly feels remote from her
Lord. When her echoing voice calls on him, complaining that she
has become a 'soul that wanders desolate' (129: 33–5, E398) the
call is apparently answered, for 'light beamd round her like the
glory of the morning' (129: 36, E398). It seems that a crisis has
been averted.

The appearance of Tharmas and Enion as children in the house
of Vala is sudden, and rather surprising. In the context of the Night
as a whole it marks an important stage in their regeneration, a
necessary rebirth. But in its immediate context, it also marks a stage
in Vala's development. The sight of her two little children draws
Vala back to her bodily house, where she feels the pull of maternal
affections: 'The Children clung around her knees she embracd them
& wept over them' (130: 6, E398). When she wakes for the second
time in her house, the prevailing mood of contentment is soon
disturbed by the recalcitrance of Enion and the weeping of
Tharmas. In the lines that follow, the tension between the children
becomes the centre of interest. Vala, who was previously led from
her house and up into the hills by her sheep, is now induced to

follow the steps of the elusive Enion 'into the garden among the fruits' (130: 32, E399). The division that seemed to be emerging in Vala's experience, between the pull of appetite and the loving care appropriate to the shepherd, is now embodied in a form that is potentially beyond her control. In this context Enion embodies that aspect of love that is fulfilled by sensuous delight, and which may lead to self-absorption. Tharmas, who wanders with the flocks, apparently embodies the caring aspect of love, the urge to protect and to have love returned. These developments foreshadow the emergence of the selfhood, its tendency to retreat from whatever threatens individual pleasure, its self-absorption and self-pity. An uneasy peace is established when Tharmas takes Enion by the hand, and she is persuaded—reluctantly—to obey the will of Vala. The incident recalls, once again, Milton's Eden, where Eve retreated from Adam when she first saw him, so that Adam had to take her by the hand (PLiv: 481–91). In Eden, the incident foreshadows the moment in Book IX when Eve separates from Adam shortly before the fall, withdrawing her hand from his (ll. 389–90). In Blake, the episode ends ambivalently, as the two children go 'straying among Vala's flocks | In infant sorrow & joy alternate' (131: 16–17, E400).[16]

Although the pastoral interlude presents a view of incarnation redeemed by innocence, its serenity is deceptive. The passage follows the development of Vala from the dawn of consciousness to motherhood, and as she discovers the nature of her world, Vala is both as innocent and as susceptible as Milton's Eve. Indeed, as I have suggested, in its gradual movement from heavenly to earthly impulses Vala's experience parallels the experience of both Adam and Eve (Vala's two dreams, like Adam's, mark the awakening of appetite and the appearance of an independent female will respectively).

The pastoral passage, then, can be read both as a prelude to Man's awakening, and as a prelude to his fall. A passage in Night VIIb, where Tharmas recalls his prelapsarian innocence, presents this second view:

[16] For an alternative reading of this interlude, see Catherine Haigney, 'Vala's Garden in Night the Ninth: Paradise Regained or Woman Bound?', *Blake, An Illustrated Quarterly*, 20 (1987), 116–24. Haigney emphasizes the sinister sexual drama of the episode, in which Vala aids Tharmas in his domination of a woman who remains unwilling.

> O Vala once I livd in a garden of delight
> I wakend Enion in the Morning & she turnd away
> Among the apple trees & all the gardens of delight
> Swam like a dream before my eyes I went to seek the steps
> Of Enion in the gardens & the shadows compassd me
> And closd me in a watry world of woe where Enion stood
> Trembling before me like a shadow like a mist like air
>
> (93: 42–94: 6, E366)

Here Tharmas obviously thinks of this incident in the gardens of Vala as the moment when his fall began. We are not shown the fall of Tharmas in these terms in *The Four Zoas*. In the heavily revised opening of the poem we 'Begin with Tharmas Parent power. darkning in the West' (4: 6, E301), and there is no mention of the gardens of Vala at this point. But some of the confused and conflicting accounts of the fall elsewhere in the poem agree that it began in Beulah, the site of this lower paradise.[17] The pastoral interlude in Night IX provides the poem's longest and most detailed account of the nature of life in this lower paradise, and contains its simplest dramatization of the central temptation of Beulah.

The fact that the pastoral myth shows Vala's susceptibility as antecedent to the unstable relationship between Tharmas and Enion may help to explain the initial importance of Vala in Blake's thinking. David Lindsay has suggested, 'in view of the persistent echoes of works written around 1789', that in this interlude 'Blake was drawing on an early poem about the soul's passage through material existence'.[18] It is possible that the copperplate text originally began with a version of the pastoral narrative (*see* Appendix 3).

The passage offers a particularly good example of how Blake read Milton—attempting to liberate the 'infernal' or imaginative truth from its containing orthodoxy. Returning to Milton from Blake, readers may be more aware of the highly ambiguous nature of an Eden which is open to both celestial and satanic visitations, where dreams may awaken dangerous appetites, and where the archetypal man suffers a division from which his fall will follow. Blake's own 'lower' paradise is a world that must be outgrown. A

[17] e.g. 21: 8–22: 41; 50: 1–27; 83: 7–26; 133: 11–21.
[18] D. W. Lindsay, 'The Resurrection of Man: A Short Commentary on Night Nine of Blake's *Vala or The Four Zoas*', *University of Capetown Studies in English*, 6 (1976), 20.

secure, protective environment may foster the inspirational joys of love, but the insularity that allows trust to develop can also lead to a contraction of sympathy. The realm of intimate personal relationships provides a microcosmic form of innocence necessary for the development of the individual, but it is an enclosed and private world, and for that reason it must be outgrown. The pastoral narrative leads to the point at which the dream of innocence might turn into the nightmare of experience, where there is a gradual awakening.

Man has to achieve a much more challenging vision of innocence, that will confront and triumph over the apparent horrors of the world, a vision of divine love that embraces all aspects of life, and transforms Enion into the loving bride of Tharmas. The narrative shows that by themselves love and instinct are unequal to the task: such innocence must be organized, which means that reason must create the conditions in which Man's sympathies can expand beyond their 'natural' limits.

Towards a Universal Community

After the growing harvest has been watered by floods from heaven, Urizen awakens to new activity:

> He pourd his light & all his Sons & daughters pourd their light
> To exhale the spirits of Luvah & Vala thro the atmosphere
> And Luvah & Vala saw the Light their spirits were Exhald
> In all their ancient innocence the floods depart. the clouds
> Dissipate or sink into the Seas of Tharmas   Luvah sat
> Above in the bright heavens in peace.
>
> (131: 32–7, E400)

Urizen no longer seeks to confine love to the place of seed, but works to extend its influence as far as possible. Nevertheless, his actions seem to reflect Man's desire to 'put off his new risen body'. In the light of reason, love is now seen as a transcendent spiritual power which elevates human aspirations beyond the immediate pleasures of sense to the possibility of deliverance from the body:

> the Spirits of Men beneath
> Cried out to be deliverd & the Spirit of Luvah wept
> Over the human harvest & over Vala the sweet wanderer
> In pain the human harvest wavd in horrible groans of woe
>
> (131: 37–40, E400)

The possibility of degeneration does not seem far away here, as Luvah weeps over Vala 'the sweet wanderer' and 'the Eternal Man was Darkend'. Like the limited, if sensuous, innocence of lower paradise, this vision in which spirit cries helplessly to spirit must be outgrown.

The resurrection of Enion (132: 14–35, E400–1) symbolizes the achievement of a more challenging innocence, in which divine love is not a distant spirit that will redeem humanity from suffering, but a presence that can be felt in the pain and sacrifice that are normal aspects of organic interdependence. At the end of Night VIII Enion began to lose her fear of death and her horror at the seemingly pointless conflict and suffering in life; she began to see all parts of life as united in sorrow. Now the fear of death departs from her like a dream, and she becomes (like matron Clay in *Thel*) a mother who lovingly nourishes all her children. At this point Man begins to see that nothing is alien to his own existence:

> the scaly newt creeps
> From the stone & the armed fly springs from the rocky crevice
> The spider. The bat burst from the hardend slime crying
> To one another what are we & whence is our joy & delight
> (132: 29–32, E401)

As Man loses his sense of alienation from the natural world he recovers his instinctive delight in the life of the body. Unlike the simple pleasure of lower paradise, this is not a childlike delight fostered by security, but a feeling that can embrace all natural hazards: Tharmas is fully humanized and at last takes Enion as his bride (132: 36–9, E401). The vision of innocence that Thel could not find is here achieved.

This 'organized' innocence is presented as the harvest of Urizen's redemptive labours. The work of harvesting parallels earlier attempts to bind the disparate elements of life into unity. In the cosmos, where the binding and garnering (30: 1–7, E319) were repressive, order was achieved by suppressing the turbulent aspects of experience. The result is a partial harmony, supplied by the lute and the lyre. In contrast, the binding activity of the harvest is accompanied by music that includes all of the poem's instruments:

> They took them into the wide barns with loud rejoicings & triumph
> Of flute & harp & drum & trumpet horn & clarion
> (132: 8–9, E400)

The golden feast which accompanies the resurrection of Enion is a counterpart of the golden feast at the beginning of the poem, from which the sorrowing Enion was excluded. At the earlier feast, the suppression of love was celebrated. Now love fuels the celebration: Luvah is no longer a transcendent spirit sitting 'Above in the bright heavens', but an immediate presence whose power is felt in the intoxicating joys of appetite as his flames serve 'the wine of Eternity' (133: 3, E401).

Brotherhood

Man's vision is still organized in sexual terms, having grown from the place of seed. The joyful union of Tharmas and Enion may imply a love without jealousy or possessiveness, the motherhood of Enion may preclude any parental sway of the kind Vala exercised over her children in lower paradise (see 131: 8–14, E399). But the potential for jealousy and repression seems inherent in all relationships that develop within the realm of sexuality. In the world of Blake's myth the vision of life as a loving community is essentially a vision of brotherhood. The narrative shows this by moving swiftly from the embrace of Tharmas and Enion to a company of Eternal Men in which the risen Man can take his place.

The existence of this community of Eternal Men might surprise the reader, since much of the preceding narrative suggests that the fallen Man contains all within him. The brotherhood of Eternals brings into focus a paradox inherent in Blake's conception of providence. When Man falls, apparently, the divine community of which he was part survives in some form. But without Man this community cannot be universal: it must be at once unfallen and imperfect. As Man now rises to rejoin his brothers, the breach is healed, and the imperfect vision of the unfallen Eternals is clarified. In contemplating the history of Man's fall, then, the Eternals are themselves emerging from error. Their shuddering reaction to the 'female form now separate', their weeping at their shadows, their view of the Generative World as 'Sin', stands in contrast to the fearless joy and love that has just been evoked. Their view of the female (133: 7, E401) involves a false antithesis, for if she is not 'born to drink up' all Man's powers, neither is she merely for the 'sport and amusement' of the male. Urizen's fall into the Caverns of the Grave begins in such a scornful underestimation of Ahania's role ('the feminine indolent bliss. the indulgent self of weariness' 43: 6, *E*328). In Man's new perception of eternal life the female exists not for 'sport', but for recreation in its full sense—for the renewal or rebirth of the creative powers. The Eternals' reaction to 'Sin' is a re-enactment of their error in 'Days of old'. The Eternal who describes the history of Man's fall is at once revealing and reconsidering a prejudicial view. The vision of human impotence ('Man is a Worm') recalls the error of the divided Orc; the idea that Man is shut off from higher life by 'walls of Gold' recalls the limited vision of the Shadow of Enitharmon (83: 10, *E*358); the reaction to Man's 'Selfish' repose ('we cast him like a seed to earth') is an act of exclusion and therefore a betrayal of brotherhood. Ironically, when Man falls the Eternals see their own shadows born in families. As a summary of Man's spiritual history, the passage suggests that he has been constantly subject to Eternal supervision which has contributed to his imprisonment in the natural world. In this view Man does not have sole responsibility for the protective structures (the limited visions of divinity and creation) which bind him. They are aspects of an ambivalent mercy: like windows, walls, and hearths, they protect the natural man at the expense of 'Brotherhood & Universal Love'. The image of the seed also suggests the positive aspect of this merciful intervention, the capacity for renewal that allows error to be recognized and outgrown. In this sense the fall is instructive for both Man and his fellow Eternals. Man's fall and regeneration reveals to the Eternals the true nature of brotherhood.

Threshing and Winnowing

As we have seen, the description of the Last Judgement tends to emphasize the distinction between the active powers of humanity and individuals who exist under their influence. Among other things, the distinction shows that the four powers have to be renewed before humanity as a whole can be regenerated. Man's progress from the place of seed to the feast of Eternal brothers is a continual expansion in his vision, which may lead readers to assume that humanity has now escaped from the selfhood completely. But paradoxically, 'Man' achieves brotherhood long before 'Men' escape the divisive effects of the selfhood. His progress is apparently an advance in the sense of possibility, which must now be realized through renewed effort.

At the outset of his recovery, Urizen recognizes that his fallen labours 'Order the nations separating family by family' (121: 16, E390). But families are not merely part of the legacy of fallen history: the pastoral interlude suggests that they are vital to human development. Nations may also be necessary as expressions of collective identity.[19] But until the individual reaches emotional maturity, these structures will tend to form the horizons of fellow feeling. Man has now learned that brotherhood is achieved only when the full power of the renovated Tharmas and Luvah has been felt. At this point, therefore, there is a shift in the distribution of labour. Los initiated the regenerative process, but as yet only Urizen has laboured with the instruments of production. Now after Urizen has begun to thresh the nations, liberating individuals from the nationalism that fosters war and deprivation, other powers start to take over. When Urizen first relaxed his control of consciousness, the rage of Tharmas and Orc erupted in chaotic vengeance which brought no escape from the heritage of cruelty. Now as Tharmas and Luvah rise again to take possession of Man, their rage is in more than one sense renewed.

The speech and actions of Tharmas (134: 2–29, E402–3) recall several biblical representations of divine anger. The description of the winnowing alludes to the wrath of God in Isaiah 17: 13. His vision of the destruction of Mystery recalls the fall of Babylon in Revelation 17 and 18, the Lord's punishment on the rebellion of Korah (Numbers 17: 30–3), the vengeance David seeks for his enemy (Psalms 55: 15), the fall of Tyrus—in which Babylon is the scourge of God (Ezekiel 26: 7–21). His vindictiveness, which triumphs with equal satisfaction over the fall of 'Pomp' and the suffering of 'delicate women & children', seems closely related to the intoxicated urge for conquest that he denounces. But the speech offers a striking contrast with his words at 96: 29–97: 17, E361–2. In the earlier passage, where he is under the influence of the

---

[19] The importance of the 'nation' in emphasized in some of Blake's late revisions to the poem, in which the Eternal Man is identified as 'Albion'. Bernard Nesfield-Cookson observes 'we should do Blake an injustice if we were to understand him as condemning the coming into being of nations. In themselves they are good; they are manifestations of the infinite variety of mankind': *William Blake: Prophet of Universal Brotherhood* (London, 1987), 186.

Shadowy Female, his pity for the oppressed leads to self-pity and tyrannical anger. Now his pitiless, even gloating rejection of the oppressive machinery of nation states seems cathartic, and it modulates into a concern for the victims of oppression.[20] Just as the winnowing separates the seed from the chaff, so his words seem to enact the emergence of human compassion from the unforgiving anger of the selfhood. The liberated victims are now joyful rather than vindictive.

As the constraints of nationalism disappear, a song of liberty unites 'every Earth in the wide Universe' (134: 30, *E*403). The black African slave becomes the representative of all of enslaved and exiled humanity, which is now free to return to the 'native land' of the soul, a state of innocence associated with youth, family, and pastoral simplicity.[21] This recalls the innocence of the place of seed, and it serves as a reminder that Universal Brotherhood demands a release not only from kings, warriors, and the cup of religion, but from the inward-looking tendencies encouraged by family feeling. If the progress towards organized innocence begins under the influence of a benign and merciful Luvah it ends under the influence of a terrifying aspect of his power, as Luvah is now commanded to make his sons bear away the 'families of Earth'.

The Vintage

At every phase of Man's history in the fallen world, the attempt to bring order to existence has involved a sacrifice of the passions. Luvah must be 'melted with woe' before the Golden World of the cosmos can be erected; Orc must be bound and elevated on the tree of Mystery before Urizen's Universal Empire can be developed. These are 'natural' perceptions of the sacrifice necessary to win a unified vision of existence. As we have seen, the vision of Universal Brotherhood calls for a quite different kind of sacrifice—the sacrifice of the selfhood. Blake's narrative has already presented several related triumphs over the selfhood—Urizen renouncing futurity, Enion losing the fear of death, Tharmas winnowing the nations. The crushing of 'human families' is the last and most violent of these, perhaps because family love is one of the most powerful and

---

[20] The lines 134: 18–23 also appear in *America*, VI: 6–11.
[21] The slave's home is 'the little Earth of Sotha'—see *America* b 20–1.

enduring influences in the life of most individuals (in *Jerusalem* Blake identified 'soft Family-Love' as the source of 'cruel Patriarchal pride,' pl. 27, E173). In the symbolism of the vintage, the sacrifice of selfhood is achieved not by denying love, but by experiencing its full power. Luvah himself presides over the sacrifice, in an action that parallels and contrasts with the repressive activity of Urizen. Luvah rising from this bright feast (135: 22, E403) mirrors Urizen rising from the earlier bright feast at 23: 9, E313. The fate of the Legions of Mystery—clusters of human families—who fall down into the wine presses is analogous to the fate of Luvah in the furnaces of affliction.

Luvah's role corresponds to that of the angels who make the sinful 'drink the wine of the wrath of God' in Revelation 14 (*see also* Isaiah 63: 1–6). But it also corresponds to Christ's role in the harrowing of hell. No longer the sacrificial victim himself ('His crown of thorns fell from his head', 135: 23, E403) Luvah descends on an errand of mercy. The merciful aspect of this descent is only apparent to the 'human odours' who have escaped from selfhood into the vision of innocence: 'How lovely the delights of those risen again from death'. To those in the winepress who have yet to attain such a vision, it seems a horrific torture:

> But in the Wine presses is wailing terror & despair
> Forsaken of their Elements they vanish & are no more
> No more but a desire of Being a distracted ravening desire
> Desiring like the hungry worm & like the gaping grave
> They plunge into the Elements the Elements cast them forth
> Or else consume their shadowy semblance Yet they obstinate
> Tho pained to distraction Cry O let us Exist for
> This dreadful Non Existence is worse than pains of Eternal Birth
> Eternal Death who can Endure. let us consume in fires
> In waters stifling or in air corroding or in earth shut up
> The Pangs of Eternal birth are better than the Pangs of Eternal
>   Death
>
> (136: 5–15, E404)

The victims are driven to the margins of Non Existence, recalling the plight of Enion who once craved on the margins of Non Entity at the earlier 'golden feast'. They give voice to the despair of those who can see nothing beyond the death of the selfhood, and who cling feverishly to what they experience as a bondage of pain. The references to the 'Elements' allude to a passage in Galatians, where

Paul addresses those who, even after they 'Have known God, or rather are known of God' turn again 'to the weak and beggarly elements, whereto [they] desire again to be in bondage' (4: 9). In Blake's myth the conflict between the terrors of the selfhood and the intoxicating fury of desire is associated with war. When Luvah descends to the vineyards he sounds 'the Song of Los' (perhaps an allusion to Blake's sequence of illuminated prophecies which describes the resurrection of Man through revolutionary wars). The winepress also appears, in a different context, in *Milton*, where the reader is informed that 'This Wine-press is call'd War on Earth' (pl. 27: 8, E124). And yet Blake's description does not focus on images of combat, but on the hellish imagery of torture, on the instruments that are typically used by tyrannic regimes to extract confessions or recantations, and to break the spirit of captives by force:

> But in the Wine Presses the Human Grapes Sing not nor dance
> They howl & writhe in shoals of torment in fierce flames consuming
> In chains of iron & in dungeons circled with ceaseless fires
> In pits & dens & shades of death in shapes of torment & woe
> The Plates the Screws and Racks & Saws & cords & fires & floods
> The cruel joy of Luvahs daughters lacerating with knives
> And whip[s] their Victims & the deadly sports of Luvahs Sons
>
> (136: 21–7, E404)

We can approach this terrible passage by considering its place in the larger pattern of the Last Judgement. We have already noted how in this Night there is a consistent pattern of repetition: a merciful vision is followed by its wrathful counterpart. The winepress is the grim counterpart of the resurrection of Enion, who is redeemed when Man loses his fear of death. Enion becomes a loving mother, a fountain of life willing to expend herself in the service of others. To the eye of innocence, creatures that are normally regarded as unproductive or alien or hostile to human life are seen as part of the divine family: Enion feeds with her milk the 'beasts & worms and creeping things'. Those imprisoned by the selfhood can only see such love as an incomprehensible sacrifice of the finite self; they will be tormented by any emotion powerful enough to threaten their sense of autonomy. Such an explanation, however, does not account for the element of sadistic glee in this passage. The vision takes to an extreme the contrast between the exuberance of those who perform the labour, and the agony of those in their power. The reference to catching the shrieks in cups of gold (137: 1, *E*405) forces a connection between the execution of criminals (whose blood was traditionally deemed to have healing properties) and the ritual sacrifices of religion. The intimations of ritual detachment and exploitation here indicate the incipient exhaustion of Luvah's power. At this point the Eternal Man darkens with sorrow, and another phase of activity is urged into being.

Urthona

Urizen, who was last referred to as working with his flail (133: 34, *E*402), does not appear again in this poem. In his place, Urthona, the last of Man's powers to be renewed, finally emerges to take control of human thought. When Urthona rises from the feast there is a description of labour that stands in contrast with the others we have so far seen:

Then Tharmas & Urthona rose from the Golden feast satiated
With Mirth & Joy Urthona limping from his fall on Tharmas leand
In his right hand his hammer Tharmas held his Shepherds crook
Beset with gold gold were the ornaments formed by sons of Urizen
Then Enion & Ahania & Vala & the wife of Dark Urthona
Rose from the feast in joy ascending to their Golden Looms
There the wingd shuttle Sang the spindle & the distaff & the Reel
Rang sweet the praise of industry. Thro all the golden rooms
Heaven rang with winged Exultation   All beneath howld loud
With tenfold rout & desolation roard the Chasms beneath
Where the wide woof flowd down & where the Nations are
  gatherd together

(137: 7–17, *E*405)

The entire agricultural process is dependent on the invention and craftsmanship of Urthona's sons 'In dens of death' (124: 21, *E*393). Now the regenerative process is almost complete the relationship between craftsmanship and rural labour is reversed: at last Urthona himself rises 'limping from his fall' and leaning on Tharmas, the blacksmith sustained by the shepherd, reviving industry closely supported by the rural economy. The human economy, that is, has been restored to what Adam Smith would regard as 'the natural course of things,' manufactures expanding only after the agricultural base has been fully developed. Urthona is recognizable as Los, freed from the constraints that once impaired his creativity. When Los laboured in the power of Tharmas, in the Caverns of the Grave, his work was a desperate struggle to transform an alien and chaotic environment into serviceable home. But Urthona himself rises only after labour has transformed the world into a source of abundance. The sequence confirms the conviction expressed in the *Marriage*, that imaginative activity is fully released only when the desire for 'sensuous enjoyment' has been satiated.

Two kinds of labour proceed under Urthona's influence, female and male. As the imaginative power, he is able to bring conflicting areas of consciousness into harmony without repressing them. When he rises, all of the female powers unite for the first time in the poem, and become productive. The description of their work at Golden Looms brings together a number of related themes. While the harvest and vintage feed the risen body, the weaving activity may clothe and protect the body at the onset of winter. The labour recalls Man's vision of eternal life, in which the female must 'sleep the wintry days | In silken garments spun by her own hands against her funeral' (122: 8–9, E391). As we have seen, if the death of the female is the fading of inspiration, the garment prevents the male's vision from degenerating into the dead world of 'mere nature', and gives promise of renewed life. The Golden Looms that ring out at the onset of winter symbolize the function of all industrial production in the regenerate community, which is to sustain rather than to absorb human creativity. As industry is no longer driven by the acquisitive and competitive ideology of materialism, it can at last become a means of uniting the nations in co-operation and putting an end to their 'rout & desolation'.

The second consequence of Urthona's rising is the making of the bread of life—the transformation of experience into knowledge. This begins after the Bacchic exuberance of the vintage has been brought to an end. When the wine has been separated from the lees, Luvah is put for dung on the ground. This is a punishment for the wicked in Psalm 83: 10 and Jeremiah 16: 4, and the allusion may signal a reaction to the sadism of the vintage (although, as Wilkie and Johnson note, it 'suggests a productive, fertilizing use even of the refuse of the winemaking process').[22] When the powers of love revive, Man 'cast them wailing' into the world of shadows, a phrase

[22] Wilkie and Johnson, *Blake's Four Zoas*, 232.

which recalls Urizen's activity as the sower, and indicates the entry into another period of sleep and renewal. The description of Urthona's activity recalls the symbolism of VIIa, where Orc is subject to the power of Urizen and his daughters ('they took the book of iron & placd above | On clouds of death & sang their songs Kneading the bread of Orc', 79: 27–8, E355). The differences between the two situations are of course as important as the similarities. Urizen's wisdom was designed to repress desire; Urthona's emerges after desire has been satiated. The bed on which Men turn is not a bed of frustrated love: the fierce agitation is powered by the instinctual force of Tharmas, not by Luvah. Whereas Orc was bound to the prescriptive wisdom of the book of iron, under Urthona men write the bitter words of stern philosophy themselves. In the power of Urizen the mill suggests the merciless reduction of individuality (80: 4, E355), but here it is associated with individual effort. The human community is a brotherhood of creative individuals, not a community bound passively together by inherited conventions. Thought may appear to be as painful now as it was for Orc (men 'knead the bread of knowledge with tears & groans,' 138: 15, E406). But while 'Men' suffer, Man regains control of the sea of space and time.

Soon after the bread of ages is made, Urthona 'took his repose in Winter in the night of Time' (138: 19, E406). This recalls the sleep of Urthona in *Europe*:

> Again the night is come
> That strong Urthona takes his rest,
> And Urizen unloos'd from chains
> Glows like a meteor in the distant north
> (3: 9–12, E61)

These lines suggest a cyclical relationship between two dominant powers in fallen history: the recurring sleep of Urthona allows Urizen to assume control of human consciousness. The seasonal pattern of the Last Judgement seems to imply a comparable cycle, as winter is the time when Urizen must take the initiative, no longer glowing like a distant heavenly body (*see* 23: 9, E313) but preparing for the return of spring by ploughing. Labour at the plough must be renewed, apparently, in order to ensure that knowledge does not consolidate into a new tyranny. The 'heavens of precious stone' in which the bread of knowledge is placed seem hard and static compared to the 'delightful Expanses' and 'vocal harmony' of the heavens described at 137: 32–3, E405. They recall the artificial quality of the Spectre, and illustrate the reification that occurs when vision is embodied in the finite form of the artefact. The characterization of Urthona as a blacksmith also points to this reification, as the blacksmith's creations must be removed from the fire to harden. As we have seen, the imagery of resurrection is predominantly that of destruction—breaking up with the plough, harrowing, reaping, flailing, crushing, grinding in the mill. Through such activities Blake dramatizes the need to relinquish the outer forms of vision continually, so that new creation can occur. His narrative foregrounds processes, and its conclusion suggests that the products of the imaginative power are not ends in themselves. The cycle of regeneration heralds the cycle of Eternal life, in which innocence must be continually reorganized. The work of Urthona clothes Man in the golden armour of science, so that he can go forward from Beulah to 'intellectual War'.

The grimness of Urthona's power has led Harold Bloom to suggest that the passage describing the mills and ovens takes us back to 'the residue of Blake's contemporary world, suffering the final afflictions of natural tyranny' and that 'Between the last "Winter in the night of Time" [. . .] and the new Sun of line 20, the world turns inside out, and reality at last appears' (E967). But the transition between the 'night of Time' and the 'fresher morning' seems to be a shift in perspective rather than a reversal, a shift that reveals the consequences of Men's efforts for Man. In the innocence of Beulah, Man appears like a new Adam surrounded by animal forms of wisdom, drawing inspiration from the natural world so that he can join the wars of Eternity.[23] But his reorganized innocence is far removed from the ignorance of Adam. The words of philosophy may be bitter, the progress towards knowledge may be filled with tears and groans, but as Blake's narrative has consistently emphasized, pain and sorrow are the price of innocence.

---

[23] In Cowper's vision of the Last Judgement in *The Task*, wild and tame animals graze together, and 'All creatures worship man, and all mankind One Lord, One father' (VI: 783).

PART III

The Major Revisions

The Major Revisions

This chapter contains the third stage of my reading. I shall reconsider the narrative as a whole, focusing primarily on the elaborate providential framework that has so far been left out of account.

Parts of the material to be considered at this stage appear in the basic text of Nights VIIb, VIII, IX. Otherwise the material appears in passages that were interpolated as follows:

1. By erasing and replacing existing text (on pages 3, 4 and 117: 1–13).
2. By adding new leaves to the manuscript (pages 19–22, 87, 90, 111, 113, 115–16).
3. By adding passages or lines in the margin or other blank spaces, notably the following: Nights I and II—5: 1–5, 29–43; 9: 9–19; 12: 25–9; 13: 8–10; 18: 11–15; 27: 10–13, 15. Night IV—55: 10–15; 56: 1–27. Night VIIa—84: 36–40; 85: 1–4, 19–21, 23–47. Night VIII—99: 4–10; 101: 43–6, 33–7; 105: 11–27; 106: 7–16; 110: 30–33.
4. By smaller, local insertions at points throughout the manuscript.

The process of revision was undoubtedly complicated, and it is clear that Blake changed his mind while he was making this revision (introducing, for example, more than one new ending to Night I, and expanding the new Night VIII by adding both marginal additions and new pages). But that does not necessarily imply that the revisions were made in a piecemeal or arbitrary fashion. As I shall attempt to show, it is possible to construct from them a more or less coherent account of the place of providence in fallen history.

9

A Christian Vision

It seems likely that when Blake wrote 'End of the Dream' on the last page of Night IX he had completed the 'Dream of Nine Nights' that the title page once announced. Perhaps this was the 'perfectly completed' poem he referred to in a letter to Butts on 25 April 1803, a poem he compared with *Paradise Lost* and the *Iliad*.[1] The comparison seems more appropriate to the linear narrative of *The Four Zoas* than to either *Milton* or *Jerusalem*.

The basic text of the ninth Night, however, contains passages that refer directly to Jesus, and which seem to be an integral part of the history of Jesus that Blake introduced to the rest of the poem in revisions (122: 1–3, 15–20, E391; 123: 20–40, E392–3). As these short passages would hardly seem to justify the retranscription of the entire Night, their presence does not lend much support to the view that this Night was transcribed several times.[2] On the other hand, the passages seem to presuppose some explanation of Jesus's role earlier in the poem, and so the original version of the eighth Night may have included some references to Jesus. In the absence of external evidence, this must remain open to question. However, it seems that some time after Blake had completed the transcription of the 'Dream' he made a series of major revisions in order to include a comprehensive history of Jesus. This history is the subject of the present chapter.

PRELIMINARIES

A History of Christianity

We do not know when Blake began the revision, or when he finally stopped work on the poem. The quotations from the Greek Testa-

---

[1] Blake did not necessarily share Frye's (influential) view that *The Four Zoas* 'was never perfectly completed into anything': *Fearful Symmetry*, 314.

[2] Gerald E. Bentley Jr. suggests that IX may have been recopied when VIIb was,

ment on page 3 must have been added after he had begun to study Greek under Hayley's supervision at Felpham. Apart from this there is very little biographical evidence to go on. For his Greek studies Blake used the 'Testament' as his 'chief master'. By the beginning of 1803 he was also learning Hebrew, and was looking forward to reading 'The Hebrew Bible' (E727). It has been suggested that the revisions may reflect a fundamental change in Blake's beliefs. Some of his letters from Felpham appear to show 'a new acceptance of Christianity'.[3] Writing to Butts on 22 November 1802, for example, Blake declared 'I am again Emerged into the light of Day I still & shall to Eternity Embrace Christianity and Adore him who is the Express image of God . . . My Enthusiasm is still what it was only Enlarged and confirmd' (E720). But it is by no means certain that Blake's 'acceptance of Christianity' ever slackened and, as we shall see, the process of revision develops issues that were already present in the poem.

The additions introduce an elaborate Christological pattern in which the descent, crucifixion, resurrection, and second coming are presented not only as parts of the history of Jesus but as stages in the larger history of Christianity itself. This history was a subject of heated contemporary debate. Since the Reformation, Protestant historians had vigorously attacked the corruption of the Roman church, and during the seventeenth and eighteenth centuries radical Protestants, Deists, and sceptics had carried the attack back into the earliest stages of Christian history. Some Protestants emphasized the essential continuity between pagan superstitions and the practices of Catholicism, claiming that the church had soon become deeply embroiled in the very idolatry it should have condemned.[4] Deists went further, adopting strategies that appeared to call into question the figurative medium of the Gospel itself, or else condemning the Scriptures outright. Matthew Tindal, for example,

'but Blake's rapidly changing ideas may have forced him to transcribe Nights VIII and IX yet once or twice again': *Vala or The Four Zoas*, 163.

[3] H. M. Margoliouth, *William Blake* (Oxford, 1951), 124.

[4] Conyers Middleton, for example, systematically related aspects of Catholic ritual to pagan antecedents in *A Letter from Rome. Shewing an exact Conformity between POPERY and PAGANISM* (London, 1729). For a helpful discussion of the development of histories of the church see Owen Chadwick, 'Gibbon and the Church Historians', in *Edward Gibbon and the Decline and Fall of the Roman Empire*, ed. G. W. Bowerstock, J. Clive and S. R. Graubard (Cambridge, Mass. and London, 1977), 219–31.

argued that Christianity was the original religion of the world, and that the essential principles of the Gospel were a 'republication' of that religion; and he implied that the form of the Scripture had helped to obscure its truth. The literal meaning of the Gospel had been discounted by the primitive fathers, but in reading the text as 'typical and prophetical' they had 'so turn'd, and twisted the Scripture, with a pious Intention to make it speak nothing but what they thought agreeable to Reason' that its meaning had been clouded.[5] Paine's attack on the Bible in *The Age of Reason* was more direct. While he admired the moral doctrines of Christ, he dismissed the history of him as 'fabulous'. The mythology of the Christian church had 'sprung directly out of the tail of heathen mythology'. Thus the 'absurd fable' of Satan's war with the Almighty was suggested by the story of Jupiter and the Giants, but the extravagant Christian mythologists had outdone their pagan forebears by deifying Satan and making him defeat 'all the power and wisdom of the Almighty'. Having dismissed the Athanasian creed as 'absurd jargon', Paine noted: 'It was upon the vote of such men as Athanasius, that the Testament was agreed to be the Word of God; and nothing can present to us a more strange idea than that of decreeing the word of God by vote.'[6] The great church councils were often attacked by radical Protestants. The Unitarian minister Joseph Priestley, for example, whose list of corruptions to the original Christian doctrine included the Trinity, the Incarnation, and the pre-existence of Christ, regarded the councils at Nice and Constantinople as milestones on the road to error.[7]

The most controversial history of the church was undoubtedly that included in Gibbon's study of the Roman Empire, which seems to have influenced Blake's treatment of Urizen's empire. Gibbon's account was presented as an impartial examination of what he termed 'the secondary causes' of Christianity's 'rapid growth', and it took account of the interrelations of religious, political, and

[5] Tindal's examples of the fathers' rejection of the literal meaning of the text include the following: 'Justine Martyr, for Instance says "None, who have the least Sense, will dare to affirm, that the Maker and Father of the Universe did appear in a small Spot of Earth; the God of the Universe can neither ascend, nor descend, or come into any Place"'. M. Tindal, *Christianity as Old as the Creation. Or, The Gospel, A Republication of the Religion of Nature* (London, 1730), 87–8, 229.

[6] T. Paine, *The Age of Reason*, with a biographical introduction by P. S. Foner (New York, 1991), 53, 55–7, 180.

[7] J. Priestley, *An History of Early Opinions concerning Jesus Christ*, 4 vols. (London, 1786), i. 320; ii. 286.

practical considerations. Gibbon described the development of the church as an evolutionary process in which the original character of Christianity was progressively modified by material interests, a gradual transformation that seems unsurprising, if not inevitable, in the given circumstances.

Blake's narrative can be seen as an attempt to accommodate and transform such critical views of Christian history. In some respects it recalls the ideas of Deists such as Tindal: the historical revelation on which the church is founded is seen as a republication of the original religion in a form that becomes involved in mystery and superstition. In other respects it recalls Gibbon's account, since Blake shows the transition from the primitive church to state religion in relation to the history of empire, and presents it as an evolutionary process whose outcome seems preconditioned by the given circumstances. But if Blake's history parallels such accounts it is also radically opposed to them, since it defends the prophetic inspiration which they tend to mock. The central problem that Blake's history has to encounter can be summarized simply—how to do justice to the liberating potential of the historical revelation of Christianity, while at the same time exposing its limitations. The myth shows that if the church descends into mystery in a 'natural' progression, that is because its faith is based on a limited vision of the natural world, which obscures the vision of Jesus; and if Jesus is revealed in a form that gives rise to superstition and idolatry, the inspirational value of that form can nevertheless be celebrated. The historical revelation of Jesus is seen as a merciful error, a vision which sustains a genuine if limited form of brotherhood, but which is doomed to lose its liberating power because it leaves the oppressive structures of empire intact. In the Last Judgement, when the entire basis of human life is completely transformed, the vision of Jesus is clarified as Man comes to see the Eternal Father 'in his brothers face'.

The Merciful Error

The merciful error is not a new concept in Blake's work. It had always been fundamental to his understanding of human knowledge. As he explained in his annotations to Lavater, 'creation is.

God descending according to the weakness of man' (E599). The finite visions of creation that imprison humanity are not only repressive errors but also limits that allow life to continue. Blake's assertion that 'Truth has bounds, error none' certainly needs to be qualified. In *The Four Zoas* fallen Man survives because there are limits to his error. But without a distinct representation of divine mercy, the dramatic method of Blake's narrative inevitably tends to suggest that the limits of error are fixed solely by the activities of Man's fallen powers. If the limits merely arise from confusion, humanity's escape from error would seem to depend ultimately on an inexplicable internal necessity, a blind mechanism of the kind Blake seeks to attack: the satire would surrender to its object.

In order to avoid this Blake has to show that the limits of error are in some sense fixed from without, by divine mercy.[8] Many of the revisions show how the spirit of Jesus enters, and operates within, the fallen world before the Last Judgement; one of the major functions of Jesus is, as we might expect, to define the limits of error. In developing a comprehensive view of divine providence, Blake was forced to confront directly some of the central problems in his own beliefs. He had always sought to emphasize the immanence of God, and to counteract the notion that God exists 'afar off'. But *The Four Zoas* shows only too clearly how far Man falls from a clear vision of God. The introduction of a supervising providence would commit Blake to showing why a merciful divinity allows Man to fall into error, and why the true nature of God has been concealed through so much of history. The machinery of providence inevitably begins to transform the poem from a cosmogonic myth into a theodicy, and brings it into a new relationship with *Paradise Lost*.

Blake does not in a formal sense attempt 'To justify the ways of God to Man'—indeed, he rejects the notion of justice on which theodicy usually depends. Unlike Milton, he avoids as far as possible discursive explanations of divine policy. However, he does begin to provide statements about the nature of eternity and divine

[8] As we have seen, intimations of divine providence occur with increasing prominence in the basic text of the Nights already examined. Urizen is conducted by 'Providence divine' to the world of Urthona (71: 25–6; 74: 31). In IX the Eternal Men claim to have supervised the fall of their brother.

providence as part of the narrative commentary. Such statements appear to have an authoritative status, since they appear to stand outside the particular temporal conditions which limit the characters' vision—even though some of them, as we shall see, call into question the possibility of a vision which transcends temporal limits. The general avoidance of discursive explanation does not free Blake from a central difficulty of theodicy, the problem of reconciling providence with free will. His sensitivity to this problem is vividly demonstrated in his identification of Milton's foreknowing God as 'Destiny' in the *Marriage*, and in his angry reaction to the slightest suggestion of predestination in Swedenborg (*E*35, 609–11). In Night VI his attempt to balance the claims of providence and will produced the longest line in the poem:

> By Providence divine conducted not bent from his own will
> Lest death Eternal should be the result for the Will cannot be
> violated
>
> (74: 31–2, *E*351)

The clumsiness here suggests that on this point Blake was unusually anxious not to be misunderstood. Throughout the narrative providence has to be shown working positively but tentatively: co-operating with the will of the fallen individual but not determining action.

However, Blake's conception of free will creates a more fundamental problem than this. Whereas Milton tells of Man's first disobedience, Blake thinks of the prelapsarian condition as one of unlimited freedom. Milton is able to confront his unfallen man with clear alternatives (to eat the forbidden fruit or not). But Blake's attempt to show the fall in terms of error rather than sin complicates the issue of responsibility, for there would be no fall if Man originally had a clear choice between truth and error. The conviction that 'Truth can never be told so as to be understood, and not be believ'd' (*MHH* pl. 10, *E*38) sustains Blake's vision of redemption, but it also implies that Man falls because in his original condition the distinction between truth and error is not absolute. It follows that the unfallen state must have the principle of error within it, not as a satanic intrusion, but as an inherent condition of existence. The merciful error is not only an essential characteristic of fallen existence, but of eternal life itself. This idea is elaborated in the complex symbolism of Eden and Beulah.

Eden

As with many of his other terms, the significance of Blake's Eden is suggested in fragmentary references, some of which diverge. In *Milton* and *Jerusalem* it is distinguished clearly from Beulah, as a higher state. But in *The Four Zoas* it appears to overlap Beulah (the term was substituted for Beulah at 5: 1, *E*302). Its inclusive character parallels that of its biblical counterpart. In *Paradise Lost* the Eden of Genesis is elaborated in a way that emphasizes its duality. Heaven and nature meet there: Adam is able to commune with his maker, and he enjoys an innocent sexual relationship with Eve. In Blake's myth the communion with God and the communion with the female represent two distinct levels of existence, Eternity and Beulah. He uses the term Eden to denote the complete cycle of unfallen existence, which includes both a full participation in the spirit of Jesus in Eternity, and an inspirational repose in Beulah. In Eden the unfallen Urthona enjoys 'Days & nights of revolving joy'. This cyclical pattern allows Blake to show that the Sons of Eden may succumb to a finite vision of nature without becoming imprisoned by it.

Eternal Brotherhood

That they all may be one
(*John 17: 21*)

The highest vision in the cycle of Eden is the vision of Jesus. Although Blake does seem to distinguish between God the Father and God the Son, Jesus is at the forefront of his thinking, because in Jesus God and Man are identified.[9] An important element of the Christological pattern introduced in the revisions is the pre-existence of Christ. The introduction of a saviour who exists eternally, from before the creation of the world, commits Blake to providing a full image of the life of Eternity (something he had tended to avoid in his earlier works):

[9] The distinction between God the Father and Jesus seems implicit on p. 3, where Blake refers to the 'Heavenly Father'. The Daughters of Beulah apparently distinguish between Jesus and God (56: 2–3). See also e.g. *Milton* 2: 12 (*E*96).

> Then those in Great Eternity met in the Council of God
> As one Man for contracting their Exalted Senses
> They behold Multitude or Expanding they behold as one
> As One Man all the Universal family & that one Man
> They call Jesus the Christ & they in him & he in them
> Live in Perfect harmony in Eden the land of life
>
> (21: 1–6, E310–11)

This divine Council presents a clear alternative to Milton's hier-archical view of heaven.[10] The Council operates as a democratic brotherhood that takes on the form of Jesus whenever it achieves unanimity. Blake's device allows divine power to function with both the authority of a democratic council and the loving intimacy of a personal saviour. In this way it resolves the difficulty that appears in Night IX, where the risen Man enjoys both the sense of community in a brotherhood of many individuals, and the sense of integrity as One Man.[11]

The Council's power of expanding and contracting the senses is a vital aspect of the narrative's vision of eternal life. The contracted senses reveal the individual as one of a multitude of separate but related individualities. The expanded senses allow that participa-tion in the universal identity and, as Milton O. Percival puts it, 'that identification of one self with another which ensures brotherhood and forgiveness of sin'.[12] The spirit of Jesus, then, is that spirit in which the individual and the universal are at one.

Beulah

For we walk by faith, not by sight

(2 Corinthians 5: 7)

A full participation in the spirit of Jesus is the highest state the mind can attain. Blake refers to it elsewhere as 'fourfold vision', the state in which each of Man's four powers act in perfect harmony (*E722*).

[10] This conception recalls Swedenborg's view of the life in Eternity: 'the universal heaven resembles the Human Form . . . therefore they call heaven the GRAND (MAXI-MUM) and DIVINE MAN'. *A Treatise Concerning Heaven and Hell*, 2nd edn. (London, 1784), 34.

[11] As John Beer notes, without the Council of God, Man must appear 'without context and therefore without possibilities of brotherhood': *Blake's Visionary Uni-verse* (Manchester and New York, 1969), 158.

[12] M. O. Percival, *William Blake's Circle of Destiny* (Oxford, 1938), 50.

If it were possible to sustain this level of vision there would have been no fall. Indeed, there would be no need for the Council of God to meet, as it would never lose its unity. But the life of Eden is said to have a temporal rhythm, and this seems to make permanent union with Jesus impossible. Enion describes the rhythm like this:

> In Eden Females sleep the winter in soft silken veils
> Woven by their own hands to hide them in the darksom grave
> But Males immortal live renewd by female deaths.   in soft
> Delight they die & they revive in spring with music & songs
>
> (5: 1–4, E302)

Enion's explanation appears in the context of her fall, and its reference to hiding suggests that it should be read as a symptom of her clouding vision. But it can be related to other statements introduced to form an interpretative commentary on the narrative. The female 'dies' as inspiration fades and Man's vision of the world becomes static and finite, but—unlike the dead world of 'mere nature'—remains a delightful, comforting presence giving promise of new life, as the cocoon gives promise of the butterfly. The male is 'immortal' in that his creative identity is never surrendered; the female is regenerate (as explained in IX, 122: 4–15, E391) because as the emanation of the male she assumes ever new forms. Since the female form is unlimited and continually changing, Blake sometimes refers to the 'emanations' of the male in Eternity.

The image of the protective veil woven by the female is a symbol of the faith that must sustain the mind in the fallow periods between creative activity (in *Paradise Lost* innocence is described as a 'veil' that 'shadowed' Adam and Eve 'from knowing ill', IX: 1054–5). An alternative and more elaborate symbolism appears in the protective creations of Beulah. The daughters of Beulah represent the faith that sustains the desire for redemptive action, and the patience required for its fulfilment. They personify not the forced obedience of those under law, but the loving obedience of the heart in tune with the loved one. They are manifestations of what St Paul refers to as 'faith which worketh by love' (Galatians 5: 6). Blake needs the symbolism of Beulah in order to clarify, among other things, the condition of the male whose female has died:

> There is from Great Eternity a mild & pleasant rest
> Namd Beulah a Soft Moony Universe feminine lovely
> Pure mild & Gentle given in Mercy to those who sleep
> Eternally. Created by the Lamb of God around
> On all sides within & without the Universal Man
>
> (5: 29–33, E303)

The condition of the sleeper in Beulah has a special importance in Blake's narrative, because it is the condition in which the cycle of Eden is broken and the fall begins. As the senses contract and the mind comes to rest on a finite vision of the world, the individual is in danger of becoming an isolated ego. With the death of the female, that is, the male may become a 'spectre', a victim of fears and anxieties that can make him forget the joys of brotherhood. The creative activities of the Daughters are needed in order to sooth and protect the emergent spectre:

> The Spectre is in every man insane & most
> Deformd   Thro the three heavens descending in fury & fire
> We meet it with our Songs & loving blandishments & give
> To it a form of vegetation
>
> (5: 38–41, E303)

Faith must create a vision of the world, a 'form of vegetation', that will comfort and sustain the Spectre, and so arrest his fall. The Soft Moony Universe of Beulah allows the finite world to be seen as the infinitely beautiful gift of a loving and merciful providence. We can see that the symbolism of Beulah inverts the Edenic relationship between males and females (the males sleep, the females wait for them to revive). There are three heavens in Beulah, an idea clarified only towards the end of the poem when Los finds new heavens and a new earth opened 'Threefold within the brain within the heart within the loins' (87: 9, E368).[13] In Beulah, it seems, divine mercy is not an idea that the mind abstracts from its experience, but a living reality apprehended in each of these three areas of life: intellectual, emotional, sexual. All imaginative creations in the fallen world derive from Beulah, as the Daughters of Beulah are daughters of inspiration, the muses of poetry and prophecy. As we shall see, the relationship between the threefold vision of Beulah and the creativity of the artist is explored in some detail as the scheme of divine providence approaches its culmination in the poem.

---

[13] There are three heavens in Swedenborg's system. See *Heaven and Hell* (no. 29).

The idea that the Daughters meet the Spectre as it is 'descending' suggests that faith creates a form of vegetation that is accommodated to the weakness of each individual. Each form of vegetation is of course a form of error, giving an illusory actuality to a finite world. But each form preserves the perception of divine mercy, and so has a protective function:

> The Daughters of Beulah follow sleepers in all their Dreams
> Creating Spaces lest they fall into Eternal Death
>
> (5: 34–5, E303)

Many degrees and forms of error thus take shape under the aegis of Beulah. For this reason Beulah exists in an ambivalent relationship with Jesus—both dependent and independent, created and creating. In this way the actions of Beulah are subtly dissociated from those of the Council. The margin that distinguishes Beulah from Eternity is, as Wilkie and Johnson have said, 'a margin of error'.[14] It allows Blake to account for the separation of fallen Man from the vision of Jesus. The Daughters of Beulah are only as strong as the faith of those in their care: they have no other means to prevent sleepers falling from their protection. For much of fallen history the Daughters are ineffectual muses who supply no knowledge of the Christian vision. In some respects their status corresponds with that of the unfallen angels in *Paradise Lost*—who are messengers, worshippers, protectors, but who do not initiate the divine plan and are not always fully possessed of its significance.

The inclusive nature of Blake's Eden allows him to show that error is a necessary condition of prelapsarian existence. For the unfallen Sons of Eden there is no simple choice to be made between truth and error. The narrative shows that there cannot be a clear distinction between them until the limits of error have been fully defined, and that these limits are defined by experience. In Blake's theodicy the fall is a fortunate fall because, through the evolutions of error, the vision of those in Eden is clarified and the faith of Beulah is strengthened. At the climax of the eighth Night, the Sons of Eden sing: 'We now behold the Ends of Beulah & we now behold | Where Death Eternal is put off Eternally' (104: 11–12, E377). Their confidence at this point is premature, as their vision is further clarified in the ninth Night, but they have begun to see fallen history as a process from which they can learn. The Daughters of Beulah

---

[14] Wilkie and Johnson, *Blake's* Four Zoas, 28.

make a complementary discovery: if there are bounds to truth, there are no limits to mercy. Initially terrified at the prospect of eternal death, the Daughters subsequently begin to see that divine mercy extends beyond death:

> Looking down to Eternal Death
> They saw the Saviour beyond the Pit of death & destruction
> For whether they lookd upward they saw the Divine Vision
> Or whether they lookd downward still they saw the Divine Vision
> Surrounding them on all sides beyond sin & death & hell

(100: 12–16, E372)

Eventually the fear of 'sin & death & hell' will be overcome completely. The narrative as a whole shows how faith depends on the power of vision. The fall begins with the failure of faith, which is a failure to see the infinite power of mercy and love.

Announcing the Theme

Above the title *Vala* on page 3 of the manuscript Blake added a quotation, in the original Greek, from Ephesians 6: 12. Blake admired the King James translation of the New Testament ('it is almost word for word', E727). But his use of the Greek here may show his sense of the inadequacy of the English rendering, which tones down its spiritual challenge.[15] I have used The New English Bible:

For our fight is not against human foes, but against cosmic powers, against the authorities and potentates of this dark world, against the superhuman forces of evil in the heavens.

The view of fallen history developed in Blake's poem is in some respects less optimistic than the view in *Paradise Lost*, because the 'powers' against which humanity must struggle are even more insidious and pervasive than Milton's Satan: they are the mental powers who shape Man's perception of his world. On the final version of the title page these four powers are identified as the primary subject of the poem (Blake's term 'Zoas' is derived from

---

[15] John E. Grant notes that Blake 'deliberately eschewed' the James Bible version of the Greek: 'Jesus and the Powers That Be', 75.

the 'zoa' or living creatures that surround the throne of God in Revelation 4). The New Testament teaches that Christ has already triumphed over 'the powers' that enslave humanity (see Colossians 2: 15). Blake's narrative shows conversely that until the Zoas are restored to unity their errors will absorb and invert the Divine Vision, leading Man to worship 'superhuman forces of evil in the heavens'.

As the poet's struggle is against 'authorities', the muse identified in his opening lines is unlike the heavenly muses of classical epic, and contrasts strikingly with the muse invoked at the beginning of *Paradise Lost*. Milton invokes the Holy Spirit, that taught Moses 'how the heavens and earth | Rose out of chaos'. The invocation is used to claim a special authority for his theodicy ('for heaven hides nothing from thy view'). In contrast, Blake's muse is not 'heavenly', but represents a challenge to established order ('shook the heavens with wrath'). She is an 'Aged Mother'—a reference perhaps to the ancient earth mother displaced by the usurping sky god, and perhaps even to the 'mighty mother', goddess of Dulness, who is celebrated at the beginning of Pope's mock heroic poem *The Dunciad*, and who threatens the collapse of the civilization Pope cherishes. As she is a 'Daughter of Beulah', her song is a limited vision which, disconcertingly, cannot give an authoritative account of its subject. The narrative can only offer a provisional view of the Zoas, because 'no Individual . . . Can know in all Eternity' the 'Natures of those Living Creatures'. Such knowledge belongs only to 'the Heavenly Father' (3: 8, 7, E301).

At the outset of his epic, Milton defines the relationship between humanity and Jesus as between 'man' and 'one greater man'. In Milton's Protestant vision of redemption through atonement, individuals are dependent on the superior qualities of the saviour: 'his obedience | Imputed becomes theirs by Faith, his merits | To save them' (*PL*xii: 408–10).[16] Blake rejected the idea of a vicarious atonement as a 'horrible doctrine', preferring instead a doctrine of redemption through at-one-ment, the identification of the human with the divine (*see BR* 337). He therefore sees the relationship between man and Jesus not as between lesser and greater, but as between individual Man and Universal Man:

[16] See C.A. Patrides, *Milton and the Christian Tradition* (Oxford, 1966), 121–52.

> Four Mighty Ones are in every Man; a Perfect Unity
> Cannot Exist. but from the Universal Brotherhood of Eden
> The Universal Man. To Whom be Glory Evermore Amen
> (3: 4–6, E300–1)

Jesus descends to the fallen world not to pay off a debt through punishment, but to reveal the unifying spirit of brotherhood. In support of this view Blake cites two references to St John. The first is Jesus's prayer to His father 'That they all may be one; as thou, Father, art in me, and I in thee, that they may also be one in us: that the world may believe that thou hast sent me' (from John 17: 21–3). The second reference also concerns the incarnation: 'And the Word was made flesh, and dwelt among us, (and we beheld his glory, the glory as of the only begotten of the Father,) full of grace and truth' (1: 14). (Blake quotes the first words of this verse in Greek.)

Only one of the fallen Zoas retains the ability to respond to the liberating spirit of Jesus: Los, the eternal prophet, the remnant of Urthona's imaginative power. In the revised poem Los will eventually become the prophet of Christian brotherhood, and his activities in this role will be, characteristically, both redemptive and repressive. The central importance of Los in Man's history is now fully acknowledged, since the fall and resurrection of Urthona are identified as major concerns of the poem. The distinction between the inspirational aspect of imagination and its capacity to enslave is immediately established. In Eden Urthona is the archetypal poet, whose imaginative creations resound in the ear, which is the ground or 'Earth' of knowledge. Such creations become heathen Gods when humanity falls, because, as Blake explained in the *Marriage*, Man begins 'Choosing forms of worship from poetic tales' (pl. 11, E38).

GIVING ERROR ITS FORM

From Eden to the Circle of Destiny

The revised narrative begins, in the heroic manner, *in medias res*. But although there is an unexplained disaster in the background, it is 'natural' to begin with Tharmas, as he is the 'Parent power' from which human consciousness emerges in its fallen state. The fall of Tharmas is now seen in relation to the seasonal rhythm of life in Eden, described by Enion (5: 1–4, E302). The death of the 'Emanations' is of course an inevitable part of this cycle, while the anxiety of Tharmas is a symptom of the emergent Spectre, which the Daughters of Beulah should comfort.

We can now interpret the fall as originating in a moment when the faith of Beulah proves too weak to soothe rising fears. As the frantic dialogue between Tharmas and Enion shows, fear transforms innocent pity into guilty self-pity (4: 7–5: 5, E301–2). The urge towards self-protection, to 'hide in secret' is rationalized as a desire to protect the creations of imagination, Enitharmon, and the outward form of the divine community, Jerusalem. But this urge to protect the outward form is the very thing that inhibits imagination and the spirit of brotherhood. It is the basis of moral law, creating 'stern demands of Right & Duty instead of Liberty'. Weaving a tabernacle for Jerusalem means building a mausoleum for her.

The myth of weaving in Eden now forms a context for Enion's weaving. If the Daughters of Beulah should comfort the emergent Spectre of Tharmas by creating a merciful form of vegetation for him, Tharmas falls beyond the point at which the finite world can be seen as an infinitely beautiful creation of mercy. Instead, Enion weaves him a joyless form of vegetation (5: 16–28, E302–3), which sustains a lesser faith than Beulah's, the blind Circle of Destiny. In the face of this grim vision, Beulah is shaken by the kind of fear that it should soothe:

> this Spectre of Tharmas
> Is Eternal Death What shall we do O God pity & help
> So spoke they & closd the Gate of the Tongue in trembling fear
> (5: 41–3, E303)

The fear of death led to the fall of Tharmas. The same fear now confirms that fall. The closing of the Gate of the Tongue can be related to the inarticulacy of the new-born child. It also indicates that within the Circle of Destiny Man will be cut off from the Word of God, from the vision of Jesus that can lead him to brotherhood. It illustrates the characteristic tendency of Beulah to protect itself from whatever threatens to overwhelm its 'comfortable notes'. In

Blake's narrative, faith survives at first by closing out despair, 'Not suffring doubt to rise up' (95: 10, E367). Only with the descent of Jesus does faith begin to triumph over its fear of eternal death.

The Circle of Destiny, which contains the hope of future restoration, forms a limit to Man's fall, and although it is a descent from the loving innocence of Beulah, it is not beyond Beulah's influence:

> The Daughters of Beulah follow sleepers in all their Dreams
> Creating Spaces lest they fall into Eternal Death
> The Circle of Destiny complete they gave to it a Space
> And namd the Space Ulro & brooded over it in care & love
>
> (5: 34–7, E303)

The Ulro has been defined in several different ways in Blake criticism, and occurs with different connotations in different contexts in the poetry.[17] The variety of uses and interpretations points to the inclusiveness of the term. Here it is merely the space within which fallen Man organizes his experience. It will therefore contain several forms of error—including the Golden World and the Caverns of the Grave. To those within, it seems the basis of reality. Seen from the higher perspective of Beulah it is a delusion from which Man can be released, and thus a manifestation of divine mercy.

Visions of Beulah

The Circle of Destiny and the space of Ulro are formless and cheerless to the primitive mind until, with the birth of Los and Enitharmon, humanity develops an imaginative perception of time and space. In the light of the providential framework, this development acquires a new significance. As soon as the two 'Infants' achieve independence from Enion, Man discovers beauty in his environment, and his primitive faith in redemption receives clearer definition (9: 9–18, E304–5). Fallen history assumes a finite measure, 'Seven thousand years', which corresponds to the traditional view that after six thousand years the millennium will arrive. Space is no longer the desolate waste over which Enion stumbled but becomes a beautiful 'Infinitude'. From the temporal point of

---

[17] For a summary of different uses of this term, see Damon, *Dictionary*, 416–17. Damon defines it as 'this material world'. Frye identifies it with the state of single vision, *Fearful Symmetry*, 48.

view this seems a natural development that accompanies the vigorous development of the imaginative powers. But from the point of
view of Beulah it appears quite differently: the new perceptions are
at once errors and gifts of mercy. They are errors because they are
based on the delusive reality of the external world: the infinite
extension of space that appears to show the power of divine providence blinds Man to the fact that Infinitude can be seen in the
smallest particle of matter; the perception of history as a finite span
pushes redemption into futurity, whereas Eternity is in the moment.
But such errors are gifts of mercy because they offer reassurance to
the fallen mind and make a kind of spiritual life possible. This
complex view is personified in the actions of Eno:

> Then Eno a daughter of Beulah took a Moment of Time
> And drew it out to Seven thousand years with much care &
>   affliction
> And many tears & in Every year made windows into Eden
> She also took an atom of space & opend its center
> Into Infinitude & ornamented it with wondrous art
>   (9: 9–13, E304–305)

Eno was the name given at one stage to the 'Aged Mother,' the
muse who inspires Blake's poem (see E819). Although she allows
glimpses into the life of Eden, the inspiration available to the
primitive prophet is limited, as Blake immediately makes clear. The
Daughters of Beulah

> saw not yet the Hand Divine for it was not yet reveald
>   (9: 17, E305)

Part of the function of Blake's providential machinery is to account
for the limitations of the fallen imagination. When Los and
Enitharmon arrive at the 'margind sea' and begin to develop a myth
of origins they are now seen to be inspired by 'visions of Beulah' (9:
33, E305). It may have been at this point that Blake intended to
introduce the elaborate sequence on pages 21–22 and 19–20,
E310–13, which explains how the Council of God reacts to Man's
fall, and which shows why the 'Hand Divine' remains hidden.[18] A

---

[18] Erdman includes this sequence after p. 18. But W. H. Stevenson has argued
convincingly that this material should be inserted after 9: 33. See 'Two Problems in
The Four Zoas', *Blake Newsletter*, 3 (1967), 14–17. Donald Ault's account of the
'embedded stuctures' of Night I appears to depend on Erdman's arrangement
(*Narrative Unbound*, fig. A.3., 38–9).

note in the manuscript indicates that the second Night now begins
at 9: 34.

Pre-existence

*the mystery which hath been hid from ages and from
generations*

(Colossians 1: 26)

The doctrine of Christ's pre-existence, so central to Milton's myth
of the fall, had been a subject of critical enquiry for a number of
Blake's contemporaries. For Deists it was part of the mythology
which shrouded the reasonable principles of natural religion. For
Unitarians like Joseph Priestley, who denied the divinity of Christ,
the doctrine was a disastrous corruption of true Christianity.[19]
Gibbon, noting that it was derived from the account of the Logos
in John's Gospel, related it not only to Plato, but indirectly to 'the
traditional knowledge of the priests of Egypt'.[20] In Blake's narrative
the pre-existence of Jesus is an eternal truth that becomes an
ancient, priestly corruption of the divine vision.

The belief in a divinity who exists from before the creation of the
world entails the notion that he conceals his true nature throughout
much of history. Between the fall of the first Adam and the coming
of the second, humanity is bereft of the knowledge of Jesus, except
through types which foreshadow His coming. The notion that God
hides Himself is something that Blake found very difficult to accept:
in *Urizen* the eternal power falls when he becomes 'a dark power
hid', 'revolving in silent activity' (*E*70–1). But however much Blake
disliked the hidden god, *The Four Zoas* shows how far man falls
from knowledge of Jesus. When Blake came to describe the divine
scheme of redemption, he attempted to resolve this problem by
setting the scheme in the context of a Urizenic conspiracy (21: 16–
22: 41, *E*311–12).

As we might expect, this crucial episode in Blake's narrative has
its counterpart in *Paradise Lost*. Milton traces the prehistory of the
fall back to the anointing of the Son as the 'great viceregent' of

---

[19] Priestley, *Early Opinions*, i. 26.

[20] Gibbon explained that 'the most ancient and respectable of the ecclesiastical
writers' had ascribed to John the purpose of confuting the heresies of the Ebionites
and the Gnostics, *Decline and Fall*, ii. 358 (ch. 21).

heaven at a full meeting of the empyreal host (*PL*v: 576 ff.), an act which provokes an envious conspiracy in Satan, who leads his host to his royal seat in the North. Seen in the light of Blake's Eden, the divine and satanic factions are both in error, as they share a concern with subordination which negates the spirit of brotherhood. In Blake's narrative the concern with subordination first emerges within a vision of Beulah, in which a conspiracy between Urizen and Luvah is seen as the origin of the fall. In reacting to a report of this vision, the Council of God is not convened by 'imperial summons' (*see PL*v: 584), but is seen as the spontaneous expression of a caring family of brothers. Jesus is not the heir of a tyrannical king against whom any disagreement must be by definition seditious, but an expression of the collective will of the divine brotherhood.

The myth of the conspiracy introduces a theme that assumes a central importance in subsequent Nights: the opposition between Urizen and Luvah is now seen as, from the very beginning, a kind of 'communing', as if fallen reason and energy become complementary expressions of the same will to power. The imagery suggests a polarization between Urizen as controller of the intellectual sun, and Luvah as controller of the Atlantic darkness of Man's affective life. This polarization begins to dissolve as each assumes the other's function (Urizen 'cast deep darkness', Luvah 'poured the Lances of Urizen'). As intellect and passion are confused, both reveal an urge to bring Man's spiritual life under the control of law. The same process is presented in alternative forms: in the imagery of kingship; in the directional symbolism (since Urizen's eternal place is in the South, his plan to control the North implies an attempt usurp the function of Urthona as the keeper of the gates of heaven); and in biblical allusions (Jerusalem, the outward form of community, is here seen as the mother of the enemies of Israel—Satan, Anak, Sihon, and Og—and therefore to be controlled).

This vision of Beulah, which expresses fear of conspiracy and of violent passions, and which concludes with an appeal for vengeance, is a limited vision, clouded by the very fears and passions it describes and condemns. Blake's scheme of providence is, like Milton's, necessarily reactive: the eternal brotherhood is forced to respond to this vision, and to that extent is governed by it. Redemption depends from the beginning on a partial submission of divine power to the forces of error. Blake's symbolism consistently emphasizes this submission. The secrecy and delay inherent in the divine plan are seen as symptoms of Urizen's apparent ascendancy. Thus while the messengers from Beulah seek immediate intervention, the Council of God withdraws into mysterious silence: 'Silently removing | The Family Divine drew up the Universal tent | . . . & closd the Messengers in clouds around | Till the time of the End' (19: 6–9, E312). This silent withdrawal seems quintessentially Urizenic: it is the fulfilment of Urizen's plan to 'infold the Eternal tent in clouds opake'.

This paradoxical submission of divine light to darkness represents a severe challenge to faith, which must survive in the face of disappointment, loss, the apparent triumph of evil, and must learn to look beyond these things. The narrative implies that without such disappointments, faith could never be fully demonstrated. The story of Lazarus is used to illustrate this point. Those who believed that Jesus could save the sick man had to sustain their belief after Lazarus had been allowed to die. In Blake's myth the messengers from Beulah who intercede for Man before the Council of God (21: 8–12, E311) echo in their appeal the messengers who summon Jesus to Lazarus (John 11: 3). Man, like Lazarus, is allowed to 'die', and those in Beulah are left with little to support their hope.

The interval between the fall and the descent of Jesus as saviour is explained by St Paul as a time during which humanity grows towards maturity and must be subject, like a child, to the authority of law (see Galatians 4: 1–5). St Augustine in De Civitate Dei elaborates the idea of a growth into maturity: he divides the span of fallen history into six epochs, which parallel the six ages of man and the six days of creation (the sixth age extends from the first coming of Jesus to His Second Coming, which initiates the seventh age). Milton presents a comparable scheme in Michael's outline of history (PL Book XII). In Blake's narrative the Council of God divides history into seven ages, or Eyes of God, each representing a development in the human vision of divinity (the scheme has been anticipated in the 'Seven thousand years' given to history by Eno). Jesus is the seventh Eye:

> they Elected Seven. called the Seven
> Eyes of God & the Seven lamps of the Almighty
> The Seven are one within the other the Seventh is named Jesus
> (19: 9–11, E312)

The vision of Jesus as an agent who can act on behalf of, and apart from, the collective brotherhood itself is an error that must eventually be clarified. It represents an abnegation of brotherhood by the Council of God, a handing-over of responsibility which relieves them from descending themselves to redeem their fallen brother. The Eyes that precede Jesus are not named until a much later point in the poem (Night VIII, 107: 42–50, E381), a fact which leaves the Daughters of Beulah—and therefore fallen humanity—in a state of ignorance concerning the shape of history. The limitations of Man's vision are further illustrated in the fall of Urthona, which is now seen as a consequence of the Urizenic conspiracy. The embalming of Enitharmon in Enion's bosom suggests the reification of Urthona's vision. When Enitharmon closes the gates of her heart 'Lest Los should enter into Beulah' (20: 7, E313), she effectively limits his prophetic potential, making him dependent on her own vision. This helps to explain why it is Enitharmon who takes the initiative, and Los who responds, when Man develops a myth of origins at 10: 9–11: 24, E305–6 and 82: 37–84: 42, E358–60 (Enitharmon's account of Luvah seizing the Horses of Light can now be seen as a version of the rebellion described by the messengers from Beulah). The gates of Enitharmon's heart will finally be broken with the birth of the Shadowy Female. In the interval, Beulah continues its protective activity by keeping alive through patience and hope the vision of community, Jerusalem. But such faith seems pitifully impotent as Jerusalem is 'lulld into silent rest' (20: 11, E313).

An Unseen Presence

The image of the divine Council that receives formal reports from Ambassadors and withdraws into secret deliberation stands in sharp contrast to the image of Jesus as a loving personal saviour. The aloofness of the Council emphasizes the gulf that develops between the life of Eden and the limited vision into which Man is falling. It may recall the critical discussions of the great church councils in the works of Priestley and Gibbon, and in particular Paine's comments on the use of the vote to determine the word of God. The figure of Jesus who 'followd the Man' (19: 12, E313) is a more personal and comforting vision, but at the end of the golden feast which confirms Man's commitment to war and repression, this figure seems powerless to prevent Man's degeneration:

> Now Man was come to the Palm tree & to the Oak of Weeping
> Which stand upon the Edge of Beulah & he sunk down
> From the Supporting arms of the Eternal Saviour; who disposd
> The pale limbs of his Eternal Individuality
> Upon The Rock of Ages. Watching over him with Love & Care
> (18: 11–15, E310)

The two trees here correspond to two mentioned in the Bible, both associated with Bethel, the place where Jacob laid his head on stones and dreamed of God's protection (Genesis 28: 10 ff.). The Oak of Weeping appears in Genesis 35: 8, at the place where a nurse named Deborah is buried. Beneath the palm mentioned in Judges 4: 5, the Israelites consulted a prophetess named Deborah, who promised them victory in war.[21] The palm tree is also associated with the crucifixion (it is called 'the Palm of Suffering' in *Jerusalem* 59: 6), while the oak tree is associated with Druid sacrifice elsewhere in Blake's work. The conjunction of the trees apparently confirms the arrival at a borderline, where Man falls beyond the protective influence of Beulah into a state in which he will sacrifice his own energies. This fall heralds Urizen's assumption of control over human life in the cosmos. It is as if, reversing the Miltonic pattern, the Son permits the Father to descend and reign over fallen man—as if mercy abdicates in favour of a tyrannical justice.

But this is only part of Blake's account of divine providence. Throughout his writings he seeks to emphasize the immanence of divine power. In *The Four Zoas* this immanence is suggested by the partial identification of Jesus as Luvah. It is Luvah who bears the greatest burden of suffering in the fallen world: cast into the furnaces of affliction, chained to the rock of a finite world, drawn on to the tree of Mystery, he is the archetypal victim. But although Luvah is weakened he is never destroyed. As Orc he inspires Los to begin the construction of Golgonooza, and his fires drive on the work of the Last Judgement. The myth now identifies Jesus as the power that sustains Luvah in all his sufferings,

---

[21] See *Blake: The Complete Poems*, ed. W. H. Stevenson, 2nd edn. (Harlow, 1989), 314–15.

and that accounts for his inspirational potential. This identification is made before each of the two eras of repression (in the Golden World, and in the Caverns of the Grave), and after each sacrifice of Luvah. As we shall see, its significance is developed on each occasion.

As Urizen descends to take control of Man's vision, and Luvah's destiny is sealed, the relationship between divine love and natural love is clarified:

> But Luvah & Vala standing in the bloody sky
> On high remain alone forsaken in fierce jealousy
> They stood above the heavens forsaken desolate suspended in blood
> Descend they could not. nor from Each other avert their eyes
> Eternity appeared above them as One Man infolded
> In Luvah[s] robes of blood & bearing all his afflictions
>
> (13: 4–9, E308)

This description of Luvah and Vala as desolate but unfallen recalls the condition of Milton's Adam and Eve between the loss of innocence and the expulsion from Eden. Milton's figures are judged and comforted by the Son as they stand on the brink of the fallen world. In Blake's narrative, the vision of Jesus clothed in Luvah's robes of blood also gives comfort while confirming loss: it anticipates the suffering to which Luvah will be condemned, and shows that he will be supported in his affliction. In this way the idea of atonement is transformed. Jesus does not take on the role of a suffering god in order to accept 'punishment' for Man's sin. Instead, he takes on the role of a guardian, continually supplying fallen man with the strength to survive his own self-inflicted punishments. This role is further clarified at the completion of Urizen's Golden World, when the first phase of Luvah's repression has been accomplished:

> For the Divine Lamb Even Jesus who is the Divine Vision
> Permitted all lest Man should fall into Eternal Death
> For when Luvah sunk down himself put on the robes of blood
> Lest the state calld Luvah should cease. & the Divine Vision
> Walked in robes of blood till he who slept should awake
>
> (33: 11–15, E321)

Blake's use of the term 'state' varies. Here it appears to mean the influence of Luvah. Between his suppression in Night II and his rebirth as Orc in Night V, Luvah is absent from the narrative. His survival as an active principle in the fallen world is now shown to be ensured by divine love. In this way the myth implies that although Jesus remains hidden through much of human history, he is nevertheless a constant sustaining presence in human life.

Defining the Limits of Error

The second phase in the history of Luvah begins in the Caverns of the Grave. Here the binding of Urizen, commissioned by Tharmas and executed by Los, shows Man's experience of the world stabilized by the power of mere blind instinct. From this act comes an awareness of the human body as a cavern of flesh with five 'inlets' or senses which are the source of all knowledge. This is the lowest level of self-awareness at which humanity can develop a vision of infinite fulfilment in the concrete particulars of experience. Here desire will be instinctively 'concentered' on the material world, and seek a limitless gratification in the 'thrilling joys of sense', even though once Orc is bound fulfilment remains tantalizingly out of reach. It is here, on the limit of Translucence, that Los will build Golgonooza on the foundations laid by Tharmas, developing an eschatological vision of history inspired by the fiery Orc. But the bound body of Urizen also provides the basis for a contrary vision of life, one dominated by the consciousness of sin and the need for law, a world pervaded by the Shadowy Female and darkened by the tree of Mystery. In reviewing the myth, then, it can be seen that Man has fallen into a world that is potentially twofold, each vision forming a limit to his fall in place of the shattered Circle of Destiny. In Blake's revisions, therefore, the binding of Urizen is seen as a decisive stage in the process by which humanity discovers the limits of error.

The ambivalent nature of Man's fallen condition is now suggested by his resemblance to a 'Polypus'. The polyp or hydra had been an object of controversy in the 1740s, on account of experiments by the naturalist Abraham Trembley. This organism inhabits stagnant ponds, produces buds like a plant, but seizes its prey with tentacles. Trembley classified it as an animal, but found that when he cut it into pieces new polyps grew from each segment. This fact seemed to imply that the soul might be divisible, and that matter could develop autonomously, independent of divine power.[22] As Nelson Hilton has pointed out, the term 'polypus' was also used in contemporary medical literature to identify a tumour or clot.[23] The Polypus thus provides a suggestive image of Man's immersion in a materialistic vision—as a diseased condition, but one which shows his remarkable ability to survive on a borderline of existence, unaware of the providence that will redeem him.

The Council of God is introduced in a pivotal passage (55: 10–56: 27, E337–8) that looks back to the initiation of the divine plan, and forward to its climax. One of the functions of this passage is to develop the significance of Luvah's robes of blood. In the fallen world Jesus must assume a form that is 'adapted to the weaknesses' of finite vision. Blake explained this in one of his earliest illuminated works: 'Therefore God becomes as we are, that we may be as he is.'[24] His quotations from St John at the beginning of the poem suggest the same idea. Jesus assumes Luvah's robes of blood not only to sustain Luvah in his sufferings, but in order to become perceivable in the fallen world. To become a Saviour he must assume willingly the roles that Luvah fills, from innocent god of love to sacrificial victim.

The reference to the Council of God over Beulah's 'mild moon coverd regions' is the first reference to Jesus 'Descending'. As the Daughters of Beulah are unable to participate in the brotherhood of Eden, their vision of divinity is limited by a sense of separation. They see Jesus as a comforting intermediary who can intercede with God on their behalf: 'for we are weak women & dare not lift | Our eyes to the Divine pavilions' (56: 3–4, E337). Their vision of Jesus corresponds to that of Martha and Mary, the sisters of Lazarus, whose words they echo: 'Lord. Saviour if thou hadst been here our brother had not died' (56: 1, E337) (see John 11: 21–3; their 'Double form' is probably another allusion to the two sisters). The

[22] As Virginia P. Dawson says, Trembley's experiments demonstrated the 'possibility of playing with Nature's designs'. Indeed, they called into question the notion of design itself, as the self-generating polypus is incompatible with the idea of a universe 'in which life in an organised body depends on the exquisite arrangements of parts': *Nature's Enigma: The Problem of the Polyp in the Letters of Bouret, Trembley and Reaumur* (Philadelphia, 1987), 20.

[23] Hilton, *Literal Imagination*, 88–9.

[24] L. W. Deen describes this as 'the root metaphor of Blake's Christianity', *Conversing in Paradise: Poetic Genius and Identity-as-Community in Blake's Los* (Columbia, Mo., and London, 1983), 23.

fearfulness of Beulah qualifies its 'loveliness and perfection', as the Daughters' desire for comfort indicates not only their terror at Eternal Death, but also their resistance to the consuming light of Eternity:

> Behold Eternal Death is in Beulah Behold
> We perish & shall not be found unless thou grant a place
> In which we may be hidden under the Shadow of wings
> For if we who are but for a time & who pass away in winter
> Behold these wonders of Eternity we shall consume
>
> (56: 6–10, E337)

The reluctance to 'consume' stands in contrast to the self-sacrificing love of Eden; at the conclusion of their speech 'The Empyrean groand throughout All Eden was darkend'. As the narrative unfolds it shows with increasing clarity that the faith of Beulah springs ultimately from the same root as the selfhood, from the same urge for self-protection. The story of Lazarus shows that the redemptive actions of Jesus not only inspire belief but also strengthen unbelief (since he gives a fresh impetus to his spiritual enemies, who begin to plot his death). The ambivalence in this description of the Daughters looks forward to the subsequent treatment of the descent of Jesus. Golgonooza and the tree of Mystery will lead respectively towards the highest and the lowest degrees of vision available to Man in the Caverns of the Grave, and each will offer a different perception of Jesus. The former will inspire an attempt to foster the spirit of brotherhood in a fallen world; the latter will promote the sacrifice of love to law.

The Daughters' urgent demand for reassurance is answered with a renewed demand for faith, and a clarification of error:

> The Saviour mild & gentle bent over the corse of Death
> Saying If ye will Believe your Brother shall rise again
> And first he found the Limit of Opacity & namd it Satan
> . . . for in every human bosom these limits stand
> And next he found the Limit of Contraction & namd it Adam
> While yet those beings were not born nor knew of good or Evil
>
> (56: 17–22, E337–8)

As these lines make clear, redemption is not a mechanical process, but depends on the power of faith. The placing of the intervention emphasizes this. The limits appear once Urizen has been bound: the providential interventions in this myth typically come after an action in the fallen world has been completed, not before. In this respect they can be seen as the products rather than the determinants of human action, so that providence does not compromise the individual will. Jesus does not forge the limits, but finds and names them, clarifying the redemptive potential of error for Los's benefit. Los, having completed his work, 'felt the Limit & saw | The Finger of God touch the Seventh furnace in terror' (56: 24–5, E338). The reference to the seventh furnace alludes to the climactic epiphany of the seventh seal in Revelation, and also portends the dawning of the seventh Eye of God. The hand of God which was concealed at 9: 17, E305 is now revealed, but there is no suggestion that Los understands what he feels or sees. He certainly feels none of the hope that comforts the Daughters of Beulah. As 'Limit Was put to eternal death', Los merely shrinks from his task.

The Limits

With the introduction of these limits we approach the heart of Blake's reinterpretation of Christianity in *The Four Zoas*, and the most complex area of symbolism in the poem. As long as desire is 'concenterd' on the natural world, individuals can sense the possibility of infinite fulfilment in their own powers and appetites. They have, that is, a 'concentering vision' of fulfilment emanating directly from their own being. The limit of Translucence, on which Los begins to build Golgonooza, is the lowest point at which such a vision is possible. The limit is passed with the birth of Vala as a Shadowy Female (85: 13 ff., E360), for this birth symbolizes the substitution of abstract ideals of love for the concrete particulars that inflame the bound Orc. Those individuals who fall into the power of the Shadowy Female lose the instinctual and amoral sense of delight in the senses and become haunted by a sense of sin. They become, that is, isolated 'spectres' contemplating a world with which they feel no vital relationship. Committed to permanent frustration, they are 'Cruel and ravening with Enmity & Hatred & War' (85: 20, E360). In drawing down Vala to the embraces of Orc, the Spectre of Urthona sought to 'annihilate' such ravening lust (84: 42, E360). But cruelty is intensified rather than diminished by repression. As soon as the Shadowy Female appears, many individuals fall into her power:

> a Cloud she grew & grew
> Till many of the dead burst forth from the bottoms of their tombs
> In male forms without female counterparts or Emanations
> (85: 17–19, E360)

This is a demonic reversal of the Last Judgement—not a resurrection, but a further death. A passage in Night VIIb shows that it corresponds to the biblical myth of the fall from heaven, which creates Satan. As the dead descend on the Shadowy Female's clouds

> in Spectrous terror
> Beyond the Limit of Translucence on the Lake of Udan Adan
> These they namd Satans & in the Aggregate they namd them Satan
> (95: 12–14, E367)

Just as Hell is the traditional limit of Satan's fall, so in Blake's narrative the 'Limit of Opacity' is the limit to which the spectres can fall beyond the Limit of Translucence. It is the boundary which saves Man from the limitless error of Eternal Death.

The limits of error are defined not only for fallen humanity, but also for those in Eternity. As we have seen, the Sons of Eden can expand or contract their senses at will, but contraction leads them to behold 'Multitude', and it can lead finally—it is now revealed—to the state of Satan in which individuals lose all sense of vital relationship with others. The collective life of the amorphous satanic 'Aggregate' is the absolute negation of true brotherhood. Once Satan has begun to appear, therefore, the limit of Contraction can be 'fixed', defining the lowest level at which some remnant of the sense of community survives. The limit of Contraction thus resembles the limit of Translucence (which disappears in Blake's later works).

In biblical tradition, the fall of Satan leads to Adam's knowledge of good and evil. In Blake's narrative the appearance of Satan allows Man, for the first time, a clear choice between degrees of vision: between the aggregate of selfhood and the community of Jerusalem. In this sense the Council of God can 'create the fallen man'. Reversing the traditional pattern, Blake's 'Adam' only appears when Man has gained the ability to know good by evil.

THE VISION OF JESUS

Preparing for Jesus

Wherefore the law was our schoolmaster to bring us unto Christ

(Galatians 3: 24)

In the Gospels the Kingdom of God proclaimed by Jesus has a dual aspect: in some statements it is conceived as imminent ('the kingdom of God is at hand', Mark 1: 15), in other statements it is identified with the Last Judgement ('the end shall not be yet', Mark 13: 7). Paul represents Jesus as having already achieved victory over the powers that held the world in thrall: 'And having spoiled principalities and powers, he made a shew of them openly, triumphing over them in it' (Colossians 2: 15). But in the so-called 'eschatological discourse' (Matthew 24–5, Mark 13, Luke 21) Jesus explains that before the Son of Man comes in glory there shall be great tribulation, and 'there shall arise false Christs, and false prophets' (Matthew 24: 24). Christianity has traditionally thought of the present kingdom as an anticipation of a future apocalyptic order, an affirmation that individuals can even now find salvation in their own lives, a fulfilment without consummation. But no matter how the present kingdom is conceived, it has to be reconciled with the continued existence of evil and unbelief in the world. For, as Blake said, 'Few believe it is a New Birth' (*E626*).

In his treatment of the descent of Jesus, Blake is concerned to explain the limitations and inevitable degeneration of the present kingdom. His account of the historical revelation acknowledges the inspirational power of the vision of Jesus, and its partial triumph over the selfhood. But it also shows, as Gibbon had shown, that the new vision of liberty inevitably declined into a sterile concern with externals. In Blake's narrative the decline is inevitable because Man remains bound by the limited vision of the prophet who ushers in the vision of Jesus.

Man's limited vision is of course the product of a historical process. Its limitations are the specific conditions which allow the spirit of Jesus to appear in the fallen world. As the identification of Jesus as the seventh 'Eye' of God suggests, Blake's new exploration

of Christianity emphasizes the historical relationship between repressive moral law and the Christian spirit of love.[25] The law serves
the divine purpose because its harrowing prescriptions help to
create the emotional conditions in which the spirit of Jesus can
appear. The birth of the Shadowy Female is now seen not only as
the prelude to war and desolation, but also as the prelude to an era
of forgiveness. It bursts the gates of Enitharmon's heart (which has
been closed to Los since Night I, separating him from the inspiring
influence of Beulah). This heartbreak not only leaves Los himself
vulnerable to the consciousness of sin (85: 23–5, E367), but also
begins to release him from the bitterness that has paralysed him
since his failure to unbind Orc. Thus another immediate consequence of the birth of the Shadowy Female is that the Spectre
'enterd Los's bosom' to inspire a spirit of brotherhood:

> Los embracd the Spectre first as a brother
> Then as another Self; astonishd humanizing & in tears
> In Self abasement Giving up his Domineering lust
> ([85]: 29–31, E367)

This marks the beginning of a long and complex conversion in Los,
but we should note that from the beginning Los has moved into the
power of his Spectre, and that as a consequence his vision of Jesus
will be subject to the Spectre's limitations.

The Spectre as Prophet

As we saw in Chapter 6, in the materialistic universe the reasoning
power of the Spectre gains ascendancy over Los, and assumes the
role of prophet. The Spectre is eloquent and persuasive as a
spiritual guide, but his vision is always limited by the world in
which he finds himself. Having helped to create a drastically
reductive view of the human body, he can recognize its limitations.
But he fails to see that these limitations are an illusion sustained by
the very power of abstract reasoning he embodies. The reasoning
power, of course, learns by experience, and the Spectre is able

---

[25] P. M. S. Dawson helpfully defines this aspect of Blake's thinking about the
moral law: 'without the realization that its impossible demands cannot be met man
could never recognize the necessity for forgiveness.' 'Blake and Providence: The
Theodicy of *The Four Zoas*', *Blake: An Illustrated Quarterly*, 20 (1987), 138. I
would add that this 'realization' is presented as an historical event rather than as an
atemporal necessity.

to advance from repressive doctrines to creative ones by responding to his own mistakes. This capacity to develop, together with his robust optimism, makes him a disarmingly persuasive figure. Some of his ideas seem very close to those expressed by Blake himself, a fact which may tempt readers to lose sight of the dramatic framework that qualifies them. The narrative shows that his attempts to liberate Man can have only limited success, and will ultimately fail.

As we have seen, at first the Spectre assumes that the limitations of the body can be escaped by denying the body completely, and by repressing the creative energies that spring from it. He sees himself as 'a masculine spirit', and while his vision of Universal Manhood (84: 4–9, E359) includes 'mild fields' and a 'sweet melodious' Luvah, it finds no place for the turbulent passions of 'the frail body', or for strenuous imaginative activity. In the new myth of redemption, the birth of the Shadowy Female forces him to see that a complete denial of the body leads merely to 'Enmity & Hatred & War', to the hellish existence of the spectres of the dead. The immediate consequences of this error are now described in that part of the narrative usually known as Night VIIb: the theology of repression allows the extension of Urizen's 'Universal Empire' and is used to justify the wanton dissipation of human energies in warfare. In the continuation of VIIa, the 'terrified' Spectre now seeks a new way to destroy the body, and thinks of 'Consummating' it 'by pains & labours' (85: 33, E368). This idea may be seen as an advance, as the creative activity of the body is now seen to be in some sense redemptive. But it is still a negative view, corresponding to the traditional assumption that labour is a punishment incurred by the fall and intended to subdue the sinful impulses of the body. The Spectre not only assumes that Los is 'but a form & organ of life . . . Created Continually by Mercy & Love divine' (86: 2–3, E368), he also assumes that Los is his own instrument: 'look upon me | Not as another but as thy real Self' (85: 37–8, E368). His seductive appeal to Los is an attempt to assimilate the disturbing 'fury' of the visionary power by encouraging it to serve the inner world of the spirit. He tells Los:

If we unite in one [,] another better world will be
Opend within your heart & loins & wondrous brain
Threefold as it was in Eternity & this the fourth Universe
Will be Renewd by the three & consummated in Mental fires
(85: 43–6, E368)

This is not a reversion to the infinite desires of Orc. Rather, it is a new understanding of the inner world that the Spectre has always attempted to protect. Intellect, emotion, and sexual desire are no longer seen as limited by the body and conditioned by nature, but as Eternal qualities that can liberate Man from his conditioning (the three worlds that he sees correspond to the three heavens of Beulah which Enitharmon sealed off in Night I). The phrase 'consummated in Mental fires' seems very close to the optimism of the *Marriage*, where Blake announces that 'the whole creation will be consumed, and appear infinite. and holy whereas it now appears finite & corrupt' (*E*39). But if the Spectre's new vision allows Man to see the fallen world as the infinitely beautiful creation of divine mercy, it does not lead him to reject the fallen world completely. In this context the term 'consummated' might suggest that the Spectre seeks to *perfect* the fallen world rather than destroy it—a suggestion confirmed by subsequent events.

Nevertheless the Spectre's vision represents a major expansion of Man's world. Now Enitharmon's gate is broken, Los can share the vision (86: 7–9, *E*368). Even though the imagination will remain subject to rational control ('controllable | By Reason's power'), for the first time since the binding of Orc, Los is inspired to build Golgonooza.

Golgonooza revisited

For as in Adam all die, even so in Christ shall all be made alive

(1 Corinthians 15: 22)

Under the influence of the Spectre Golgonooza becomes once more a refuge, a vision that allows a partial liberation from the external world. Its association with Golgotha begins to assume a new significance, as here Man discovers the ability to cast off his old self and rise in the spirit of Jesus. It is founded on the fallen world hammered into shape in IV, the caverned universe in which the two limits of Satan and Adam have already been 'felt'. But it allows Man to see beyond this world into the threefold innocence of Beulah:

A Threefold Atmosphere Sublime continuous from Urthonas world
But yet having a Limit Twofold named Satan & Adam

(87: 10–11, *E*368)

This kind of technical exposition becomes increasingly prominent in the myth as Blake becomes more concerned with the boundaries and borderlines of different degrees of vision, and with paradoxical conjunctions between them. The conjunction here seems particularly important. The law-bound world of the Caverns of the Grave opens into a sublime and merciful vision that is quite unlike that world. When Los stands on the limit of Translucence, he is transfixed by contrary impulses. The vision of new heavens and new earth does not diminish his sense of own unworthiness, but if anything intensifies it, rendering him more susceptible to the power of the tree of Mystery. This can be seen in his new commitment to self-restraint:

> I will quell my fury & teach
> Peace to the Soul of dark revenge & repentance to Cruelty
> (86: 11–12, E368)

When Los embraces the Spectre and Enitharmon, 'Enitharmon trembling fled & hid beneath Urizens tree'. Blake's narrative, like Milton's, shows that the revelation of the redemptive potential of the Lamb was historically dependent on a full participation in the consciousness of sin. It was out of guilt and fear that the Christian yearning for forgiveness emerged. The condition of the sinners in Golgonooza corresponds to that of Milton's 'first parents' after their fall. Milton's Jesus descends as both redeemer and judge: he clothes the 'inward nakedness' of Adam and Eve with 'his robe of righteousness', and he condemns the sinners to death. Like Milton, but in quite different terms, Blake shows the Christian vision emerging from an attempt to reconcile the demands of mercy and justice. Jesus is seen when repentance leads to forgiveness, as Los attempts to comfort Enitharmon:

> look! behold! take comfort!
> Turn inwardly thine Eyes & there behold the Lamb of God
> Clothed in Luvahs robes of blood descending to redeem
> O Spectre of Urthona take comfort O Enitharmon
> Couldst thou but cease from terror & trembling & affright
> When I appear before thee in forgiveness of ancient injuries
> Why shouldst thou remember & be afraid. I surely have died
>   in pain
> Often enough to convince thy jealousy & fear & terror
> (87:42–9, E369)

But Los's spirit of forgiveness is balanced by the guilt which inspires fear of and desire for punishment: Enitharmon sees the Lamb of God descending not to redeem but to 'give us to Eternal Death'. The Spectre, being a rational 'medium' between Los and Enitharmon, seeks a reconciliation of mercy and justice, a 'ransom' through good works. He now recognizes that the lust of the spectres of the dead is a manifestation of their spiritual nakedness. Having once scorned 'the frail body', he concludes that without a 'Created body', or a 'concentering vision' for its desires, 'the Spectre is Eternal Death' (87: 39, E369). It is a perception that gives a new sense of purpose to Man's creative powers.

Clothing Inwardly: Art as Initiation

Before the spectres can be given a new body, they must be rescued from the torments of anxiety and frustration. The way of salvation is discovered at the Gate of Luban (Luban is the name of the moon ark in Bryant).[26] The Gate is the point at which the positive and negative aspects of Los's vision meet, where the porches of Golgonooza and the branches of the tree of Mystery converge. From here, life appears to offer a grim alternative between 'Urizen's war', in which energy is enslaved by abstract systems and, for the souls of the victims of battle, an afterlife of 'happy obscurity' in Enitharmon's bosom (a counterpart to Orc's vision of 'the Grey obscure' beyond the bounds of Science, 80: 42, E356). To break this purposeless closed cycle, Los now begins to develop a redemptive view of art:

> Stern desire
> I feel to fabricate embodied semblances in which the dead
> May live before us in our palaces & in our gardens of labour
> Which now opend within the Center we behold spread abroad
> (90: 8–11, E370)

Gibbon emphasized that the early Christians abhorred images and every art and trade that was concerned with their production. In his account, images were introduced by the successors of Constantine, and their use developed from a desire to set up memorials to the

---

[26] Raine, *Blake and Tradition*, i. 232.

dead.[27] The idea that Christians abhorred images would have been incomprehensible to Blake, who consistently emphasized that Christianity was founded on the divine image, on the appearance of divinity in human form. In his account the desire to erect images 'in which the dead May live before us' forms an essential foundation of the historical revelation of Christianity (the references to palaces and to gardens of labour suggest public memorials). In this context, however, the idea of resurrecting the dead through art assumes a significance that is quite unlike anything in Gibbon. The idea can be illuminated by a passage in Blake's prose description of his design for the Last Judgement:

If the Spectator could Enter into these Images in his Imagination approaching them on the Fiery Chariot of his Contemplative Thought if he could Enter into Noahs Rainbow or into his bosom or could make a Friend & Companion of one of these Images of wonder which always intreats him to leave mortal things as he must know then would he arise from his Grave then would he meet the Lord in the Air & then he would be happy (E560)

This passage implies that an imaginative response to a work of art does not merely bring a perceiving subject into relation with an aesthetic object. It releases the individual from the selfhood (the time-bound 'subject' disappears), and it demands an intimate, sympathetic understanding that transforms an object into a friend and companion. In contrast to abstract reasoning, art appeals to every area of human response. It offers 'spiritual sensation', a perception of the infinite in its minutely organized concrete particulars. It may draw inspiration from nature, but it transforms the transitory images of the temporal world into works of 'permanence' and significance. And it encourages the imaginative sympathy that is the ground of love and brotherhood. In this way art can be thought of as offering an initiation into the vision of Jesus.

In historical terms, Blake's association of Christianity with the transformation of the prophet into an artist suggests the movement from a tradition in which the primary function of prophetic vision is the control of the passions, the reinforcement of moral virtue, to one in which the primary function is to liberate the spirit from its sleep of death. It is when the inspirational effect of prophetic vision is recognized above its doctrinal content that it becomes art. In his

[27] Gibbon, *Decline and Fall*, v. 262 (ch. 49).

late engraving of the Laocoön, Blake claimed that 'Jesus & his Apostles & Disciples were all Artists' (*E*274).

As soon as Los begins to create the 'permanent' forms of art, the spectres of the dead find reassurance in them (90: 41–3, *E*371). Nature becomes again a source of comforting repose and inspiration, as its forms are clothed once more with veils of innocence that protect the beholder from the vision of Eternal Death. Redeemed from the isolation of their spectrous condition, individuals become a family 'of brothers & sons & daughters', corresponding to the New Testament vision of those made alive in Jesus. The feelings of love that are liberated within this family are a new expression of the power of Orc, who thus becomes a father to Los's children, and in them finds some alleviation of his repression.

Urizen the earth-bound reason cannot be made to surrender his tyrannical moral conscience, nor the hypocritical pity that springs from it. But art reveals the spiritual form of such Urizenic principles: Rintrah, defined by Damon as 'the just wrath of the prophet', and Palamabron, a genuine 'sympathy for the oppressed'.[28] Urizen is divided, and becomes the instrument of Christian salvation: 'Startled was Los he found his Enemy Urizen now In his hands' (98: 64–5, *E*371). In Los's own attitude to his work there is a comparable transformation: he begins his labours in the consciousness of sin, and thinks of his creations as a potential 'Sacrifice'. But the experience of love overcomes the fearful urge to sacrifice, and at this point the new Adam begins to appear.

Clothing Outwardly: Nature Regenerated

> *ye have put off the old man with his deeds; And have put on the new man*
>
> *(Colossians 3: 9–10)*

Leopold Damrosch Jr. is surely right to insist 'we should not exaggerate the power of art in Blake's system'. As he explains, 'Anything that Los can make is a temporary structure ... that serves as a stay against chaos, until the apocalypse arrives and man can "converse" in visionary forms'.[29] *The Four Zoas* shows that art

---

[28] Damon, *Dictionary*, 321, 349.
[29] L. Damrosch Jr., *Symbol and Truth in Blake's Myth* (Princeton, NJ, 1980), 321–2.

clothes the spirit. But in itself art does not cause the systems of empire to crumble. It opens into the infinite, but is founded on the world of finite forms where Urizen reigns. Los's activity as an artist does not lead directly to the Last Judgement therefore, but back into the world of fallen nature. However, it allows the fallen world to be seen in a quite different light, and in this respect it provides an initiation that corresponds to the death and rebirth offered in baptism (see Colossians 2: 12). The new life put on by the baptized Christian is conceived not only as a life of the spirit, but also of the body: 'Know ye not that your bodies are the members of Christ?' (1 Corinthians 6: 15). In Blake's narrative the entry into Golgonooza means the death of the spectrous self and the putting-on of a new bodily existence, discovering a new delight in the senses, and a new feeling of kinship with others.

In this way Los's commitment to art helps to 'fix' the limit of contraction, as it defines the lowest point at which individuals can experience a genuine sense of community. Those in the fallen world beyond Golgonooza must live without any sense of vital connection with their world or with others. Man is now free to choose between two visions of life, a choice corresponding to the knowledge of good and evil that characterizes the fallen Adam. From the point of view of Eternity, Man has been lying dormant in the womb of nature since his fall, totally submerged in error. Now, at this late stage in human history, the Council of God meets 'upon Gilead & Hermon | Upon the Limit of Contraction to create the fallen Man'. Gilead and Hermon are mountains which overlook the promised land; throughout Night VIII biblical allusions create a parallel between the history of Man's awakening, and the history of the Israelites' possession of the promised land, their struggles with hostile kingdoms, the development and subsequent capture of Jerusalem, and the triumph of Babylon. 'Contraction' suggests not only constriction but also birth. As soon as the Limit of Contraction is fixed, Man begins to wake, and reposes once again in the saviour's arms (see 18: 12–14, E310, where he sank down from the supporting arms of the Eternal Saviour). His seven sneezes recall the awakening of the Shunammite's son in 2 Kings 4: 35, and signal the advent of the seventh Eye of God foreshadowed at the end of Night IV. Now both Los and Enitharmon feel the divine hand on them with love and awe (in contrast to the terror felt by Los in IV).

Rebirth

Once the inner worlds have been opened, the body is no longer seen as a closed cavern which isolates the individual from all other forms of life, nor as a source of evil passions that must be repressed, but—as Wilkie and Johnson put it—'as the delightful work of an artist who loves his vocation'.[30] The creation of this new vision of the body is the work of Enitharmon's looms in Cathedron. While Los creates 'permanent' forms of art, Enitharmon creates transient bodies of vegetation which 'Opend within their hearts & in their loins & in their brain | To Beulah' (100: 20–1, E373). As in Beulah itself, each vision is accommodated to the weakness of the individual: 'some were woven single & some two fold & some three fold | In Head or Heart or Reins' (100: 23–4, E373). The image of the garment implies a dualistic distinction between the body and the spirit, but the dualism is placed in a dramatic context, at a level of vision that must be surpassed at the Last Judgement, just as Los and Enitharmon must be united in the body of the risen Urthona.[31] Although the body here represents a limited vision, it is the first creation that arises from the inspired labour of both male and female. In the process of creation the male is neither victimized by nor a tyrant over the female. The outward expression corresponds to the inward conception.[32]

The vision of the body as a garment indicates the emergence of a new view of identity. If the individual can be released from the ravenous lusts of the selfhood, then apparently 'habitual' traits such as envy and jealousy must be seen as aspects of the state from which the individual has been liberated, not as aspects of identity. Compared with the determinist vision of Urizen, such a vision represents an expansion of free will, and it implies that no individual is beyond redemption. The distinction between individuals and states is not expounded until page 115, but it has already influenced the presentation of the relationship between Jesus and Luvah, and it helps to account for the new prominence given to 'gates' in Blake's myth.

[30] Wilkie and Johnson, *Blake's Four Zoas*, 171.
[31] See M. D. Paley, 'The Figure of the Garment,' in *Blake's Sublime Allegory*, ed. Stuart Curran and Joseph (Madison, Wis., 1973), 124.
[32] Judith Lee argues that 'as characters' in this narrative the emanations grow 'towards the state of self-affirming interdependence', 'Ways of Their Own: The Emanations of Blake's *Vala, or The Four Zoas*', *ELH* 50 (1983), 132.

The gate is the meeting-point between two states, the point at which a radical transformation in consciousness is possible. When we awaken from sleep, we pass through such a gate, experiencing at once a kind of death and a kind of rebirth. As we have seen, the gates lie in the control of Urthona, the Zoa who shapes fundamentally the perception of time and space. In his unfallen form Urthona is a figure like St Peter through whose power the individual can enter into the brotherhood of Eden. In the Caverns of the Grave he resembles Milton's Death guarding the gate of Hell: in V his Spectre builds 'enormous iron walls' between which Urizen must pass in order to reach Orc. Now Los becomes a keeper of the gates of Golgonooza, building the walls 'against the stirring battle' of Urizen, 'That only thro the Gates of Death they can enter to Enitharmon' (101: 40–1, E374). As in V, Golgonooza is designed to protect Enitharmon—this time from the machinations of Urizen. Now the object is not simply to exclude the hostile influences of doubt and despair, but to draw in the victims of such dehumanizing forces.

The machinery of the gates may seem cumbersome, but it allows the conflict between faith and doubt to be visualized as a process influenced at every stage by intelligent and benevolent powers. It may be helpful to summarize the process. The transition from innocence to experience is now symbolized as a descent from the protective custody of Beulah to the horrors of Urizen's empire. This is a fall which faith is not strong enough to prevent ('For nothing could restrain the dead in Beulah from descending | Unto Ulros night,' 99: 19–20, E372). The dead descend to a life of spectrous frustration through the gate of Pity. This descent is a kind of birth which is governed at once by the seductive pity of the Shadowy Female and the merciful pity of Enitharmon. The spectres are redeemed from the war of Urizen and Tharmas through the gate of Death (by putting off the spectrous self), and are reborn through a third gate, the gate of Luban, into a new life woven in Cathedron's looms. Enitharmon thus presides over the gates of birth (Pity and Luban) through which individuals enter the world of nature, while Los controls the gates of death, through which individuals enter the organized world of the spirit. The individual is implicitly free to choose whether to remain in the power of the spectrous self or not, which means that the state of Satan can be further clarified as it is progressively separated and isolated from Golgonooza.

Jerusalem

For as the body is one, and hath many members, and all the members of that body, being many, are one body: so also is Christ

(1 Corinthians 12: 12)

At this point the primitive church begins to take a recognizable form, and the narrative begins to present a history of its gradual transformation into an elaborate state institution. The sequence can be illuminated by considering Gibbon's account of this process. Gibbon was not only concerned with the veracity of doctrines, but with their institutional effectiveness. He argued that the primitive church was strengthened by the doctrine of a future immortality 'universally proposed', and by the millennial vision of a New Jerusalem in which the redeemed would 'possess their human nature and senses' and enjoy a miraculous abundance. The church thrived on its oppositional character, on its holy war against the empire of evil, a war in which 'The edification of the New Jerusalem was to advance by equal steps with the destruction of the mystic Babylon'. Despite Gibbon's notoriously sceptical tone, his account does some justice to the vigour and idealism of the early church. But in his analysis this society—based on the communality of goods, existing without legislation, united only by the ties of faith and charity—seems doomed to move towards hierarchy, law, and division. For Gibbon, the ideals of the primitive church are unsustainable, since 'the most perfect equality of freedom requires the directing hand of a superior magistrate'. The abolition of communal property, the slide from the language of exhortation to that of command, the allegorizing of the New Jerusalem and its subsequent rejection as heresy—these events are presented as aspects of a natural 'progress'. The establishment of Christianity as the state religion of Rome—that Babylon to which it was once opposed—is related to the practical needs of Rome: 'the passive and unresisting obedience which bows under the yoke of authority, or even of oppression, must have appeared in the eyes of an absolute monarch the most conspicuous and useful of the evangelic virtues.'[33]

In Blake's narrative, the primitive church is composed of those who enter the protection of Golgonooza, and it takes the form of

---

[33] Gibbon, *Decline and Fall*, ii. 7, 26, 27, 44 (ch. 15); 313 (ch. 20).

Jerusalem. As in Gibbon's account, its evolution into a hierarchical institution is shown to be inevitable. But here the process is seen to be determined not by an unquestioned notion of what is natural, but by the historical limitations of Man's vision. This may become clear if we consider the appearance of Jerusalem:

> Thus forming a Vast family wondrous in beauty & love
> And they appeard a Universal female form created
> From those who were dead in Ulro from the Spectres of the dead
> And Enitharmon namd the Female Jerusa[l]em the holy
> Wondring she saw the Lamb of God within the Jerusalems Veil
> The divine Vision seen within the inmost deep recess
> Of fair Jerusalems bosom in a gently beaming fire
>
> (103: 37–104: 4, E376)

The vision of Jesus in Jerusalem here is the appearance of the spirit of brotherhood and love within a united, but fallen, community. Jerusalem is the body of Jesus as it appears at the highest level of vision available to Man in his fallen condition: a Universal Female rather than a Universal Man. The imagery emphasizes the limited nature of what is revealed—Jesus remains distant, veiled, his consuming power cooled to a gently beaming fire. As long as Los remains in the power of his Spectre, and clings to the vision of a finite world, his response to Jesus will be partial, and his creativity will eventually decline into contemplation, or a mere tracing of the same dull round.

The placing of this revelation gives a particularly clear indication of how Blake is reinterpreting the New Testament. In the Bible the creation of the manifold church is made possible by the previous incarnation of God as a single individual. In Blake's narrative the living church of individuals united in brotherhood represents a higher vision of 'incarnation'. The more limited vision of Jesus as a historical person who became a sacrificial victim occurs subsequently in the Satanic realm of single vision. Frye explains this aspect of Blake's Christianity very clearly:

The belief, with its implications, that Jesus existed on earth two thousand years ago, which is the literal or historical core of the New Testament, is, whether in itself true or false, not the basis of the Christian religion. . . . The Jesus about whom a biography can be written is dead and gone, and survives only as Antichrist. The Evangelists tell us not how Christ came, but how he comes: they are concerned not with a vanished past but with the imagination's 'Eternal Now'. The timid will protest that we are here in danger of dissolving the reality of Christianity into a vaporous allegory: Blake's answer is that the core of reality is mental and present, not physical and past.[34]

TOWARDS STATE RELIGION

Satan

Those who stay outside the gates of Death remain in the power of the Shadowy Female, their energies bound by Urizenic law and dissipated in the 'bestial' strife of imperial war, laborious workmanship, and slavery. The new spirit of love poses a terrible threat to such an Empire (Urizen is 'terrifid,' 101: 1–3, E373). Unlike the fiery desire of Orc, love which offers itself freely for others cannot be suppressed, or brought to market. It stands quite outside the system of values on which the economy of Urizen depends. In the light of this merciful love, the implicit kinship between the tyrannical will of reason and the raging hunger of natural appetite becomes more obvious: while Urizen and the serpentine Orc appear to be opposites, their conflict is a kind of 'communing' in which each provides a justification for the rage of the other. Urizen's stratagems of war are now seen as a desperate response to the spiritual revolution that threatens his Empire, an attempt to 'undermine the World of Los'. But the attempt to strive with a love that expresses itself through forgiveness merely exposes even more clearly the true nature of the selfhood:

> Terrified & astonishd Urizen beheld the battle take a form
> Which he intended not a Shadowy hermaphrodite black & opake
> The Soldiers namd it Satan but he was yet unformd & vast
> Hermaphroditic it at length became hiding the Male
> Within as in a Tabernacle
>
> (101: 33–7, E374)

The hermaphroditic form is a revelation of the communing between contraries that sustains Urizen's system: aggressive selfishness dressed in principles of love and pity; the urge for domination

---

[34] Frye, *Fearful Symmetry*, 342–3.

masquerading as its supposed opposite. This, however, is not the final form of Satan, for as yet the 'love' and 'pity' of the Shadowy Female are instruments of Urizenic suppression, rather than its driving force. The turning-point in the history of Urizen's Empire arises when reason itself begins to succumb to the power of the Shadowy Female. This is a moment that Blake 'opens out' in the narrative in several different ways.

As we have seen, the Shadowy Female is 'in love with tears', fixed in contemplation of a lost saviour. The only kind of redeemer that can renew her faith is one who renews her sense of loss. In confronting her, Urizen confronts the despair that his entire system has been designed to avert. As he is overwhelmed by her he undergoes a conversion that parallels Los's, experiencing his own struggle with sin and his own repentance. But whereas Los is released from the guilty consciousness of sin by the spirit of forgiveness, Urizen succumbs absolutely to its power, and absorbs only a self-protective meekness. This meekness provides the basis for a new church that will negate Jerusalem: not a family connected by a spirit of forgiveness, but an 'aggregate' of spectrous individuals united by their commitment to moral law. This new church, the synagogue of Satan, is the basis of Christianity as a state religion. Blake's narrative suggests that a community in which brotherhood is reconciled with law cannot rid itself of tyranny: every individual becomes a tyrant, committed to suppressing his own and others' individuality for an abstract conception of the general good. Blake's Satan is composed of

> multitudes of tyrant Men in union blasphemous
> Against the divine image. Congregated Assemblies of wicked men
> (104: 29–30, E378)

The repressive will no longer has to be hidden under the guise of the Shadowy Female's 'love': it is now legitimized by that love, and can sacrifice innocence in its name. The hermaphroditic form of Satan is thus reversed: the tyrant male displays itself fully, while the 'love' that motivates it becomes hidden.

As the two communities of Jerusalem and Satan emerge, it becomes apparent that each will have a different perception of Jesus. The song of the Sons of Eden (104: 5–10; 113: 1–37; 104: 11–17, E376–7) is a 'Hymn on the Morning of Christ's Nativity' which, paradoxically, celebrates two different visions of incarnation. It begins by celebrating the appearance of the divine vision in Jerusalem as the prelude to a full revelation of Jesus, 'Who now beginneth to put off the dark Satanic body' (104: 7, E376). But it ends with a recognition that a further descent into error is necessary, and that in fact the Lamb has yet to 'Assume the dark Satanic body' (104: 13, E377).

The song shows how those in Eden expand their awareness of error, and perceive its limits, by observing the process of redemption. The Sons see the relationship between Los and Urizen as a continuous opposition between two unchanging states, rather than an opposition that emerges at one point in history. Their view represents the Christian vision of history as a conflict between two cities, one dedicated to love of God, and one to love of self. As the vision of time becomes simpler, so the geography becomes more complex:

> Eastward of Golgonooza stands the Lake of Udan Adan In
> Entuthon Benithon a Lake not of Waters but of Spaces
> Perturbd black & deadly on its Islands & its Margins
> The Mills of Satan and Beelzeboul stand round the roots of
>   Urizens tree
> For this Lake is formd from the tears & sighs & death sweat
>   of the Victims
> Of Urizens laws. to irrigate the roots of the tree of Mystery
>
> (113: 23–8, E377)

Golgonooza and Udan Adan represent two kinds of conviction, between which every fallen individual is torn. Fulfilling artisan labour is opposed to alienated labour in mills. In the Satanic economy desires cannot take shape but are dissolved in despair. In contrast, Los gives the passions and affections of the spectrous dead a definite form, while in the looms of Cathedron the body becomes a work of beauty, clothed 'With gifts & gold of Eden'. The spectres reborn in Golgonooza are not immune from the forces of Urizen, but must contend actively with them (Israel is exhorted to cross the river Arnon in order to contend in battle with her enemy: Deuteronomy 2: 24). The clothing of Golgonooza is an armour of faith that can be destroyed in the struggle, for Urizen offers an alternative clothing, a 'faith' in justice and moral law, which makes virtues of passivity, unquestioning ignorance, and 'bitter compunction'. The figure of Rahab epitomizes the desire to reduce individuals to despairing obedience to law.

By the end of their song the Sons of Eden appear to have revised their view of the redemptive process. They conclude that the opposition between these two visions of life would be unending but for the decisive intervention of Jesus, and that Jesus can only redeem the spectres by descending into the lowest depths of error. But their hope must still be tested. When they say 'Come Lord Jesus come quickly', Satan appears.

The Dark Satanic Body

Los said to Enitharmon Pitying I saw
(104: 31, E378)

This incomplete line marks the turning-point in Los's role as prophet of Jesus, as it is the point at which he begins to see Jesus as a victim. In this way the descent of Jesus is shown to be the result of the prophet lapsing from vision to memory (Los speaks in the past tense). From this point onwards, the redemptive activities of Golgonooza are seen no more. The next time Los is described at his anvil, he is no longer working. The creative spirit has departed from Jerusalem.

In the realm of single vision Jesus is not seen as a unifying spirit of forgiveness that appears within a community. Since the community is understood to be an aggregate of autonomous individuals regulated by law, Jesus can only be seen as an individual whose actions must judged according to the law. It is inevitable that such a person should be numbered among the transgressors, because he will refuse to condemn them: 'The Victims fled from punishment for all his words were peace' (109: 4, E378). The very fabric of a regulated society is threatened by true forgiveness. The Assembly that judges Jesus, with its 'Twelve rocky unshapd forms', sacrifices the spirit in order to preserve the letter. As David Lindsay points out, it 'can be identified not only with Pilate but also with the twelve-stone druidical circle of Exodus 24: 4, the foes of Israel in Deuteronomy 25: 17–19 and the heretical party attacked in Revelation 2: 9; and their vindictive decision, as is noted in Mark 15: 28, accomplishes the prophecy of Isaiah 53: 12'.[35]

[35] D. W. Lindsay, 'Prelude to Apocalypse: A Short Commentary on Night VIII of Blake's *Vala or The Four Zoas, Durham University Journal*, 70 (1977–8), 181–2.

If Jerusalem is the highest expression of brotherhood possible in the fallen world, the Synagogue of Satan is the lowest, unified only by the delusive power of the Shadowy Female. As such it provides a false counterpart not only to the activities of Golgonooza, but also to those of Eden. Just as Jesus, the unifying spirit of Eden, must assume a finite form in the fallen world, so the Shadowy Female assumes a 'form of vegetation' as the Synagogue of Satan consolidates around her. This incarnation symbolizes the creation of rituals, regalia, and artefacts through which the enticing power of holy fears and repressive humility is given a material expression. The scarlet robes are at once the counterpart of Luvah's robes of blood, and of the body created in Golgonooza as a 'concentering vision' for the satanic spectres. If prophetic art works to liberate the imagination, the powerful glamour of religious forms is designed to seduce the individual into conformity with law. In her vegetated form, therefore, the Shadowy Female is identified with the great harlot Mystery of Revelation 17: 3–5. Her name, Rahab, is the name of a harlot in Joshua 2, and of an ancestor of Jesus in Matthew 1: 5.[36] Her robes can be identified with those placed on Jesus in mockery at his trial, as in Luke 23: 11. The Daughters of Rahab—particular codes and rituals—are known collectively as Tirzah. Tirzah is described as 'comely as Jerusalem' in The Song of Solomon 6: 4. She is named as the last of five daughters who win the right of a female inheritance in Numbers 27, and is associated in Blake's myth with the tyrannical power of the female will, and with the five senses of the caverned body. The Daughters of Rahab are named after pagan kingdoms: Amalek, Canaan, and Moab. The prominence of the females in this scene of judgement serves partly to emphasize the paradoxical derivation of cruelty from the Shadowy Female's love and pity. In the song of Tirzah (105: 31–53, E378–9) the sacrificial victim is the object of a possessive and sorrowful desire. Condemnation and worship, damning and blessing are married here, as 'pity' triumphs over the creative potential of the individual. The victim is bound down to a minimal, fruitless vision of the temporal world, the mere 'stems of vegetation'. The biblical names in this song all have some association with division or with a deadly urge for conformity. Ephraim and Manasseh were

[36] Harold Bloom points out that Rahab is 'an orthodox type of the church': *Blake's Apocalypse: A Study in Poetic Argument* (New York, 1963), 259.

two sons of Joseph: their land was divided by the river Kanah. Mount Ebal is associated with the division of the tribes by Moses (*see* Deuteronomy 27: 13), while Gilead is also associated with family divisions (*see* Genesis 31: 23 ff.). Shechem was both a town in Ephraim, and the prince of the Hivites. Jacob's sons insisted that the Hivites be circumcised, and afterwards killed them.

The crucifixion is the final stage in the descent of Jesus, the moment at which forgiveness itself assumes the false body of holiness. It is the point at which the sacrificed transgressor is 'forgiven' by those who condemned him, and is recognized as Lord and King. Such forgiveness is a mockery, as it transforms the willing sacrifice of the victim into an act of atonement, through which law receives its ultimate sanctification. It is not only Jesus who descends in the crucifixion, but Los and Jerusalem as well. Once the prophet has lapsed from vision to memory, his art becomes merely an instrument of orthodoxy, which transforms the vision of eternal life into a prison of the spirit. Los, like Joseph of Arimathea, places the crucified body in a sepulchre he had hewn 'for himself'. When Jerusalem is separated from the spirit of Jesus she becomes merely an orthodox church weeping over the sepulchre of the crucified body.

At the Tomb

The supposition that Jesus has already begun 'to put off the dark Satanic body' is certainly premature. Blake's narrative shows that there is no resurrection before the Last Judgement, because until then there is no true Christian brotherhood. The interval between the crucifixion and resurrection extends through the 'two thousand years' of subsequent history (110: 33, E385), during which time Los and Jerusalem merely worship at the tomb. Blake's version of the visit to the sepulchre leads not to a revelation of the spirit, but to a revelation of the power of error:

> But when Rahab had cut off the Mantle of Luvah from
> The Lamb of God it rolld apart, revealing to all in heaven
> And all on Earth the Temple & the Synagogue of Satan & Mystery
> Even Rahab in all her turpitude
>
> (113: 38–41, E379–80)

Rahab cuts off the mantle of Luvah from the Lamb not in order to liberate Christian love, but in order to exclude it entirely from her vision. The worship of Jesus as a sacrificial victim is revealed as another manifestation of a state religion that will sit in judgement on sinners.

The passage that follows (113: 48–55; 115: 1–51; 116: 1–6, E380–1) is sometimes regarded as either a synopsis or a sketch of what Blake was planning for the Bard's song in *Milton*, possibly indicating that Blake 'had abandoned any intention to make the *Zoas* a finished, free-standing work'.[37] However the material here is an integral part of the revised narrative of *The Four Zoas*. Los is cast in the role of the angel questioned by Mary in the tomb. But as Los himself has created the sepulchre, and worships at it, he can tell of no resurrection. His radical reinterpretation of fallen history has its counterpart in Luke 24, where, as the disciples fail to recognize the risen Jesus on the road to Emmaus, they learn to reinterpret the Old Testament, and to see Christ's mission as the culmination of God's plan for history (Luke 24: 27, 'And beginning at Moses and all the prophets, he expounded unto them in all the scriptures the things concerning himself'). Los's reaction at this point parallels his reaction in Night V, where he lost his creative impetus after Orc had been bound. His encounter with Rahab is presented with pervasive irony. The previously clear opposition between Golgonooza and Entuthon Benithon dissolves as Rahab stands among his furnaces. His creative labours have ceased. No longer seeing his triumph over the selfhood as a continuous process of forgiveness, he assumes that his salvation is assured ('I was once like thee'). No longer seeking to inspire through his art, he seeks to bring his listener to penitence through a direct appeal to her conscience. Such preaching necessarily involves the accusation of sin, and manifests the spiritual pride it seeks to destroy. In short, while Los attempts to expose the true nature of Mystery, he succumbs to its seductive power, 'with tenderness & love not uninspired' (113: 44, E380).

Los's entire view of history is coloured by his sense that he has been redeemed from error, while others remain in it. He appears to accept responsibility for the human condition, as he sees that his sons and daughters determine the shape of history (his sons include

[37] Wilkie and Johnson, *Blake's* Four Zoas, 192.

the twelve tribes of Israel, and the founders of major epochs of Christianity). However, the story of Satan and his brothers does not explain Los's fall from his station, but explains the separation of part of fallen humanity from the redemptive influence of Golgonooza. In this respect it shows how the Christian preoccupation with the two cities, of the redeemed and the worldly, begins to shape the sense of history, and to limit the perception of divine mercy. For Los now sees Satan's space as cut off and separate from Golgonooza, remote from its creative influence, whereas the narrative has shown (and the placing of Rahab emphasizes) that Los's world is continuous with Satan's. Los re-enacts the error of the Council of God at the beginning of the narrative, which removed itself from fallen humanity and assigned the task of redemption to an elected redeemer instead of descending to embrace the fallen one in an act of brotherhood. His account of the seven Eyes of God elaborates the Council's divine plan. The six Eyes that precede Jesus are visions of divinity limited by the selfhood.[38] They are all derived from the Bible, although Blake's scheme is not bound by biblical chronology. The sequence implies a gradual movement from absolute tyranny towards willing self-sacrifice and brotherhood. The first is Lucifer, the embodiment of pride 'That made the world as a wilderness' (Isaiah 14: 12 ff.). Molech, the second, is the god to whom the Ammonites sacrificed children. Elohim, the third, is the name of God generally used in Genesis until the time of Abraham. As an 'Eye of God' the name represents a new attitude to sacrifice, since Elohim is seen as a creator who sacrifices his creation: 'Elohim created Adam to die for Satan'. Shaddai is the name of God generally used from Abraham to Moses ('the Almighty'). Blake characterizes him as 'angry', but as infant sacrifice stopped under Abraham, he represents a further advance in man's vision. Pachad, or Pahad, a name which appears in Genesis 31: 42, is translated in the King James version as 'fear'. Perhaps Blake associates the name with 'fear of the Lord' which in Isaiah 2 abolishes idols and humbles pride. The sixth, Jehovah, is the law-giver. As we have seen the law is a necessary preparation for the spirit of brotherhood. Thus although Jehovah is 'leprous' he stretches his hand 'to

[38] For a full interpretation of the Eyes of God see Frye, *Fearful Symmetry*, 360–1. Rachel V. Billingheimer offers a comprehensive discussion of sources and interpretations in 'Blake's "Eyes of God": Cycles to Apocalypse and Redemption', *Philological Quarterly*, 66 (1987), 231–57.

Eternity', initiating the descent of Jesus. In Los's account the willing death of Jesus does not inspire new imaginative effort ('what can we purpose more') but merely reinforces the conviction that Los's errant children should return to the fold of Golgonooza:

> Lo Enitharmon terrible & beautiful in Eternal youth
> Bow down before her you her children & set Jerusalem free
> (116: 1–2, E381)

This appeal sounds very oddly in the mouth of one who claims to have renounced pride.

Blake appears to use the story of Satan here ironically, then, in order to reveal the errors of Christian tradition. The expulsion of Satan begins in a denial of the spirit of brotherhood, and in the disruption of creative labour. But the spirit of brotherhood is denied on both sides. The great solemn assembly condemns Satan in a way that parallels the judgement of Jesus by the Synagogue. Satan becomes the pitying transgressor, condemned by the wrath of the righteous. Los sees Satan as a tempting Jehovah, luring the sons of Israel into a false promised land which is in fact a world of death. But as a preacher Los has a similar role: having enclosed the Mantle of Luvah in the Sepulchre hewn for himself, he seeks to convert his listener in the name of the Lamb. The story of Satan, in its manifold ironies, shows that as soon as individuals lapse from the creative spirit of brotherhood and forgiveness to the accusation of sin, they will impute their own sins to others, and become that very evil they seek to renounce. This passage does not testify to what Bloom describes as 'a dramatically matured Los, the patient apocalyptic worker of Jerusalem' (E964). Instead it shows a Los who has become the archetype of the reforming prophet, one who cries out against the corruptions of the church in an effort to preserve its original purity.[39]

Urizen's confrontation with Rahab now provides the immediate context of Urizen's final seduction by the Shadowy Female. As we have seen, in Blake's narrative there is no resurrection before the Last Judgement. The orthodox belief that the crucified body of Jesus rose from the tomb is a mystery of the kind fostered by Rahab: the account of Rahab appearing before Urizen corresponds

---

[39] For an illuminating reading of comparable material in the 'Bard's Song' in Blake's *Milton* see P. Otto, *Constructive Vision and Visionary Deconstruction* (Oxford, 1991), 40 ff.

to the Gospel accounts of Mary Magdalene bearing news of the resurrection to the disciples. If Urizen's entry into the sphere of religion begins with an attempt to control the sense of mystery he feels in the presence of a material universe, it culminates in his 'Embrace' of a mystery that flies in the face of his own principles of order (106: 23–4, E381). Whereas Los's conviction of sin led to a vision of redemption though forgiveness and creative labour, Urizen's leads to the Christianity of single vision, in which all human will appears sinful, and redemption depends on the power of a superhuman god. The mystery is compounded as Christianity becomes a state religion, as the fallible will of the ruling power is sanctified, and the dragon form becomes an object of worship:

> Rahab triumphs over all she took Jerusalem
> Captive A Willing Captive by delusive arts impelld
> To worship Urizens Dragon form to offer her own Children
> Upon the bloody Altar. John Saw these things Reveald in Heaven
> On Patmos Isle & heard the Souls cry out to be deliverd
>
> (115: 1–5, E385)

In Revelation St John sees very clearly that the forces of evil operate most rampantly immediately before the coming of God's kingdom: the satanic dragon form worshipped in Revelation 13 heralds the approach of the true Christ. As Blake's Rahab presides over the final consolidation of error she is in this sense an instrument of providence, just as òne of her namesakes in the Bible plays a key part in the Israelites' entry into the promised land.

Blake's Rahab is the false counterpart of Jesus, dressed in her own scarlet robes. In order to complete her role as counterpart she must also be judged and sacrificed by the Synagogue of Satan, and separated from her robes. Rahab's robes are put off when, as in the scepticism of some Enlightenment writers, or in the natural religion of Deists, Man seeks to free his vision from the outward forms of Mystery, without attempting to free himself from the limited vision that gives rise to Mystery. This is another revolutionary gesture that is bound by false horizons, a 'communing' between Orc and Rahab:

> [Rahab] secretly left the Synagogue of Satan
> She commund with Orc in secret She hid him with the flax
> That Enitharmon had numberd away from the Heavens
> She gatherd it together to consume her Harlot Robes
> .   .   .   .

> The Synagogue of Satan therefore uniting against Mystery
> Satan divided against Satan resolvd in open Sanhedrim
> To burn Mystery with fire & form another from her ashes
> For God put it into their heart to fulfill all his will
>
> The Ashes of Mystery began to animate they calld it Deism
> And Natural Religion as of old so now anew began
> Babylon again in Infancy Calld Natural Religion
>
> (115: 10–13, 18–24, E386)

The biblical story in which Rahab harbours Israelite spies in her own city provides the model for the hiding of Orc here (*see* Joshua 2: 6). Blake's use of it may reflect the covert nature of Deistical attacks upon revealed religion in the eighteenth century.

With the emergence of Deism we have arrived at the final consolidation of error. The inspired struggle of the eternal prophet against the forces of Urizenic error has dwindled into the stagnant opposition between Jerusalem the uninspired church, and the Babylon of Deism. All of the redemptive hopes inspired by the descent of Jesus lead to the unfulfilled present in which Blake writes. At this point the redemptive mission seems to have reached an abortive conclusion. Although Jesus submits willingly to the process that Orc was compelled to undergo, his sacrifice seems no more liberating than Orc's. The divine purpose of this submission to Rahab may be to expose error, so that it can be rejected: 'All mortal things made permanent that they may be put off' (107: 36, E383). But once the divine light has been swallowed up in darkness there seems to be no obvious reason why it should ever re-emerge.

In a revised beginning of Night IX, the 'Last Judgment' begins like this:

> And Los & Enitharmon builded Jerusalem weeping
> Over the Sepulcher & over the Crucified body
> Which to their Phantom Eyes appear'd still in the Sepulcher
> But Jesus stood beside them in the Spirit Separating
> Their Spirit from their body. Terrified at Non Existence
> For such they deemd the death of the body. Los his vegetable hands
> Outstretchd . . .
>
> (117: 1–7, E386)

Los's terror at the vision of Jesus has a precedent in Luke, where the resurrected Christ is greeted in fear by his disciples (*see* Luke 24:

37, 'But they were terrified and affrighted, and supposed that they had seen a spirit'). Los's vision of Jesus as a power that separates spirit from body apparently shows the influence of his Spectre, and his reaction to the vision seems quite uncomprehending. Blake's account of fallen history ends where it begins, with the terror of death, and his history of Christianity shows, as Paine would say, 'Satan . . . defeating . . . all the power and wisdom of the Almighty'. If Los pulls down the heavens while he confuses the death of the body with Non Existence, his action appears to be motivated neither by faith, nor by an enlightened commitment to putting off the selfhood in forgiveness, but by a suicidal despair. Blake's new vision of the Christian mission introduces many expressions of hope to the grim vision of fallen history, and consistently attempts to show that divine providence co-operates with the creative activities of Los. Nevertheless the poem shows that as long as Man remains bound in his fallen state, the divine vision will be absorbed in error. Man can only be redeemed by grace, in the form of a providential misinterpretation. Once he has made this leap in the dark, then his powers can be liberated for the difficult labours of the Last Judgement.

THE LAST JUDGEMENT REVISITED

As the culmination of Blake's account of divine providence, the Last Judgement describes the emergence of a new vision of Christian brotherhood, based on a new understanding of the relationship between male and female powers. In the Christian vision that develops under the influence of the Shadowy Female, the female assumes a determining role. The distribution of labour in Golgonooza ensures that the weaving of the females creates the groundwork of vision (the females clothe the spirit in a body that opens inward to Beulah). The divine vision that appears in Golgonooza is mediated by Enitharmon, who names Jerusalem, and who sees the Lamb 'within Jerusalems Veil' (104: 1–4, E376). This veiled and modulated revelation is the closest Los and Enitharmon approach to the divine vision. The sequel, in which the

Lamb is sacrificed before Rahab, and Jerusalem weeps over the empty sepulchre, is a consequence of this veiling. The sequence as a whole is a re-enactment of the pattern seen in Orc's relationship with the Shadowy Female. The male is sacrificed, the female mourns his apparent absence. As a representation of organized religion in general, and of institutional Christianity in particular, this pattern shows that divine love is buried by the finite material forms that ostensibly give it expression.

When Los destroys the heavens he renounces the outer world on which Golgonooza was built, and in which the dogma and rituals of institutional religion operate. The dismantling of the heavens leads to the closing of the distance that has been maintained throughout history, between the Council of God and fallen humanity: 'All the Sons of Eternity descended into Beulah' (118: 40, E388). It also leads swiftly to the consummation of Rahab and Tirzah (118: 7 ff., E387). The twenty-seven folds of Orc's serpent form (119: 3–4, E388) are not explained here; they may be related to the twenty-seven churches referred to in Milton 37: 35–43, E138). Once Jerusalem has been separated from the powers that enslaved her and from those that formed her, the flames of Orc begin 'to enter the Holy City'. This corresponds to the destruction of Jerusalem by fire in 2 Kings 25: 9, and it prepares for the emergence of a New Jerusalem.

In the rest of Night IX there are two references to the role of Jesus in the basic text. The first is a vision of Jerusalem descending out of heaven at 122: 1–20, E391; the second is a vision of throne of God, at 123: 20–39, E392–3. Both derive from Revelation, where the throne of God appears first (in Revelation 4), while the descent of Jerusalem is the climax of the book (Revelation 21). In Blake's myth the order is reversed, so that the narrative characteristically proceeds from mercy to judgement, from the Lamb of God to the Son of Man enthroned on a cloud of blood. The sequence forms a parallel with the eighth Night. In VIII, the Lamb descends through Jerusalem's gates to be judged and punished by the Synagogue of Satan amid 'Twelve rocky unshapd forms' and the twelve divisions of Rahab. In IX he descends from Jerusalem's gate and appears subsequently as a judge 'surrounded by twenty four venerable patriarchs'. His descent in VIII is accompanied by Los's pity; his second coming in IX occurs in a scene of wrath.

Jerusalem and the Lamb

The first vision appears after the resurrection and death of Ahania, where Urizen and Man have to confront the instability inherent in all creative activity. It is a crisis that demands faith, and the demand is answered in part by a vision of the Lamb and Jerusalem, which introduces Man's description of the seasonal life of eternity:

> Behold Jerusalem in whose bosom the Lamb of God
> Is seen tho slain before her Gates he self renewd remains
> Eternal & I thro him awake to life from deaths dark vale
> (122: 1-3, E391)

This time the revelation is Man's vision, not Enitharmon's, and the Lamb appears without a veil. The sense of distance in the earlier vision is here replaced by a recognition of identity: Man's own experience of death and renewal seems intimately related to, and dependent on, the death and self-renewal of the Lamb. The vision heralds Man's new conception of the relationship between males and females, which is the reverse of his previous view: now females must die and be reborn, while 'Immortal' males exist in their absence. This new pattern shares some of the limitations of the pattern it replaces: the female's duty to learn obedience in this matter turns her into a victim of the male, rather than a spontaneous self-sacrificer. The place of male labour in this cycle ('The winter thou shalt plow') makes the female seem a reward for his effort. In this respect Jerusalem seems quite unlike other females. No longer the joint creation of Enitharmon and Los, she is created by the Lamb himself, and descends as a gift from heaven:

> Thus shall the male & female live the life of Eternity
> Because the Lamb of God Creates himself a bride & wife
> That we his Children evermore may live in Jerusalem
> Which now descendeth out of heaven a City yet a Woman
> Mother of myriads redeemd & born in her spiritual palaces
> By a New Spiritual birth Regenerated from Death
> (122: 15-20, E391)

As a celestial gift, Jerusalem seems remote from the world of human labour. The comforting image of Jesus as the Lamb, and of Jerusalem as a protective mother, is the limited vision of an innocence in which individuals must become as children. The vision may lead us to think that a spirit of universal peace and forgiveness is about to prevail, but actually the reverse is true. When the 'bursting Universe explodes' the process of rebirth begins in unforgiving anger and violence.

The Son of Man

The Cloud of the Son of Man appears 'after the flames', a sequence which—like the transition from fire to cloud in Night V—perhaps indicates an obscuring or mystification of vision. The venerable patriarchs seem remote from the ideal of brotherhood to which Man is progressing. They suggest an invincible paternal authority in contrast to the comforting maternal vision of the Lamb. The vision is apparently an expression of Man's desire to sanctify vengeance: it is explicitly associated with the refusal of brotherhood and forgiveness (123: 20–32, E392–3). However, the patriarchs are surrounded by four 'Wonders of the Almighty', which correspond to the four 'beasts' (or 'zoa' in Greek) that surround the divine throne in Revelation 4: 6, and which recall the 'living creatures' mentioned in Ezekiel 1: 4–25.[40] These creatures are neither maternal nor paternal: they are 'Fourfold each in the other reflected'. They anticipate the brotherhood that Man will achieve in the company of fellow eternals, where each sees the Eternal Father in his brother's face. Although they are not explicitly identified with Urizen, Urthona, Luvah, and Tharmas, they are a model of the fourfold unity announced at the beginning of the poem. Their presence here points to the inadequacy of Man's vision of Jesus as *either* a messianic Son of Man *or* as a self-sacrificing Lamb. In either form Jesus is seen as a saviour who descends from above to answer human wishes, rather than a power that operates within Man himself. In this sense both are limited visions that have to be passed through. This point is emphasized as Man and Urizen, seeing the Cloud of God, strive to enter the consummation and are repelled. Redemption is to be achieved by a gradual transformation of Man's own powers, rather than by sudden retribution, or an instant illumination. Here the noise that accompanies the progress of judgement is not the thunder that accompanies sudden wisdom in Revelation (see 6: 1 and 14: 2), but the noise of rural work.

---

[40] See Margoliouth (ed.), *Vala*, 148.

Resurrection depends on the renovation of the body, which is not achieved until Enion becomes the bride of Tharmas. The feast that accompanies this union is equivalent to the supper celebrating the marriage of the Lamb to Jerusalem in Revelation. Jesus is now not a remote power, but present in the body—or fully incarnate. The description of the Eternals, who learn from Man's history and expand their understanding of brotherhood and love, is glossed by a reference to Ephesians 3: 10, which reads: 'To the intent that now unto the principalities and powers in heavenly places might be known by the church the manifold wisdom of God.' This recalls the epigraph of the poem, which is directed at spiritual wickedness in heaven. Previously Man has thought of divine love descending from heaven to earth, while the eternals have looked down on what they regard as sin. The error of the Council of God, which thought of redeeming Man by electing a representative, instead of surrendering its own purity and descending to re-establish brotherhood, has now been clarified. Neither Jesus nor Jerusalem seem necessary as separate symbols in the poem now that this brotherhood has been achieved.

In the context of this history of Jesus and Jerusalem, the co-operative weaving of the females at 137: 11–17, E405 forms a conclusion to the revision of relationships between the sexes. The reference to the nations gathered together possibly alludes to the final redemption of the nations in Jeremiah 3: 17. Unlike Enitharmon, these females do not weave the body—they only begin their weaving after the body has been renovated. Their work can be related to the creation of the garments in which females 'sleep the wintry days' (122: 8, E391), the protective veil of innocence that must sustain Man in his winter. The females, that is, have taken on the protective work previously assigned to Beulah, and the last strand of the providential machinery of the myth has been reabsorbed into the immediate experience of humanity.

PART IV

Final Changes

Final Changes

This stage of my reading focuses on an incomplete series of revisions, which were probably the last changes Blake made to the poem. These include:

1. a revision of the title page
2. minor changes in Nights I and II at 4: 3; 19: 8; 21: 7, 9, 15; 23: 1
3. the long addition at 25: 6–33
4. minor changes in Nights III and IV at 41: 3, 10, 13, 15; 56: 13.

Buried Beneath the Ruins

Towards Milton *and* Jerusalem

The moment at which Los initiates the Last Judgement by rending down the heavens, is the moment of liberation to which all of Blake's prophetic works are moving: the present moment, located for Blake within the era of institutional Christianity and, more specifically, within the period dominated by the visionary power of Milton and by the challenge of the Enlightenment. *The Four Zoas* presents this moment in the context of a universal history, by viewing the historical process as if from the outside—as a linear sequence whose causes and consequences can be laid out for inspection. In the two great illuminated prophecies, *Milton* and *Jerusalem*, history is often seen as from within, as it appears to the 'me' who inscribes the poem—as if the past must be viewed in relation to the conditions that appear to constitute the present. In *Milton* Blake the poet has to clarify the Miltonic legacy that inspires his own work. In *Jerusalem* he addresses those whom he seeks to liberate: the Public who may buy his works; the Jews whose traditions have helped to shape the mental horizons of that public; the Deists who make war on Christianity; the Christians who betray their own vision and despise 'the labours of Art & Science'. These works explore, more closely than *The Four Zoas* could do, the errors that dominate the present age and that must be cast off before the Last Judgement can begin.

It seems likely that Blake had already begun work on *Jerusalem*, and perhaps on *Milton* as well, before he stopped working on *The Four Zoas*.[1] Both *Milton* and *Jerusalem* are presented as though conceived at Felpham, where Blake probably transcribed part of the

---

[1] e.g. the Song of the Females of Amalek in Night VIII (105: 31–53, E378–9) also occurs in *Jerusalem* (67: 44–68: 9, E221), and appears to have been taken from there (line 105: 46 may have been transcribed as a half line because Blake decided to exclude the second half, which appears in *Jerusalem*, 67: 61, with two more lines not included in *The Four Zoas*).

proof text of *The Four Zoas*.[2] It is possible that, at one stage, he was working on all three poems at once. As *The Four Zoas* was not produced in illuminated printing, critics have tended to assume that it was superseded by the other two poems, and effectively abandoned. In what sense, then, did Blake 'stop working' on *The Four Zoas*? Before we attempt to answer this question, it may be helpful to review briefly the narrative that we have already examined.

Forms of History

The reasoning historian, turner and twister of causes and consequences, such as Hume, Gibbon, and Voltaire; cannot with all their artifice, turn or twist one fact or disarrange self evident action and reality. Reasons and opinions concerning acts, are not history. Acts themselves are alone history . . . (A Descriptive Catalogue of Pictures 1809 (E543–4))

Blake's angry dismissal of the reasoning historian masks an interest which this book has tried to clarify. The Enlightenment ambition to reveal the inner springs of social development by a systematic analysis of causes and consequences, was an ambition that Blake himself shared. Like the historical and social discourses with which it engages, *The Four Zoas* is concerned with evolutionary processes, with large patterns of growth and decline, and with the ideology that governs them. This concern determines the poem's relationship with the Bible and *Paradise Lost*: as we have seen, the narrative recreates some of the major narrative patterns of these texts (the process of creation, the escape from Egyptian bondage, the building of Pandæmonium, Satan's journey through Chaos) and episodes in which major revelations or confrontations occur (Satan tempting Eve beneath the forbidden tree, Satan confronting Sin at the gates of Hell, God foreseeing the fall, etc.). *Paradise Lost* lends itself particularly well to Blake's enterprise since, like *The Four Zoas*, it presents history as a continuous and closely plotted sequence of causes and effects. In quite different ways both works strive to establish a universal perspective that will encompass and explain the entire span of fallen existence. But *The Four Zoas* also resembles Enlightenment stadial histories, in that it sees the same

---

[2] *Milton* includes a vision set in the garden of Blake's cottage at Felpham (pl. 36, E137). The address 'To the Public' at the beginning of *Jerusalem*, refers to the poet's 'three years slumber on the banks of the Ocean' (pl. 3, E145).

processes at work in all cultures. This means reducing material developments to one pattern (for example, one movement through periods of hunting, pasturage, agriculture, and commerce); and it means suggesting fundamental similarities between different myths and traditions (Orc as Prometheus, Dionysus, Isaac, Christ; Urizen as Lear, Oedipus, God the Father, etc.). The method produces history in an archetypal form that can illuminate widely different periods of historical time.

In the revisions to *The Four Zoas* which show the history of Jesus, one can detect the emergence of a new approach to history, which is also a new approach to narrative. These revisions tie the myth to a particular historical time-scale: the two thousand years of history since the advent of Christ are superimposed onto the archetypal pattern. In the references to biblical locations, in Los's extraordinary genealogy, in the account of the seven Eyes of God, names assume a new significance. Unlike Blake's invented, archetypal names, the biblical names tie the myth unequivocally to one history, one tradition. One can see here, I think, the beginnings of a movement away from the presentation of history (and of narrative) as a continuous sequence of causes and effects whose universality is suggested by its power to synthesize and systematize a range of different contexts and traditions; a movement towards a narrative that is rooted more firmly in particular traditions whose universality is suggested by other means. This movement can be seen as a renunciation of the Enlightenment influence, an attempt to free the 'acts' of history as far as possible from the generalizing arrangement or 'disarrangement' of them.

This movement accompanied, or perhaps prepared the way for, Blake's new interest in national history. As Susan Matthews points out, in 1785 William Hayley (later Blake's patron at Felpham) had urged poets to write epics using British myths and legends.[3] Around the turn of the century a number of English poets, including John Ogilvie, Joseph Cottle, and John Thelwall, shared an ambition to create such a national epic. This ambition can be related in general terms to the increasing influence of nationalism during the period following the French Revolution, a development that marks the end

---

[3] '*Jerusalem* and Nationalism', in *Beyond Romanticism: New Approaches to Texts and Contexts 1780–1832*, ed. S. Copley and J. Whale (London and New York, 1992), 89. See also M. Butler, 'Romanticism in England', in *Romanticism in National Context*, ed. R. Porter and M. Teich (Cambridge, 1988).

of the Enlightenment concern to create a universal history.[4] In Blake's case the interest in national history centred on the development of a new myth of origins that would have a universal significance. His interest in ancient British antiquities seems to have been fed by a number of contemporary theories, in which the Druids were identified with the bards, and were credited with building Stonehenge and other prehistoric monuments. From his friend Owen Pughe, translator of the Welsh Triads, he may have learned that the religion of the Ancient British bards was related directly to that of the biblical Patriarchs.[5] Blake's response to such theories is encapsulated in his assertion that Britain was 'the Primitive Seat of the Patriarchal Religion', and that 'Albion was the Parent of the Druids' (*Jerusalem* pl. 27, E171). As well as considering the relationship between the British and Hebraic traditions, Blake also turned to the traditional British history as presented by Geoffrey of Monmouth, by Spenser, and by Milton in his *History of England*. This, of course, was precisely the kind of history that the Enlightenment had dismissed as absurd fantasy: rooted in folklore and legend, rich in imaginary acts, devoid of historical reasoning.

Blake's attempt to revise *The Four Zoas* in the light of this interest was probably the last stage in the poem's composition, and may have been an attempt to transform the poem into a national epic: in some places the Eternal Man was identified as Albion, and other additions relate the history of the fallen world to ancient British origins. Changes to the title page suggest that the work acquired its present title *The Four Zoas* only at this stage.[6] In the narrative, the first sign of this revision appears on page 3, where Urthona's Emanations are identified as 'Fairies of Albion afterwards Gods of the Heathen' (4: 3, E301). Other changes establish a connection between Druidic and Hebraic tradition. The Council

---

[4] See G. Barraclough, 'Universal History', 85.

[5] For a discussion of the possible sources of Blake's interest in British Antiquities see Damon, *Dictionary*, 108–10; M. D. Paley, *The Continuing City: William Blake's Jerusalem* (Oxford, 1983), 54–7, 241–2; Butler, 'Romanticism in England', 49–50. Owen Pughe's translations of ancient Welsh poetry appeared in *The Heroic Elegies and Other Pieces of Llywarc Hen* (London, 1792) and in the *Myvyrian Archaiology of Wales*, 3 vols. (London, 1801–7). By 1809 Edward Davies' *Myths and Rites of the British Druids* (London, 1809) would have been available to Blake.

[6] The following revisions were made to the title page in pencil: 'Vala or' deleted; 'The Four Zoas' and 'The Torments of Love & Jealousy' substituted; 'Albion' inserted ('of Albion the Ancient Man').

of God originally convened above Mount Gilead (associated in the
Bible with visions of God that promote non-communication and
division, Genesis 31: 25; Judges 7: 3). It now convenes above
Snowdon (associated in Gray's poem 'The Bard' with Druidism and
with the demise of the bardic tradition). The Ambassadors from
Beulah no longer kneel down in Beth Peor, where Moses was
buried, but in Conway's Vale (21: 15, E311), where Gray's bard
plunges 'to endless night'. The most extensive revision is the long
passage inserted in the margin on page 25, where Urizen begins to
construct the Golden World:

Petrifying all the Human Imagination into rock & sand
Groans run along Tyburns brook and along the River of Oxford
Among the Druid Temples. Albion groand on Tyburns brook
Albion gave his loud death groan The Atlantic Mountains trembled
Aloft the Moon fled with a cry the Sun with streams of blood
From Albions Loins fled all Peoples and Nations of the Earth
Fled with the noise of Slaughter & the stars of heaven Fled
Jerusalem came down in a dire ruin over all the Earth
She fell cold from Lambeths Vales in groans & Dewy death
The dew of anxious souls the death-sweat of the dying
In every pillard hall & arched roof of Albions skies
The brother & the brother bathe in blood upon the Severn
The Maiden weeping by. The father & the mother with
The Maidens father & her mother fainting over the body
And the Young Man the Murderer fleeing over the mountains

Reuben slept on Penmaenmawr & Levi slept on Snowdon
Their eyes their ears nostrils & tongues roll outward   they behold
What is within now seen without they are raw to the hungry wind
They become Nations far remote in a little & dark Land
The Daughters of Albion girded around their garments of
    Needlework
Stripping Jerusalems curtains from mild demons of the hills
Across Europe & Asia to China & Japan like lightenings
They go forth & return to Albion on his rocky couch
Gwendolen Ragan Sabrina Gonorill Mehetabel Cordella
Boadicea Conwenna Estrild Gwinefrid Ignoge Cambel
Binding Jerusalems Children in the dungeons of Babylon
They play before the Armies before the hounds of Nimrod
While The Prince of Light on Salisbury plain among the druid
    stones . . .

                                        (25: 6–33, E314–17)

The passage introduces an approach to history quite unlike that adopted in the rest of the poem. There is a vestigial narrative here, which elaborates the idea that Albion is the unified form of humanity, and that his fall destroys Jerusalem, instigates Druidic sacrifice, and divides the human community into nations. But the handling of time dissolves chronology, just as the handling of space avoids the creation of a scenic context. Albion's fall is continually identified with, and re-enacted in, its divisive consequences. Tyburn's brook runs past the place of execution in the London of Blake's own day, where 'Druid' sacrifice is still practised. The river of Oxford runs past temples of learning that are also Druidic in their promotion of a theology that can endorse such justice. 'Lambeths Vales', which skirt the Thames, were once Blake's home, and are also the home of the Archbishop of Canterbury, the spiritual descendant of the priestly Druids. Water is associated with both sacrifice and division. The Atlantic mountains recall the continent of Atlantis, the destruction of which divided England from America, a division re-enacted in the War of Independence. The river Severn, which divides England from Wales (the last home of the Ancient Britons) was the site of civil war—the battles of Shrewsbury and Tewkesbury. The theme of division is continued in the references to Reuben and Levi, both of whom founded Israelite tribes (they are identified as Druids here, and as sons of Los in Night VIII, 107: 4, E380). The Daughters of Albion, whose names come from Geoffrey of Monmouth and Milton, take on the functions attributed to Vala, Tirzah, and Rahab. They help to petrify the imagination by transforming mild demons of the hills (which may recall Urthona's 'Fairies') into tyrannical Gods. The reference to their stripping of Jerusalem's curtains, and to their garments of needlework, recalls the contrast established elsewhere in the poem between the protective veil of innocence and the naturalistic web that stifles creativity. Nimrod is traditionally identified as the builder of the tower of Babel, an edifice here related to Stonehenge (believed to be a temple for Druid sacrifice).

The passage achieves its effects by juxtaposition rather than conflation, by creating a field in which parallels and associations draw attention back and forth, without a focusing plot. Only once are we invited to rest our attention on a scene—the description of maiden, parents, and Young Man—which reads like the caption of a painting, and which serves to focus the emotion of the passage. It must have become clear to Blake that this kind of material could not be integrated into the existing narrative of the poem in the way that the revisions concerning Jesus were. This approach to history dissolves the kind of distinctions that the rest of *The Four Zoas* explores—between the primitive and the civilized, for example, or between the cosmos and the scientific universe. It is hardly surprising that the revision was not continued at any length beyond this point.

A Ruinous Tradition

This incomplete revision is one of several loose ends in the narrative. The others are textual difficulties, which arise mainly because the instructions in the manuscript concerning the beginning and ending of some Nights are unclear. Apart from minor lacunae and awkward transitions, there are two major areas of difficulty, which have already been noted in passing: the ending of Night I, and the two Nights VII. As editors have found workable solutions to both of these problems, I shall not review them now (*see* Appendix 4). What concerns me here is the fact that the existence of these loose ends has helped to sustain the traditional view that the poem is a chaotic ruin.[7] This tradition has not only influenced general views of the poem's status (as I mentioned in my Preface), but also, it seems, specific points of interpretation. The idea that the revisions concerning Los's conversion allegorize directly a conversion that Blake himself underwent, and that the added material looks forward directly to *Milton* and *Jerusalem* rather than to the ninth Night of *The Four Zoas*, has become deeply entrenched.[8] The assumption that these revisions signal Blake's own renunciation of revolutionary apocalypse and his endorsement of an inner regeneration has had a significant influence on the received view of Blake's political and spiritual development during the late 1790s and early 1800s.[9]

---

[7] Stephen Cox sums up the traditional view of *The Four Zoas*: 'Blake's project clearly leaves the reader in the position of an archaeologist contemplating an irregular and many layered ruin', *Love and Logic* (Ann Arbor, 1992), 168.

[8] I make the same assumption in 'The Revision of the Seventh and Eighth Nights of *The Four Zoas*', *Blake: An Illustrated Quarterly*, 12 (1978), 115–33.

[9] See e.g. E. D. Hirsch Jr., *Innocence and Experience: An Introduction to Blake* (New Haven, 1964), and Cantor, *Creature and Creator*, 58–61.

In view of the strength of these assumptions, I end my study by restating briefly some of its conclusions. First, there is little evidence to support the view that Blake revised the poem so much that it went through many drafts. Blake's process of revision invariably tends to complicate and fragment the narrative, while the basic text of much of the poem seems remarkably homogeneous. Secondly, although the manuscript has a chaotic appearance in places, there seems little reason to suppose that the revisions were made in an arbitrary or piecemeal fashion, or that they represent an attempt to keep up with the rapidly changing events of contemporary history. Most seem designed to elaborate and/or clarify issues already present in the text, while many—including those concerned with the role of Jesus—are closely interrelated. Third, the assumption that the revisions show an abandonment of revolutionary hopes in favour of inner regeneration must be challenged. The reading given here suggests precisely the opposite: inner regeneration without revolutionary action is presented as doomed to fail, just as revolutionary action is doomed to fail until and unless there is a complete rejection of selfhood.

Blake's poem may be fractured and in places confusing, and it presents some textual problems that may never be fully resolved. But to characterize it as a ruin is to recoil from, instead of engaging with, its complexities. Of the major narrative poems in English, *The Four Zoas* is one of the least read. If we could free it from some of the prejudices and bewildering editorial practices with which we have surrounded it, more readers might begin to see it as one of the most rewarding.

Appendix 1:
A Note on the Illustrations

As Magno and Erdman show, an optimistic interpretation of the illustrations can find meaning in practically all of them, even in tentative sketches and accidental stains.[1] However, the condition of the manuscript provides evidence that may qualify such optimism. Consider the following cases:

1. The illustrations accompanying the first three pages of the narrative have been finished quite carefully—the pencil outlines reinforced in some places with ink, the figures and backgrounds washed with several colours. Those on the next two pages have less finish, those on pages 8 and 9 even less, while the images on pages 10–11 are very rough sketches.

2. An illustration on page 15 (of an old man with wings and flowing white hair and beard, who grasps a large rope) has some touches of grey and brown wash. This page was interpolated into a text that has many less finished drawings.

We might conclude from (1) that Blake began with the intention of illustrating every page carefully, but soon became less careful, or even bored, and that (2) indicates a temporary revival of interest in careful illustration. But the unfinished sketches on the verso of page 15 (i.e. page 16) lend little support to the latter idea. There is another possible explanation for (2): that the drawing was made before the leaf became part of this manuscript. It might, for example, have been a preliminary sketch for Edward Young's *Night Thoughts*, for which Blake made many designs between 1795 and 1797 (it resembles in some respects two other *Night Thoughts* designs: NT 197 and 226).[2] A sketch on the verso, over which Blake transcribed the text, would support this idea: like the one on page 108, it resembles a pencil sketch on the verso of Blake's design for the *Night Thoughts* frontispiece (vol. i).

But if the drawings on pages 15–16 could be trial sketches for *Night Thoughts*, might not this also apply to the more elaborately coloured sketches on pages 3–5 of the manuscript? Could the female on page 3, for example, have been a first version of, say, the seductive figure of Earth in NT 185? Could the winged archer with the huge serpent on page 4 have

---

[1] See Magno and Erdman, 'The Four Zoas'.
[2] The numbers refer to *William Blake's Designs for Edward Young's 'Night Thoughts'*, ed. Erdman, Grant, Rose, and Tolley.

been a discarded version of the serpentine Leviathan and rider in *NT* 349? Could the winged figure that lies upon a wavy sea on page 5 have been a first version of *NT* 57, which shows two winged figures in the sea? I know of no additional evidence that lends support to these suggestions, nor of any that might categorically refute them,[3] but it is not difficult to entertain such possibilities, since we know that many of the illustrations in the manuscript—all of the *Night Thoughts* proofs—*were* originally designed for another text. That does not mean that Blake made no effort to introduce them to the manuscript at points that seemed generally appropriate. Since his visual and verbal symbolism centres on a limited number of themes, it would not be difficult to find such points (the old man on page 15 would seem appropriate at very many points in the manuscript, since it would always be interpreted as an image of Urizen). But the evidence of makeshift and improvisation may qualify the assumption that in every case Blake intended a detailed allegory of some sort, or that he was producing a fully integrated 'composite art'.[4] Some designs illustrate the text in a direct and obvious way, some are imaginative illuminations, some offer general thematic parallels, some seem related to the text very tenuously (if at all), while some are so unfinished that even description of them is difficult. Any attempt to read all of the illustrations in the same way must overlook the considerable variations in Blake's practice.

[3] The extensive revisions on the first three pages, and the possibility that the illustrations may have been retouched by Blake, make it difficult to determine whether the text pre-dates or post-dates the illustrations.

[4] The phrase was coined by Northrop Frye, and adopted by W. J. T. Mitchell, primarily with reference to Blake's illuminated books. N. Frye, 'Poetry and Design in William Blake', *Journal of Aesthetics and Art Criticism*, 10 (1951), 35–42; W. J. T. Mitchell, *Blake's Composite Art: A Study of the Illuminated Poetry* (Princeton, NJ, 1978).

Appendix 2: Interim Revisions

On page 48 of the manuscript Gerald E. Bentley Jr. has detected a mirror-image of a page of Hayley's first Ballad, and an indentation probably caused by the impression of a copper plate. Bentley suggests that this proof page was used as a backing-sheet when Blake was printing engravings for the Ballads at Felpham.[1] Blake's engravings for the first Ballad are dated '1 June 1802'. As it seems unlikely that Blake would temporarily remove a page of his manuscript to use it as a backing-sheet, it seems reasonable to conclude that the writing on page 48 was transcribed after the proof had been used in this way. If the basic text of the proof pages was mostly transcribed at about the same time, and the copperplate text was transcribed in 1797 as the title page suggests, there may have been an interval of at least five years between the transcription of the proof text and the copperplate text.

One series of revisions appears to belong to this interval. At several points in the copperplate text Blake erased 'Eternal' from the phrase 'Eternal Man', and substituted other epithets. 'Fallen' is the most common substitute, but 'Wandering', 'Slumberous', and 'Ancient' also appear (the last term was substituted on the title page and twice in the text). Blake's general method in these alterations—erasing the original text, writing the revisions first in pencil, and then confirming them in ink—indicates a concern for the physical appearance of the copperplate text. On page 48 of the proof text (line 13) Blake began to write 'Ancient,' but then substituted 'Eternal Man,' which is the phrase generally used throughout the proof text. 'Fallen Man' and 'Ancient Man' would thus seem to be interim terms, adopted after Blake had transcribed the copperplate text, but dropped when he began to transcribe the proof text. From this evidence it would seem that Blake revised Enitharmon's 'Song of Death' in the interim period, for here 'Fallen' replaced 'Eternal' (10: 10, E305).

Another revision that seems to have been planned in the interim period survives on the fragment page 141, where Blake first used the term 'ancient man', and then changed this to 'Eternal Man' (deleted text in italics; additions in square brackets):

Beneath the veil of ?*Enion* [Vala] rose Tharmas from dewy tears
The *ancient* [eternal] man bowd his bright head & Urizen prince
     of light

[1] Bentley, Vala, *or* The Four Zoas, 161.

Astonish lookd from his bright Portals calling thus to Luvah
O Luvah in the ————————————————————————————————
Astonishd lookd from his bright portals. Luvah king of Love
Awakend Vala. Ariston ran forth with bright ?Onana
And dark Urthona rouzd his shady bride from her deep den
[*Awaking from his stony slumber*]
Pitying they viewd the new born demon. for they could not love
After their sin ——————————————————————————————————
Male formd the demon mild athletic force his shoulders spread
And his bright feet firm as a brazen altar. but. the parts
To love devoted. female, all astonishd stood the hosts
Of heaven, while Tharmas with wingd speed flew to the sandy shore [*ocean*]
He rested on the desart wild & on the raging sea
He stood & stretchd his wings &c ———————————————————————

With printless feet scorning the concave of the joyful sky
Female her form bright as the summer but the parts of love
Male & her brow radiant as day. darted a lovely scorn
Tharmas beheld from his high rocks & ——————————————————————

(141: 1–20, E845)

The fragment appears to develop an account of the fall which involves
two pairs of characters who do not appear (as far as we can tell) in the
original copperplate text: Ariston and Onana, with Urthona and his shady
bride. Blake may have been trying to form a mythical structure that would
correspond to his later scheme of four 'Zoas.' The fourth pair would
presumably have been Urizen and Ahania. Perhaps Tharmas and Enion,
and Los and Enitharmon were once thought of as products of the fall
rather than as prelapsarian powers (Tharmas is perhaps the child of Vala
here, as in the pastoral interlude of Night IX). When Blake continued this
passage in pencil on the verso of the leaf, he made three attempts to
describe the mating of Tharmas and Enion. The second attempt describes
a conception followed by a separation. In the third attempt, Tharmas
conceives from Enion:

> From Enion pours the seed of life & death in all her limbs
> Frozen in the womb of Tharmas rush the rivers of Enions pain
> Trembling he lay swelld with the deluge stifling in the anguish
>
> (142: 8–10, E846)

These tentative notes seem to present an alternative to the sexual union
described on page 7. Blake apparently got as far as making tentative pencil
notes of a comparable revision on page 7. Erdman notes:

Under lines 1–3 . . . are three erased lines in Blake's usual hand, the last word of the
1st line being 'threatening.' Partly under these but beginning in the top margin is a
pencil passage of six lines, the 1st three legible (but short, as if only beginnings
of lines):

> When Tharmas shook his billowy hair
> Two forms of horror howld beneath ?it
> A male & female witherd
>
> (*E821*)

These lines, partly underneath the first layer of ink revisions at the top of the page, are probably among the earliest additions to the page. As in the fragment, Tharmas appears to be sexually female, giving birth to 'two forms of horror'. This tentative revision was not adopted, although in 8: 2, which refers to the birth of Los and Enitharmon, Blake deleted in pencil 'little infants wept' and added 'Then forms of horror howled' (an alteration over which Blake vacillated before rejecting it).

The Tharmas of the fragment—a monstrous winged demon who is compared to a metallic artefact, and whose birth is associated with 'sin'—is presumably the prototype of the Spectre of Tharmas who mates with Enion in the revised myth. The concept of the Spectre allowed Blake to distinguish between different forms of Tharmas and of Urthona, and it played an important part in the structure of the four 'Zoa' scheme. By the time Blake began to transcribe the proof text, Los and the Spectre of Urthona had been identified as fallen forms of Urthona.

Appendix 3: The Gardens of Vala

It is possible that erased copperplate text on pages 3–7, at the beginning of Night I, originally contained an account of Tharmas's fall from the gardens of Vala. The pastoral interlude in Night IX has more than 170 lines—far too many to be accommodated on the first four-and-a-half pages of the manuscript (page 4 originally had 19 lines of copperplate text, page 6 had 12 lines). However, two of the phrases deciphered from the copperplate text by David Erdman also appear in the pastoral interlude: 'light of day' and 'the crystal sky' (see E819–20). An account of Tharmas's fall from Vala's gardens would necessarily involve a transition from the pastoral world to the 'watry world of woe' that Tharmas usually inhabits. There is a precedent for this kind of transition in *Visions of the Daughters of Albion*, where Oothoon takes her flight from Leutha's pastoral vale to the desolate coastline of Theotormon's reign. In *Visions* this transition leads to a fierce coupling with the monstrous Bromion. The erased text of pages 3–7 of *The Four Zoas* leads into the account of the tempestuous coupling of Tharmas and Enion, which survives in the text of page 7. The fragment page 141, which appears to be an attempt to revise the description of this coupling and of the events leading up to it, shows how Tharmas arises 'beneath the veil of Vala . . . from dewy tears' (*see* Appendix 2). This may refer to Tharmas's transition from the innocence of Vala's gardens (where he weeps 'dewy tears' 130: 18) to the rugged fallen world of the 'desart wild' and the 'raging sea'.

It seems possible that Blake had developed a myth similar to that in the pastoral interlude by the time he was working on *Thel*, where Luvah is mentioned by name. There Luvah appears to be an Apollo figure (the cloud tells Thel 'our steeds drink of the golden springs | Where Luvah doth renew his horses' (3: 7–8, E4). When Blake was planning *Thel* he made sketches which suggest that he thought of matron Clay's house as a fine building with pillars, like Vala's bodily house.[1] In the ninth Night interlude, the gradual movement from Vala's joyful relationship with Luvah towards the unstable relationship of Tharmas and Enion represents a gradual movement towards the complications of the fallen world. In *Thel* there is no such gradual transition, but an abrupt confrontation with the horrors of experience, described on the final plate.

[1] For a discussion of the composition of *Thel* see *William Blake: The Early Illuminated Books*, ed. M. Eaves, R. N. Essick, and J. Viscomi (London, 1993), 71–4.

Appendix 4: Two Textual Problems

1. An instruction on page 9 indicates that Night II begins at line 34, but the end of Night I is announced elsewhere, at two different places (at the foot of page 18 and at the foot of the inserted page 19). Presumably the Night heading on page 23 originally read 'Night the Second', but there is no sign of the word 'Second' here. At one stage Blake inserted 'Third' in this heading, and twice he inserted 'First', but each insertion was cancelled. Some editors ignore the instruction on page 9, and assume that Night II begins on page 23. But W. H. Stevenson (1989) accepts the instruction on page 9, and suggests that the material on pages 19–22 should be inserted after 9: 33, to form the end of the first Night. I find his arguments convincing (see chapter 9).

2. There are two seventh Nights, beginning on pages 77 ('VIIa') and 91 ('VIIb') respectively. It seems likely, as Gerald E. Bentley Jr. suggests, that in the process of revising and expanding the eighth Night Blake divided it into two Nights, of which the first became VIIb.[1] Sub-sequently Blake divided VIIb in two and transposed the portions. Both VIIa and VIIb seem integral parts of the narrative, but the instructions in the manuscript do not show clearly how they should be integrated with the rest of the poem. There would seem to be several possible explanations for this problem:

(a) When Blake changed the Night heading on page 23 to read 'Night the First', he intended to renumber the following Nights, and to treat the original Night I as a Preludium (or exclude it). In this case he must have changed his mind when he erased 'Night the First' on page 23.

(b) When Blake deleted 'A Dream of Nine Nights' from the title page he had abandoned the nine-Night structure, intending perhaps to renumber the Nights from one to ten (VIIb perhaps following VIIa). In this case he either forgot to put the renumbering into effect, or changed his mind about it.

(c) Blake left instructions (with the manuscript or separately) which have since been lost (see his instructions concerning the order of *Songs of Innocence and of Experience*, E772).

(d) Blake left instructions in the manuscript which are too scant and ambiguous for us to interpret with certainty.

Both (a) and (b) involve a renumbering of the Nights. As Blake did not renumber them in this way we would have to conclude that he effectively

---

[1] Bentley, Vala, *or* The Four Zoas, 162–3.

abandoned the poem, or that he wanted to confront the reader with a radically 'indeterminate' text. Both (c) and (d) might involve a conflation of the two Nights VII into one.

I doubt if we have enough evidence to accept any of these explanations as conclusive. However, the 'Albion' revisions appear to be later than those concerning Jesus (which probably caused the reorganization of the seventh Nights). This suggests that Blake did not stop working on the poem until he abandoned the Albion revisions. In any event we are left with a problem that editors have to make uncomfortable decisions about. Several different ways of integrating the material in these Nights have been proposed. It is generally accepted that the one adopted by David Erdman (1982) produces the most satisfactory reading text (although there are no signs that Blake himself intended such an arrangement).[2]

[2] For a full discussion of this problem see *Blake: An Illustrated Quarterly*, 12 (1978).

Select Bibliography

Editions of Blake

BENTLEY, G. E. JR. (ed.), *William Blake: Vala, or* The Four Zoas: *A Facsimile of the Manuscript, a Transcript of the Poem, and a Study of Its Growth and Significance* (Oxford, 1963).

—— (ed.), *William Blake's Writings* (2 vols.; Oxford, 1978).

EAVES, MORRIS, ESSICK, ROBERT N., and VISCOMI, JOSEPH (eds.), *William Blake: The Early Illuminated Books* (London, 1993).

ELLIS, E. J. and YEATS, W. B. (eds.), *The Works of William Blake: Poetic, Symbolic, and Critical* (3 vols.; London, 1893).

ERDMAN, DAVID V. (ed.), *The Poetry and Prose of William Blake* (New York, 1965).

—— *The Complete Poetry and Prose of William Blake.* With a Commentary by Harold Bloom. (New York, 1982).

—— GRANT, JOHN E., ROSE, EDWARD J., and TOLLEY, MICHAEL (eds.), *William Blake's Designs for Edward Young's 'Night Thoughts'* (2 vols.; Oxford, 1980).

KEYNES, GEOFFREY (ed.), *The Writings of William Blake* (3 vols.; London, 1925).

—— (ed.), *Blake: Complete Writings* (Oxford, 1966; rev. 1969, 1971, 1972).

MAGNO, CETTINA TAMONTANO, and ERDMAN, DAVID V. (eds.), *'The Four Zoas' by William Blake: A Photographic Facsimile of the Manuscript with Commentary on the Illustrations* (Lewisburg, Va., London, and Toronto, 1987).

MARGOLIOUTH, H. M. (ed.), *Vala: Blake's Numbered Text* (Oxford, 1956).

OSTRIKER, ALICIA (ed.), *William Blake: The Complete Poems* (Harmondsworth, 1977).

SLOSS, D. J. and WALLIS, J. P. R. (eds.), *William Blake's Prophetic Writings* (2 vols.; Oxford, 1926).

STEVENSON, W. H. (ed.), *Blake: The Complete Poems* (2nd edn.; Harlow, 1989).

Primary Sources

ADDISON, JOSEPH, 'An Oration in Defence of the New Philosophy, Spoken in the Theatre at Oxford, July 9 1693', included in *A Week's Conversa-*

tion on the Plurality of Worlds, by Monsieur de Fontenelle (London, 1737).

ADDISON, JOSEPH, STEELE, RICHARD, *et al.*, *The Spectator*, ed. Donald F. Bond (5 vols.; Oxford, 1965).

The Anti-Jacobin—or Weekly Examiner, Monday 19 February, 1798; Monday 26 February, 1798; Monday 2 April, 1798.

BACON, FRANCIS, *Of the Advancement and Proficience of Learning or the Partition of Sciences*. Interpreted by Gilbert Wats (Oxford, 1640).

—— *The Philosophical Works of Francis Bacon*. Transl. Peter Shaw (3 vols.; London, 1733).

—— *The Advancement of Learning*, ed. William Aldis Wright (Oxford, 1900).

BENTLEY, G. E. JR., *Blake Records* (Oxford, 1969).

BOYLE, ROBERT, *A Free Enquiry into the Vulgarly Receiv'd Notion of Nature* (London, 1685).

BUFFON, GEORGES-LOUIS, *Barr's Buffon: Buffon's Natural History* (10 vols.; London, 1792).

BUNYAN, JOHN, *Grace Abounding and The Pilgrim's Progress*, ed. Roger Sharrock (Oxford, 1966).

BURKE, EDMUND, *Reflections on the Revolution in France*, ed. Conor Cruise O'Brien (Harmondsworth, 1968).

BURNET, THOMAS, Archaeologiae Philosophicae; or, The Ancient Doctrine Concerning the Originals of Things (London, 1736).

BUTLER, JOSEPH, *The Analogy of Religion* (5th edn.; London, 1754).

CLARKE, SAMUEL, *A Collection of Papers which Passed between the Late Learned Mr Leibniz and Dr Clarke in the Years 1715 and 1716. Relating to the Principles of Natural Philosophy and Religion* (London, 1717).

—— *A Discourse Concerning the Being and Attributes of God* (London, 1712).

—— *A Discourse Concerning the Unalterable Obligations of Natural Religion and The Truth and Certainty of the Christian Religion*, in *A Collection of Theological Tracts*, ed. Richard Watson (4 vols.; London, 1785).

COLERIDGE, SAMUEL TAYLOR, *The Collected Works of Samuel Taylor Coleridge, Volume I: Lectures 1795 on Politics and Religion*, ed. Lewis Patton and Peter Mann (London and Princeton, NJ, 1971).

CONDORCET, ANTOINE-NICOLAS DE, *Outlines of an Historical View of the Progress of the Human Mind* (London, 1795).

COOPER, ANTHONY ASHLEY, *Anthony Ashley Cooper, Third Earl of Shaftesbury: Standard Edition*, ed. Gerd Hemmerich and Wolfram Benda (6 vols.; Frommann-Holzborg, 1981-9).

COWLEY, ABRAHAM, *Poems*, ed. A. R. Waller (Cambridge, 1905).

CUDWORTH, RALPH, *The True Intellectual System of the Universe* (London, 1678).

—— *A Treatise Concerning Eternal and Immutable Morality* (London, 1731).

DARWIN, ERASMUS, *Zoonomia: Or the Laws of Organic Life* (2 vols.; London, 1794–6).

DAVIES, EDWARD, *Myths and Rites of the British Druids* (London, 1809).

DERHAM, WILLIAM, *Physico Theology, or, a Demonstration of the Being and Attributes of God from his Works of Creation* (4th edn.; London, 1716).

FERGUSON, ADAM, *An Essay on the History of Civil Society* (1767), ed. Duncan Forbes (Edinburgh, 1966).

GEDDES, ALEXANDER, *The Holy Bible* (London, 1792).

GIBBON, EDWARD, *The History of the Decline and Fall of the Roman Empire*, ed. J. B. Bury (7 vols.; London 1909–14).

GLOVER, RICHARD, *Leonidas* (5th edn.; London, 1770).

GODWIN, WILLIAM, *Enquiry Concerning Political Justice* (2 vols.; London, 1793).

HOBBES, THOMAS, *Leviathan*, ed. Richard Tuck (Cambridge, 1991).

HORSLEY, SAMUEL, *A Sermon, preached before the Lords Spiritual and Temporal, on Wednesday, January 30, 1793. Being the Anniversary of the Martyrdom of Charles the First* (London, 1793).

HUME, DAVID, *Writings on Religion*, ed. Anthony Flew (La Salle, Ill., 1992).

—— *The History of Great Britain* (2 vols.; Edinburgh, 1754).

—— *David Hume: The Philosophical Works*, ed. Thomas Hill Green and Thomas Hodge Grose (4 vols.; Aalen, 1964).

—— *Enquiries concerning Human Understanding and concerning the Principles of Morals*, ed. L. A. Selby-Bigge (3rd edn., rev. P. H. Nidditch; Oxford, 1975).

HUTCHESON, FRANCIS, *An Essay on the Nature and Conduct of the Passions and Affections* (London, 1728; repr. Menston, Yorkshire, 1972).

KEATS, JOHN, *The Letters of John Keats 1814–21*, ed. Hyder Edward Rollins (2 vols.; Cambridge, Mass., 1958).

LOCKE, JOHN, *An Essay Concerning Human Understanding*, ed. Peter H. Nidditch (Oxford, 1975).

—— *Two Treatises of Government*, ed. Peter Laslett (Cambridge, 1988).

LUCRETIUS, *Lucretius Carus of the Nature of Things in Six Books*. Transl. Thomas Creech (London, 1714).

MACKINTOSH, JAMES, *Vindiciae Gallicae* (London, 1791). A facsimile reprint, with introduction by Jonathan Wordsworth (Oxford, 1989).

MACPHERSON, JAMES, 'A Dissertation Concerning the Poems of Ossian', in

The Works of Ossian, Son of Fingal. Translated from the Galic [sic] *language by James Macpherson* (London, 1765).

MANDEVILLE, BERNARD, *The Fable of the Bees, or Private Vices, Publick Benefits*, ed. F. B. Kay (2 vols.; Oxford, 1924; repr. Indianapolis, 1988).

MARX, KARL, *The Poverty of Philosophy* (London, 1956).

MICHAELIS, JOHN DAVID, *Introduction to the New Testament*. Transl. Herbert Marsh (Cambridge, 1793).

MIDDLETON, CONYERS, *A Letter from Rome. Shewing an exact Conformity between* POPERY *and* PAGANISM (London, 1729).

MILLAR, JOHN, *The Origin of the Distinction of Ranks* (London, 1779).

MILTON, JOHN, *The Poems of John Milton*, ed. John Carey and Alastair Fowler (London and New York, 1968, 1972).

—— *The Complete Prose Works of John Milton*, ed. Don M. Wolfe, *et al.* (8 vols.; New Haven, Conn. and London, 1973).

MONTESQUIEU, BARON DE, *The Spirit of the Laws, translated from the French of M. de Secondat Baron de Montesquieu* (2 vols.; Edinburgh, 1793).

MUNBY, A. N. L. (ed.), *Sale Catalogues of Libraries of Eminent Persons, Volume 2: Poets and Men of Letters* (London, 1971).

NEWTON, ISAAC, *Newton's Principia*, ed. Florian Cajori (2 vols.; Berkeley and London, 1934, 1962).

—— *Opticks*. With a foreword by Albert Einstein, an introduction by Sir Edmund Whittaker, a preface by Bernard Cohen, and an analytical table of contents by Duane H. D. Roller (New York, 1952, 1979).

OGILVIE, WILLIAM, *An Essay on the Right of Property in Land With Respect to its Foundation in the Law of Nature* (London, 1781).

PAINE, THOMAS, *Political Writings*, ed. Bruce Kuklick (Cambridge, 1989).

—— *The Age of Reason*. With a biographical introduction by Philip S. Foner (New York, 1991).

PLATO, *The Cratylus, Phaedo, Parmenides and Timaeus of Plato*. Transl. from the Greek by Thomas Taylor (London, 1793).

POWER, HENRY, *Experimental Philosophy; in Three Books* (London, 1664).

PRICE, RICHARD, *A Discourse on the Love of our Country* (London, 1789).

PRIESTLEY, JOSEPH, *An History of Early Opinions concerning Jesus Christ* (4 vols.; London, 1786).

PUGHE, OWEN, *The Heroic Elegies and Other Pieces of Llywarc Hen* (London, 1792).

—— *Myvyrian Archaiology* (London, 1801–7).

RAMSAY, CHEVALIER [ANDREW MICHAEL], *The Travels of Cyrus in Two Volumes* (London, 1730).

ROBERTSON, WILLIAM, *The History of America* (1771), in *The Works of William Robertson* (11 vols.; Chiswick, 1824).

—— *The Progress of Society in Europe*, ed. Felix Gilbert (Chicago and London, 1972).

ROUSSEAU, JEAN JACQUES, *A Discourse to which the Prize was adjudged by the Academy of Dijon in the year 1750*. Transl. R. Wynne (London, 1757).

—— *A Discourse Upon the Origin and Foundation of the Inequality among Mankind* (London, 1761).

SMITH, ADAM, *The Theory of Moral Sentiments*. With an introduction by E. G. West (Indianapolis, 1976).

—— *An Inquiry into the Nature and Causes of the Wealth of Nations*, ed. R. H. Campbell, A. S. Skinner, and W. B. Todd (2 vols.; Oxford, 1976).

—— *Essays on Philosophical Subjects*, ed. W. P. D. Wightman and J. C. Bryce (Oxford, 1980).

SPENCE, THOMAS, *The Political Works of Thomas Spence*, ed. H. T. Dickinson (Newcastle upon Tyne, 1982).

SPINOZA, BENEDICT DE, *Tractatus Theologico-Politicus*. Transl. Samuel Shirley (2nd edn.; Leiden, New York, Copenhagen, and Cologne, 1991).

SPRAT, THOMAS, *History of the Royal Society*, ed. Jackson I. Cope and Harold Whitemore Jones (London, 1959).

SWEDENBORG, EMMANUEL, *A Treatise Concerning Heaven and Hell* (2nd edn.; London, 1784).

TINDAL, MATTHEW, *Christianity as old as the Creation. Or, The Gospel, A Republication of the Religion of Nature* (London, 1730).

VOLNEY, CONSTANTINE, FRANÇOIS DE, *The Ruins, or a Survey of the Revolutions of Empires* (3rd edn.; London, 1796).

VOLTAIRE, *Candidus, or All for the Best, translated from the French of M. Voltaire* (Edinburgh, 1773).

WARBURTON, WILLIAM, *The Divine Legation of Moses Demonstrated* (10th rev. edn.; 3 vols.; London, 1846).

WATTS, ISAAC, *An Essay Towards the Encouragement of Charity Schools* (London, 1728).

WESLEY, JOHN, *Primitive Physick. Or, An Easy and Natural Method of Curing Most Deseases* (14th edn.; Bristol, 1770).

Secondary Sources

ABRAMS, M. H., *Natural Supernaturalism: Tradition and Revolution in Romantic Literature* (New York, 1971).

ACKLAND, MICHAEL, 'The Embattled Sexes: Blake's Debt to Wollstonecraft in *The Four Zoas*', *Blake: An Illustrated Quarterly*, 63 (1982–3), 172–83.

ACKLAND, MICHAEL, 'Blake's Critique of Enlightenment Reason in *The Four Zoas*', *Colby Library Quarterly*, 4 (1983), 173–89.

AERS, DAVID, 'Representations of Revolution from The French Revolution to *The Four Zoas*', in *Critical Paths: Blake and the Argument of Method*, ed. Dan Miller, Mark Bracher, and Donald Ault (Durham, NC and London, 1987), 264–5.

AULT, DONALD, *Blake's Visionary Physics* (Chicago and London, 1974).

—— *Narrative Unbound: Revisioning William Blake's* The Four Zoas (New York, 1987).

BARRACLOUGH, G. 'Universal History', in *Approaches to History: A Symposium*, ed. H. P. R. Finberg (London, 1962), 83–9.

BEER, JOHN, *Blake's Visionary Universe* (Manchester and New York, 1969).

BENTLEY, G. E., JR. *Blake Books* (Oxford, 1977).

BILLINGHEIMER, RACHEL V., 'Blake's "Eyes of God": Cycles to Apocalypse and Redemption', *Philological Quarterly*, 66 (1987), 231–57.

BISHOP, MORCHARD, *Blake's Haley: The Life, Works, and Friendships of William Hayley* (London, 1951).

BLOOM, HAROLD, *Blake's Apocalypse: A Study in Poetic Argument* (New York, 1963)

BORDO, SUSAN R., *The Flight to Objectivity: Essays on Cartesianism and Culture* (New York, 1987).

BROOKS, HAROLD F., 'Blake and Jung: Blake's Myth of the Four Zoas and Jung's Picture of the Psyche', *The Aligarh Critical Miscellany*, 1 (1988), 47–74.

BUTLER, MARILYN, 'Romanticism in England', in *Romanticism in National Context*, ed. Roy Porter and Mikuláš Teich (Cambridge, 1988), 37–67.

CANTOR, PAUL A., *Creature and Creator: Myth-Making and English Romanticism* (Cambridge, 1984).

CHADWICK, OWEN, 'Gibbon and the Church Historians', in *Edward Gibbon and the Decline and Fall of the Roman Empire*, ed. G. W. Bowerstock, John Clive, and Stephen R. Graubaud (Cambridge, Mass., and London, 1977), 219–31.

CHASE, MALCOLM, *The People's Farm: English Radical Agrarianism 1775–1840* (Oxford, 1988).

COX, STEPHEN, *Love and Logic: The Evolution of Blake's Thought* (Ann Arbor, 1992).

DAMON, SAMUEL FOSTER, *William Blake: His Philosophy and Symbols* (Boston, 1924).

—— *A Blake Dictionary* (London, 1973).

DAMROSCH, LEOPOLD JR., *Symbol and Truth in Blake's Myth* (Princeton, NJ, 1980).

DAWSON, P. M. S., 'Blake and Providence: The Theodicy of *The Four Zoas*', *Blake: An Illustrated Quarterly*, 20 (1987), 134–43.

DAWSON, VIRGINIA, *Nature's Enigma: The Problem of the Polyp in the Letters of Bouret, Trembley and Reaumur* (Philadelphia, 1987).

DEEN, LEONARD W., *Conversing in Paradise: Poetic Genius and Identity-as-Community in Blake's Los* (Columbia and London, 1983).

DE LUCA, VINCENT ARTHUR, *Words of Eternity: Blake and the Poetics of the Sublime* (Princeton, NJ, 1991).

DICKINSON, H. T., *British Radicalism and the French Revolution 1789–1815* (Oxford and New York, 1985).

DILLENBERGER, JOHN, *Protestant Thought and Natural Science* (London, 1961).

DISALVO, JACKIE, *War of Titans: Blake's Critique of Milton and the Politics of Religion* (Pittsburgh, 1983).

ERDMAN, DAVID V., 'The Binding (et cetera) of *Vala*', *The Library*, 5th ser., 19 (1964), 112–29.

—— 'The Suppressed and Altered Passages of *Jerusalem*,' *Studies in Bibliography*, 17 (1964), 1–54.

—— *Blake: Prophet Against Empire* (Princeton, NJ, 1954; 3rd edn., Princeton, NJ, 1977).

ESSICK, ROBERT N., '*The Four Zoas*: Intention and Production', *Blake: An Illustrated Quarterly*, 18 (1985), 216–20.

—— 'William Blake, Thomas Paine, and Biblical Revolution', *Studies in Romanticism*, 30 (1991), 189–212.

FAIRCHILD, B. H., *Such Holy Song: Music as Idea, Form and Image in the Poetry of William Blake* (Kent, Oh., 1980).

FERGUSON, REBECCA, *The Unbalanced Mind: Pope and the Rule of Passion* (Brighton, 1986).

FEYERABEND, P. K., 'Explanation, Reduction, and Empiricism', in *Scientific Explanation, Space, and Time* (Minnesota Studies in the Philosophy of Science, 3; Minneapolis, 1962), 28–97.

FISHER, PETER, *The Valley of Vision: Blake as Prophet and Revolutionary* (Toronto, 1961).

FOX, SUSAN, 'The Female as Metaphor in William Blake's Poetry', *Critical Enquiry*, 3 (1977), 507–19.

FRYE, NORTHROP, *Fearful Symmetry: A Study of William Blake* (Princeton, NJ, 1947).

—— 'Poetry and Design in William Blake', *Journal of Aesthetics and Art Criticism*, 10 (1951), 35–42.

FULLER, DAVID, *Blake's Heroic Argument* (London, New York, and Sydney, 1988).

GALLANT, CHRISTINE, *Blake and the Assimilation of Chaos* (Princeton, NJ, 1978).

GEORGE, DIANA HUME, *Blake and Freud* (Ithaca, NY and London, 1980).

GLECKNER, ROBERT, *The Piper and the Bard* (Detroit, 1957).

GOODWIN, ALBERT, *The French Revolution* (5th edn.; London, Melbourne, and Auckland, 1970).

GRANT, JOHN E., 'Visions in *Vala*: A Consideration of Some Pictures in the Manuscript', in *Blake's Sublime Allegory*, ed. Stuart Curran and Joseph Anthony Wittreich Jr. (Madison, 1973), 141–202.

—— 'Jesus and the Powers That Be in Blake's Designs for Young's *Night Thoughts*', in *Blake and His Bibles*, ed. David V. Erdman, with an Introduction by Mark Trevor Smith (West Cornwall, Conn., 1990), 71–115.

HAIGNEY, CATHERINE, 'Vala's Garden in Night the Ninth: Paradise Regained or Woman Bound?', *Blake, An Illustrated Quarterly*, 20 (1987), 116–24.

HILL, CHRISTOPHER, *Milton and the English Revolution* (London, 1977).

HILTON, NELSON, *Literal Imagination: Blake's Vision of Words* (Berkeley, Los Angeles, and London, 1983).

HIRSCH, E. D., JR., *Innocence and Experience: An Introduction to Blake* (New Haven, 1964).

HIRSCHMAN, ALBERT O., *The Passions and the Interests: Political Arguments for Capitalism before its Triumph* (Princeton, NJ, 1977).

HOOYKAAS, R., *Religion and the Rise of Modern Science* (Edinburgh and London, 1972).

JACOB, MARGARET, *The Newtonians and the English Revolution 1689–1720* (Hassocks, Sussex, 1976).

KING-HELE, DESMOND, *Erasmus Darwin and the Romantic Poets* (London, 1986).

KOYRÉ, ALEXANDER, *Newtonian Studies* (London, 1965).

KUHN, ALBERT J. 'English Deism and the Development of Romantic Mythological Syncretism', *PMLA* 71 (1956), 1094–116.

KUHN, THOMAS S., *The Copernican Revolution* (Cambridge, Mass., 1957).

—— *The Structure of Scientific Revolutions* (2nd edn.; Chicago and London, 1970).

LAPRADE, W. T., *England and the French Revolution 1789–97* (New York, 1970).

LEASK, NIGEL, *The Politics of Imagination in Coleridge's Critical Thought* (Basingstoke, 1988).

LEE, JUDITH, 'Ways of Their Own: The Emanations of Blake's *Vala*, or *The Four Zoas*', *ELH* 50 (1983), 131–53.

LINCOLN, ANDREW, 'The Revision of the Seventh and Eighth Nights of *The Four Zoas*', *Blake: An Illustrated Quarterly*, 12 (1978), 115–33.

—— 'Blake's Lower Paradise: The Pastoral Passage in *The Four Zoas*,

Night the Ninth', *Bulletin of Research in the Humanities*, 84 (1981), 470–8.

—— 'Blake and the Natural History of Creation', *Essays and Studies* (London, 1986), 94–103.

—— 'Blake and the Reasoning Historian', in *Historicising Blake*, ed. Stephen Clark and David Worrall (London, 1994), 73–85.

LINDSAY, DAVID W., 'The Resurrection of Man: A Short Commentary on Night Nine of Blake's *Vala* or *The Four Zoas*', *University of Capetown Studies in English*, 6 (1976), 15–23.

—— 'Prelude to Apocalypse: A Short Commentary on Night VIII of Blake's *The Four Zoas*', *Durham University Journal*, 39 (1978), 179–85.

LOVEJOY, ARTHUR O., *The Great Chain of Being: A Study of the History of an Idea* (Cambridge, Mass. and London, 1936 and 1964).

McGANN, JEROME J., 'The Idea of an Indeterminate Text: Blake's Bible of Hell and Dr Alexander Geddes', *Studies in Romanticism*, 25 (1986), 303–24.

MANN, PAUL, 'The Final State of *The Four Zoas*', *Blake: An Illustrated Quarterly*, 18 (1985), 204–9.

—— '*The Book of Urizen* and the Horizon of the Book', in *Unnam'd Forms: Blake and Textuality*, ed. Nelson Hilton and Thomas A. Vogler (Berkeley and Los Angeles, 1986), 49–68.

MARGOLIOUTH, H. M., *William Blake* (Oxford, 1951).

MATTHEWS, SUSAN, 'Jerusalem and Nationalism', in *Beyond Romanticism: New Approaches to Texts and Contexts 1780–1832*, ed. Stephen Copley and John Whale (London and New York, 1992), 79–100.

MEE, JON, *Dangerous Enthusiasm: William Blake and the Culture of Radicalism in the 1790s* (Oxford, 1992).

MEEK, R. L., *Social Science and The Ignoble Savage* (Cambridge, 1976).

MELLOR, ANNE K., 'Blake's Portrayal of Women', *Blake: An Illustrated Quarterly*, 63 (1982–3), 148–55.

MITCHELL, W. J. T., *Blake's Composite Art: A Study of the Illuminated Poetry* (Princeton, NJ, 1978).

MORTON, A. L., *The Everlasting Gospel: A Study in the Sources of William Blake* (London, 1958).

NESFIELD-COOKSON, BERNARD, *William Blake: Prophet of Universal Brotherhood* (London, 1987).

NEUBERG, VICTOR E., *Popular Education in Eighteenth-Century England* (London, 1971).

NISBET, ROBERT, *History of the Idea of Progress* (London, 1980).

NURMI, MARTIN, 'Negative Sources in Blake', in *William Blake: Essays for Samuel Foster Damon*, ed. Alvin H. Rosenfeld (Providence, RI, 1969).

OLIVER, W. H., *Prophets and Millennialists: The Uses of Biblical Prophecy in England from the 1790s to the 1840s* (Auckland, 1978).

OTTO, PETER, 'The Multiple Births of Los in *The Four Zoas*', SEL 31 (1991), 631–53.

—— *Constructive Vision and Visionary Deconstruction: Los, Eternity, and the Productions of Time in the Later Poetry of William Blake* (Oxford, 1991)

PALEY, MORTON D., 'Blake's *Night Thoughts*', in *Essays for S. Forster Damon*, ed. A. H. Rosenfeld (*Providence*, RI, 1969), 131–57.

—— *Energy and Imagination: A Study in the Development of Blake's Thought* (Oxford, 1970).

—— 'The Figure of the Garment,' *Blake's Sublime Allegory*, ed. Stuart Curran and Joseph (Madison, 1973), 119–39.

—— *The Continuing City: William Blake's Jerusalem* (Oxford, 1983).

PATRIDES, C. A., *Milton and the Christian Tradition* (Oxford, 1966).

PERCIVAL, MILTON O., *William Blake's Circle of Destiny* (Oxford, 1938).

PIERCE, JOHN B., 'The Shifting Characterization of Tharmas and Enion in Pages 3–7 of Blake's *Vala or The Four Zoas*', *Blake: An Illustrated Quarterly*, 22 (1988–9), 93–102.

—— 'The Changing Mythic Structure of Blake's *Vala or The Four Zoas*', *Philological Quarterly*, 64 (1989), 485–508.

POCOCK, J. G. A., *The Machiavellian Moment* (Princeton, NJ, 1975).

—— 'Between Machiavelli and Hume: Gibbon as a Civic Humanist and Philosophical Historian', in *Edward Gibbon and the Decline and Fall of the Roman Empire*, ed. G. W. Bowerstock, John Clive, and Stephen R. Graubaud (Cambridge, Mass., and London, 1977), 103–19.

PUNTER, DAVID, 'Blake: Social Relations of Poetic Form', *Literature and History*, 8 (1982), 182–205.

RAINE, KATHLEEN, *Blake and Tradition* (2 vols.; Princeton, NJ, 1968).

ROSSO, GEORGE ANTHONY JR., *Blake's Prophetic Workshop: A Study of The Four Zoas* (Lewisburg, London, and Toronto, 1993).

ROTHENBERG, MOLLY ANNE, *Rethinking Blake's Textuality* (Columbia, Mo., and London, 1993).

RUBEL, MARGARET MARY, *Savage and Barbarian: Historical Attitudes in the Criticism of Homer and Ossian in Britain, 1760–1800* (Amsterdam, Oxford, and New York, 1978).

SCHORER, MARK, *The Politics of Vision* (New York, 1946).

SHAVIRO, STEVEN ' "Striving with Systems": Blake and the Politics of Difference', in N. Hilton, *Essential Articles for the Study of William Blake, 1970–84* (Hamden, Conn., 1986), 271–99.

STEMPEL, DANIEL, 'Blake, Foucault, and the Classical Episteme', *PMLA* 96 (1981), 388–407.

STEVENSON, W. H., 'Two Problems in *The Four Zoas*', *Blake Newsletter*, 3 (1967), 14–17.

SUTHERLAND, JOHN, 'Blake and Urizen', in *Blake's Visionary Forms Dramatic*, ed. David V. Erdman and John E. Grant (Princeton, NJ, 1970), 250-1.

TANNENBAUM, LESLIE, *Biblical Tradition in Blake's Early Prophecies: The Great Code of Art* (Princeton, NJ, 1982).

THOMPSON, E. P., *The Making of the English Working Class* (Harmondsworth, 1968).

—— *Witness Against the Beast: William Blake and the Moral Law* (Cambridge, 1993).

TUVESON, ERNEST LEE, *Millennium and Utopia: A Study in the Background of the Idea of Progress* (Berkeley and Los Angeles, 1949).

VISCOMI, JOSEPH, *Blake and the Idea of the Book* (Princeton, NJ, 1993).

WEBSTER, BRENDA S., *Blake's Prophetic Psychology* (Athens, Ga., 1983).

WESTFALL, RICHARD S., *Science and Religion in Seventeenth-Century England* (Michigan, 1973).

WHITE, DOUGLAS H., *Pope and the Context of Controversy: The Manipulation of Ideas in* An Essay on Man (Chicago and London, 1970).

WHITE, HAYDEN, *Metahistory: The Historical Imagination in Nineteenth-Century Europe* (Baltimore and London, 1973).

WHITNEY, LOIS, *Primitivism and the Idea of Progress in English Popular Literature of the Eighteenth Century* (Baltimore, 1934).

WILKIE, BRIAN and JOHNSON, MARY LYNN, *Blake's Four Zoas: The Design of a Dream* (Cambridge, Mass. and London, 1978).

WORRALL, DAVID, *Radical Culture: Discourse, Resistance and Surveillance, 1790-1820* (Hemel Hempstead, 1992).

YOUNGQUIST, PAUL, *Madness and Blake's Myth* (University Park, Pa., and London, 1989).

Index